REBELLION AND RIOT

REBELLION AND RIOT
Popular Disorder in England during the Reign of Edward VI

Barrett L. Beer

The Kent State University Press

Library of Congress Cataloging in Publication Data
Beer, Barrett L.
     Rebellion and riot.

     Bibliography: p.
     Includes index.
     1. Great Britain — History — Edward VI, 1547-1553.
     2. Riots — England — History — 16th century. I. Title.
     DA345.B4   942.05'3   81-19341
     ISBN 0-87338-269-2   AACR2

For Jill, Peter, and Caroline

CONTENTS

PREFACE

Although the story of the Edwardian rebellions of 1549 has been told many times, no one has attempted to examine all forms of popular disorder from 1547 to 1553. The best accounts of the rebellions have focused either on the Western Rebellion in Cornwall and Devon or Kett's Rebellion in Norfolk. My objective has been to view popular discontent as a national threat to law and order that expressed itself in diverse ways throughout the various regions of Tudor England. I have attempted to show the interrelationship between the local communities and the central government even though surviving records tell us more about government policy than the strategy of local leaders and rebels. Any study of popular discontent during the reign of Edward VI must emphasize the rebellions, but I have also given attention to riots, conspiracies, and lesser manifestations of unrest. Tudor chroniclers, preachers, and politicians were more interested in the suffering of the gentry and urban oligarchy than the circumstances that caused the commons to rebel, and they enthusiastically recounted the military campaigns and executions that led to the restoration of order. For the most part modern historians, sharing the distaste of the Tudors for the common man and popular agitation, have written accounts that were highly sympathetic to the government and the ruling aristocracy. My approach has been quite different. I have placed the rebels and the popular leaders and causes at the center of the stage but have sought to present a balanced account that considers the interests of each side and strives to understand why the commons, aristocracy, and government behaved as they did.

It is a pleasure to acknowledge the assistance that I have received in the preparation of this book. A project of this scope could not have been attempted had it not been for the pioneering work of F. W.

PREFACE

Russell and Frances Rose-Troup. I have also benefited from the valuable research of S. T. Bindoff, W. K. Jordan, Stephen K. Land, and Julian Cornwall. Archivists and librarians at Kent State University, the British Library, Public Record Office, Devon Record Office, Duchy of Cornwall Office, Essex Record Office, Guildford Museum and Muniment Room, Inner Temple Library, Norfolk and Norwich Record Office, Surrey Record Office, and elsewhere were extremely helpful. The Rev. David Bickerton, Rector of Sampford Courtenay, Devon, kindly answered my query about the parish church. Miss Betty R. Masters, Deputy Keeper of the Records at the Corporation of London Records Office, read an earlier version of Chapter 7, which was published as "London and the Rebellions of 1548-1549," in the *Journal of British Studies,* 12 (1972). Professor Conrad Russell invited me to present a paper on Robert Kett to his seminar at the University of London, and he and his colleagues responded with generous criticism. My greatest scholarly debt, however, is to Professor Roger B. Manning, who read the completed manuscript and made many valuable suggestions for its improvement. The Kent State University Research Council funded a large portion of the research in England. Mrs. Marjorie Evans carefully typed the final draft of the manuscript. Important debts of a more personal kind are owed to Mr. H. T. Parker, who provided hospitality for my family in London, and to Jill Parker Beer, who typed early drafts of the manuscript and helped me in more ways than could possibly be recounted here.

June 30, 1981

Spelling, punctuation, and capitalization have been modernized in all quotations. Dates are given in the New Style.

A prince ought to take more care of his people's happiness than of his own, as a shepherd ought to take more care of his flock than of himself. Certainly it is wrong to think that poverty of the people is a safeguard of public peace. Who quarrel more than beggars do? Who long for a change more earnestly than the dissatisfied? Or who rushes in to create disorders with such desperate boldness as the man who has nothing to lose and everything to gain?

Thomas More, *Utopia*

1. REBELLION AND POPULAR DISORDER IN TUDOR ENGLAND

The lost world of sixteenth-century England reveals itself through a variety of contrasting faces. Some we remember vividly, while others are merely vague shadows. The face of the Tudor monarchy is best remembered, and for centuries the deeds of kings, queens, and courtiers have formed the very essence of Tudor history. Few epochs have produced personalities rivalling Henry VIII, Anne Boleyn, and Elizabeth. Intensive study of the monarchy, its institutions, and its laws has revealed a face of fascinating complexity. If the monarchy has a serious rival for the attention of posterity, it is the face of the church because of the revolutionary change unleashed by the Reformation. The establishment of the Church of England, the dissolution of the monasteries, the drama of persecution and martyrdom all loom large in the pages of history. The Tudors understood the importance of the monarchy and the church and wanted future generations to remember as well.

The sixteenth century had other faces — less romantic, less exciting faces — that also made a strong impression on contemporaries. There were the shadowy faces of the great majority of Tudor men and women, the yeomen, husbandmen, artisans, laborers, and servants, who comprised the commons of England. A hierarchical society expected the commons to work, pay rent and taxes, and obey the laws of the monarchy and church. The simple, contented face of the common man or woman dutifully fulfilling his small role in society frequently gave way to the face of hunger, the face of despair, and the face of anger. And anger often led to quarrels, riots, and rebellions. The rulers of Tudor England knew the face of rebellion and riot all too well, and they hated and feared what they saw. But when they recorded the history of their age, they chose to assign the commons to the margins of that history and to see their complaints and protests as ugly blemishes on the face of the body politic.

1

If contemporaries wanted one face of the Tudor age to be forgotten, it was the frightening face of popular disorder. The best interests of the crown and aristocracy required law and order, and while the privileged classes claimed for themselves the right to resort to violence when required, they agreed with the crown that the commons must be kept down. In maintaining order the crown and aristocracy could count on the support of the church, as its interests were also served by domestic tranquility. For centuries the institutional church prospered through its support of the state, but the church abandoned the more radical implications of the Christian Gospel, and by the sixteenth century became dependent on the crown rather than the Christian community as a whole for its protection. The clergy spoke for the church and favored close ties with the crown and aristocracy. The late medieval church may have offered the sure way to salvation, but during the long and troublesome years that constituted mankind's sojourn on earth, the institutional church taught little beyond acceptance of one's lot in life and obedience to lord and master. If the commons turned to politics, they found that the late medieval constitution offered few opportunities for effecting change and obtaining redress of grievance. Parliament was an assembly of landlords and royal officials, while the justices of the peace governed the countryside in their own interest. As the Tudor political system did not encourage popular participation in government, the alternative was often direct action, namely rebellion and riot.

The remarkable success of the Tudors in controlling and repressing popular discontent, particularly in comparison with the preceding Lancastrian and Yorkist era and the century that followed the death of Elizabeth, gave rise to the notion that their government served the best interests of all. The Tudors wished to be remembered as benevolent sovereigns ruling over a happy and contented people, and generations of historians accepted their claims at face value. Sharing the outlook of Tudor intellectuals, modern historians preferred to study the sixteenth century from the top downwards, to examine the policy of ministers of the crown, and to participate vicariously in the seductive pleasures of courtly life. In these pursuits the commons were of little importance, and the protests of the inarticulate together with the unruly behavior of the rude multitudes were merely unfortunate obstacles blocking the progress of culture and good government.[1]

Although disorder was abhorred and banished from the minds of decent, God-fearing subjects, rebellion and riot were as much a part of Tudor England as the divorces of Henry VIII and the ill-fated romances of his daughter, Elizabeth. Each of the Tudor sovereigns faced at least one major rebellion and countless smaller disturbances and conspiracies. Henry, Earl of Richmond was himself a successful rebel who deposed Richard III and founded a new dynasty. Little more than a decade of Tudor rule had passed when the Cornish, much grieved by

The counties of England and Wales.

taxation in support of a war with Scotland, revolted against Henry VII and marched to Blackheath before suffering defeat. In 1536 the Pilgrimage of Grace defied the authority of Henry VIII. This rising, centered in Lincolnshire and Yorkshire, embodied a complex variety of political, religious, and social issues.[2]

The most menacing rebellions of the century occurred between 1548 and 1549 when over half the counties in England seethed with angry social and religious protests. Traditionally seen as two separate revolts — the Western Rebellion in Cornwall and Devon and Kett's Rebellion in Norfolk — the risings were actually more extensive and had much in common. The commons and their leaders claimed loyalty to the young King Edward VI but defied the policies of his uncle, Edward Seymour, Duke of Somerset and Lord Protector. Somerset's government, strongly influenced by religious and social reformers including Hugh Latimer, Sir Thomas Smith, and John Hales, aroused mistrust from many gentry and commons. Lacking confidence in the central government, local leaders were hesitant about enforcing its laws and upholding order. Conflict between court and country ensued as local communities and leaders attempted to thwart the Protector's reforms. Polarization also took place within the church, where Protestant bishops, supported by Somerset and the Council, pushed aside defenders of the Henrician religious settlement. Conservative bishops suffered imprisonment while their adherents among the parish clergy turned to rebellion. Throughout the length and breadth of England the upper gentry and town oligarchs encountered vigorous popular opposition as the commons protested against a host of local grievances: enclosure of common pasture, rising rents, and the enforcement of Protestant religious reforms. Leadership of the commons came from the lesser gentry, yeoman farmers, parish priests, and artisans of whom Robert Kett, the Norfolk tanner, was the most energetic.

The rebellious commons suffered defeat in every part of the country at the hands of the king's army. The embittered aristocracy sought a scapegoat for the costly risings and in October 1549 deposed Somerset as Lord Protector. His agrarian policy was misconceived and ill-executed and his leadership indecisive in the face of the rebellious commons, but until midsummer when the whole country teetered on the brink of disaster his government enjoyed at least a measure of support from the Privy Council and the aristocracy. Only when Exeter was under siege and Robert Kett defeated a royal army and occupied Norwich was it easy to see the failure of Somerset's policies. The vengeance of the aristocracy was not confined to Somerset, for the defeated commons suffered savage repression as the countryside was pacified. The Council, under the leadership of John Dudley, Earl of Warwick, turned to policies that combined repression with cautious financial and social reform. As in the past, the government assigned a higher priority to protecting the privileges of the propertied classes than to satisfying the grievances of the commons.[3]

The overthrow of Somerset and the execution of Kett and other rebel leaders signalled the end of the Edwardian rebellions but not of popular discontent. Riots and smaller popular disturbances continued until the king's death in 1553. Better harvests, greater price stability, and above all the vigilance of the Council and local leaders prevented recurrence of a major rising. Edward VI had been dead less than a year when Sir Thomas Wyatt recruited and led a large rebel army to the walls of London at Ludgate. Opposition to Queen Mary's decision to marry Philip of Spain prompted Protestant leaders to plan risings in the West, the Midlands, and the Southeast. Only in Kent did the commons rally to the standard of rebellion in significant numbers. Yet Wyatt's Kentish rebels might have successfully deposed the queen if support from London had been forthcoming.[4]

Rebellion played a smaller role during the reign of Elizabeth, but even Gloriana felt the sting of revolt in 1569 when the earls of Northumberland and Westmorland restored the Latin mass at Durham Cathedral, called for the arrest of Sir William Cecil, the queen's leading adviser, and demanded the restoration of Roman Catholicism. Less threatening than the mid-Tudor rebellions, the rising of the northern earls revealed the deep-rooted discontent of the aristocracy and its tenants. The last rising of the Tudor era took place in 1601, only two years before the death of Elizabeth, when the Earl of Essex, frustrated by his loss of royal favor, led 200 supporters up Fleet Street, London, in a desperate and futile attempt to restore his political ascendancy.[5] A survey of Tudor rebellions leads to the inescapable conclusion that every rebel captain whether artisan or earl and every popular cause — religious, political, or economic — suffered defeat. What is remarkable and usually overlooked by historians is the courage of generations of Tudor rebels to resist oppression and go down to defeat in the face of overwhelming odds.

Although popular disorder was endemic throughout the sixteenth century, the pattern of rebellion and riot was extremely diverse. The rebellion of Henry Tudor in 1485 began as a royalist conspiracy against the Yorkists, and the dynastic interests of the Courtenays and Mary Stuart played important roles in later risings. When political opposition to the Tudors was not dynastic, it usually included conflict between court and country. For example, the northern aristocracy in 1536 and 1569 and the western gentry in 1549 vigorously opposed policies emanating from the court. The leadership of Thomas Cromwell and William Cecil aroused regional discontent; remote counties feared centralizing reforms of all kinds; and in 1549 the western gentry saw the Edwardian Reformation as little more than the program of court politicians supported by a clique of heretical clergy. After Henry VIII's break with Rome in the 1530s, religion emerged as a divisive issue that fired political and social instability. Only under Edward VI did Catholics and Protestants rise at the same time. Religious unrest during the reigns of Henry VIII and Elizabeth came primarily from Catholics opposed to the royal supremacy, the monastic dissolution, and innovations in the church, while Mary's opponents were exclusively Protestant. Real or imagined social and economic grievances played a part in many rebellions, particularly the Cornish Rebellion of 1497, the Pilgrimage of Grace, and Kett's Rebellion in Norfolk. Riots almost always stemmed from economic issues; frequently heard grievances concerned rent payments, food prices, enclosure, and property rights.

Popular disorder would be easier to understand if it were possible to write an equation showing the interaction of rational political, religious, and economic motivation. Unfortunately the minds of Tudor rebels and rioters were not so logical as modern historians would like. The commons' political perceptions were affected by an imperfect understanding of the past and a limited comprehension of the present. Loyalty to a powerful magnate could cause a tenant or servant to join a rising in which he had no legitimate interest. Naïve and credulous commons fell prey to rumors that excited the emotions and clouded the mind. Prophecies, as Keith Thomas has shown, were employed "in virtually every rebellion or popular rising which disturbed the Tudor state."[6] Vague and ambiguous prophecies purported to foretell the future and frequently encouraged resistance to government policy. Thomas has also delineated important links between orthodox Christian beliefs and magic, astrology, and witchcraft. The occult influenced men and women of all ranks and degrees, and confused seemingly clear-cut divisions arising from the Reformation. Mischievous priests often persuaded ignorant commons to favor a course of action that served only the interests of a clerical faction or religious party. Social and economic issues — poorly understood by the best minds of the century — also evoked responses from peers, gentry, and commons that conflict with modern views of enlightened self-interest.

As Tudor rebellions had diverse and often contradictory causes, so too was there diversity of leadership. Because the Tudor dynasty was founded on usurpation, the kings and queens had most to fear from cousins with royal blood in their veins and nobles whose offspring were potential claimants to the throne. Although the victims of Tudor justice included the Duke of Buckingham, the Marquis of Exeter, the Duke of Suffolk (father of Lady Jane), the fourth Duke of Norfolk, and Mary, Queen of Scots, such persons were more important as symbols around which the commons might rally than as actual leaders of rebel forces. The nonroyal peerage made a larger contribution to Tudor rebellions. Lord Audley led the Cornish in 1497, Lord Darcy joined the Pilgrimage of Grace, and the earls of Northumberland and Westmorland raised the

North against Elizabeth. Every major rebellion received support of one kind or another from the landed gentry or from mayors and other town officials. The most famous of the gentry were Robert Aske, Humphrey Arundell, and Sir Thomas Wyatt. The mayor of Bodmin in Cornwall was a major participant in the Western Rebellion of 1549, while the mayor of Norwich protested that he assisted Robert Kett only to protect the city. If there is a common characteristic to be found among rebellious peers, gentry, and urban officials, it is alienation from the crown and court. Living in remote counties, denied lucrative offices and a respected place in the counsels of the monarch, hostile to the official religion of the day, these frustrated members of the Tudor aristocracy sought to reassert themselves through alliances with the commons.

Before any rising could attract attention from outside the locality where it began, it had to arouse enough popular support to challenge the maintenance of order by justices of the peace and other local officials. The support of the commons, those who ranked below the gentlemen, determined the strength of every rebellion. Ranging from prosperous yeomen to the very poor living on charity, the commons varied enormously. If we accept Lawrence Stone's estimate that the peers and gentry comprised about 2 percent of the population,[7] the commons made up the other 98 percent. Yeoman farmers, a numerous and thriving class in the early sixteenth century, formed the buffer dividing the commons from the aristocracy. Husbandmen, like the yeomen, occupied a family farm but worked less land and kept fewer livestock.[8] Ranking below the peasant farmers came agricultural laborers, who made up about one-fourth to one-third of the total population.[9] Artisans and apprentices filled the towns and villages, while servants worked in the households of the aristocracy. The number of poor and unemployed commons increased during the mid-Tudor period. In the towns John Pound estimated that as much as one-third of the population was "below the status of wage-earner."[10] The existence and indeed growth of a very substantial portion of the population that enjoyed merely subsistence in good times and often lacked adequate food, housing, and clothing created an environment in which disorder thrived.

The aristocracy understood the plight of the commons and feared the fury of the unruly mob. Throughout the century government propagandists, pamphleteers, and preachers denounced all forms of disorder and exhorted the populace to obey the law. In the literature of obedience, it was generally assumed that violent, irrational behavior was the identifying characteristic of the commons. A less prejudiced attitude would not deny the existence of an unwashed rabble but would emphasize that most of the commons were law-abiding subjects. The great majority of Englishmen — rich and poor — accepted the natural and historical order. Few longed to overturn the monarchy, exterminate the aristocracy, or divide the land on the basis of need. People tended to be optimistic and hopeful, for there was no other way to endure the toil of daily life. At mid-century the commons often looked back to a golden age of plenty at the end of the fifteenth century when their fathers and grandfathers enjoyed abundant land, paid low rents, and ate meat almost every day. They abandoned their traditional conservatism only when faced with adverse circumstances. Although everyone who was regularly employed possessed property of one sort or another, the commons had little or no voice in governing the society in which they lived. Rebellion was a means of political expression as well as an act of violence.

The commons contributed leadership as well as manpower to rebellions. Among the unemployed and very poor there was little, if any, leadership potential. Yeomen, husbandmen, and artisans, on the other hand, served as leaders as well as followers. The best-known leaders drawn from the ranks of the commons included the Cornish blacksmith, Michael Joseph, and the Norfolk tanner, Robert Kett. The typical popular leader worked at the local level, often under the direction of peers or gentry. The Edwardian rebellions produced a host of daring rebel captains about whose exploits surviving records are tantalizingly sketchy. The most resourceful men inevitably avoided capture and thus left behind only a heroic oral tradition.

The objectives of popular leaders were usually limited to redress of specific local grievances, but a few, inspired by radical prophecies and folk legends, entertained larger ambitions. Seventeenth-century radicals, who were guided by the King James (1611) version of Acts 17:6, sought to turn the world upside down.[11] Their Tudor predecessors could not have been similarly inspired, because earlier translations of the Bible give different versions of this text. If mid-Tudor rebels turned to scripture, the English translation of Erasmus's *Paraphrase of the New Testament* would have been a likely choice. There disorderly Christians were rebuked not as persons attempting to turn the world upside down but only as "these that trouble the world."[12] Modern historians, who have studied the goals of sixteenth-century rebels, disagree as to whether their objectives were radical or conservative.

Rebellious commons, gentry, and peers failed in each attempt to gain concessions from the crown. The causes of failure were as complex as the rebellions themselves. The easy explanation is simply that the rebels lacked sufficient support and that the government outsmarted and out-generaled its opponents. Compared with Charles I, who was destroyed by his rebellious subjects, the Tudor monarchs were shrewder and more ruthless. The extreme provincialism of sixteenth-century rebels worked against their success. Although much of the country suffered from disorder in 1549, individual rebel leaders never attempted to coordinate their military efforts or to prepare petitions for redress of grievances with broad national appeal. In 1554 Sir Thomas

Wyatt and his fellow conspirators had an attractive unifying cause — the queen's marriage to Philip of Spain — and they planned risings in enough different places to cripple the government, but only Wyatt successfully executed his assigned responsibilities. By contrast, risings limited to the poor and sparsely populated counties of northern England or Cornwall were doomed from the very beginning. Another cause of failure was inadequate financial support. In the 1640s Parliament financed the war against the king; Tudor rebels relied on private capital and plunder. The rebel armies also lacked cavalry, firearms, and an adequate supply organization. Operating from hand-to-mouth, the sixteenth-century rebels managed to muster large forces for only a few weeks at a time. Government commanders benefited from the rebels' inadequate military organization and bought valuable time through negotiation and stalling tactics. Rebel captains naively trusted the crown and were repeatedly deceived by time-consuming parleys and false promises. Guided by medieval precepts that the king could do no wrong and that wicked councillors were the real enemy, Tudor rebels misunderstood the cause of their oppression. The best efforts of rebel leaders could not succeed until they overcame the mystique of monarchy and identified the crown as the cornerstone of an unjust society.

Although rebellions erupted with regularity throughout the sixteenth century, riots were an even more frequent form of popular disorder. An ordinary riot was a small affair and required a company of only three persons "assembling and forcibly attempting the unlawful act which they intended."[13] A large-scale riot, on the other hand, might develop into a rebellion. No one has yet determined how many riots took place during the Tudor period, but G. R. Elton has noted that "breaches of the peace were distinctly commonplace and could arise from the most trivial of causes."[14] The Court of Star Chamber under Cardinal Wolsey heard thirty-five cases of riot.[15] Roger B. Manning, using only Star Chamber records, was able to study no fewer than seventy-five cases dealing with enclosure riots from the reigns of Henry VIII and Edward VI.[16] During the reign of Mary, quarter sessions in Middlesex indicted twenty-eight persons for rioting; twenty-nine others were indicted for quarrelling and inciting to breach of the peace.[17] Riots may have occurred less frequently after 1558, but Peter Clark refers to some thirteen riots in Elizabethan Kent, with the greatest number taking place in the 1590s.[18] If prerogative courts, common-law courts, and local courts were investigated for the whole century, the total number of riots would certainly reach into the hundreds.

Tudor chroniclers abhorred riots as much as rebellions and unless they were directed against foreigners or Roman Catholics rarely wrote sympathetic accounts. Historians study riots primarily through court records, which contain contradictory and distorted testimony. A person seeking to recover damages for the destruction of property invariably exaggerated the number of rioters and the extent of violence. Litigants attempting to try land titles in the Court of Star Chamber might refer to riots that were altogether spurious. The rioter claimed to be a peace-loving subject provoked by prior acts of violence or victimized by violation of local customs and parliamentary statutes. Manning argued that in twenty-nine of seventy-five Star Chamber cases concerning early Tudor enclosure riots "the casting down of hedges was procured by peers or gentry; . . . in only twelve instances can we confidently state that the levelling of hedges was initiated by yeomen, husbandmen, laborers, or craftsmen."[19] The aristocracy, according to Manning, instigated riots in pursuit of quarrels with other gentry or peers to enforce uniform agricultural practices among tenants and to provoke intervention of Star Chamber in local disputes. The Elizabethan riots studied by Clark involved a surprising number of women. The rank and file were drawn from the commons and were usually migrants, small urban craftsmen, laborers, and the poor.

The rioter — like the rebel — was a man of action. Too angry, too frustrated, too shortsighted to wait on the slow-turning wheels of Tudor justice, he sought an immediate remedy. While the rebel hoped to arouse an entire village or parish or perhaps the whole county, the rioter took aim at a single target and usually accomplished his objective within a few hours. The most typical victim of the enclosure riots studied by Manning were outsiders, particularly merchants buying their way into the gentry and farmers of leases. In Elizabethan Kent, Clark identified corn merchants, rack-renting lawyers, aliens, suspected Catholics, and iron masters as the principal enemies of rioters. From the perspective of modern historians, the objectives of Tudor rioters appeared "conserva-tive, limited, and deferential," but neither the crown nor the justices of the peace would have accepted such an assessment.[20] The rulers of Tudor England, fearful of the many-headed monster unleashed when the commons rioted, countered with repression.

The spectre of rebellion and riot extended far beyond the shores of sixteenth-century England. The violent protests of peasants and towns-people echoed from the Baltic to the Mediterranean. While some historians see popular disorder as an aberration lying outside the mainstream of early modern history, Marc Bloch argued otherwise. "To the historian, whose task is merely to observe and explain the connec-tions between phenomena," he wrote in *French Rural History*, "agrar-ian revolt is as natural to the seigneurial regime as strikes, let us say, are to large-scale capitalism."[21] French rebels, like their English counter-parts, fought with great courage although they were "almost invariably doomed to defeat and eventual massacre."[22] Agrarian rebellions in the two countries were similar, but the French experience offers several extraordinary examples of popular disorder.

Religious riots in French cities and towns have been termed "rites of violence."[23] In 1562 Calvinist pastors at Gien and Rouen goaded the faithful with the text of Deuteronomy 12:1-3: "And ye shall overthrow their altars, and break their pillars and burn their groves with fire; and ye shall hew down the graven images of their gods, and destroy the names of them out of that place." In each instance iconoclastic riots followed. A few days before the outbreak of massacres at Bordeaux in 1572, a Jesuit preached "on how the Angel of the Lord had already executed God's judgment in Paris, Orleans, and elsewhere, and would also do so in Bordeaux."[24] The so-called judgment of the Lord in Paris referred to the savage massacre of St. Bartholomew's Eve when Catholics killed Huguenot leaders and several thousand coreligionists.

At Romans in the Dauphiné hungry peasants and artisans fomented one of the most bizarre insurrections of the century. Over four thousand men, women, and children crowded into Romans in 1580 and acted out their revolt in the streets of the city, exclaiming that "before three days are out Christian flesh will be selling at six deniers the pound." Fearing the cannibalism of the rebels, the rich, organized as a party of law and order, jousted, tilted, and banqueted with the rebels. Each side issued letters of defiance. The festivities were a prelude to bloody combat in which the gentlemen butchered the rebels "like hogs." Emmanuel Le Roy Ladurie called the Carnival of Romans a "psychological drama or tragic ballet whose actors danced and acted out their revolt instead of discoursing about it in manifestos." The carnival was an "abortive episode of social inversion" that ended symbolically when the local judges had an effigy of the chief rebel hanged upside down by the heels.[25]

Of all the sixteenth-century rebellions the German Peasant War of 1525 claimed the greatest number of lives. The war began with riots in Swabia, spread from Alsace to the lands south of Bavaria, and engulfed Franconia, the Palatinate, and Thuringia. The peasants sought religious liberties and freedom from economic oppression. To the Lutherans the war posed an unwanted dilemma, and Luther's decision to oppose the peasants limited the future effectiveness of his movement. The German aristocracy fought the peasants to protect the established social and economic system. By April 1525 an estimated 300,000 rebels were in arms. Led by radical preachers, a few lesser nobles, and men drawn from the middle classes, the peasants burned, plundered, and killed. Hajo Holborn concluded that acts of violence against persons were rare but rowdyism was widespread.[26] The process of pacification, however, was barbaric, leaving 100,000 peasants dead. For the past decade the Peasant War has been the subject of intense controversy among historians.[27] Marxist historians, guided by economic determinism, regard it as "the most significant revolutionary mass movement of the German people" until 1918.[28] Western scholars have emphasized political and religious aspects of the war, but recent research has pointed the way toward a non-Marxist social interpretation.[29]

A quarter century later, when England appeared on the brink of a similar disaster, Sir William Paget remembered the Peasant War. The strong hand of Henry VIII was gone, and Edward VI reigned under the tutlege of his uncle, Protector Somerset. Paget, who had served as secretary to the late king, criticized the policies of Edward's government and feared that his country would suffer the agony of Germany if the risings were not immediately extinguished.[30] Paget's fears were exaggerated, but the England of Edward VI stood on the threshold of the worst popular rebellions of the Tudor era.

And the first degree is to look backward, whether at your first setting forward, you took not a wrong way as (saving your favor) I think you did; for you have cared to content all men (which is impossible and specially being subjects in such a subjection as they were left) and be loth or rather afraid to offend any. Extremities be never good, and for my part I have always hated them naturally too much in our old majesty's time (I speak with reverence and in the loyalty of a true heart to my sovereign lord that was and that now is) and too much in our majesty's time that now is. . . . Then all things were too straight and now they are too loose; then was it dangerous to do or speak though the meaning were not evil; and now every man hath liberty to do and speak at liberty without danger.

Sir William Paget to Protector Somerset, Christmas Day, 1548

2. THE ENGLAND OF EDWARD VI

In 1547 Englishmen of all ranks and degrees mourned the death of Henry VIII, a titan among kings who successfully defied the Pope and wrested Boulogne from the French. Henry, for all of his failings, remained popular among the great majority of his subjects. The king's robust zest for life counted for more among the commons than his failure to live up to the expectations of his early admirers. Now that the old man was gone, attention inevitably focused on his nine-year-old-son, Edward VI.

Everyone rejoiced at the young king's festive coronation, for not many could remember his father's accession in 1509. At the same time there was apprehension, because it was plain to all that a small boy could not govern the country. Before the establishment of the Tudor dynasty, factionalism, court intrigue, and even civil war had accompanied minority rule, but that was part of the distant past. King Edward was said to be a young Josiah, a just and powerful lawgiver under whom the country would rise to new heights of greatness. The aristocracy may have doubted whether the frail and studious child would ever equal much less exceed his father's renown. The king's potential for leadership, however, was not the major concern of the vast majority of the population whose world centered on the village or hamlet. Among the commons few had any reason to expect that life under Edward VI would be better than in the past, but all must have prayed to God that it would not be worse.

The will of Henry VIII named most of the late king's councillors to advise Edward during his minority. Among the familiar faces were Edward Seymour, Earl of Hertford, the king's uncle; Thomas Cranmer, Archbishop of Canterbury; John Dudley, Viscount Lisle; and Sir William Paget. The most striking omission from the minority Council was Stephen Gardiner, Bishop of Winchester, who had fallen into disfavor with Henry immediately before his death. Although the king's will implied rule by a council of equals, common sense dictated that one person should exercise leadership. The choice of Edward Seymour as Protector was logical considering his kinship with the king and his political and military roles during the closing years of Henry's reign. As Protector, Seymour had responsibility for the king's education — both political and religious — and authority for the direction of the government's foreign and domestic policies. Shortly after Seymour was named Protector, the leading councillors assumed new titles, said by Paget to be the desire of the deceased king. Accordingly Seymour became Duke of Somerset, and William Parr, Earl of Essex, the brother of Queen Catherine, became the Marquis of Northampton. Dudley and Thomas Lord Wriothesley were created earls, receiving the titles of Earl of Warwick and Earl of Southampton, respectively. Also advanced to the peerage as barons were Sir Thomas Seymour, Somerset's younger brother; Sir Richard Rich; Sir William Willoughby; and Sir Edmund Sheffield, who later died fighting rebels at Norwich.

The major restructuring of the government from a regime dominated by an all-powerful king to a protectorate charged with the duty of ruling in behalf of a nine-year-old child was accomplished with minimal opposition. The most important casualty was the controversial Thomas Wriothesley, Earl of Southampton, who was removed as Lord Chancellor but later rejoined the Council.[1] From the outside the most formidable opponent of the Protectorate was Stephen Gardiner, Bishop of Winchester, whose omission from the Council caused him to oppose the program of his former colleagues. The government of Protector Somerset might have been merely a caretaker regime attempting to steer a steady but unadventuresome course if the country had not faced religious, social, and economic problems at home and challenges in Scotland and on the continent.

1. Problems of the Realm

Although parliamentary legislation from the reign of Henry VIII officially defined the religious settlement, religious instability troubled the government from the day of Edward's accession. The Reformation under Henry VIII abolished papal authority in England and established the king as the supreme head of the church. Subsequent legislation dissolved the monasteries and placed chantry lands at the king's disposal. The fall of Thomas Cromwell, the chief architect of the Henrician Reformation, destroyed hopes of reformers that the Church of England might adopt the doctrines of continental Protestants as the church's official creed. To the end of his life Henry VIII remained unalterably opposed to Lutheranism as well as the more advanced Protestant doctrines, and the Act of Six Articles, 1539, defined the king's religion in highly orthodox terms. The Six Articles reaffirmed the doctrine of transubstantiation and repudiated communion in both kinds, that is, the practice of offering the cup as well as the bread to the laity. The Articles also forbade the marriage of priests, stated that private masses were agreeable to God's law, and required auricular confessions "to be retained and continued, used and frequented in the Church of God." The purpose of the act was to strengthen the realm through religious uniformity, a principle that remained close to the hearts of Tudor sovereigns from Henry VIII through Elizabeth. To assure compliance with the law, the Act of Six Articles provided extreme penalties for offenders. Persons denying transubstantiation either in words or writing were guilty of heresy and were to be burned at the stake. Those who preached, taught, or obstinately denied any of the other articles were to die by hanging as felons.[2] If guiding principles lay behind the king's religion, they were a commitment to royal supremacy and religious uniformity augmented by reforms eliminating some of the worst features of late medieval Catholicism.

Statutes might define the doctrines of the Church of England, but they did not reflect the beliefs and practices of all Englishmen. Protestantism existed illegally before Henry began divorce proceedings against Queen Catherine and continued through the Marian persecution. Men and women of all ranks and degrees had considerable freedom to think and believe as they pleased so long as they did so in private and continued to practice outward conformity. Zealots and troublemakers obviously suffered when they fell into the net of royal justice as Thomas Bilney, John Lambert, and Anne Askew tragically discovered. Rigorous enforcement of religious uniformity was beyond the competence of any Tudor government; moreover, certain features of the Henrician settlement worked to weaken its effectiveness. Most historians are agreed that the most radical innovation of Henry VIII was the authorization of the English Bible. The Latin Vulgate remained a closed book to the great majority of the laity, but the English Bible revealed the word of God to anyone who could hear or read. When Henry, beginning to grasp the difficulties inherent in maintaining religious uniformity in a society where the vernacular Bible was readily available, legislated to restrict its use, the battle to control men's minds was already lost.

Another weakness of the king's religion was the penetration of the Church at the highest level by clerics whose personal views were closer to the continental reformers than the orthodoxy of the Act of Six Articles.

The Archbishop of Canterbury, Thomas Cranmer, remained in the king's high favor to the end and served as a constant reminder to conservative clerics that the dynamism of reform, gravely weakened by the fall of Cromwell, survived at the highest level within the church. Although forced to resign his bishopric, Hugh Latimer was still a source of inspiration to reform-minded clergy who patiently awaited an opportunity to rid the church of its Catholic doctrines and ceremonies.

Henry VIII set a poor example for his subjects by tolerating a degree of religious freedom at court that mocked his laws establishing uniformity. The king apparently believed that one law governed the commons of England while another higher but more flexible law bound the king and his friends. Fully aware of Cranmer's religious leanings, Henry playfully teased the archbishop saying," Ah, my chaplain, I have news for you. I know now who is the greatest heretic in Kent!"[3] But the king continued both to befriend the prelate who served him longer and better than any other and to protect him from enemies. In 1543 Henry actually offered to appoint Cranmer as commissioner to investigate charges that were made against him. The king's leniency may also be seen in the protection of his sixth and last queen, Catherine Parr. The unpredictable old man allowed articles to be drawn up against his wife, but when she begged his pardon, the king instantly submitted to her pleas of innocence. "By St. Mary," he said, "you are become a doctor, Kate, to instruct us (as we take it), and not to be instructed by us."[4]

Rumors and court intrigue connected other courtiers, particularly the associates of Queen Catherine and Cranmer, with heresy and left little doubt that Protestant doctrines were making deep inroads at court. When Anne Askew was examined in 1546 for denying transubstantiation, Sir Richard Rich and another councillor pressured her to reveal the names of her sympathizers. Anne replied that she knew of no others. "Then they asked me of my lady of Suffolk, my lady of Sussex, my lady of Hertford, my lady Denny, and my lady Fitzwilliams. I said that if I should pronounce anything against them, I were not able to prove it."[5] Prior to Henry's death informed sources reported that Edward Seymour, Earl of Hertford and John Dudley, Viscount Lisle were tilting toward Protestantism, but little concrete information about the religious views of Seymour, Dudley, or other lay courtiers has survived. Some probably developed leanings toward the teaching of Luther, Zwingli, or Calvin through casual reading and conversation without acquiring a deep understanding of continental Protestantism, while a few experienced a conversion to evangelical Christianity that made them dissatisfied with the Henrician settlement.

Christian humanism was another important but ambiguous religious force at the court of Henry VIII. Whereas it was once believed that English humanism perished with Thomas More and John Fisher, it is now recognized that humanism survived the deaths of the Catholic martyrs as well as the fall of Thomas Cromwell. But Christian humanism led its adherents along a variety of paths. Some, following the lead of Tyndale, Melancthon, and Calvin, espoused Protestantism, while others, upholding the traditions of Erasmus and More, remained sympathetic to the Roman Catholic Church. Still others developed an intensely personal form of Christian piety based upon the life and teachings of Christ, nondogmatic beliefs that placed greater emphasis upon inner devotion than the outward adherence to formal statements of belief. Queen Catherine was the most influential patron of humanism during the last years of Henry's reign. As patron of scholars, author of works of pietistic devotion, and supervisor of the education of Prince Edward, Henry's last queen maintained and promoted the spirit of Christian humanism at the court.[6]

The effect of conflicting religious currents during the last years of Henry VIII's reign on Prince Edward and the future religious development of England has been the subject of intense debate. Historians, following the interpretation of S. T. Bindoff, believe that England would probably have become a Protestant country if Henry had lived a few years longer. They contend that the aging king came to recognize Protestantism as the religion of the future and began preparations to reform the church by converting the Latin Mass into a service of Holy Communion, a radical departure from the doctrine established in the Six Articles of 1539. An even more dramatic sign of a shift in the king's religious views is seen in his appointment of Protestant tutors to educate his son and heir and the omission of Stephen Gardiner, Bishop of Winchester from the Council named to rule until Edward came of age. Lacey Baldwin Smith was the first historian to challenge this widely held view. He argued that Henry's behavior was diametrically opposed to his newly acquired beliefs:

> During the entire time that Henry was presumably allowing reformers to educate his son in the Protestant faith, he was systematically burning and maiming the disciples of that creed; in the same month (August 1546) that he is supposed to have contemplated turning the Mass into a communion he was busy enforcing a proclamation for the public burning of all heretical books; and during the spring and summer of 1546 he sanctioned the martyrdom of seven Protestants, demanded the abject recantation of Dr. Edward Crome, and broke out in a towering rage against his Queen's somewhat mystical and humanistic religious views.[7]

In refuting the notion that Henry VIII was in the process of converting to Protestantism at the time of his death, a subtle but essential distinction must be drawn between politics and religion during the last years of the reign. The fall of the Howards — the Duke of Norfolk and his son, the Earl of Surrey — and the rise of the Earl of Hertford and Lord Lisle signaled political but not religious changes within the king's Privy Council. At no time during the reign of Henry

VIII did the composition of the Council have a direct connection with the introduction of new religious policies. Moreover, the Act of Six Articles, the legal basis of Henrician Catholicism, was a parliamentary statute, not a royal proclamation or Privy Council warrant. The exclusion of Gardiner from the minority Council resulted from a poorly timed quarrel with the king and not from Henry's repudiation of Gardiner's religious views. The idea that Protestant tutors assumed responsibility for the education of Prince Edward resulted more from the errors of historians than from the king's disenchantment with Catholic theology. Although John Cheke and Richard Cox later became prominent Protestants, there is no evidence that they held or practiced their beliefs openly before 1547. Cheke and Cox were chosen to tutor the prince because of their humanistic learning, educational experience, and loyalty to the crown. Edward was but nine years of age when his father died, scarcely an age to undertake a serious study of the relative merits of Catholic and Protestant doctrines. When Richard Cox reported on Edward's educational progress, he mentioned the prince's declension and conjugation of Latin nouns and verbs and his study of *Aesop's Fables*, but as a wise and compassionate teacher Cox appropriately excluded both the Schoolmen and John Calvin's *Institutes of the Christian Religion* from the educational fare of his young royal charge.[8]

Edward became king and supreme head of the Church of England the moment Henry was dead but never directed the affairs of church and state as his father had done. Real political power rested with Protector Somerset and the Council, while Protestant reformers among the clergy, led by Cranmer, won political support for a program of religious reform. Denied the support of Henry VIII's conservatism and iron will, the opponents of Protestantism promptly retreated in disarray. Even the pragmatic political conservatism of Sir William Paget was rejected by his friend and former confidant, Somerset. Before the end of 1547 Parliament repealed the Six Articles and ordered that communion should be administered to the laity in both kinds. With this legislation the Henrician religious settlement was laid to rest.

Serious social and economic problems weakened the government and contributed to unrest among the commons. While some problems were the direct result of government policy, others were caused by conditions beyond human control. For example, the wars of Henry VIII and the resulting financial crisis might have been avoided if the country had had wiser political leadership, but the problems arising from population growth went beyond human understanding and the competence of any sixteenth-century government. Tudor governments did not know what the population of England was and did not think demography of sufficient importance to warrant taking a census. Contemporaries had no understanding of the problems of rapid population growth because their experience was confined to a period of population decline. Population fell after the Black Death and continued to fall until possibly as late as the 1530s. A recent estimate places the population of England at 2.3 million in the 1520s, only slightly higher than the population in 1377, a date at which population was substantially below the highest level before the Black Death. In the early sixteenth century population growth occurred in select areas including London, the surrounding counties, and thinly settled counties such as Sussex and Worcestershire. After 1530 the population began to grow very rapidly, reaching 3.75 million by 1603, an increase of 63 percent. The social and economic effects of population growth are subjects of continuing study and controversy, but there can be no doubt that that growth contributed to increased domestic demand for food and manufactures, caused a shortage of land, and stimulated the upward movement of prices.[9]

When Edward VI became king, prices — based on the Phelps Brown-Hopkins index of consumables — were 46 percent higher than in 1540. Prices fell in 1548 only to resume upward movement in 1549. In 1549, the year of the rebellions, prices were 11 percent higher than they had been the previous year. Using the Bowden index of the price of agricultural products, the rate of inflation was even greater as prices rose 21 percent between 1548 and 1549. The onset of inflation in the sixteenth century, often termed the Price Revolution, created serious problems for the government. Like population growth, inflation was poorly understood by the best minds of the period even if its outward manifestations were far more visible. The government faced a worsening financial crisis as expenditures, particularly for war, rose more rapidly than income. The government was unable to increase its overall income rapidly enough to keep pace with inflation, because the landed classes, who were similarly caught in the inflationary squeeze, were reluctant to assume larger tax burdens. A short-term remedy begun by Henry VIII and continued by Protector Somerset was debasement of the coinage. Debasement proceeded along three lines: coins were reduced in weight, the content of gold and silver in coins was reduced, and old coins were increased in value. When debasement ended in 1551, the money supply had increased two times, and the coinage came to consist almost entirely of silver. Debasement, although conceived as a remedy for problems of inflation, actually contributed to it by increasing the amount of money circulating in an economy that experienced little increase in either agricultural or industrial production. The profit to the crown was considerable, amounting to £1,270,000 between 1542 and 1551, according to the best estimate. The Great Debasement was at once "an imperative fiscal device" to prevent bankruptcy and a fraud which the government perpetrated against the people of England.[10]

Throughout the sixteenth century the overseas trade of England consisted chiefly of raw wool and unfinished woolen cloth. The export of wool declined as more and more domestic wool was marketed abroad in the form of cloth. Cloth was manufactured primarily in the West Country, East Anglia, and Yorkshire, and exported through London to the Low Countries. Peter Ramsey estimated that as much as 88 percent of cloth exports was shipped from London at the accession of Edward VI. The country's dependence on woolen cloth as the single most valuable commodity for export combined with the concentration of the trade at London made Tudor governments highly responsive to the political and economic interests of London merchants and financiers. With the profits of the woolen trade, England purchased a wide variety of goods abroad, especially wines, spices, and jewelry, all of which were items especially prized by the upper classes. The needs of the commons, on the other hand, were largely satisfied by domestic production.[11]

That the export of cloth and wool expanded during the early sixteenth century is clearly established, but there is controversy concerning the rate of growth and the effects of debasement of the coinage. If the calculations of J. D. Gould that woolen exports (cloth plus wool) increased as little as 13 percent during the first four decades of the century are correct, discontent among weavers and others in the textile industry at mid-century would be more readily understood. Yet Gould also believes that cloth exports remained quite stable for the first four years of debasement — 1544-48 — and actually showed a small increase between 1548 and 1550. On the basis of these estimates, overseas trade can be seen as one factor contributing to social unrest, but hardly as a direct or immediate cause of the rebellions of 1549.[12]

Students of economic history occasionally fail to appreciate that the problems of greatest concern to the government and upper classes were not always of equal importance to the people of England as a whole. Sir Thomas Smith was correct in a legal sense when he said that the consent of Parliament was the consent of every man, woman, and child in the country, but it would be nonsense to pretend that Parliament or any other institution of central government set the welfare of the people as its highest priority.[13] Major conflicts of interest divided those who ruled Tudor England from those who were governed by the king's laws. Although the government of Protector Somerset continually teetered on the brink of bankruptcy, the financial health of the government was not a pressing concern to yeomen farmers, copyholders, and small tradesmen, whose interests were limited to the local community. Similarly, the inflation of prices is of considerable interest to economic historians, but the commons were only adversely affected when real wages and income actually declined. Nor could the value of the pound at Antwerp have a direct effect on the well-being of a peasant whose simple needs were satisfied almost entirely by domestic production. If the county was the natural milieu of the country gentleman, it was the village or perhaps the neighboring field or commons that mattered to the common man.

He was less interested in the national effects of the enclosure movement and the shortage of arable land than in the immediate situation affecting his family and friends. Whereas a poor harvest meant loss of income to the gentry, it often meant extreme privation or starvation to the poor.

The best evidence presently available suggests that the sixteenth century witnessed "a progressive decline in the average standards of living."[14] The peasant living in the fifteenth century under the Yorkists enjoyed a higher standard of living than his grandchildren who lived under Henry VIII. At mid-century the gap between real wages and prices began to grow, and it reached the widest point in 1597. In the 1540s and 1550s the real wages of an urban laborer may have fallen as much as 50 percent, causing his diet to consist of an increasing proportion of bread in comparison to meat. W. G. Hoskins estimated that the working class spent as much as 80 to 90 percent of its income on food and drink and that a third of the population lived below the poverty line. Although a declining standard of living for the country as a whole seems firmly established, significant local variations indicate that all persons were not affected in the same way, and intense controversy continues about the causes of the decline.[15]

Rising population and the resulting shortage of arable land forced the tenant to pay higher entry fines and rent for the land that he farmed. Enclosure of open fields, once seen as the major cause of rural poverty, diminishes in importance with the knowledge that most of the countryside was not enclosed until the nineteenth century. The poor sheep, villains of Sir Thomas More's *Utopia,* apparently reproduced less rapidly than the *homo sapiens* who sheared off their fleece and ate their flesh. And it has been argued that the sheep's dung was as important as the wool, because dung was required to fertilize the lighter soils in order to feed the growing number of bread-hungry mouths. The introduction of convertible or up-and-down husbandry increased agricultural production and ended the inefficient maintenance of permanent pasture and permanent arable lands, but the new practices also eliminated rights of the small farmer to pasture his livestock on the village commons. Agricultural innovations, despite their potential advantages to large landowners, were too risky to be tried by the ordinary peasant, while the poorer cottage-dweller with ancient rights on the common had no arable land with which to experiment. On the eve of the rebellions, the commons were caught in the grip of economic forces beyond their understanding. Few, if any, can have comprehended the actual effects of population growth, enclosure, and convertible husbandry. On the other hand, the annual harvest was an economic reality requiring no expert interpretation. The country enjoyed a good grain harvest in 1547, a less abundant one the following year, and, significantly, a poor harvest in 1549.[16]

Henry VIII left behind extensive foreign commitments that required careful attention and shrewd management. The reign ended with England in possession of Boulogne — the solitary symbol of Henry's success on the continent — and nominally at peace with France. Although supported by a weak alliance with Charles V, England saw relations with France deteriorate rapidly after the aggressive Henry II succeeded to the throne of Francis I. Boulogne stood as a continuing source of embarrassment to the French and a burdensome financial liability to its English occupiers. The situation in Scotland complicated English relations with the European powers. Henry VIII had tried unsuccessfully to force Scottish compliance with a treaty of 1543 calling for the marriage of the young Scottish queen to Prince Edward, an alliance intended to create a Greater Britain under English leadership. The Scots resisted English pressures and turned to France, their traditional ally, for assistance. At the time of his death, Henry was supporting a Protestant pro-English faction that had seized St. Andrew's Castle and was also planning a large-scale invasion of Scotland for the summer of 1547.[17]

Protector Somerset pursued a dynamic foreign policy that was essentially Henrician. He strengthened Calais and Boulogne against anticipated French attacks and prepared to invade Scotland. The French capture of St. Andrews in July 1547 effectively forced Somerset's hand, but the Protector, who had served as Henry's commander against the Scots, had his own ideas for the conquest of Scotland, a policy that curiously combined Protestant evangelism with English manifest destiny. Leading a powerful army of 18,000 into Scotland in September, Somerset crushed a larger enemy force at Pinkie. Somerset quickly returned to London but left behind an army of occupation. Garrisons stretched from Inchholm on the Firth of Forth to Dundee and Roxburgh, with a force of 2,500 positioned at Haddington that devastated the area from Dunbar to Edinburgh. Somerset's determination to garrison Scotland marked a major departure from previous efforts at conquest which allowed the Scots an opportunity to recover after a single military defeat. If Somerset's approach was a tactical improvement upon prior English strategy, it was costly in manpower and supplies and almost certain to provoke French intervention. Predictably, a French army of 6,000 landed in June 1548, forcing the English onto the defensive. In the face of growing difficulty, most of the garrisons were withdrawn, and English military power in Scotland became concentrated at Haddington and Broughty Craig, at the mouth of the River Tay. Meanwhile, France further harrassed the English with attacks on Calais and Boulogne. Even before the outbreak of the rebellions a rapidly deteriorating situation both in Scotland and on the continent confronted Somerset and his military commanders. In April 1549, Sir William Paget was so depressed with the state of affairs that he wrote, "All things in manner going backward and unfortunately, and every man almost out of heart and courage, and our lacks so well known as our enemies despise us and our friends pity us." Demands for reinforcements and supplies gradually brought the government to the brink of bankruptcy.[18]

2. Climate of Opinion

With the accession of Edward VI the climate of informed opinion became distinctly more favorable to religious and social reform. The voice of religious reform, muted but never silenced after the passage of the Six Articles in 1539, sounded throughout the land. To the reformers the Henrician religious settlement constituted only the first step toward a church purged of corrupt and superstitious practices. Fasting, images, and the Latin mass came under heavy attack. Close on the heels of agitation for religious change was the social and economic criticism of the Commonwealth writers, the most outspoken of whom were Hugh Latimer, John Hales, and Robert Crowley. Concern for the poor who suffered at the hands of oppressive landlords was heard throughout the early sixteenth century. In *The Tree of Commonwealth,* Edmund Dudley, the disgraced minister of Henry VII, called on Henry VIII and the nobility to show compassion for the poor. Later Sir Thomas More levelled a powerful attack on human pride and acquisitiveness in *Utopia,* while Cardinal Wolsey heard complaints of the poor in the Court of Requests and attempted to restrict enclosures. In the 1530s Thomas Cromwell employed Parliament as the logical instrument for the reform and renewal of the commonwealth. Even if Henry VIII's great minister "did not manage in nine years to stamp out poverty or bring contentment to all sorts and conditions of men, he could lay claim to considerable achievements." Cromwell's sheep and enclosure legislation created a sound basis for stabilizing the agrarian economy. His Poor Law, according to G. R. Elton, "marked the real beginning of a national system of relief which was unique among the nation-states of Europe."[19]

In 1547 Protector Somerset emerged as the heir of Dudley, More, Wolsey, and Cromwell. Although the development of his religious, political, and social ideas remains obscure, Somerset took the lead in patronizing and promoting reform. Commonwealth writers and politicians maintained close ties with him and the Seymour family. His policy, wrote M. L. Bush, "was designed not to change society but to prevent radical change."[20] Archbishop Cranmer's leadership was less visible, even though his personal commitment to the Protestant cause was greater than that of any other member of the young king's Council. Cranmer's biographer, Jasper Ridley, saw him as "a man who had spent sixteen years as a servile servant of a despot and had lost whatever capacity for leadership he may once have possessed."[21] Unfortunately

Ridley's judgment flies in the face of impressive evidence that Cranmer was the most important architect of religious reform. He alone among Edward's councillors possessed the experience and ability to transform the Henrician Church into a Protestant Church. If Cranmer lacked the will to seize the initiative himself, it appears that Somerset created an environment that allowed the archbishop to achieve objectives which Henry VIII had opposed. A decade earlier Cromwell had given Cranmer the necessary political support; in 1547 Somerset strove to play the same role. Preachers, theologians, and liturgists knew Cranmer as their friend and supporter notwithstanding his previous deference to Henry VIII.

An objective appraisal of the climate of opinion in the first years of Edward's reign requires not only an examination of the political and religious leadership, but also an evaluation of preaching and pamphleteering. Contemporary chroniclers left little doubt that change was in the wind, while the protests and complaints of Henricians who saw power and influence slip from their hands add the necessary confirmation that the death of Henry marked the end of an era. Until the outbreak of rebellion in 1549, the reformers moved from strength to strength, and the articulation and implementation of their programs constitute an important watershed in the history of the sixteenth century.

In a preindustrial and semiliterate society, the pulpit was the most important means of shaping public opinion. Tudor monarchs and their ministers not only lacked the vehicles of mass communication but also failed to use public oratory to inform, direct, and inspire the subjects of the crown. Although courtiers and foreign ambassadors usually knew what policies were favored by the crown, the ordinary citizens of Westminster and London relied on gossip and rumor unless informed by a royal proclamation, parliamentary statute, or the public execution of the spokesman for a defeated cause. The counties of Tudor England were a world to themselves. The gentry and burgesses knew well enough what was happening, usually through contacts at court or in London, but they were often a step or two behind those closer to the center of power. The husbandman or townsman, on the other hand, knew only what he was told or managed to overhear. Uninformed gossip and wild rumors, blended with generous doses of wishful thinking, often comprised the commons' understanding of government policy, unless they were informed otherwise by the parish priest. From the beginning of Edward's reign, reforming clergy launched a massive propaganda offensive from the pulpit and called for sweeping religious and social reforms. Although the overall tenor of the preaching represented policies favored by Protector Somerset and Archbishop Cranmer, overzealous preachers promised more than the government could deliver.[22]

The role of sermons in shaping public opinion may be seen by analyzing sixty-two sermons preached at London and Westminster from the accession of Edward VI to the outbreak of rebellion in the summer of

1549. Thirty-seven of the sermons were preached in public, the most important places being Paul's Cross, St. Bride, and St. Mary Spittal. At Paul's Cross and St. Mary Spittal, preachers spoke from outside pulpits to large crowds of Londoners. Most of the other sermons were preached before King Edward and the court. Although several preachers, notably Stephen Gardiner, Bishop of Winchester, defended the Henrician settlement, about fifty-five of the sermons were given by Protestant reformers. No fewer than seventeen sermons, over a fourth of the total, were preached by Hugh Latimer, the former bishop of Worcester. Other prominent reformers who preached on more than one occasion were Nicholas Ridley, Miles Coverdale, John Cardmaker, Henry Holbeach, Richard Cox, William Barlow, and Roger Tonge. Almost all had close ties with Archbishop Cranmer, Protector Somerset, and the court.[23]

The religious views of the preachers were clear and unequivocal. They denounced the Henrician settlement, the Six Articles, fasting, images, and the Latin Mass. They exhorted the king, the Council, and Parliament to reform the old religious order. William Barlow, Bishop of St. David's preaching at Paul's Cross on November 27, 1547, "showed a picture of the resurrection of our Lord made with vices [movable joints] which put out his legs of sepulchre and blessed with his hand and turned his head; and there stood afore the pulpit the image of our Lady which they of Paul's had lapped in seercloth." In his sermon Barlow "declared the great abomination of idolatry in images with other feigned ceremonies contrary to scripture to the extolling of God's glory and to the great comfort of the audience." Following the sermon, the chronicler, Charles Wriothesley, who may have been present himself, recorded that boys broke the idols into small pieces of rubble.[24] Several conservative clerics, trimming their views in response to the growing pressure for Protestant reform, repudiated their former teachings. Dr. Richard Smith recanted, burned two of his own books, and renounced the "old papistical order" at Paul's Cross. Another, Dr. Peren, justified images in a sermon at St. Andrew Undershaft on April 23, 1547, but like Smith recanted in a sermon given two months later.[25]

Hugh Latimer, the most influential preacher of the period considering both the quantity and the quality of his sermons, was a religious reformer of long standing.[26] Imprisoned by Henry VIII, Latimer was released from the Tower at the beginning of the new reign and went to live with Cranmer at Lambeth. When he resumed preaching on January 1, 1548, the most powerful voice of the English Reformation was heard for the first time in eight years. Latimer defended the Royal Injunctions of 1547, which embodied the first substantial measures of Protestant reform, and then unleashed a withering attack on bishops and other clergy who refused to preach the Gospel. Unpreaching prelates, said Latimer

are so troubled with lordly living, they be so placed in palaces, couched in courts, ruffling in their rents, dancing in their dominions, burdened with ambassages, pampering of their paunches, like a monk that maketh his jubilee, munching in their mangers, and moiling in their gay manors and mansions, and so troubled with loitering in their lordships, that they cannot attend to it.[27]

Latimer also turned to the social question, a far more delicate and politically dangerous issue. In the famous "Sermon of the Plough," preached at St. Paul's, he berated the rich citizens of London for their covetousness, pride, and cruelty. In times past, he said, Londoners were full of pity and compassion, "but now there is no pity; for in London their brother shall die in the streets for cold . . . and perish there for hunger." He entreated the nobility to set a good example for the commons: "For truly, such as the noblemen be, such will the people be." Speaking before King Edward at Westminster in 1549, Latimer inveighed against "extortioners, violent oppressors, engrossers of tenements and lands through whose covetousness villages decay, and fall down, the king's liege people for lack of sustenance are famished and decayed." He continued, "We have good statutes made for the commonwealth, as touching commoners and enclosers, many meetings and sessions, but in the end of the matter there cometh nothing forth." On the one hand, he lamented the decline of the yeomanry, the class from which he came; on the other, he berated the rich lawyers, merchants, landlords, and judges, who were the instruments of the commons' oppression.[28] No economist, Latimer attributed the misery of the rural poor to rent-raisers rather than to the inflation of prices that was potentially harmful to all social classes. The eight surviving sermons preached before the outbreak of rebellion severely criticize the rich for their oppression of the poor, but the sermons taken as a whole cannot be described as propaganda for the Commonwealth cause. As Latimer directed the larger portion of his wrath against corrupt clergy, whoredom, and dicing, his sermons made a greater contribution to Christian prophecy than to social reform.

Outside of London a very similar pattern appears. From one end of England to the other Protestant preachers assailed the Henrician compromise and demanded immediate reforms. One of the most zealous was Thomas Hancock, an Oxford graduate, licensed to preach by Archbishop Cranmer. At Christ Church, Hampshire, Hancock interrupted the priest during mass to denounce the sacrament of the altar; later at Salisbury in the presence of Bishop Gardiner, he "inveighed against the superstitious ceremonies, as holy bread, holy water, images, copes, vestments and at the last against the idol of the altar proving it to be an idol, and no God by the first of St. John's Gospel." Hancock's radicalism caused him to be examined at the Wiltshire assizes only to be released when a rich woolen-draper agreed to post bond for him. Hancock subsequently appealed his case to Protector Somerset, who intervened in his behalf and secured cancellation of the bond. For the remainder of Edward's reign, Hancock preached at Poole, evoking the same strong opposition as he had encountered at Salisbury, but he enjoyed the protection of Somerset and Sir William Cecil. Although there is little evidence that Hancock or any of the other preachers combined religious radicalism with either social or political protest, the Council issued a proclamation on April 24, 1548, prohibiting all preaching throughout the realm except by clergy licensed by the king, the Protector, or the Archbishop of Canterbury. With the protection of Somerset extended to the likes of Thomas Hancock, the proclamation had little effect, and consequently an absolute ban on all preaching was temporarily invoked by another proclamation in September of the same year.[29]

Although it is extremely difficult to assess the role of preachers in reflecting and shaping the climate of opinion, the task of making similar judgments in regard to the Commonwealth writers is even more hazardous. Preachers may be easily categorized on the basis of their religious views in that those calling for reform enjoyed the favor and encouragement of the Protector's government. Indeed, preachers defending the Henrician settlement are strikingly absent from the London chronicles and were probably no more vocal in the countryside. The presence of large numbers of reformers in the pulpit is in no way surprising since preaching was the vehicle of communication favored by Protestants for spreading the word of God. Moreover, we know that the Edwardian preachers had an audience. They spoke before the king and court and to crowds assembled at Paul's Cross, addressed Parliament, and preached to sympathetic congregations in London parish churches. There is every reason to believe that those who listened to the sermons liked what they heard. The sermons therefore both reflected and molded public opinion. In contrast, we know very little about such Commonwealth writers as William Forrest and Robert Crowley. In the case of such works as "Policies to Reduce this Realm of England unto a Prosperous Wealth and Estate," the first problem is identification of the author. Forrest and the anonymous author of "Policies" dedicated their works to Somerset, but to what end? Possibly they saw him as a leader who was receptive to their ideas about social reform. Another reason would be to seek one of the many appointments that the Protector was able to bestow. Commonwealth writers and humanists, taken as a group, were as ambitious in seeking profitable employment as other Tudor careerists.[30]

Equally problematical is the task of assessing the influence of the Commonwealth pamphleteers. It is likely that some of the readers were Privy Councillors, administrators, members of Parliament, and influential clergymen. G. R. Elton wisely cautioned against ascribing excessive importance to the printed word when he wrote, "Few men of action ever learned their jobs or ideas from books."[31] Yet there was a rapidly increasing demand for books during the early sixteenth century. Some fifty editions of the New Testament in English had been printed by 1557, while the number of books published annually in England increased from fifty-four in 1500 to over two hundred at mid-century. The growth of literacy stimulated the demand for books. Although it is impossible to determine with certainty the level of literacy in early Tudor England, readers were found in most social classes and walks of life. Sir Thomas More thought "far more than four parts of the whole divided into ten could never read English," an estimate of literacy approaching 60 percent that modern authorities regard as too high. At the other extreme was Stephen Gardiner, Bishop of Winchester, who declared that "not the hundreth part of the realm" was able to read in 1547. The most recent research indicates that as late as the 1640s, illiteracy was 70 percent among men and 90 percent among women. Whatever the level of literacy may have been, the total number of persons subjected to the influence of English books would have to include the nonliterates who heard books read aloud or discussed. The Commonwealth writers must have believed that an audience for their books existed or else they would not have bothered to go into print.[32]

Only a few of the best-known Commonwealth treatises appeared before the outbreak of rebellion. The anonymous manuscript, "Policies to Reduce This Realm of England unto a Prosperous Wealth and Estate," began by defining "the flourishing estate of the realm." It observed that "surely in my judgment it consisteth chiefly in being strong against the invasion of enemies, not molested with civil wars, the people being wealthy, and not oppressed with famine nor penury of victuals." The author also stressed the king's need for a full treasury to command the respect of his subjects and to defend the realm against foreign enemies. After stating the characteristics of a prosperous realm, the book proceeds very logically to give specific policy recommendations that would achieve these ends. The fall or devaluation of the pound in Flanders, not debasement, was seen as the major cause of rising prices. If the royal mints paid lower prices for gold and silver, prices would fall. The mints could be assured of adequate supplies of lower-priced bullion by increasing the country's agricultural and industrial production. The author contended that the concentration of wealth, particularly sheep, in the hands of a few led to higher prices and lower agricultural productivity. He called for a tax on sheep and measures to increase the amount of land under cultivation. Import duties levied on foreign manufacturers were recommended to benefit a long list of craftsmen including cappers, pinners, worsted-weavers, cutlers, and linen-spinners. Only iron, steel, copper, pitch, and tar should be excluded from the import duty. The author argued that the country was impoverished by special interests or privileged minorities — covetous merchants, monopolistic sheepfarmers, horders of plate, rackrenters, and enclosers of common lands. His sympathies lay with the small farmers and craftsmen, whose productivity, if properly encouraged, would restore England to a prosperous state.[33]

William Forrest's "Pleasant Poesye of Princely Practice," dedicated to Protector Somerset, also denounced the rich oppressors of the poor, but Forrest was more a prophet or social critic than a proponent of economic reform. For him, times were out of joint:

> The world is changed from that it hath been
> not to the better but to the worse fare:
> more for a penny we have before seen
> then now for four pence, who list to compare.

High rents and prices impoverished the yeomanry, who were no longer able to defend the country against its foreign enemies. Once-proud Englishmen were reduced to the servile status of other Europeans. Forrest criticized the merchants of the staple whose wool exports deprived clothworkers of employment. He decried depopulation as well as inflation of prices. For the rent formerly paid for a house with common rights and arable land, a poor man must accept only an "old rotten house" and a small garden. Conditions had become so bad, said Forrest, that "thousands there be that right gladly would wed if they had holdings to cover their head."[34]

The most eloquent of the Commonwealth writers was Robert Crowley, who combined vigorous Protestantism with compassion for the oppressed commons. In *An Information and Petition against the Oppressors of the Poor Commons...*, he called on the king's councillors and members of Parliament to support social as well as religious reform. Godly men, said Crowley, are at work preaching the word of God, but the danger is that the plight of the poor will be "passed over with silence." Engrossers of farms, rackrenters, enclosers, leasemongers, and usurers felt the sting of Crowley's prose: "Woe be unto you therefore that do join house unto house, and couple one field to another, so long as there is any ground to be had." He estimated that 90 percent of the houses in London were rented by leasemongers rather than by the owners. Because of grinding poverty men were forced to rob and steal. With the zeal of a prophet Crowley implored the rich to mend their ways: "Now harken you possessioners and you rich men, lift up your ears, ye stewards of the Lord, mark what complaints are laid against you in the high court of the living God." He called upon the king's councillors to accept even heavier responsibilities. "Know that your office is to distribute and not to scrape together on heaps," he wrote. "Consider that you are but ministers and servants under the Lord our God, and that you shall render a straight account of your administration." Crowley believed in the power of Parliament to redress social grievances and to establish a Christian Commonwealth in which all men could be brothers. He was not a demagogue calling for the commons to rise up against their oppressors.[35]

Protestant reformers saw an obvious connection between religious and social reform. To Robert Crowley and Hugh Latimer the personal gospel and the social gospel were identical and inseparable. The author of "Policies to Reduce This Realm of England" took much the same view when he wrote, "Now that the true worshipping of God is by the virtuous inclination of the king's majesty and by the godly diligence of [Protector Somerset] so purely and sincerely set forth, it is likewise to be trusted that God of a boundant mercifulness toward us will use the king's majesty and your grace to be also his ministers in plucking up by the roots all the causes and occasion of . . . decay and desolation."[36] Unfortunately, the reformers were not wholly in step with public opinion. Although there was popular support for religious reform based on traditional anticlericalism, Lollardy, and continental Protestantism, the reformers owed their success to the favorable attitudes of Somerset, the Council, and Parliament. Protestantism as embodied in the established church was imposed on the commons by the ruling elite or the political nation of Edwardian England. In most places popular opinion accepted or at least tolerated official religious change.

Social reform was entirely different. Support for social reform came primarily from the unenfranchised — small landholders, artisans, and the poor — who experienced the grievances recounted by the Commonwealth writers. During the reign of Henry VIII, men were taught that obedience to the state came before one's own well-being; after 1547 the Commonwealth advocates believed that new policies should begin to redress long-standing social and economic grievances. They succeeded in winning the ear of Protector Somerset but found the Council and Parliament less sympathetic. The Council and Parliament, reflecting the legitimate vested interests of the peerage and gentry, could accept Protestantism but not programs that threatened to reduce their incomes and encouraged assertiveness among the commons.

The fact that few Commonwealth tracts appeared prior to the rebellions undermines any notion that these writers stimulated, encouraged, or provoked popular unrest.[37] The reformers' objective, as Crowley made very clear, was to impress upon the Council and Parliament the seriousness and extent of suffering among the commons. The question was not, as Sir William Paget arrogantly put it, whether conditions among the poor were significantly worse than in the past, but whether the regime of King Edward could make life better for all sorts and conditions of men.[38] The Commonwealth writers were not rabble-rousers inciting the peasants to pull down fences. As spokesmen of the inarticulate masses, they called on government to undertake legislative reforms. They failed in part because their educational and propagandistic efforts were barely under way when the outbreak of rebellion destroyed any hope that the aristocracy would support measures favorable to their tenants.

3. The Progress of Reform

The first three years of the reign of Edward VI saw the most sweeping religious innovations in English history. Edward's first Parliament, meeting in November 1547, dismantled the Henrician religious settlement by repealing the Six Articles and also instituted communion in both kinds. A. G. Dickens regarded the Chantries Act of 1547 as the most important legislation "so far as ordinary Englishmen were concerned," because it repudiated Catholic teachings on purgatory and masses for the dead. Although the legislation attempted to alter traditional practices, a broad section of population benefited from the grammar schools, almshouses, hospitals, and other charitable institutions that were endowed with the property of the dissolved chantries. The next year Somerset, pushing forward with Protestant reforms, issued a royal proclamation appointing a new Order of Communion which inserted English prayers into the Latin mass. By May 1548 English language services were conducted unofficially at St. Paul's and other London churches.[39]

These important first steps toward liturgical reform paved the way for the introduction of Cranmer's first Book of Common Prayer in 1549. The English service was sufficiently ambiguous to encourage a variety of interpretations of the doctrines that it contained, but Philip Hughes perhaps most closely appreciated the attitudes of Catholics and Henricians when he wrote, "In this First Prayer Book of King Edward VI, not only is the ancient sacramental ritual everywhere greatly changed, but the rubrical directions more than once leave no doubt that the changes have been made in order to give effect to this new heretical doctrine which Cranmer and his associates undoubtedly held."[40] The 1549 Act of Uniformity required all clergy to conduct services according to the Prayer Book under threat of life imprisonment for the third offense. Persons attacking the Prayer Book or forcing a priest to use a different service were subject to fines and loss of all goods for the third offense. The new Protestant church of Edward VI, like its Henrician predecessor, was authoritarian and intolerant of dissenting beliefs.

Parliamentary legislation in 1549 permitting clerical marriage rounded out the first phase of the Edwardian Reformation. Protestant clerics, following the lead of Martin Luther, had taken wives many years earlier, but Henry VIII effectively resisted the practice in England. The Edwardian legislation, far from encouraging clergymen to enter the state of holy matrimony, merely voided all previous laws and canons preventing it. The preamble to the statute held that it was better for ministers of the Church of God "to live chaste, sole, and separate from the company of women and the bond of marriage," but grudgingly conceded that the "godly use of marriage" was preferable for those too weak to avoid fornication. Notwithstanding its conservative rationale, the Act to Take Away All Positive Laws Against Marriage of Priests marked a radical departure from previous practices. Many clerics hastened to take advantage of their newly acquired rights although some prominent reformers including Cranmer and Miles Coverdale, the translator of the English Bible, had previously married in defiance of clerical celibacy.

Whereas the hand of Thomas Cranmer is readily apparent in the formulation of religious policy, the genesis of support within the Council for political and social reform remains highly obscure. In the absence of information to the contrary, it must be assumed that Somerset himself was the foremost advocate of reform in the secular sphere. The councillors best qualified to transform ideas into practicable administrative procedures, proclamations, or parliamentary legislation included Sir William Paget, Sir Thomas Smith, Sir William Petre, William Paulet, Lord St. John, and Richard, Lord Rich. Yet the biographers of Smith, Petre and Rich contend that none of them was important as a policy-maker.[41] Paget, although personally closer to Somerset than any of the others, gradually lost influence with the Protector and by the end of 1548 was writing letters highly critical of the reform program. Smith, a new face in politics who left Cambridge to advance himself in Somerset's household, believed in social reform, but his views on important matters such as the coinage ran contrary to Somerset's policies. Paulet and Thomas Wriothesley, Earl of Southampton both possessed considerable administrative ability and experience, but the contribution of the former is unclear, while the latter, having been removed as lord chancellor, can scarcely have worked closely with Somerset in developing domestic policy. John Dudley, Earl of Warwick, like Paget a friend of Somerset, exercised considerable influence within the Council and most likely supported political reform. Yet Warwick, who was more of a soldier than an administrator, never concerned himself with such tasks as drafting legislation or royal proclamations.

Somerset never relied entirely on the Privy Council in shaping political and social policy, for he organized a remarkable household of advisers that included Commonwealth reformers. Among the inner circle, whose role was criticized by Paget as he felt his own influence wane, were Sir John Thynne, John Hales, and William Cecil. In addition Somerset maintained close ties with Hugh Latimer, the Protestant preacher and advocate of Commonwealth principles. It is highly probable that these personal advisers were as important as the Council in helping Somerset develop a domestic program.[42]

The reform program upon which Somerset's reputation rests included parliamentary statutes, royal proclamations, and administrative initiatives, but the exact roles of the Protector, the Privy Council, and Parliament in the process of policy-making are poorly documented. Somerset, notwithstanding his extensive authority as Protector, governed with a Council that frequently disagreed with his policies and a Parliament that showed increasing signs of independence. He undoubtedly preferred parliamentary support for his reform measures and worked with his supporters to gain the support of both houses. With the exception of his jealous brother, Thomas, Lord Seymour, the opponents of Somerset's reform objected initially to his policies rather than to his position of leadership. Moreover, Somerset's own political and social principles seem to have undergone significant modification as he became increasingly influenced by John Hales and the Commonwealth writers. The complex interaction of Somerset, the Council, and Parliament explains the diversity and indeed the contradictions found in the political and social reforms of the Protectorate. Political reforms reflecting the interests of the aristocracy generally received support from the Council and Parliament, while programs intended to ease the plight of the poor were implemented only through the use of the royal prerogative.

The domestic reforms enacted by Parliament in 1547 reveal a curious mixture of political and social principles. The great repeal act (1 Edward VI c. 12) for which Somerset has been highly praised, repealed the heresy laws and treason legislation enacted during the reign of Henry VIII. The preamble to the act is said to embody Somerset's idealistic credo, while its best-known clauses removed from the statute books the most oppressive features of Henrician despotism.[45] But the liberalism of this legislation benefited mainly the aristocracy, the class that suffered most heavily because of the Henrician treason laws. The commons, on the other hand, had little to fear from the treason laws because the felonies with which they were most likely to be charged also carried the death penalty. The repeal act, in addition to modifying the law of treason, favored the peerage by extending benefit of clergy to peers on the first offense irrespective of their ability to read Latin in all cases except murder. Another section of the act actually revived a statute of Henry VIII (27 Henry VIII c. 17) against servants stealing goods or cattle from their masters. The repeal act may be seen primarily as a measure of political reform benefiting the ruling elite who were represented in Parliament and the Council. It is indeed difficult to see how any of Somerset's fellow councillors, however conservative they might be, could have been harmed by this statute.

The worst blot, however, on Somerset's reputation as a reformer with strong sympathies for the poor is found in the notorious Vagrancy Act of 1547 (1 Edward VI c. 3) imposing slavery as punishment for refusal to work. The act provided that two justices of the peace, "hearing the proof of the idle living of the said person . . . approved to them by two honest witnesses or confession of the party," might have the individual branded with a letter *v* and enslaved for a period of two years. Runaway slaves were condemned to perpetual slavery for the first offense and death as a felon for the second. On the other hand, a man so enslaved might be freed before the two-year term elapsed if he obtained suitable employment. In an age of savage punishments for vagabonds and sturdy beggars, when beating, branding with hot irons, and compulsory apprenticing of pauper children were the law of the land, the Vagrancy Act of 1547 with the unique and innovative provision for enslavement stands as a landmark in the history of human oppression.

How did the legislation pass the two houses of Parliament and obtain the royal assent, given in the king's name by Protector Somerset? Because of the inadequacy of parliamentary records, C. S. L. Davies found it impossible to reconstruct the legislative history of the statute but believed it originated in three vagrancy bills introduced into the Lords. The upper house quickly produced and passed without opposition an amended bill, which was accepted by the Commons. Davies concluded that the act "may not have been a government measure in its origin" and that the slavery provisions were reviewed by a committee of lawyers and judges. There is no evidence that Somerset or his supporters in the Lords and Commons opposed the legislation. By giving the royal assent on 24 December, the last day of the parliamentary session, Somerset confirmed the government's approval. The fact that the vagrant's act, like so much Tudor legislation, was never enforced and was repealed immediately after Somerset's fall from power serves as a reminder that Edwardian parliamentarians were wise enough to recognize and remedy their mistakes.[44]

Somerset prorogued Parliament on December 24, ending a session of seven weeks. The extent to which the legislation that was passed reflected the desires of Somerset, the Council, or Parliament itself will probably always remain a subject for debate. Historians sympathetic to Somerset credit him with inspiring and supporting the good legislation and assign blame for the bad to a vaguely defined group of opponents, an interpretation that is untendable in view of existing documentation. The rejection of forty-eight bills of which twenty-three, according to W. K. Jordan's calculations, were concerned with economic problems suggests a generally conservative posture among parliamentarians.[45] Although Somerset managed Parliament with a gentle touch, allowing it to exercise its inclinations toward independence, the Protector's choice of proclamations the next year as the means of implementing his social reforms — notwithstanding Parliament's legislation against proclamations — indicates that he saw Parliament as a body unsympathetic to the plight of the poor.

The proclamation of June, 1548, announcing the appointment of a commission to enforce legislation against enclosures, stands as the chief monument to Somerset's concern for the peasantry. As the proclamation makes absolutely clear, legislation against enclosures had never been enforced effectively. Thus, the threat to enclosure came not from the laws themselves, but from the will of the government to enforce the law. The language of the proclamation with its references to "the insatiable covetousness of men" and the "misery and poverty" of the peasantry indicates the extent to which Somerset had been won over to the Commonwealth attitude toward social reform. The enclosures commission headed by the resolute John Hales conducted investigations in the Midlands during the summers of 1548 and 1549. The proclamation required tenants to give the commissioners information about offenses committed by their landlords and offered hope that Somerset's government would act to redress all legitimate violations of parliamentary legislation against enclosures.[46]

The work of John Hales and the other commissioners did not end the enclosures problem, but historians, after accepting this overall assessment, hold widely differing views regarding the significance of Somerset's agrarian program. Historians well-versed in the popular literature of the period see the enclosures commission as an appropriate government response to distress of the agrarian poor. Other authorities, more concerned with actual agricultural conditions and demographic trends, contend that the commission dealt with the wrong problems. The most extensive period of enclosure preceded the accession of Henry VII in 1485, while the boom in sheep-farming ended about the time that Somerset issued the famous proclamation. The real problem, on the basis of demographic evidence, was a shortage of land to produce food for a rapidly growing rural population.[47]

The disagreements among modern historians merely echo the attitudes of contemporaries to Somerset's enclosure policy. The Commonwealth faction saw the Protector as the champion of social justice and a true believer in Christian compassion for the poor. Among the Tudor aristocracy he had fewer admirers. The gentry, who regarded the enclosures commission as an attempt to undermine their governance in the countryside, interfere with rights of private property, and encourage disobedience among the commons, successfully countered its effectiveness. Within the Council questions were raised about Somerset's use of the prerogative in issuing the proclamations and about the effect of the policy on law and order. Sir William Paget was the most articulate and outspoken critic of Somerset's program, but the Earl of Warwick and other councillors shared many of his fears. When Parliament reassembled in November 1548, John Hales tried unsuccessfully to obtain passage of three bills intended to benefit the Commonwealth. A bill against regrating of victuals, containing the provision that "graziers nor no man should buy any cattle and sell the same again within a certain time," passed the Lords; but, as Hales later recounted, met vigorous opposition in the Commons: "[The bill] which if you had there heard debated and had seen how it was tossed and to whose hands at length it was committed, and how it was deferred, if you should have seen men's affections wonderfully, perchance you would have said that the lamb had been committed to the wolf to custody." The opposition of the gentry, acting through its representatives in the House of Commons and supported by the larger part of the Council, obstructed Somerset's efforts to assist the poor.[48]

The hostility of the gentry toward the enclosures commission did not deter Hales and the Commonwealth reformers from offering measures of social and economic reform to Parliament when it reconvened. Although most of the bills failed to pass, Hales and his supporters secured enactment of the famous sheep tax. The tax was intended to generate revenue that was desperately needed by the government and to discourage wool production. In theory, arable farmers threatened with enclosure would be the beneficiaries. The amended version, entitled the Act for the Relief, 2 and 3 Edward VI c. 36, included a poll tax on sheep, a levy on cloth exports, and a relief on personal property. In its final form the act accomplished substantially less than Hales had originally intended. A provision whereby a sheepowner became liable to pay the poll tax on his sheep only if his obligation exceeded the amount paid by way of the relief levied on personal property eased the burden placed on graziers. As M. W. Beresford has shown, "A man whose sheep tax totalled 10s. would pay nothing unless his relief on goods had been assessed at less than that sum. If his sheep tax did exceed his property tax, then he was only to pay the difference." This complicated legislation also failed to produce revenue, because the rebellions broke out before officials completed assessing the liabilities of the sheepowners. Over a month before the ill-fated sheep tax was initially introduced in the Commons, Sir William Paget, with uncanny prescience, advised Somerset to raise revenue in a different way. He should, said Paget, ask only for the traditional subsidy, which was what the people expected, and he predicted that a new tax on sheep and cloth would yield very little.[49]

The social and economic reforms initiated by Somerset's government combined good intentions with poor results. The enclosures commission and the sheep tax reflected the Christian idealism of the Commonwealth reformers. On the other hand, Somerset's prodding of the Court of Requests, often seen as a further example of his concern for the poor, has recently been viewed as merely an attempt to promote traditional justice along conventional lines.[50] And the odious Vagrancy Act embodied neither high ideals nor justice for the poor. For his limited achievements Somerset paid an extraordinarily high price. He lost the confidence of the Privy Council and aroused distrust among the gentry, whose support was assiduously cultivated by more successful Tudor rulers. Without the support of the gentry, the government could not raise the revenue needed to prevent bankruptcy. As for the peasantry and the poor, Somerset promised more than he could deliver. The commons, confused and bewildered by the wide gulf separating the intentions of the government from the actions of Parliament, local officials, and landowners, resorted to direct action and finally rebellion to press their claims for social justice.

The commons of Cornwall and Devonshire rose against the nobles and gentlemen, and required not only that the enclosures might be disparked, but also to have their old religion, and act of six articles restored.

John Stow, *Annales of England*, London, 1605

3. THE WESTERN REBELLION

Significant popular unrest began first in the West of England when the Cornish, inspired by the clergy, opposed the government's religious reforms. Discontent spread into the neighboring county, Devon, and in 1549 grew into one of the largest rebellions of the Tudor century. The great Western Rebellion arose over local grievances and remained regional in its focus. The rebels first challenged the authority of local officials and later, after a complete collapse of law and order, demanded redress from the king and his ministers. Although the rising was initially directed against religious innovation, it soon acquired important political and social dimensions. The rebellion looked to the past and reflected the attitudes of a remote and an intensely provincial society.

The world of Devon and Cornwall was small, inward-looking, and parochial. Although all Englishmen were subjects of Edward VI and governed by the laws of Parliament, every man, woman, and child retained strong local loyalties and social ties. For the gentry the county, not the nation, was the natural political environment. The gentry controlled local government and vied for election to the House of Commons either as knights of the shire or as representatives of small boroughs that were all-too willing to entrust their limited interests to wealthy and influential rural neighbors. Although London was emerging as a social and political magnet drawing the gentry toward the capital, the countryside with the comforts of rural life and the easier prestige of county politics continued as the more powerful force. Provincialism was even more the way of life for ordinary men and women. They toiled in the fields, worked in villages and hamlets, worshipped in the parish church, drank and whored in local inns, traded in the small market towns, and at the end of difficult and often short lives came to rest in a graveyard among relatives and close neighbors. Poor roads, the absence of mass communications, and long hours of back-breaking labor discouraged interest in the outside world. The history of

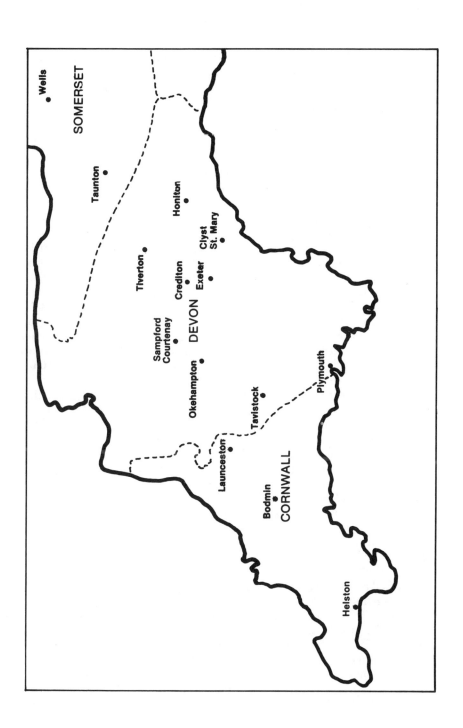

early Tudor England was a composite of family, social, and occupational groups living in communities that enjoyed extensive political autonomy in local affairs, a high degree of economic self-sufficiency, and often unique cultural traditions. Nowhere was the provincialism of Tudor England more apparent than in Devon and Cornwall.

From the days of the Anglo-Saxon invasions to the Reformation of Henry VIII, the geographical location of Devon and Cornwall shielded the western counties from innovation and change. The Westcountrymen were ignorant and suspicious of the outside world, an alien world, which for its part showed only intermittent interest in the small, impoverished communities of Devon and Cornwall. Located over 150 miles from London, the city of Exeter stood as the last bastion of civilization before the rugged Celtic society of Cornwall. The traveler, proceeding westward from Exeter, faced a difficult journey of 64 miles across the moors before reaching Bodmin, while Helston lay another 45 miles farther to the west. On Dartmoor the land rose to more than 2,000 feet above sea level. The West of England with 500 miles of coastline and a short 35-mile boundary joining it to the rest of England embraced the sea, but in the reign of Edward VI the maritime fame of the region belonged to the future. In the early sixteenth century London and other ports to the east had the advantage of closer proximity to European centers of trade. The sea did bring the warm, moist air from the Gulf Stream that gave the West short, mild winters. Although other counties were favored with better soils, Devon and Cornwall remained green nine months each year. The longer growing season, the absence of early frosts and heavy snowfall, were coveted gifts in an area otherwise little favored by nature.

Tudor Cornwall, wrote A. L. Rowse, was "a homogenous society of its own, defined by language and having a common history underneath, like Brittany or Wales or Ireland, reaching back beyond Normans and Saxons, beyond even Rome in these islands, to an antiquity of which its people were still dimly conscious." Cornish was a Celtic language related to Welsh and Breton. Although the gentry abandoned their native tongue, the common people, particularly in the remote western parts of the county, retained it throughout the sixteenth century. In 1532, when Henry VIII invited wrestlers to court, two Cornishmen, described as "proper fellows for the feat," were sent to London with the warning that "their English is not perfect." At the beginning of the seventeenth century John Norden reported: "In the west part of the country . . . the Cornish tongue is most in use among the inhabitants, and yet . . . though the husband and wife, parents and children, master and servants do mutually communicate in their native language, yet there is none of them in manner but is able to converse with a stranger in the English tongue, unless it be some obscure people that seldom confer with the better sort." The retention of the Cornish language obviously accentuated the county's geographical isolation from the mainstream of English culture, while memories of a heroic Celtic past submerged by Saxon and Norman conquerors nurtured feelings of bitterness and resentment. At worst the Cornish saw themselves as a conquered people whose culture, liberties, and prosperity had been degraded by the English.[1]

The Cornish earned their living as farmers, tin-miners, and fishermen. The standard of living, compared with the more prosperous counties of eastern England, was low. The local historian, Richard Carew, recalled conditions in the mid-sixteenth century when ordinary husbandmen had "little bread corn, their drink water or at best whey, for the richest farmer in a parish brewed not above twice a year." The husbandmen's clothing was "coarse and ill-shapen; . . . their legs and feet naked and bare to which sundry old folks had so accustomed their youth that they could hardly abide to wear any shoes, complaining how it kept them over hot." Carew also described living conditions:

> Suitable hereunto was their dwelling and to that their implements of household: walls of earth, low thatched roofs, few partitions, no planchings [flooring] or glass windows and scarcely any chimneys other than a hole in the wall to let out smoke; their bed straw and a blanket as for sheets so much linen cloth had not yet stepped over the narrow channel between them and Britain. To conclude a mazer and a pan or two comprised all their substance.[2]

Good agricultural land was scarce throughout Cornwall; in fact Joan Thirsk characterized the county as a "series of cultivated oases set in a large expanse of moor, the only continuous stretches of fertile land lying on the coast. The population was too small to feel any compulsion to colonize fresh land or improve the use of old."[3] As most of the land was enclosed, tenants and landlords lived in greater harmony than in East Anglia and the Midlands. Commonfields and pastures survived primarily around the towns where the poorer inhabitants kept a cow or two to provide milk and cheese for their families. Much of the rugged countryside was useful only as pasture, and poor pasture at that, for the sheep were small and produced an inferior grade of wool commonly known as "Cornish hair."

In addition to agriculture, tin-mining offered extensive employment. Cornwall had the most productive tin mines in England and provided one of the country's most valuable exports. Tin deposits occurred across the entire length of Cornwall and extended into Devon, but the center of the industry gradually moved westward. For the miners the work was difficult and dangerous. In some cases the men worked at depths of 250 and 300 feet beneath the surface. Ventilation systems were primitive, making the air exceedingly foul. When the narrow shafts collapsed, the miner might be buried alive, or if water burst into the mine, he risked drowning. Hazards increased as the mine shafts pushed deeper into the earth. Because of working conditions, miners usually

41

spent only four hours each day below the surface. In Cornwall as elsewhere in Europe the miner was poorly compensated for his labor. Mine owners, various middlemen, and a bevy of petty officials controlled production in Cornwall, while London merchants, the pewterers, strove to monopolize marketing and export. To make matters worse for the ordinary miner, production declined during the sixteenth century, and the price of tin failed to keep pace with the rising cost of food and mining equipment. If opportunities in agriculture were poor, those in mining were even worse. Many miners in fact turned to farming later in the century as the mining industry declined. Contemporary writers agreed that living conditions among the tin-miners were the worst in Cornwall. Low wages combined with the short period that the miner could work in the deeper shafts encouraged drunkenness, idleness, and an ugly disposition favorable to violence and rebellion.[4]

Acute poverty together with Cornwall's sense of political and cultural oppression created severe problems of law enforcement. Local government in Cornwall, as in all English counties, was the responsibility of the landed aristocracy. Although the Courtenay family had been influential in Cornish affairs until the execution of the Marquis of Exeter in 1538, the county had no resident nobility. Richard Carew succinctly observed that "the king hath there no cousins."[5] As justices of the peace, the gentry ruled the countryside, protected their own vested interests, and enforced the king's laws. Geographical isolation encouraged widespread intermarriage among the gentry and a conservative outlook. Few of the Cornish gentry were strong supporters of the religious reforms of Henry VIII and Edward VI. Local government differed from the pattern in other counties because of the crown's extensive landholdings and the tin-mining industry. The Duchy of Cornwall, in the words of A. L. Rowse, was the "peculiar institution"[6] in that it administered manors, castles, parks, and boroughs on behalf of the king. During the reign of Henry VIII the wealth of the Duchy increased with the addition of the Courtenay lands and a rich harvest of monastic property. The Duchy nominated the sheriff and also controlled tin-mining through the office of lord warden of the stannaries. The stannary courts, held under the authority of the lord warden, had criminal and civil jurisdiction over all tinners in the county. A stannary parliament, consisting of twenty-four stannators appointed by the mayors of Lostwithiel, Truro, Launceston, and Helston, governed the tinners primarily in the interests of the mine owners and tin dealers.[7] Considering the county's small population and poor standard of living, Cornwall suffered from over-governance through a complicated local regime that was more effective in collecting fees and employing petty officials than in serving the needs of the larger community.

During the half-century prior to the rebellion, Cornwall experienced a major uprising and several lesser stirs. In 1497 the Cornish rose in opposition to Henry VII's oppressive taxation. The first Tudor king needed money to fight Scotland and with parliamentary approval levied the heaviest tax of the reign. The tax was of two types, two fifteenths and tenths, a tax on movable property, and a subsidy, a regressive income tax that placed a heavy burden on persons of low income. The Cornish objected to paying any taxes but particularly opposed local assessments for the subsidy and held that they should not be responsible for financing wars in distant Scotland. The rebellion began in the parish of St. Keverne in western Cornwall and quickly spread throughout the county. The principal leaders were Michael Joseph, a forceful and defiant blacksmith of St. Keverne, and Thomas Flamank, a Bodmin lawyer, who was the son of one of the commissioners for the collection of the subsidy. The rebellion also received substantial support from the lesser gentry. Following the centuries-old practice of attributing unpopular policies to the influence of evil councillors, the rebels held Cardinal Morton and Sir Reginald Bray, Henry VII's leading ministers, responsible for the oppressive taxes. In an effort to free the king, to whom they pledged complete loyalty, from the grip of wicked councillors, the Cornish rebels with support from Devon and Somerset marched on London. At Wells, James, Lord Audley joined the rebels and assumed the leadership of a force said to number 15,000. The rebels met surprisingly little resistance as they marched across the breadth of England until the decisive battle with the king's army at Blackheath outside London. Overwhelmed by superior numbers and artillery, the Cornish and their allies sustained a crushing defeat.[8]

After Henry VII's victory over the rebels outside London, Perkin Warbeck, an imposter claiming to be the heir of the Yorkist king, Edward IV, landed in Cornwall hoping to rally the people to his cause. Warbeck, calling himself King Richard IV, recruited an army of about 6,000 which he led to the gates of Exeter. When the citizens of Exeter refused to admit him, Warbeck led an unsuccessful attack on the city from the north. The king's army marched to the west to relieve Exeter, but before it arrived, Warbeck fled to an abbey where he sought sanctuary. The attempt to raise Cornwall in the name of a Yorkist imposter was utterly futile. The initial revolt which culminated in the march to London offered at least the possibility of success, but Perkin Warbeck's badly timed effort combined a discredited cause with an inept leader. On the other hand, the 1497 rebellion alerted the king to the widespread disaffection in Cornwall and served as a pretext for severe repression. The leaders of the first rising, Joseph, the blacksmith, Flamank, and Lord Audley were hanged, drawn, and quartered, while the pathetic Warbeck became the king's prisoner. Henry VII punished the rebellious Cornish with heavy fines levied on each parish, reminding the people, both rich and poor, that the power to tax was indeed the power to destroy. As A. L. Rowse remarked, Cornwall was "impoverished and wasted" for its sedition and treason, and the resulting exhaustion "kept the county quiet for a half a century."[9]

The Reformation under Henry VIII began a generation of sweeping changes in Cornish religious life although the reforms followed the national pattern devised by the king, Thomas Cromwell, and Parliament. Cornwall accepted the royal supremacy and acquiesced in the dissolution of the monasteries. A long history of hostility between the Cornish towns and the monasteries made the implementation of the government's policies less difficult, while the gentry eagerly sought to acquire a generous share of monastic land as soon as it was certain that the monasteries could not be saved.[10] In 1536, when the Pilgrimage of Grace inflamed the North, many preconditions of rebellion were present in Cornwall, yet the county remained curiously quiet and actually supplied men for the army sent to suppress the northern insurrection. After the rising had been put down, evidence of Cornish unrest appeared when Sir William Godolphin learned that a friend had been asked to paint a banner of the five wounds of Christ for the parishioners of St. Keverne, the home of Michael Joseph, leader of the 1497 revolt. The banner was to portray Christ holding a banner in his hand, the Virgin Mary holding her breast in her hand, and the king, queen, and commons kneeling before Christ humbly petitioning that the traditional religious holidays be retained. Godolphin reported that the county was extremely quiet, and it does not appear that the banner was ever produced, much less displayed at St. Keverne.[11]

The tranquility of Cornwall at the time of the Pilgrimage of Grace has been attributed to lingering memories of 1497; yet few persons could have had vivid personal recollections of those events, while the potentially more volatile younger generation was not born until the sixteenth century. If there was little visible unrest, apprehension and uncertainty lurked in the minds of the commons, for Henry VIII's Reformation upset traditional religious life throughout Cornwall. Simple, credulous folk saw monasteries dissolved, heard that customary holidays were to be eliminated, and feared that Thomas Cromwell's newly mandated parish registers might be used to compile vital statistics for heavier taxation. The parish clergy, the only educated persons with whom the commons had day-to-day contact, were directed to amend the Latin mass with Bible readings and prayers either in English or Cornish.[12] The laity might grumble about the worldly pretensions of the clergy and voice a variety of anticlerical sentiments, but when their daily lives were affected by strange, innovative practices, they were highly susceptible to clerical exhortations for the preservation of the true Catholic faith.

The neighboring county of Devon, compared with Cornwall, had the advantages of better geographical location, larger population, and greater wealth. Although the wealth of both Devon and Cornwall increased very rapidly between 1334 and 1515, they ranked far below Middlesex, Somerset, and Essex, the three most affluent counties.[13] While Cornwall was notorious for its turbulence, Devon enjoyed a reputation of loyalty to the early Tudor monarchs. The men of Exeter refused to join Perkin Warbeck and the Cornish rebels in 1497, and for its loyalty Henry VII gave the city a sword of state and cap of maintenance that are still carried before the mayor on ceremonial occasions.

The wealth of Tudor Devon was both agricultural and industrial. "Most of the northern half of the county, except around Bideford and Barnstaple, was pastoral country, rearing many sheep and cattle, and fattening some in the valleys, for supplying meat to ships' victuallers."[14] The best arable land lay in the lower river valleys and coastal plains, especially the vale of Exeter, along Torbay, and the region south of Dartmoor known as the South Hams. Until the fall of the Marquis of Exeter in 1538, the Courtenays were the dominant landowners in the Exe valley. Henry VIII's destruction of this ancient family left a power vacuum in the county that was later filled by John Russell, Earl of Bedford and his descendants. Elsewhere the gentry, yeomen, and leasehold farmers, often protected against rising rents by ninety-nine year leases, cultivated the soil and fattened cattle and sheep. Less fortunate were the farm laborers who in the early sixteenth century made up about a third of the rural population. Although Devon was generally regarded as enclosed, common fields could be found in the more fertile valleys and along the coast.[15]

The economic growth of Devon in the early sixteenth century resulted from increased production of woolen cloth rather than from agricultural expansion. Inferior grades of cloth were produced in Devon throughout the middle ages, but until the fifteenth century the local market absorbed most of the output. Although the cloth industry was primarily rural, Exeter, Barnstaple, and Totnes became major centers for manufacture and overseas trade. In the early sixteenth century about one-tenth of all English cloth exports passed through the port of Exeter. The major achievement of the Exeter merchants was "to develop a market, largely in France and in the Mediterranean countries, for cheap, light-weight, brightly-coloured cloths."[16] The cloth industry brought large profits to merchants who were able to take advantage of expanding overseas markets; to the poor inhabitants of the Devon countryside the industry offered important opportunities for occasional or by-employment whereby meager incomes from agriculture might be supplemented.

Disorder erupted in the west in 1547 when Protector Somerset authorized a general visitation of the church to enforce newly issued ecclesiastical injunctions, which required the removal of images and other superstitious objects from parish churches. The injunctions of 1547 differed very little from those issued a decade earlier by Thomas

Cromwell. A disturbance occurred in the hundred of Penwith, the most westerly district of Cornwall, when William Body, the Archdeacon of Cornwall, attempted to enforce the government's religious policies. Surviving records tell us only that a "tumult" ensued as Body delivered the injunctions. The Privy Council held Body responsible for the disturbances because in violation of instructions he summoned the clergy to attend upon him to avoid the bother of visiting each individual parish. Misunderstanding the new policy, the clergy of Penwith assumed that the government intended to confiscate the religious images rather than have them removed and preserved in the churches to prevent private sales or embezzlement. The councillors ordered Body committed to ward for a week and bound by recognizances to appear before them to answer for his misbehavior. They also required several opposition leaders committed to ward in an effort to convince the clergy that the Council intended to enforce the injunctions and maintain order.[17]

The tumult in Penwith and what followed later at Helston may have been caused as much by the actions of William Body as by a disagreement or misunderstanding regarding religious innovation. Ten years earlier while in the service of Thomas Cromwell, Body leased the archdeaconry of Cornwall for thirty-five years from Thomas Winter, son of Cardinal Wolsey. Officials of the diocese of Exeter challenged the lease in the episcopal court, and Body sought to protect his interests in Star Chamber and the Court of King's Bench. During the course of what proved to be a protracted and bitter controversy, Body scuffled with John Harris, commissary of the Bishop of Exeter, and allegedly attempted to draw a dagger before being overpowered. From all we know of him, Body was hot-tempered and undiplomatic, but he may have been provoked by Harris and other church officials who labored long and hard to prevent him from exercising his duties as Archdeacon of Cornwall. The Cornish clergy disliked all outside interference and were especially outraged when a complete outsider, who was a layman and an ambitious careerist, obtained the highest church office in the county. The fact that Body's rights were upheld in London courts was a poor recommendation in remote Cornwall.[18]

William Body was next heard of at Helston, a decayed market town and parliamentary borough, in April 1548. Just what he was doing there remains a mystery, but we know that he was brutally murdered on the fifth by an angry mob led by Martin Geoffrey, a priest from the neighboring parish of St. Keverne. Farmers and fishermen from surrounding villages, according to Frances Rose-Troup, rendezvoused near Helston and proceeded to attack Body, who sought protection in a private home. After the killing the mob moved to a cemetery where Geoffrey spoke emotionally of the righteousness of their cause. John Pyers, a mariner from St. Keverne, vowed to rescue any person taken into custody for the murder. "From the cemetery, pushing and jostling, the throng moved to the market place."[19] Here John Resseigh, a yeoman farmer from Helston, harangued the assembled crowd and called for the restoration of the Henrician religious settlement until Edward VI reached the age of twenty-four.

By April 7, the multitude of rebellious Cornish increased to 3,000. "In the excitement this mixed and unruly assembly committed divers thefts, spoliations, and other evil deeds." To restore order the gentry summoned assistance from the surrounding countryside. At Morval parishioners sold a chalice to pay men sent to Helston. "At St. Nighton's they sold a small chalice and a bell 'by the assent of the whole parish for meat, drink, and horses for the carrying of men' to the West; Lanteglos sent twenty-six men, Boconnoc eighteen. There were similar payments at Launceston and Stratton in the north." Reinforcements rushed into western Cornwall from as far away as Plymouth. The rebels were soon subdued, but there were threats against justices of the peace, who tried to bring the accused before the quarter sessions. The commons charged that if the regular sessions were held at Helston, they would turn out in large numbers to obstruct justice. Faced with such formidable opposition, the justices "changed the venue and committed those apprehended to the sheriff's keeping to be produced before a special commission of oyer and terminer at Launceston."[20]

As the actions of Body at Helston are unknown, it is difficult to determine the motives of his murderers. Body was obviously enforcing the Edwardian Reformation; whether he was actually casting down images in Helston must remain a matter of conjecture.[21] The ringleaders were charged with high treason and tried at Launceston and London. Most were found guilty and sentenced to death. The lesser figures were pardoned by royal proclamation. The twenty-eight rebel leaders initially denied pardon included the priest, yeomen, husbandmen, mariners, fishermen, a smith, a miller, and a groom. They lived in the area surrounding Helston, mainly in the parish of St. Keverne, but it is surprising that only John Resseigh was said to be a resident of Helston, the scene of the murder. By the end of October the government pardoned most of the leaders, including William Kilter and Pascoe Trevian, whom Frances Rose-Troup and A. L. Rowse credited with the actual killing of Body.[22] John Kilter, on the other hand, apparently did not receive a pardon and was probably one of the murderers. However, the only rebels definitely known to have suffered execution were Martin Geoffrey, the priest, and an unidentified man hanged at Plymouth. Most of the trials took place at Launceston, where a number of persons were executed. Geoffrey was sent to London for trial and later was hanged, drawn, and quartered at Smithfield. The dismembered priest's head ornamented London Bridge, while quarters of the corpse were displayed on four gates of the city of London.[23]

As a popular religious rising, the Helston affair of 1548 exudes a foul stench. If Body was in fact defiling the parish church or the hospital of St. John, the only other religious institution in the parish, it is indeed curious that only one local man apparently bothered to oppose him. Records are silent about the role of the Helston parish clergy, but John Harris, Body's adversary when he was trying to establish his rights to the archdeaconry of Cornwall, was superior of the hospital of St. John. Perhaps Harris intrigued behind the scenes to settle an old grudge. Although the Duchy of Cornwall was the largest landowner in the district, John Winslade, who was later implicated in the rising at Bodmin, had property in Helston, Constantine, and St. Keverne.[24] Was it a mere coincidence that the Kilters were residents of Constantine and that the majority of the rebel leaders came from St. Keverne, ten miles away?

Obviously, insufficient evidence survives to suggest that John Harris, John Winslade, and Martin Geoffrey conspired to murder the hapless Body. Yet the numerous pardons granted months after the disorder ended hint that the government may have learned that many of the men had been duped by the Cornish gentry and clergy, whose target was Body, not the religious reforms legislated by Parliament. If we knew more about the circumstances that induced Martin Geoffrey to lead his band of followers from St. Keverne to Helston and something of the last months of the life of William Body, the puzzling aspects of this episode might be explained.

A year elapsed between the murder of Body and the rising at Bodmin in 1549. The government did little to popularize its religious policies although the king's chaplain, Joseph Tonge, and Miles Coverdale were sent to preach in the West. If the Helston disturbance was a direct cause of what followed, the connections are extremely tenuous. The former was confined to the western part of the county, while the Bodmin rising began in the eastern district and spread throughout the county and into Devon. At Bodmin, as at Helston, the immediate cause of hostilities remains highly obscure although lower clergy opposed to the progress of the Reformation played a prominent role in arousing the gentry and commons.

Bodmin, according to A. L. Rowse, was "the largest and busiest of Cornish towns with a population of 2,000 — almost twice that of any other." Before the Reformation the burgesses quarrelled with the prior, who enjoyed extensive and lucrative privileges in the town, and later there was considerable litigation connected with the sale of the priory's property, but none of this seems to have inspired the uprising in 1549. However busy Bodmin may have been as the county town of Cornwall it was included among the declining towns of the West in parliamentary legislation of 1540 and was little improved at the end of the sixteenth century. Houses lay along a single main street that extended for a mile.

Steep hills rose on either side of the street, admitting little light to the dwellings below. Carew noted that privies were built on the slopes, so that whenever it rained foul-smelling sewage ran down into the open sewers of the main street. Contemporaries regarded Bodmin as an ugly and dirty place; in fact Carew thought it was the most unhealthy town in all of Cornwall. The only clue to the town's response to the Edwardian Reformation comes from Carew's anecdote about the organization of schoolboys into factions favoring and opposing the new religion. After considerable controversy one of the boys fashioned an improvised gun with which he killed a calf, perhaps symbolizing the idolatry of Catholicism. Whatever meaning the killing was intended to convey, the fun quickly ended when the master of the free school soundly whipped the mischievous and destructive culprits. Although it would be unwise to ascribe too much significance to the pranks of schoolboys, the division of the school into competing factions demonstrates conclusively that the allegedly conservative town of Bodmin numbered among its residents a few who very vigorously, if ineffectively, voiced their support of religious reform.[25]

About Easter, well-armed rebels from all parts of Cornwall converged on Bodmin and pitched their camp at the end of the town.[26] Commons from the town and countryside, supported by the mayor and clergy, sought leadership from the gentry. Humphrey Arundell, a gentleman living at Helland a few miles from Bodmin, quickly assumed leadership of the rebels. Other men of substance active from the beginning were John Winslade, Esq., and Thomas Holmes, a yeoman farmer. Establishing his headquarters at the ruined fortress of Castle Kynock near Bodmin, Arundell organized the rebel military force. On the basis of fragmentary evidence, it appears that the chief adversaries of the rebels were those gentry who refused to support the rising. One group of loyal gentry together with their wives and families sought refuge at St. Michael's Mount, a coastal fortress in western Cornwall separated from the mainland at high tide. Arundell, formerly commander of the small garrison at St. Michael's Mount, led the assault against the castle. Carew described the fighting, in which the rebels first won "the plain at the hill's foot, by assault, when the water was out and then the even ground on the top, by carrying up great trusses of hay before them to blench the defendents sight and dead their shot." The defenders of the Mount could not resist, "for no sooner should anyone within peep out his head over those in flanked walls but he became an open mark to a whole shower of arrows." The tactical advantages of the attackers together with superior numbers and "the women's dismay and decrease of victuals" forced St. Michael's Mount to surrender. The victorious rebels robbed the defenders of their goods, "imprisoned their bodies, and were rather by God's gracious providence, than any want of will, purpose or attempt, restrained from murdering the principal persons."[27]

The victorious rebel army returned to Castle Kynock and attracted enthusiastic supporters as it passed through the villages and countryside. John Militon, sheriff of Cornwall, stood powerless while Humphrey Arundell imprisoned dozens of opposition gentry. The rebels, according to Davies Gilbert, appealed to King Edward for redress of religious grievances. Waiting for the reply, they threatened the lives of the imprisoned gentry and paraded through the streets of Bodmin crying, "Kill the gentlemen! We will have the Six Articles up again and ceremonies as they were in King Henry VIII's time." Arundell and his fellow leaders resolved to march on London as their forefathers had done during the reign of Henry VII. Armed with clubs, swords, and cannon, and flying the banner of the Five Wounds of Christ, the army marched eastward along two routes. One force marched directly toward Devon across the barren waste of Bodmin Moor. The other advanced by way of Liskeard and Menheniot toward Plymouth.[28]

The Cornish rebels swept all before them, for the gentry were either unwilling or unable to mount effective resistance. A few found protection on the fortified island of St. Nicholas (now Drake's Island) in Cawsand Bay. Less fortunate were those who sought the protection of Sir Richard Grenville at Trematon Castle near Saltash. Grandfather of the Elizabethan seaman of the same name, Grenville had enriched himself through military service and was one of the major landowners in Cornwall. Trematon might have held out had not many of its defenders slipped over the walls and defected to the rebels by the dark of night. Grenville was forced to parley, and when he appeared outside the gate, rebels "stepped between him and home, laid hold of his aged, unwieldy body, and threatened to leave it lifeless" if the castle did not surrender immediately. The rebels, having seized the castle, plundered everything in sight. Frightened and indignant gentlewomen "without regard of sex and shame were stripped from their apparel to their very smocks," and several suffered broken fingers as gold and silver rings were unceremoniously removed. Sir Richard Grenville was himself removed from Trematon and jailed at Launceston.[29]

The stirring in remote Cornwall fathered an insurrection that inflamed a large part of western England. Unfortunately, the fragmentary sources leave many unanswered questions regarding the Cornish revolt. Although all authorities agree that religion was the mainspring, little evidence of religious reaction has survived. If the rebellion began as early as Easter, there would have been no Book of Common Prayer to overthrow, and the use of English, which the Cornish rejected so vehemently, would have been familiar from the reign of Henry VIII when vernacular prayers and Bible readings were added to the Latin liturgy. Nor is it clear whether the gentry were attacked because of their wealth and social standing or because they remained loyal to the government of Protector Somerset. Class hatred may indeed explain why the rebels robbed and plundered their genteel victims, but the compelling need of the rebel army for food and supplies as it marched eastward to Devon was probably a more powerful driving force than any ideological impulse. If enclosures of fields, commons, and parks motivated the Cornish, little evidence of the commons' wrath survives. It does appear likely, however, that the towns and countryside of Cornwall lay firmly under their control as the rebels crossed into Devon. On the other hand, the realities of life — both for gentry and commons — under the rebel regime of 1549 must remain one of the mysteries that the past will not divulge.

Rebellion came to Devon when the Cornish crossed the Tamar, the river dividing Devon from Cornwall, and attacked Plymouth, the heavily fortified port that protected England's southwestern coast. Unfortunately the date of the initial attack on Plymouth and details of rebel activity are unknown. The Cornish, perhaps aided by supporters in Devon, burned a structure known as the "steeple" containing "all the town's evidence." The Plymouth historian, R. N. Worth, speculated that the steeple may have been a bell tower attached to the guildhall in which records were stored.[30] Plymouth Castle, guarding the harbor, successfully resisted the rebels and held out through the entire course of the Western Rebellion. In July rumors reached London that the mayor of Plymouth had traitorously surrendered the town, and the Council ordered a fleet of ships to take the castle and apprehend the mayor. A few days later the Council learned that the rumor was erroneous and reported that "the matter of the town [was] not to be so evil as we heard."[31]

The village of Sampford Courtenay, on the northern edge of Dartmoor, was the site of the first recorded disturbance in Devon. Located just off the main road that ran from Launceston in Cornwall, across the Tamar, to Okehampton and Crediton, Sampford Courtenay was well-positioned to learn quickly of the goings-on among the Cornish. News traveled rapidly through the countryside; the rumormongers of the Tudor era rarely underestimated the seriousness of a popular uprising. As its name reminds us, the village had formerly belonged to the Courtenay family, the most powerful magnates in the West of England. The Courtenays were never enthusiastic supporters of the Henrician Reformation, and their Yorkist ancestry inevitably aroused suspicion. Only a decade before the rebellions, Henry Courtenay, Marquis of Exeter, had been executed for his part in a conspiracy to raise men in Devon and Cornwall. Sampford Courtenay subsequently passed to Henry VIII's last queen, Catherine Parr, and reverted to the crown upon her death in 1548, but it is likely that Courtenay sympathizers in the village kept old traditions and loyalties alive.[32]

On Whitsunday, June 9, William Harper, rector of Sampford Courtenay, celebrated Holy Communion according to the new Book of Common Prayer for the first time. Harper, who had been appointed by Queen Catherine, simply obeyed the Act of Uniformity which required the introduction of the new liturgy on that Sunday. In most parishes the reformed service gave little offense to the commons, for it retained traditional priestly vestments and bore more than superficial resemblance to the older liturgies. The fact that the service according to the Book of Common Prayer was entirely in English can hardly have been profoundly disturbing to parishioners who had heard the vernacular inserted in the Latin mass since the 1530s. Nonetheless, the Prayer Book provoked hostility at Sampford Courtenay. On the following day, as the priest began once again to use the new service, a group of angry parishioners, led by Thomas Underhill, a tailor, and a laborer named Segar, demanded restoration of the Latin liturgy. When the priest replied that he must obey the law of the land, Underhill and his associates argued — quite erroneously — that the last will and testament of Henry VIII forbade any religious change until Edward VI came of age. Acts of Parliament affecting religion passed during the king's minority, they contended, were invalid. Faced with pressure and perhaps intimidation from the whole parish, the priest gave in and restored the Latin mass. The contemporary Exeter historian, John Hooker, upon whose account of the Western Rebellion all later historians are dependent, reported that the commons were ecstatic. The news, "as a cloud carried with a violent wind and as a thunder clap sounding at one instant through the whole country . . . [is] carried and noised even in a moment throughout the whole country, and the common people so well allowed and liked thereof that they clapped their hands for joy and agreed in one mind to have the same in every of their several parishes."[33]

If Hooker exaggerated the speed with which news spread and the enthusiasm of the commons for rebellion, subsequent events leave little doubt that the rural population of Devon had not been won over to the religious policies established by Parliament at distant Westminster. On the other hand, the disturbance at Sampford Courtenay was initially a small affair, probably involving only a few hundred persons. It was precisely the type of local disorder that should have been quelled by justices of the peace. Hooker tells us that the justices responded to the challenge and met at Sampford Courtenay. Sir Hugh Pollard, Anthony Harvey, Alexander Wood, and Mark Slader hurried to the troubled village, but the rebels refused to meet with them until the justices agreed to leave their men, probably armed retainers and servants, behind and come to a small close outside the village. The justices and rebels "had conference a pretty while together" and then departed "without anything done at all." Although the justices and their allies outnumbered the rebels, they refused to enforce the law and punish offenders.

John Hooker, outraged at their behavior, denounced the justices as "white livered" cowards who were afraid of their own shadows. Unfortunately we may only speculate about their true motivation. Perhaps Hooker's calculations were incorrect, and the justices saw clearly that they were outnumbered, for the entire gentry in the area cannot have been more than five percent of the total population. Another possibility is that the justices sympathized with the commons of Sampford Courtenay. If the justices were prepared to accept the Book of Common Prayer and obey the Act of Uniformity passed by Parliament, they may have opposed either the government's sheep tax or its enclosure policy.

The only representative of the landed class bold enough to defy the rebels was William Hellyons, a franklin, who

> so earnestly reproved them for their rebellion and so sharply threatened them of an evil success that they all fell in a rage with him: and not only with evil words reviled him, but also as he was going out of the Church house and going down the stairs, one of them named Lithibridge, with a bill struck him in the neck and immediately notwithstanding his pitiful requests and lamentations, a number of the rest fell upon him and slew him and cut him in small pieces.

Hellyons was subsequently buried in the churchyard as a heretic with his body placed north and south. Later a Protestant ballad hailed him as a martyr.[34]

Although the rebellion spread to other parts of Devon, Sampford Courtenay remained a major center of strength for the commons. On June 29 Protector Somerset and the Privy Council assigned the highest military priority to the "appeasing of the multitude assembled at Sampford Courtenay" and outlined a complex strategy for its capture. The grievances of the villagers apparently were not limited to rejection of the Book of Common Prayer, for the councillors in London learned that rumors were circulating to the effect that geese and pigs would be taxed after the new sheep tax was collected. They had also heard of a list of grievances drawn up by the ringleaders which included an article alleging that the newly promulgated religious reforms would restrict the frequency of infant baptism. Both allegations were wholly false, but they show the importance of rumors and misinformation among persons whose outrage encouraged them to believe almost anything uttered against the government.[35]

Shortly after the rising at Sampford Courtenay, the Devon men joined forces with the Cornish. Pushing toward the east, the combined forces captured Crediton, an important market town only seven miles north of Exeter. Before the Norman Conquest Crediton had been the seat of a bishopric, but later the town yielded its ecclesiastical position to Exeter and suffered substantial economic decline after the Black Death in the fourteenth century. Tudor Crediton, however, regained at least a part of its past glory as a thriving wool town. The wool mart flourished and drew buyers from Exeter, its larger and wealthier neighbor to the south. The rebels' position at Crediton posed a growing danger to the county because of the town's proximity to Exeter and because it lay on the major road connecting south Devon communities with the port of Barnstaple.

The worsening situation caused Protector Somerset's government to dispatch Sir Peter Carew and his uncle Sir Gawen to Exeter with instructions to pacify the countryside. Both were prominent Devon gentry, but Sir Peter had been living on his wife's estates in Lincolnshire, while Sir Gawen served at court. If the Carews were handicapped by an extended absence from their native county, they were men whom the Council could trust for loyalty to the regime and its religious policies; the same could not be said of many other Westcountry gentry. After conferring with authorities at Exeter, Sir Peter Carew led a small force toward Crediton. The rebels, informed of Carew's advance, resolved to stand their ground and fortified the town as best they could. They "entrenched and rampired the highway at the town's end leading towards Exeter and had hanged up great plough chains upon them and fortified the same with men and munition." Men armed with bows and arrows took up positions in barns that paralleled the road opposite the hastily constructed rampire.[36]

The defenders of Crediton held their ground as the advance guard of Carew's horsemen came into view. Seeing the well-defended rampire blocking the road, the gentry dismounted and went forward on foot in hope that the rebels would come forward and parley. But the commons did not respond with the deference to which the gentry were accustomed. The sturdy rebels defiantly refused to budge from their positions; they would not come forward to negotiate with Carew and hear his offer of pardon. A few of the bolder ones shouted words of abuse. John Hooker, the friend and biographer of Sir Peter Carew, recorded the confrontation with dismay. He could account for the astounding display of irreverence and discourtesy of the commons toward their betters only by invoking the untimely intervention of heavenly bodies: "No offers of persuasions nor motions of conference" were allowed, he said, because "the sun being in Cancer and the mid-summer moon at full" clouded the rebels' minds with such arrogance that "as the man of Athens they would hear no man speak but themselves and thought nothing well said but what came out of their own mouths."[37]

Rather than accept the rebels' defiance, Carew and his men attempted to advance across the rampire but were driven back "by them which kept the rampires and especially by such as were within the barns." The hail of arrows took its toll, and within minutes the wounded littered the road. In an attempt to avoid defeat, Mr. Fox, a retainer of one of the gentry, set fire to the barns. As the flames spread through the thatched roofs and dry straw of the buildings where the rebels hid, the occupants fled for their lives in all directions. Ten rebels died in the ensuing tumult.[38] Carew's men remounted and advanced into Crediton, but the victory was hollow since everyone except the very poor and elderly had fled into the countryside. The victors of Crediton—like Napoleon at Moscow—achieved nothing of value. No rebels meekly accepted pardon; no ringleaders were captured, and no army was destroyed. Carnew simply retraced his tracks southward and returned to Exeter.

Supported by a fresh grievance, the burning of the barns at Crediton, the rebels were better able to win over new converts. Leaders might now appeal to peasants and artisans, who previously found little fault with the Book of Common Prayer, using the argument that the gentry were bent on their destruction and would, if necessary, smoke them from their homes like vermin. As Hooker admitted, "the fame and rumour of the burning of the barns was so spread throughout the whole country that the next day the people like a swarm of wasps were up in sundry places." Later, when Sir Peter Carew returned to London, Protector Somerset and Lord Rich blamed him for starting the fires, for they undoubtedly realized that Carew's foolish act of desperation served only to intensify social conflict. Opposition to Protestant religious reforms caused the initial risings in Cornwall and Devon, but the charred barns and houses of Crediton stood as grim reminders of the widening cleavage between the landowning gentry and the masses of working men and women.[39]

Shortly after the burning of the Crediton barns, the revolt spread to Clyst St. Mary, a village about two miles southeast of Exeter, where a local squire arrogantly accosted an old woman on her way to church. The episode is of particular interest as it involves Walter Raleigh, Esq., father of the famous Elizabethan courtier, Sir Walter. The elder Raleigh was riding toward Exeter when he overtook an old woman walking to the parish church of Clyst St. Mary. Seeing that the woman had rosary beads in her hands, Raleigh asked her what she did with them. Her response was unsatisfactory to a gentleman of the reformed religion, and Raleigh seized the opportunity to lecture her on the laws newly passed by Parliament and to emphasize—and perhaps exaggerate in an intimidating manner—the penalties prescribed for those who would not abandon foolish popish superstitions. The exact words of the woman are unknown, but it is unlikely that the elderly pedestrian dared to insult the squire on horseback for fear that she would be punished with something more than words. Later, when the woman joined her neighbors at church, she spoke her mind without equivocation. Offended and indignant, she charged that Raleigh threatened to burn the commons out of their houses and pillage their property if they refused to discard rosaries and give over holy bread and water. Although the old woman almost certainly exaggerated as she related her conversation with Raleigh, her friends believed what she said and quickly proceeded to fortify Clyst St. Mary against attack.[40]

Walter Raleigh's words did not go unanswered, for a party of villagers set off in hot pursuit after him. The townspeople overtook him, abused him with insolent talk, and forced him to seek refuge in a chapel. John Hooker reported that Raleigh might have been murdered had he not been rescued by mariners from Exmouth. Although he escaped successfully, his luck ran out a short time later when he was captured and imprisoned in St. Sidwell's Church outside Exeter for the duration of the rebellion. While there is no reason to believe that Walter Raleigh treated the old woman with more disrespect than was customary according to accepted gentry standards, the unfortunate meeting at Clyst St. Mary served to provoke people already frightened by the barn-burning at Crediton and threatened by Protestant religious reforms.

The news that Clyst St. Mary was fortifying itself against the gentry reached Exeter quickly. On Sunday, June 23, Sir Peter Carew accompanied by a small military force advanced toward Clyst St. Mary to restore order. Reaching the bridge outside the town, they found their way barred by a hastily constructed barricade. Carew dismounted and went forward on foot to talk with the rebels. As he approached the bridge, John Hammon, the rebel gunner and a blacksmith by trade, aimed his weapon and threatened to shoot. Carew drew back and then offered to send a messenger. After a short delay, while the rebels debated whether to admit any of Carew's men, they agreed that three of the gentry might come forward for negotiations. The conference began about ten o'clock in the morning and continued into the afternoon. The remainder of Carew's force, waiting outside Clyst St. Mary near the barricaded bridge, grew restless and began to argue among themselves about the wisdom of storming the town. Several rode to the river's edge and began to test the depth of the water in the event that it was decided to attack the town by fording the river. But they found the tidal waters of the River Clyst too deep for easy crossing. The rebels, seeing Carew's men probing the river, cried out in alarm with such vigor that the three gentlemen, who had been admitted, feared for their safety. The panic subsided, and soon afterwards the three negotiators returned from the town but curiously refused to disclose to Carew what they had discussed with the rebels.

The whole party rode back to Exeter, "supped all together, and after supper ended, and all the serving men avoided out of the room, Sir Peter Carew demanded of them what they had done and what agreement they had made." The three negotiators replied that the rebels had offered "to keep themselves in good and quiet order and to proceed no further in their attempts" if the king and the Council would restore the Henrician religious settlement. Carew and Sir Piers Courtenay, sheriff of Devon, angrily denounced the three for having negotiated in such a sinister way.

Carew and Courtenay contended that rather than having considered such terms they should have attacked Clyst St. Mary that very day. But others among them spoke in favor of appeasement. Indeed the argument became so loud and disorderly that rebel sympathizers nearby could not fail to overhear what was being said. In the end the gentry could not agree on a course of action. As Hooker wrote, "on each side words were so multiplied that they brake asunder without any further dealings; and every man shifted for himself, some one way, some another way."[41] The political and religious consensus of the Devon gentry had collapsed.

News of the gentry's disagreement spread rapidly among the rebels. The failure of the gentry to restore Henrician Catholicism and the crippling divisions within their ranks convinced the rebels to seize the initiative. At once they began to block roads around Exeter, "casting great trenches, and laying great trees overthwart the same." Gentry departing Exeter to return to their homes were taken by surprise and imprisoned. Throughout the county the landowning classes suffered from indecision and panic. Some surrendered themselves to the mercy of the rebels, while others went into hiding. Within a few days the rebels controlled the entire countryside around Exeter. With roads blocked in all directions, the city of Exeter was cut off from the rest of the country and forced to fend for itself.

Exeter, the major city of the West, was a tempting prize to the rebels, but its ancient walls protected it from attack. The city's leaders were able and vigilant, and they maintained close ties with the government in London. In November 1547 the mayor and council dutifully reported an unlawful assembly outside East Gate to the Protector.[42] Two weeks before the debacle at Clyst St. Mary, the city fathers strengthened the watch and ordered that only honest and discreet persons be appointed. They also tried to head off possible discontent among the poor by providing firewood at a reduced rate.[43] The main danger to Exeter came from the conservative religious attitude of its citizens. There were, according to Hooker, two sorts of people in Exeter: "The one and the greater number were of the old stamp and of the Romish religion. The other being of the lesser number were of a contrary mind and disposition, for they wholly relied themselves to the reformed religion, and to the king's proceedings, and endeavoured themselves to obey and follow the same." The Protestant preachers, Miles Coverdale and Joseph Tonge, may have "marvellously" persuaded the people, as Hooker thought, but John Veysey, Bishop of Exeter and most of the local clergy remained firmly committed to the Henrician settlement.[44]

The rebel leaders, recognizing the large number of Catholic sympathizers in Exeter, asked the citizens to join their cause. Messengers approached the mayor, John Blackaller, and requested that the gates of Exeter be opened so that the rebel army might have free access to the city. The leaders wanted to cooperate more closely with friends inside and use the wealth of Exeter to support their cause. Although many of the city fathers shared the rebels' religious views, they had greater loyalty to the king and the city. Possibly they had an even deeper commitment to themselves, their families, and their wealth, for they rightly feared that the rebel army, once given the freedom of the city, might confiscate property to finance the rebellion. For these reasons, the mayor refused to collaborate with the rebels. The leaders, having sustained an initial rebuff, appealed to the mayor a second time. Gentle persuasion gave way to threats to besiege and capture Exeter if the city refused to ally with the rebels. The mayor refused to budge. Repeating his previous refusal, he denounced the rebels as wicked men who were enemies against God, the king, and the entire country. The mayor and council proceeded to defend Exeter, while the rebels began a siege on July 2 with the threat that the city would be plundered if it did not immediately open its gates.

With superior numbers, the rebels took the initiative. Rebel control of the surrounding countryside forced the closing of the city's markets and created a serious food shortage. Conduits bringing water into Exeter were broken, but the citizens managed to survive because the city contained springs with "good sweet waters." Rebel gunners battered the city gates while sharpshooters positioned in houses near the wall fired on citizens walking in the streets. John Hooker described the defensive measures taken to flush out the rebel marksmen: "Upon which occasion the citizens set some part of the suburbs on fire and some part which was next to the walls they beat and brake down, and so drove the rebels out of those holes." The rebels attempted to breach the walls by placing explosives in tunnels dug under West Gate. John Newcombe, a tinner from Teignmouth and friend of one of the alderman, discovered the tunnel and foiled the miners working beneath the wall. "He took a pan of water and did put the same on the ground and by shaking of the water in the pan, he by removing the pan from place to place came at length to the very place where the miners were working and forthwith he countermined against the same, and wrought so near into it until that he might and did see and look into it." Newcombe arranged for each resident in the area to draw a large tub of water and on his command to empty the tubs into gutters leading toward West Gate. He channelled the water into the area that had been countermined so that the rebels' tunnel and explosives were flooded. Later a heavy rain further assisted Newcombe and the defenders of Exeter.[45]

Inside the city the mayor and aldermen worked to defend the walls and maintain a united front toward the rebels. The failure of the gentry to control the countryside and the uncertainty surrounding the advance of a relief force created an atmosphere of anxiety and fear. When the siege began, the mayor could not be sure how much support the rebels had among the townspeople. A few Catholic sympathizers left Exeter and joined the rebels. Others met together within the besieged city, discussing possible strategies for opening the gates to the rebels, and communicated with their allies by shooting arrows to which messages were attached over the walls. John Wolcott, merchant and common councillor, was apparently the most important citizen with leanings toward the rebel cause. One day, while inspecting the gates, Wolcott and two confederates suddenly left the city through West Gate and conferred with the rebels. Although we do not know what was discussed, Wolcott returned to the city only over the objections of the rebels, and his companions were held as hostages. John Hooker, obviously taking a poor view of the entire proceeding, said that Wolcott promised more than he could deliver and was severely blamed for his actions.[46]

The Catholic faction tried to gain control of the city during an assembly of all "commoners" at Guildhall. Every man arrived at the meeting wearing his armor, and the Catholics comprised the majority. Richard Taylor, a clothier, nearly caused a panic when he raised his bow and took aim at one of the Protestant leaders. Before releasing the arrow, Taylor's hand slipped, and he mistakenly shot his best friend, John Peter, who would have been killed instantly had the arrow not hit a rib bone. The mishap foiled the plans of the Catholics and allowed the mayor's supporters to regain control. John Peter, a customs officer, not only lived but later became mayor, whereas Richard Taylor, the inept archer, died in prison as a debtor.[47]

Although neither John Wolcott nor Taylor accomplished anything of importance, the Catholics persisted in their attempts to deliver Exeter to the rebels. There was an unsuccessful plot to have the soldiers at Exeter Castle admit rebels through the postern gate. During negotiations with city leaders, the rebels demanded hostages selected from the most prominent citizens in the hope that they might be persuaded to join their company. On Sunday, August 4, only two days before Lord Russell's army broke the siege, rebel sympathizers attempted to raise the city. Walking into the streets in every quarter of Exeter, armed men cried out: "Come out these heretics and two-penny book men! Where be they! By God's wounds and blood we will not be pinned in to serve their turn. We will go out and have in our neighbors; they be honest, good, and godly men." The mayor and magistrates, learning of the rising, successfully pacified the mob and sent John Vincent, John Sharke, and "others bellwethers of this flock into their houses." Only in South Street near the gate was there fighting, but few were injured, "other than a broken pate or two," because "the warders of that gate at that time were against them."[48]

Astute leadership by John Blackaller, the mayor, and the Protestant citizens explains Exeter's successful resistance to the five-week siege. The city fathers refused all overtures from the rebels, and citizens of both Catholic and Protestant leanings put civic loyalty before religious belief. Sacrifice and self-discipline were the order of the day. After the siege ended the twenty-four councillors charged one of their colleagues, Nicholas Reve, a brewer, with selling beer and ale at excessive prices and dismissed him from their number.[49]

The defenders of Exeter benefited from the city's sturdy walls and its location in a highly defensible situation.[50] Although the cathedral and parochial clergy were conservative Henricians, they remained loyal to the mayor and magistrates. The poor posed the greatest danger to the city's survival, for a hungry and unruly mob might have overwhelmed the solid citizenry and opened the gates to the rebels. The mayor, alert to the needs of the poor, instituted an effective relief program. Officials collected a poor rate from the more wealthy citizens and received contributions from the parish churches. The money was distributed among the poor on a weekly basis. Steps were taken to provide what food was available to the poor either at no cost whatsoever or at a very low price. When cattle were caught near the walls, the meat was divided fairly among all inhabitants. Exeter had adequate supplies of dried fish, rice, prunes, raisins, and wine, but not bread flour. In this extremity, Hooker recounted, "The bakers and householders were driven to seek up their old store of puffins and bran, wherewith they in times past were wont to make horsebread, and to feed their swine and poultry, and this moulded up in cloths, for otherwise it would not hold together, and so did bake it up, and the people well contented therewith." Following the guiding principle that the poorer the people were "the better they were considered and the more carefully provided for," the Protestant leadership successfully united both rich and poor and saved Exeter from the rebel besiegers.[51]

The rebel leaders, anticipating the early capitulation of Exeter, grew increasingly frustrated. As the days passed into weeks, the forces raised by the government increased in strength and threatened to dislodge the rebels from their positions surrounding Exeter. The situation became so desperate that one of the gunners proposed the destruction of the city with fireballs. This gunner, "a stranger and an alien, who was a very skillful gunner and could handle his piece very well," had already killed a man in North Street with a shot fired from St. David's Hill. The gunner was so confident of his ability that he boasted that the city could be burned to the ground in only four hours. The plan was well-advanced when Robert Welsh, vicar of St. Thomas near Exe Bridge, intervened. "Do you what you can by policy, force or dint of sword to take the city," he protested; "I will join with you and do my best. But to burn a city which shall be hurtful to all men and good to no man, I will never consent thereunto, but will here stand with all my power against you." The vicar argued with such vigor that the plan to burn Exeter was abandoned. If the Western rebels rejected mass destruction, reminiscent of the burning of Crediton, they nonetheless caused severe damage to the city and dealt harshly with their opponents.

John Hooker expressed great shock at the execution of Kingwell, a tinner from Chagford and servant of John Charles of Tavistock. The rebels hanged Kingwell because he had secretly conveyed letters between Lord Russell and his master. A staunch and uncompromising adherent of the reformed religion, Kingwell not only refused the rebels' efforts to convert him to their beliefs but also tried to escape from his captors. Hooker held that Kingwell was hanged on the orders of Vicar Welsh primarily for his religion; yet as a spy he was equally deserving of the death penalty.[52]

Warfare, especially emotional conflict over deeply held religious and social principles, brings forth both the best and worst in men. During the long siege of Exeter each side fought enthusiastically and at times heroically to attain its objectives. Similarly, the rebels as well as the defenders of Exeter were responsible for cruel acts for which no apology will suffice, but one incident stands out, indicative of the social malaise affecting England in the mid-sixteenth century. In the midst of the fighting, a party of Exeter men organized a sally through the postern gate at the house of Lord Russell. The force killed a few rebels, took prisoners, and captured several pieces of ordinance. One of the men, John Goldsmith, had the misfortune of being captured by a rebel, "who offered in taking of him with his bill to have slain him." Faced with this threat, Goldsmith fell down and surrendered. He kept his handgun charged as he yielded himself, and as his captor looked the other way, Goldsmith fired his gun into the rebel's belly, killing him. Goldsmith robbed the corpse and brought it back into Exeter with him. In the eyes of Hooker and most of his compatriots, John Goldsmith had scored the "best success" of the day. The defenders of Exeter viewed the rebels merely as "refuse, the scum, and the rascals of the whole county" to whom no code of decency or honor applied. The rebel taking Goldsmith prisoner had higher ideals or else he would have killed him as he lay on the ground. The man paid for the error with his life.[53]

The Western rebels apparently had no military objectives other than the capture of Exeter. If Exeter had finally surrendered, it is unlikely that the rebels could have used it to any greater advantage than Robert Kett used Norwich. The rebels concentrated their entire military force at Exeter and thereby allowed the government in London badly needed time to move forces to the West. The rebels' strategy, as revealed by their military operations, was limited to objectives in Devon and Cornwall. They gained control over most rural areas in the two counties but never looked beyond the horizons of the West. If the leadership communicated with their counterparts in Somerset, Wiltshire, Hampshire, and Oxfordshire, no evidence of a grand strategy has survived. The rebel leadership consisted of local men, who undoubtedly regarded the penetration of the Southeast, the Midlands, and East Anglia with the same apprehension that they would have had for a military campaign in a foreign country. An advance to the north or east would have required a command structure, disciplined units, and an elaborate supply system. All of these requirements were beyond the military competence of the rebel leaders, even the well-equipped Cornish. Moreover, the rebel rank and file was even more parochial in its outlook than the leaders. The commons deployed at Exeter were primitive rebels, simple farmers and artisans, who were provoked and led into direct action against their betters but lacked the vision to transform a local rebellion into a national revolution.[54]

It is necessary to reconstruct the actions of the Western rebels from the early stirring in Cornwall to the siege of Exeter, using sources completely hostile to the rebel cause. The rebels — country gentlemen, priests, townsmen, and peasants — left behind no letters, no strategic plans, and no narratives. When the history of the Western Rebellion was first written, it was set down by John Hooker, an Exeter antiquarian loyal to the crown and the Protestant Reformation. Other information comes from the central government, privy councillors, and military commanders who fought against the rebels. Each writer accepted without question the hierarchical social structure of Tudor England and the solemn obligation of the common man to obey his master. Contemporaries as well as historians writing in the nineteenth and twentieth centuries found the repression of the rebels more interesting than the rebellion itself. The dreams and objectives of the rebels were largely ignored because they were wicked. The goals of the government, on the other hand, were in accordance with the laws of God and man.

Modern historians, wishing to probe beyond a moralistic narrative of events, sought to explain the causes of the Western Rebellion. The judgment of John Hooker that the cause was "only concerning religion which then by act of Parliament was reformed" was authoritative, simplistic, and seductive.[55] Writers interested only in identifying a single cause found Hooker's explanation amply supported in the records of the sixteenth century. The first major challenge to this view came from A. F. Pollard in 1900. In *England under Protector Somerset,* he asserted

> The cause [of the rebellions] everywhere but in Devon and Cornwall was admittedly social, and even there it is almost certain that the same feeling was at the bottom of the revolt, though it was captured by the priests in the interests of the Roman Catholic religion. The enclosure of their commons was a more potent irritant with the agricultural labourers than the alteration in the form of their belief, or even the destruction of images in their churches; and the western rebellion has many of the characteristics of a social movement. There was not a peer or a man of wealth implicated in it, and with the exception of the priests the leaders were of the same class as those who headed the rising in Norfolk.[56]

Pollard's interpretation did not long hold sway and prompted the rebuttal of Frances Rose-Troup, *The Western Rebellion of 1549,* published in 1913, a work that has stood as the most authoritative account down to the present.[57]

Since Pollard was more interested in the reputation of Protector Somerset than the social question, Rose-Troup easily reestablished the primacy of religion. Like the sixteenth-century writers, she limited her inquiry to a quest for a single cause. It was easy to show that Pollard had gone wrong in emphasizing peasant resistance to enclosures in Cornwall and Devon, and her biographies of the ringleaders demolished Pollard's assertion that men of wealth and property abstained from the rebellion. In a vigorously argued final chapter, Rose-Troup surveyed almost every extant contemporary source to prove that religion was the overriding cause of the rebellion.

With an impressive mastery of source materials and a determination to find a single cause, Rose-Troup may have won the battle against Pollard but most assuredly lost the larger struggle to understand the aspirations of the rebels. Her book discredited Pollard's perception of the social question, but not the social question itself. If we move away from her narrow frame of reference, we find that Pollard was right in suggesting that the rebels were motivated by more than a single objective. As Rose-Troup herself showed, the Western rebels were a heterogenous group of clergy, gentry, townsmen, and peasants. The rebel ranks included no fervent supporters of the Book of Common Prayer, but on other matters they were less single-minded than Rose-Troup cared to believe. In truth the mind of the rank-and-file rebel was less tidy and less oriented to causal theories than early twentieth-century historians could imagine. And, while Protestant polemicists of the sixteenth century might identify Popery as the chief obstacle to mankind's progress, the uneducated commons thought in limited and localized terms. Although we can never fully understand the behavior of the inarticulate masses of the Tudor period, the rebels of 1549 have communicated their motives and objectives in three different ways. First of all, the rebels speak to us through their actions. Secondly, formal statements of demands reveal the outlook of at least one segment of the rebel leadership. Finally, testimony of the opposition — of Protector Somerset, Lord Russell and other privy councillors and military commanders — fills some of the gaps left by the rebels' silence.

No one has ever doubted that religion was one of the major forces motivating the Western rebels. The actions of the rebels, their formal grievances, and all of the correspondence and literature generated by the rebellion testify to this essential truth. Protestant preachers and propagandists exaggerated the importance of religion in order to mask the rebels' social and economic grievances, but they grounded their arguments upon real evidence. On the other hand, the Protestant polemicists refused to recognize the distinction between Roman Catholicism and the king's religion established by Henry VIII, and they denounced all those

THE ARTICLES OF US THE COMMONERS OF DEVONSHIRE AND CORNWALL IN DIVERS CAMPS BY EAST AND WEST OF EXETER

1. First, we will have the general council and holy decrees of our forefathers observed, kept and performed, and whosoever shall gainsay them, we hold them as heretics.

2. Item, we will have the laws of our sovereign lord King Henry the VIII concerning the six articles to be in use again as in his time they were.

3. Item, we will have the mass in Latin as was before and celebrated by the priest without any man or woman communicating with him.

4. Item, we will have the sacrament hang over the high altar, and there to be worshipped as it was wont to be, and they which will not consent, we will have them die like heretics against the holy catholic faith.

5. Item, we will have the sacrament of the altar but at Easter delivered to the lay people, and then but in one kind.

6. Item, we will that our curates shall minister the sacrament of baptism at all times as well in the week day as on the holy day.

7. Item, we will have holy bread and holy water made every Sunday, palms and ashes at the times accustomed, images to be set up again in every church, and all other ancient old ceremonies used heretofore by our mother the holy church.

8. Item, we will not receive the new service because it is but like a Christmas game, but we will have our old service of mattins, mass, evensong, and procession in Latin not in English, as it was before. And so we the Cornishmen (whereof certain of us understand no English) utterly refuse this new English.

9. Item, we will have every preacher in his sermon and every priest at his mass pray specially by name for the souls in purgatory as our forefathers did.

10. Item, we will have the whole Bible and all books of scripture in English to be called in again, for we be informed that otherwise the clergy shall not of long time confound the heretics.

11. Item, we will have Dr. Moreman and Dr. Crispin, which hold our opinions, to be safely sent unto us and to them we require the king's majesty to give some certain livings to preach among us our catholic faith.

12. Item, we think it very meet because the lord Cardinal Pole is of the king's blood should not only have his free pardon but also sent for to Rome and promoted to be first or second of the king's council.

13. Item, we will that no gentleman shall have any more servants than one to wait upon him except he may dispend one hundred mark land, and for every hundred mark we think it reasonable he should have a man and no more.

14. Item, we will that the half part of the abbey lands and chantry lands in every man's possession, howsoever he came by them, be given again to two places where two of the chief abbeys was in every county, where such half part shall be taken out and there to be established a place for devout persons, which shall pray for the king and the commonwealth, and to the same we will have all the alms of the church box given for these seven years, and for this article we desire that we may name half of the commissioners.

15. Item, for the particular griefs of our country, we will have them so ordered as Humphrey Arundell and Henry Bray, the king's mayor of Bodmin, shall inform the king's majesty, if they may have safe conduct under the king's great seal, to pass and repass with a herald of arms.

16. Item, for the performance of these articles we will have four lords, eight knights, twelve esquires, twenty yeomen, pledges with us until the king's majesty have granted all these by Parliament.

opposed to the Edwardian reforms as Catholics, Papists, and rank traitors. In 1549, when Stephen Gardiner and Edmund Bonner were steadfastly defending the Henrician settlement, dispassionate observers could distinguish between the late king's religion and the Church for which More and Fisher died. By the reign of Elizabeth, however, when John Hooker wrote his history of Exeter, the religious issue had polarized to the point where the important differences between Henrician Catholicism and Roman Catholicism were too subtle and irrelevant to attract much attention. A careful examination of the rebels' religious demands leads to the conclusion that their views were closer to those of Henry VIII than the Pope.

The rebels' religious demands are found in a series of undated articles, the last of which contains sixteen articles and was compiled outside Exeter.[58] The first two articles embody the constitutional proposals of the rebel leaders and emphasize their identification with the Henrician church. The first article is very general and merely calls for religious policies in accordance with the "general council and holy decrees of our forefathers," while the second specifically demands reenactment of the Act of Six Articles of 1539. The rebels did not call for reconciliation with the Holy See, nor did they propose repeal of the Act of Supremacy establishing the king as the Supreme Head of the Church. The rebel articles add little to the theological concepts contained in the Six Articles. They reject communion in both kinds and demand masses for the dead and the use of images. The most important difference between the articles and the Henrician church lies in the former's repudiation of the authorized English Bible. The rebels would have "the whole Bible and all books of scriptures in English to be called in again, for we be informed that otherwise the clergy shall not of long time confound the heretics." Whereas Henry VIII had favored the authorized vernacular Bible as a vehicle for teaching the people the word of God, the Western rebels placed their trust in the clergy.

The rebels were most vehement in their rejection of the liturgical innovations contained in the Book of Common Prayer. They demanded the restoration of the Latin mass and denounced the prayer book as a "Christmas game." Disregarding the extensive use of English, the Cornish insurgents argued against the new service on the grounds that "certain of us understand no English." The articles called for lay persons to receive the communion only at Easter rather than at more frequent intervals; in fact, the rebel position is contradictory because another article states that the Latin mass should be celebrated "by the priest without any man or woman communicating with him." The authors of the articles must have intended Easter as the only exception. In accordance with late medieval custom, they demanded that the sacrament should hang over the high altar and "there to be worshipped." The rebels misread the prayer book's teaching on infant baptism and insisted the baptisms take place on weekdays as well as on Sunday; the prayer book did not forbid private baptismal services during the week but merely admonished the people to bring their children to church on Sundays and holy days so that the entire congregation might participate in the sacrament. The liturgical demands reflect the worst features of late medieval piety. The conservative, parochial-minded clergy, who were undoubtedly the authors of the rebel demands, were complete strangers to both Catholic and Protestant proposals for liturgical reform, and their liturgical ideals merely reaffirmed traditional practices.[59]

Opposition to the dissolution of the monasteries was less intense among the Western rebels than among the supporters of the Pilgrimage of Grace in 1536. The passage of time placed a stamp of finality on Henry VIII's destruction of the monasteries that explains the difference in attitude. The early stirrings in Cornwall indicate dissatisfaction with the dissolution of the chantries and the confiscation of church property deemed superstitious, but what is known of the rebels' action gives little indication that they undertook corrective action in districts falling under their control. The rebel proposals, expressed in the formal grievances, were quite moderate compared to the demands of the Pilgrims thirteen years earlier. The Western rebels asked only that half of the abbey and chantry lands be restored to refound two religious houses in each county. The location of the houses was to be "where two of the chief abbeys was within every county." To sustain the abbeys the rebels demanded that "we will have all the alms of the church box given these seven years." The rebels also asked that half of the commissioners named to implement the monastic restoration should be nominated by them. Their willingness to accept but half a loaf represents a degree of moderation that was entirely unappreciated by Protector Somerset and the Protestant reformers.

The religious objectives of the rebels extended beyond liturgical and institutional concerns, for their formal grievances referred to three church leaders, Reginald Cardinal Pole, Richard Crispin, and John Moreman. The latter two were Henrician divines who suffered imprisonment after the accession of Edward VI, but Pole, the de facto head of English Roman Catholics, had been attainted for treason. During the Pilgrimage of Grace the Pope had commissioned Pole to organize support for the rebels.[60] Active in a variety of diplomatic schemes to impede the Reformation, Pole was the enemy of Henrician Catholics as well as Protestant reformers. The Western rebels demanded that Pole receive pardon and be "promoted to be first or second of the king's Council." It has escaped the notice of previous historians of the rebellion that Pole was apparently perceived as a political leader rather than as an ecclesiastic. Since the rebels never called for the removal of Somerset as Lord Protector, they must have assumed that Pole would serve in the Privy Council in association with him and the other reformers. It is difficult to understand why the clerical authors of the rebel demands did not call for Pole's appointment to a position within the Church. If the rebels had wished to name a replacement for Thomas Cranmer, Archbishop of Canterbury, Pole would have been the obvious choice.

Richard Crispin and John Moreman, former canons of Exeter, had a strong following among the clergy in Devon and Cornwall. Both were enemies of Simon Haynes, who was appointed Dean of Exeter in 1537 upon the dismissal of Pole from that position. Dean Haynes destroyed images of saints, removed the shrine of Bishop Lacy from Exeter Cathedral, and proposed the replacement of the dean and chapter with a pastor and twelve preachers of the Gospel. Crispin and Moreman, on the other hand, were clerics whose views coincided with the rebels, and they demanded that the two be released and sent to the West so that they could "preach amongst us our Catholic faith."[61]

Pole, Crispin, and Moreman were also of political significance, for they evoked memories of Catherine of Aragon and the Yorkist claim to the throne. Pole and Moreman had opposed the divorce of Henry VIII and befriended Queen Catherine. The spectre of the White Rose of York may be seen in Pole's descent from George, Duke of Clarence, the brother of Edward IV, and the Pole family's close ties with Henry Courtenay, Marquis of Exeter.[62] Pole's mother, the Countess of Salisbury, his brother, Lord Montague, and the Marquis of Exeter had been executed by Henry VIII. Richard Crispin was another link with the Yorkist faction and Courtenay rule in the West, because he had served as chaplain to the Marquis of Exeter. It may have been inevitable that churchmen favored by the rebels in 1549 would have Courtenay associations, but from the beginning of the Devon rising at Sampford Courtenay to the formulation of demands for the release of Crispin and Moreman and the return of Pole, there is an indication that the rebels remembered the good lordship of the Courtenays. Although any notion that the Western Rebellion attempted to revive the Yorkist cause must be rejected, the very mention of the name of Cardinal Pole aroused as much anxiety in the era of Protector Somerset as it had during the reign of Henry VIII.

The significance of the rebels' social and economic grievances has aroused the greatest controversy among historians. Although Frances Rose-Troup argued persuasively for the primacy of religion, she failed to eliminate social discontent as a contributing factor. The rebellions of 1549 obviously occurred in an atmosphere of economic distress, for people of all ranks and degrees suffered from rising prices and a poor harvest. The growing shortage of arable and pastoral lands, caused by increasing rural population, affected the poor most adversely and set peasants against the landlords. Yet a generalized description of social conditions at mid-century, using data unavailable to Rose-Troup in 1913, does not by itself establish a cause for the Western Rebellion or explain the behavior of the rebels. With price indices and demographic data the historian may identify periods of hard times when no major disturbances took place. In 1549 a number of counties in the Midlands and the North, subject to the same distress that prevailed throughout the country, remained generally peaceful. Two western counties, Gloucestershire and Dorset, experienced no large-scale disorders. Therefore, general social and economic conditions explain the actions of the Western rebels only when they can be linked directly to the situation in Devon and Cornwall.

The circumstances of the Western Rebellion and the behavior of the rebels point toward social conflict. Among the leadership there was hostility of the sort that historians of the seventeenth century associate with the antipathy between the court and country before the English Revolution. The secular leaders of the Western Rebellion were preeminently country-type politicians. Although Humphrey Arundell, John Winslade, and Sir Thomas Pomeroy had impressive pedigrees and substantial landholdings, not one of them served at court under either Henry VIII or Edward VI. The opening of the new reign in 1547, rather than opening doors to new talent, merely continued the influence of Henrician careerists such as Sir William Paget, Sir William Petre, and Sir Richard Rich. Arundell, Winslade, and Pomeroy had a recognized standing in the West, but they were not numbered among the gentry elected to Parliament as knights of the shire or appointed to the commission of the peace. These backwoods gentry, alienated from their betters on both the provincial and national levels, identified with rebels of lower social status and viewed the policies of Somerset as the program of the dominant court party. The other rebel leaders were in a very similar position. The mayors of Bodmin and Torrington obviously counted for little among the urban leadership of Tudor England, while the conservative clergy discovered that they had backed the wrong side when the Protestant reformers forced the Henricians from positions of influence within the church.

The behavior of the rebels leaves little doubt that the gentry were the principal adversaries, for the commons expressed anger and resentment toward the ruling elite throughout Devon and Cornwall. While the formal demands of the rebels touched on the social question only in regard to limiting the household servants of the gentry and restoring church lands, the rebels' actions are a better guide to their disposition. One of the first targets of the Cornish was the gentry at St. Michael's Mount, who were attacked and robbed during the early weeks of the rebellion. At Bodmin the rebels intimidated captured gentry and cried out, "Kill the gentlemen!"[63] Sir Richard Grenville, one of the largest landholders in Cornwall, was abused as the rebels seized Trematon

Castle. When the insurrection spread to Devon, the rebels easily persuaded the priest at Sampford Courtenay to restore the Latin Mass, but they brutally murdered William Hellyons, the only gentlemen bold enough to resist them. The burning of the barns at Crediton is yet another example of the class strife that was ignited as a result of the rebellion. Throughout the long siege of Exeter the city fathers feared a revolt among the poor and wisely instituted a program of poor relief to guard against this danger. From beginning to end the Western Rebellion found the commons fighting on one side and the leading gentry families on the other.

The testimony of eyewitness observers and contemporary commentators corroborates evidence drawn from the rebels' actions and confirms the existence of social conflict. John, Lord Russell, commander of the king's army, charged that the Cornish gentry, especially "the meaner sort," had oppressed the poor. After the rebellion ended he heard complaints that some poor men were oppressed

> with extreme and unreasonable compositions, some grieved with unjust exactions by their landlords, some spoiled by one gentleman, some utterly undone and impoverished by another; . . . and the whole commons universally vested with such extremity, wrong and oppression as . . . no slander or reproach was ever heard or reported like unto this, which at the present to the great disfavour and discredit of all the gentlemen of the shire is generally spread and bruited in every honest man's mouth.[64]

Another eyewitness, an anonymous writer identified only by the initials "R. L.," described the rebels as sturdy vagabonds, who "would have no justice," and a "band of thieves [who] would have no state of any gentlemen." He identified Underhill, the tailor of Sampford Courtenay, not Humphrey Arundell, as the "first captain" of the rebels. The causes of the rebellion, according to the anonymous "R. L.," were complex but included serious economic grievances. He was uncertain whether the fault lay more with gentry who increased rents or with farmers who raised prices. The remedy, however, lay with Parliament

> where when the argument is at an end, it may be established by a law, whereof there was never more likelihood, because the amendment thereof will help so many as well lords and gentlemen as all other commoners, no man having cause repine against it, but such as gather, not to spend and improve their livings, not for their charges, as many gentlemen have done, but for their coffers.[65]

His arguments leave little doubt that in his judgment a portion of the blame for social distress had to be laid at the feet of rapacious gentry who raised rents, not to cover rising costs, but to line their pockets at the expense of the poor commons.

The anonymous writer as well as Lord Russell imply that the traditional concept of good lordship had declined in the West. Although the truly good lord may have been more myth than reality, the commons expected fair rents, secure employment, legal protection, and a general attitude of generosity. The good lord cared for his tenants as a father would care for his children. In good times the lord rewarded his tenants with food, gifts, and entertainment. He assisted the poor and sick with alms. When crops failed, the good lord would be expected to distribute grain among the tenants to tide them over until the next harvest. By the mid-sixteenth century the traditional good lord had given way to the agricultural entrepreneur, whose eye was fixed firmly on profits.[66]

Contemporary commentators, removed from the heat of rebellion either in time or place, agreed on the importance of social issues. Writing from London, the staunch reformer John Hooper observed, "The people are sorely oppressed by the marvellous tyranny of the nobility."[67] The ambassador of Charles V, Van der Delft, echoed Hooper's sentiments when he said that the nobles had usurped the peasant's rights, leaving no pasture for sheep and cattle and reducing diets to nothing more than bread and water.[68] When Thomas Cranmer, Archbishop of Canterbury preached against the rebellions, he criticized not the gentry but "ruffians and sturdy idle fellows which be the causes of their own poverty."[69] Nicholas Udall, the government pamphleteer, also spoke of "idle loitering ruffians that will not labor nor can by any other ways get anything to maintain them withal but by an open and common spoil."[70] Chroniclers and historians, among whom John Hooker was most prominent, repeated the official position of the government that the worst elements of the lower classes — the scum of society — rebelled either because they were seduced by Catholic priests or because they coveted their neighbors' wealth.

The Western rebels charged the gentry with failing to provide good lordship, the paternalism that allowed the rich and poor to live together in harmony, but did not protest against enclosure of the commons or rough grazing land. When A. F. Pollard cited enclosure as a cause of the Western rebellion, he failed to present persuasive supporting evidence and invited the rebuttal of Frances Rose-Troup whose mastery of local sources and examination of the rebel demands reaffirmed the primacy of religion. Since her book appeared in 1913, no new evidence has come to light upon which a case for enclosure riots can be based. Yet there are chronicle accounts that undoubtedly encouraged Pollard to write as he did. John Stow stated categorically that the rebels demanded "that the enclosures might be disparked," while John Foxe made an ambiguous reference to attacks on enclosures.[71] Similar statements recur in the chronicles of Raphael Holinshed and Richard Grafton. In a letter of June 29 to Lord Russell, Protector Somerset mentioned a commission "for the inquiry of decays and unlawful enclosures," and the anonymous eyewitness, "R. L.," spoke of plucking down enclosures and enlarging commons but failed to give an example of this kind of activity.[72] Without references to enclosure riots that give details of time and place, any conclusions that enclosure was a significant ingredient in the Western Rebellion must be extremely tentative.

A stronger case can be made for the Act of Relief, the newly enacted tax on sheep and cloth, as a grievance motivating the Western rebels. In articles submitted to Lord Russell that have not survived, the rebel leaders demanded to have the relief granted to the crown by Parliament remitted. Considering that historians still disagree about the purpose and mechanics of this complex statute, it is safe to assume that the men of Devon and Cornwall regarded the measure simply as a tax harmful to sheep-farmers and clothiers.[73] New taxes were no more popular in the sixteenth century than in later periods of history. The commons probably opposed the Act of Relief not only because it was specifically aimed at their principal occupations, but also because they perceived it as an instrument of oppression devised by the court gentry in collusion with the Protestant reformers surrounding the king in London.

Somerset, in a reply to the rebels published in the name of Edward VI, defended the act. He argued that it would produce revenue badly needed to repay debts inherited from the reign of Henry VIII, to garrison Scotland, and to pacify the rebellious countryside. Somerset stressed that he had already granted "two eases" or concessions in enforcing the statute, namely, that only graziers with flocks in excess of 100 would be taxed and that clothiers would be required to give only "notes [sic] of the number and contents of their cloth without valuation or appraising of them" until the Council reviewed the matter.[74] Rebels, who were equally confused by the intricacies of liturgical reform and tax legislation, were not appeased. After the rebellion ended, Lord Russell himself asked that the Act of Relief not be enforced in the West, but Somerset and the Council refused.[75] The next year Parliament repealed it, laying to rest a statute that caused far more trouble than it was worth.

As the opposition to the sheep and cloth tax spread through the countryside, rumors were heard that the legislation was only the beginning of a new program of fiscal oppression. The commons misunderstood the sheep and cloth tax, a measure that went far beyond the comprehension of ordinary people, and feared the worst. Hence simple minds were receptive to suggestions that the government wanted even more. Before the end of June, Somerset had learned of "special bruits and rumors" alleging that geese and pigs were soon to be taxed.[76] Holinshed referred to "false forged tales" that went further: "The people should be constrained to pay a rateable tax for their sheep and cattle and an excise for everything that they should eat and drink."[77] In the emotionally charged atmosphere that pervaded the West, rumor of anticipated economic wrongs could be as powerful a stimulant as grievances that were real.

Antigentry behavior, complaints against the tax on sheep and cloth, criticism of large households, and receptivity to rumors grossly distorting the government's tax program tend to refute Hooker's view that the rebellion was directed solely against Protestant religious reforms. The rebels, whether peasants or townspeople, protested against social and economic conditions that seemed to be growing worse. Their complaints were usually inarticulate protests that showed little understanding of the true economic situation, yet the thrust of their outrage was very clear. Even Somerset heard the commons' complaints "of dearth of victuals."[78] Although Somerset and his supporters were committed to social reforms intended to ease the plight of the commons, the Western rebels misunderstood his intentions and interpreted his policies entirely differently.

The rebels could neither comprehend the government's social program nor trust the gentry upon whose shoulders the implementation of the new policies rested. Their response was direct action. The question of whether Somerset's government or the gentry was more responsible for popular unrest is not easily answered. The gentry could charge the court politicians with initiating unsound policies that aroused fear and suspicion among themselves and the commons. In defending the government, Somerset could counter that Parliament had approved most of his program. The attack on enclosures was, of course, based on prerogative powers exercised through royal proclamations, but Parliament had legislated against enclosure in the past. Somerset could also argue that the gentry had acted selfishly and that they had been negligent in enforcing the law. The gentry — the traditional political nation of Tudor England — failed to maintain good lordship among their tenants and neighbors throughout the countryside, and when minor disturbances began in Cornwall and Devon, they were incapable of restoring order.

When it became apparent that the gentry and local officials could not manage affairs in the West, intervention by the government was imperative. The paramount question was simply how the West might be pacified. Somerset suffered from many limitations as a national leader, but he was not so inept as to side with the rebels. He sympathized with the plight of the poor and favored policies intended to benefit the Commonwealth. But neither Somerset nor any other Tudor politician favored direct action by the people.[79] In responding to the rebellion, Somerset had only two choices. The first option, suggested by Sir William Paget and presumably supported by other Henrician hardliners, was to crush the rebels quickly and decisively without much concern for human life.[80] The alternative was to move slowly, offer generous pardons to rebels willing to return home, and hope that divisions among rebel leaders, lack of discipline, and supply shortages would cause the rising to disintegrate from within. Somerset's personal instincts inclined him toward the second course of action. The lack of manpower and money made his choice nearly imperative.

Somerset might have been more successful if the Western Rebellion had been an isolated event, but beginning in the spring of 1549, he faced a series of worsening crises. The execution of his brother, Thomas, Lord Seymour of Sudeley, for treason damaged the family reputation and weakened his authority. French intervention in Scotland the previous summer thwarted Somerset's design for the conquest of that country and caused severe financial problems for the government. At home the outbreak of rebellion throughout the country was unanticipated because Somerset believed social reforms would remedy legitimate grievances among the commons. The Protestant clergy assumed that the people would rejoice at their deliverance from the bondage of Popish superstition, but the Western Rebellion proved them wrong. Although Somerset was warned to proceed more cautiously, the rush of events overwhelmed the government and forced it to react defensively.[81]

Surviving evidence provides only an incomplete picture of the government's response to the first news of the Western Rebellion. If Somerset and his colleagues received intelligence reports from Cornwall and Devon, the accounts have not survived. Preachers were sent to the West to proclaim the reformed Gospel, while Somerset waited for the gentry to restore order. Later Somerset and the Council dispatched the Carews — Sir Peter and Sir Gawen — to help the gentry resist the rebel force. At this stage Somerset took the position that the disorders were the result "rather of ignorance than of malice" on the part of "light and naughty persons." Such offenders were to be pardoned in the hope that they would "behave themselves towards us as the duty is of loving and obedient subjects."[82] Those who refused pardon were to be apprehended. The Carews could not implement Somerset's policy; and when Sir Peter returned to London sometime after June 24, he was greeted with indignation. Somerset and Lord Rich angrily berated him for burning the barns at Crediton and for exceeding his authority.[83]

Before Sir Peter Carew returned to London to report his failure, Somerset and the Council assigned John, Lord Russell the formidable task of pacifying the West. The recipient of generous grants of monastic land in Devon, Russell presided over the short-lived Council of the West designed by Thomas Cromwell as a scheme for more efficient local administration. Unlike Cromwell, Russell survived the reign of Henry VIII and retained his influence as a privy councillor under Edward VI. Russell divided his time between the court and the Westcountry. As a result of service to Henry VIII and Somerset, he never managed to build up the degree of regional influence necessary to control the West. Yet in 1549 Lord Russell was the only councillor with enough experience and authority to have any chance of pacifying the rebels.[84]

Russell, accompanied by a small military force, proceeded to Salisbury and then advanced to Hinton St. George in Somerset. As there had been disturbances in both Wiltshire and Somerset, he moved with extreme caution to protect himself against encirclement and attacks from the rear. At Hinton St. George he met Sir Peter Carew en route to London and learned what had occurred in Devon. Russell then crossed into Devon and established his headquarters at Honiton. On the basis of the frustratingly incomplete correspondence between Russell and the Council, two completely different perceptions of the situation emerge. Somerset and the Council viewed the Western Rebellion as a small-scale affair similar to the risings in Wiltshire and Somerset. What was required, according to the Council, was a show of force, vigorous exhortations to stiffen the resolve of the justices of the peace and gentry, and gentle persuasion of the rebels encouraging them to return home.[85]

A Council letter signed by Somerset, Sir William Petre, Sir Anthony Wingfield, and Sir Anthony Denny, written June 29 after the rebels' first articles of complaint had been received, suggests that the government was hopelessly out of touch with the rapidly deteriorating situation. The councillors incorrectly assumed that the main rebel force was still at Sampford Courtenay and recommended a strategy for its recovery. They also proposed the use of spies to subvert the rebellion from within:

> Two or three trusty likely persons may be addressed thither with good wise instructions to become partakers of the said multitude and to profess much earnestness therein to the intent to get some credit and authority amongst them and so to proceed two or three days, as you shall appoint them. And afterward upon the rumours to be brought of your lordship's power thither and upon the bruit of their offences, the terror of committing treason, the fear of a king's execution, yea, and upon knowledge that they have been seduced by false disposed people, and furthermore upon the fear of their own lives, the same men so suborned may wax faint and so fall to fear by degrees that it may be without suspect and not only to begin to flee themselves but also to move all others that to do.[86]

The councillors assumed that the rebels could be duped easily and induced to abandon their leaders. These hopelessly erroneous assumptions were made at a time when the rebel army, vastly larger than the force accompanying Russell, was laying siege to Exeter. The government's inept directive may have resulted from Somerset's leniency toward the rebels but was more likely the result of misinformation and poor communications.

If the events of the same period, the last week of June, are viewed from the provinces, a very different picture emerges. Nothing could have been further from Lord Russell's mind than an assault on Sampford Courtenay. He feared that he might be forced to retreat into Dorset from his advanced position at Honiton. Consideration was given to Sherborne, located just across the Dorset border, as a rallying point for checking the rebels' eastward advance. Russell rejected the idea, explaining, "It cannot appear to our judgments that the town of Sherborne doth stand upon any such strait as the same with any mean force shall be a stay to the passage of the rebels eastward; nor that they can be well-impeached of the said passage by any other straits of that country otherwise than by an army able to withstand them in the face."[87] Russell's small army and the growing strength of the rebels left him with no choice other than a defensive strategy. Conditions became so bad that he withdrew from Honiton, but Sir Peter Carew, having returned to the West, met him en route and persuaded him to remain in Devon. Rumors circulated freely throughout the countryside and included a false report that Exeter had fallen.

Although Somerset and Russell never fully agreed on the best strategy for defeating the rebels, Somerset quickly recognized the need for action and issued a series of royal proclamations. Perhaps the most positive approach was the proclamation of July 2 to regulate the price of cattle, sheep, butter, and cheese. R. W. Heinze characterized the Protector's other proclamations as "ranging from merciful pardons to irresponsible threats."[88] In one breath Somerset offered pardon to rioters; in the next he decreed martial law against those who persisted in rebellion. He initially placed great hope in a proclamation declaring the forfeiture of all rebel lands and property, an attempt to "set a terror and division among the rebels themselves." The proclamation not only authorized the forfeiture of property but also offered the same to those who supported the government.[89] The notion that rebels willing to risk their lives in armed combat would abandon their cause merely to protect their property rested on an absurd fallacy. Somerset thought the proclamation might induce the Cornish to abandon their allies in Devon but only ten days before the relief of Exeter admitted that it had "wrought no great effect in Devonshire." Somerset had more faith in the efficacy of royal proclamations than most of his fellow councillors. Sir William Paget criticized Somerset's policies long before the rebellions, and by late July Sir Thomas Smith was willing to admit that firm military action was "better than ten thousand proclamations and pardons for the quieting of the people."[90]

In spite of the barrage of royal proclamations, weeks passed before Lord Russell could advance toward Exeter. Historians studying the lengthy communiques that passed from the government in London to Russell have disagreed sharply regarding the wisdom of the government's directives and Russell's perception of rebel strength.[91] In the ensuing debate both Russell and Somerset have found champions, but the real issue is less a matter of personalities than geographical location. Somerset and the Council, based in London, received only fragmentary accounts of the situation in the West and had to contend with rebellion in other areas as well as the aggressive designs of the French. At Honiton, on the other hand, Russell concentrated only on reducing the rebel force surrounding Exeter and controlling the countryside. He refused to advance toward Exeter until his army was possessed of overwhelming strength. Russell may have been excessively cautious, but it is difficult to fault his judgment that a defeat at the hands of the rebels was a catastrophe to be avoided at all cost. As Russell's letters from the West have not survived, all attempts to judge his strategy must be based on the government's correspondence.

The combined strength of the Cornish and Devon rebels blocked Russell's forward advance while unrest in Somerset, Dorset, and Wiltshire posed a threat from the rear. When he found it difficult to recruit loyal men in the Western counties, he asked for reinforcements from other regions. He requested large contingents of foot soldiers and foreign mercenaries. He needed bows, arrows, shot, and powder as well as ready money to pay the soldiers. As late as July 18, Russell complained to the government about the insufficiency of his army. Somerset and the Council, viewing events from the perspective of London, called for economy. The councillors argued that if Russell's men shot too many arrows, the rebels would simply gather them up for a counterattack. The rebellions obviously placed inordinate demands on the government's military and financial resources.[92]

Somerset promised to send Lord Grey to Devon but only after he defeated rebels in Oxfordshire and Buckinghamshire. A promise to send a large force under the Earl of Warwick never materialized because he was dispatched to fight Robert Kett in Norfolk. Unexplained delays retarded the appearance of a force recruited by Sir William Herbert. Unable to give Russell the support that he wanted, Somerset and the Council recommended better use of small, mobile cavalry units. To make matters worse, the government heard rumors that the French were preparing to attack Cornwall and advised Russell to protect ports along the coast. Somerset and the Council were aghast on July 28, when they heard that Russell expected Sir William Herbert to bring as many as 10,000 foot. According to their calculations, the combined rebel strength of Cornwall and Devon could not "make above 7,000 men, tag and rag, that should come to fight, and yet some we are sure they leave behind to keep their houses and the town, and one thousand of them is in Exeter."[93]

As Somerset directed the military buildup in the West, he kept a watchful eye on Princess Mary, the elder daughter of Henry VIII. Mary was excluded from the government of Edward VI, and she resisted all efforts of the king and Council to persuade her to conform to the reformed religion. Her response to the Western Rebellion was of great concern to the government, because she was the recognized heir to the throne. If Mary gave even the slightest encouragement to the Catholic leaders in the West, Somerset's position might have been rendered untenable. The Council suspected that one of her chaplains was active among the rebels at Sampford Courtenay and wrote an anxious letter asking assistance in restraining alleged rebels. Mary stoutly protested the innocence of all of her servants and stressed that she had no lands or acquaintances in Devon. Somerset undoubtedly breathed a sigh of relief, but he and the Protestant leadership continued to scrutinize her activities very carefully.[94]

Lord Russell, although frustrated by Somerset's directives and generally indifferent to the government's difficulties with Princess Mary, the Norfolk Rebellion, and the French, could confidently assume that time was on his side. So long as Exeter resisted the siege, the main rebel force was unlikely to attack him at Honiton. Loyal gentry began to rally to Russell's standard as newly arrived supplies and men strengthened his small army. In addition to money raised by the government, three Exeter merchants, Thomas Prestwood, John Bodley, and John Periam, drawing on credit at Bristol, Taunton, and elsewhere, offered badly needed financial assistance.[95]

The story of Russell's advance to Exeter — a tale related with great satisfaction by each generation of historians from the time of John Hooker to the present — was anticlimactic.[96] He first attacked Ottery St. Mary, burning the town before returning to Honiton. Later, on about July 28, the rebels took the offensive and advanced to Fenny Bridges only three miles from Honiton. The next morning Russell's army captured the bridge across the River Otter and drove the rebels from an adjoining meadow. The rebels did not yield easily, for Hooker wrote of the "good store of blows and bloodshed" that resulted in the injury of Sir Gawen Carew. The arrival of some two hundred Cornish reinforcements commanded by Robert Smith of St. Germans permitted the rebels to counterattack, but the force was too small to turn the tide. Russell pursued the retreating rebels for three miles, abandoning the chase only after hearing unfounded rumors that another rebel band was approaching from the rear. The fighting at Fenny Bridges claimed at least one hundred rebel lives, while government deaths were put at only three. After his limited victory, Russell returned again to Honiton. His spirits were buoyed by the arrival of Lord Grey of Wilton accompanied by the horsemen who had defeated rebels in Berkshire, Buckinghamshire, and Oxfordshire.

Supported by an experienced commander, Russell marched out of Honiton toward Exeter on Saturday, August 3. The army, leaving the main road, passed through the burned town of Ottery St. Mary and crossed over the downs toward Woodbury. The army pitched camp near the windmill of a loyal gentleman, Gregory Carye, but quickly came under heavy attack from rebels advancing from Clyst St. Mary.[97] The army managed to drive off the first attackers and were in the midst of a religious service conducted by Miles Coverdale when the rebels suddenly reappeared. Hooker's account at this point is unclear, but it appears that indecisive skirmishing followed as the rebels began to concentrate their men for a major attack. According to Hooker, as many as 6,000 assembled in the vicinity of Clyst St. Mary. On Sunday morning Russell's army fought its way into the town only to be attacked from the rear: "One of the chief captains of these rebels named Sir Thomas Pomeroy, knight, kept himself in a furze close, and perceiving the army to be past him, and having them with him a trumpeter and a drum slager, commanded the trumpet to be sounded and the drum to be stricken up." At the sound, Russell and the army were startled, "supposing verily that there had been an ambush behind them to have entrapped and enclosed them." The army promptly retreated, abandoning wagons "laded with munition, armor, and treasure." Russell regrouped but found the town too well defended for a direct attack. Every house was fortified and filled with rebels.

To avoid heavy casualties to the army, Russell ordered the town burned. Sir William Francis, a Somerset man, led an advanced party into Clyst St. Mary through a "deep and narrow" lane where the rebels "being upon the banks upon every side of the way with their stones so beat him that they struck his headpiece fast to his head and whereof he died." The fires were nonetheless ignited, but the rebels, joining together in the middle of the town, fought determinedly. Some died by the sword, some were burned to death, while others drowned in the River Clyst trying to escape the slaughter. At least five hundred rebels were killed and about twenty of Russell's soldiers. Among one hundred archers fighting with Sir William Francis, seventy-nine were injured.[98]

After Clyst St. Mary was recovered, the army proceeded toward Clyst Heath, a large open space west of the river. The way was blocked by rebels, who barricaded the bridge with timber and placed a gun at the far end. The gunner killed the soldier leading a frontal attack across the bridge, but before the gun could be reloaded a party of soldiers who forded the river captured the gun emplacement from the rear. The bridge was quickly cleared, and the army, led by Lord Grey, advanced to the heath. No sooner had the army occupied this position than Grey spied another rebel force: "Looking backward toward Woodbury, he saw . . . a great company assembled and marching forward." He reported the situation to Lord Russell, and they concluded that "the prisoners whom they had before taken at the windmill and in the town, who were a great number and which, if they were newly set upon, might be a detriment and a peril unto them, should be all killed." The executions began immediately, "every man making a dispatch of his prisoners." In this matter-of-fact prose, John Hooker reported the slaughter of what may have been several hundred men.[99]

The rebel reinforcements approaching from the east apparently never materialized, but during the night others camped around Exeter made their way to Clyst Heath. Along the lower side next to the road, they built trenches and positioned guns. Dawn came, and the rebel guns opened fire at the royal army camped above. Russell promptly divided the army into three parts and ordered the encirclement of the rebels. Trapped on every side, the sturdy and determined rebels fought to the last man: "In the end," wrote Hooker, "they were all overthrown, and few or none left alive." After the battle Lord Grey remarked that never in his military career had he seen men fight with greater "valor and stoutness." Estimates of the dead at Clyst Heath vary, but Sir Hugh Paulet reported that two thousand rebels died. Of the king's men, there were forty fatalities and over one thousand injured.[100]

When the rebels besieging Exeter heard of the carnage at Clyst Heath, they abandoned their posts and retreated westward. On August 6, Russell, marching northward from Topsham where he camped after the battle, approached the gates of Exeter. To reduce the risk of plundering a city already critically short of food, Russell kept his men outside the walls. The relief of Exeter led to the capture of several important rebel leaders including Sir Thomas Pomeroy; Robert Paget, an Exeter man who was the brother of Sir William, the privy councillor; and Edward Drew. Although the heavy hand of repression soon followed Russell's arrival, the citizens of Exeter — both rich and poor — welcomed the victorious army. Loyal residents of the surrounding countryside had less cause to rejoice, because shortly after the siege was raised, Sir William Herbert arrived with a thousand ill-disciplined Welsh, who, according to Hooker, arrived "too late to the fray, yet soon enough to the play." The unruly soldiers pillaged at their pleasure, and the "whole country" was "put to the spoil."[101]

The Western rebels sustained a bloody and costly defeat at Clyst St. Mary, but they remained in control of districts to the west of Exeter. As the camps surrounding Exeter were poorly located to resist the advancing relief army, the decision to retreat and regroup at Sampford Courtenay reflected sound strategy on the part of Humphrey Arundell and other leaders. The surviving force, largely Cornish, was still inspired by priests who fought bravely and died in battle with their parishioners. The ten days that Lord Russell remained at Exeter gave the rebels time to regroup and regain confidence. Nevertheless, the rebels were much weaker than before Clyst St. Mary, whereas the royal army now swelled to between eight and ten thousand men as reinforcements arrived from Wales and the surrounding countryside where once-timid Devon gentry recovered their courage and enthusiastically backed the winning side.[102]

On August 16, Russell, surprised to learn of the rebels' strength at Sampford Courtenay, marched westward from Exeter by way of Crediton. A preliminary skirmish claimed the life of Maunder, the shoemaker, one of the chief rebel captains. At Sampford Courtenay, Russell found his enemy "strongly encamped." Lord Grey and Sir William Herbert fired into the camp with their guns as pioneers prepared the way for a frontal attack. Russell, who remained behind with the transport, came under attack by Humphrey Arundell's Cornish. The most able and daring of the Western rebels, Arundell "wrought such fear in the hearts" of the army that Russell wished that his force was even stronger. But in the end the sheer weight of numbers overcame the courageous rebels. Grey withdrew enough troops from the attack on Sampford Courtenay to resist Arundell, while Herbert, "pressing still upon them, never breathed til he had driven them to a plain fight." Sampford Courtenay fell with the loss of five or six hundred defenders including Thomas Underhill, who had been in command there since June. Other units of the royal army defeated Arundell and pursued him until nightfall as he retreated into Cornwall.[103]

The Western Rebellion ended in Cornwall where it began. Humphrey Arundell and a few devoted followers fled to Launceston where they tried unsuccessfully to rally the town. By August 20, Launceston was safely in government hands, and Arundell was in prison. Farther to the west the army also reoccupied St. Michael's Mount. In the weeks that followed, Cornwall paid a heavy price for its role in the rebellion as Sir Anthony Kingston and other officials summarily hanged men suspected of participating in the revolt. The leaders were taken to London for trials and executions. The last remnants of the once-mighty rebel army escaped annihilation at Sampford Courtenay, fled to North Devon, and made a final stand at Kingweston in Somerset.

Robert for lack of grace pretending to do good thereby to the commonwealth said he would assist them with body and goods, whereupon of a small company at the first not above five or six persons they increased to servants and vagabonds that they would not be resisted, and the same Robert with them after they had ended their purpose at Wymondham came forward to Norwich . . .

Nicholas Sotherton, "The Commoyson in Norfolk 1549"

4.   ROBERT KETT AND THE COMMOTION IN NORFOLK

The Commotion in Norfolk, like the Western Rebellion, had an inauspicious beginning. The initial stirring of obscure men in rural Norfolk signalled no national crisis, and the grievances of those who toiled in the fields were no more distressing than the complaints of commonfolk in other parts of England. Although Robert Kett quickly entered into the light of recorded history, contemporaries who recounted the story of the rebellion regarded the deeds of the rebels as less important than the achievements of the upholders of law and order. The temporary humiliation of the gentry was recorded with great compassion, but the slaughter of simple men and boys merely served to exemplify God's judgment upon the wicked. Nicholas Sotherton, Alexander Neville, and Raphael Holinshed wrote the first histories of the Norfolk Rebellion, and as spokesmen for the victors they emphasized the plight of the gentry and the citizens of Norwich and praised the soldiers who crushed the rebel host. Yet, emerging from the records of the past is a faint but clearly visible track that leads back to the summer of 1549 when Robert Kett, the tanner of Wymondham, shook the foundations of Tudor England.

Disturbances began early in June when inhabitants of the market town of Attleborough and their neighbors "threw down certain new ditches" made by John Green, Gent., of Wilby. The villagers charged that Green enclosed a portion of common pasture belonging to Attleborough. For several weeks the men had heard rumors that enclosures were being destroyed in Kent and other parts of southern and eastern England. It was undoubtedly one of the bolder fellows, who, seeing that nothing of the sort had occurred in his neighborhood, inspired a handful of his friends to demolish Green's offending ditches.[1] Although enclosure riots and isolated acts of vandalism were common in the early sixteenth century, the attacks on enclosures in 1549 were apparently inspired by the belief that the government of Protector Somerset favored direct action by peasants to implement the king's proclamation against illegal enclosures. The men of Attleborough, therefore, thought they acted lawfully in righting what they saw as the wrongs of a local landlord. Having accomplished their objective, the men returned home.

Several weeks later, on Saturday, July 6, crowds of people gathered at Wymondham, a market town located about halfway between Attleborough and Norwich, to attend a play called Wymondham Game commemorating the translation of St. Thomas Becket to the see of Canterbury. Festivities began on Saturday, continued through Sunday, the feast day, and ended on Monday. While some came to Wymondham simply to attend a religious play, others met secretly to plan further destruction of enclosures. A few left Wymondham on Tuesday for Morley, a mile away, and cast down the enclosures of Master Hobart before returning to Wymondham "where they practised the like feats." At this point Holinshed, the only sixteenth-century authority on the earliest phase of the Norfolk Rebellion, remarked that "as yet they took no man's goods by violence."[2]

The rebels' next victim was John Flowerdew, Gent., of Hethersett.[3] A successful lawyer who acquired a substantial landed estate, Flowerdew was unpopular in Wymondham because he removed lead and freestone from the abbey church at the time of the dissolution. He was so angry at the destruction of his enclosures that he offered the rebels 3s. 4d. to demolish those of his neighbor, Robert Kett. When Kett heard the objections to his enclosures, he agreed that his hedges and ditches should be "thrown down and made even with the ground." Kett not only complied with the rebels' demands but added that he was ready to repress and subdue "the power of great men" so that they would repent of their great pride. Promising to revenge the "hurts done unto the weal public and common pasture by the importunate lords," Kett joined the rebels and vowed "that he would never be wanting to their good, and that they should have him not only a companion, but a captain, and in the doing of so great a work, not a fellow, but a leader, author, and principal."[4] By offering his leadership to the rebels, Kett transformed an angry but ill-directed local mob into a potentially powerful rebel force.

Although our knowledge of Robert Kett is extremely limited, one thing is certain: the leader of the Commotion in Norfolk does not conform to the modern stereotype of an alienated political activist or social revolutionary. First, Kett was not a youthful firebrand but an elderly grandfather of about fifty-seven. Life in the sixteenth century was short. At middle age a man's body was frequently tormented with painful chronic ailments ranging from toothache to kidney stones and gout. The best medicines of the day often merely increased one's discomfort; hence the sensible skepticism about the value of treatment by physicians and surgeons. Henry VIII, once a vigorous and powerful man, died at fifty-five, his body racked by disease. His father, Henry VII, the victor of Bosworth, was dead at fifty-two. The life-span of the royal Tudors corresponded to the normal pattern of the period. By fifty a man had reached an age when death could be expected; he was neither in the prime of life nor expected to exhibit an image of zestful middle age such as is characteristic of our own perpetually youthful society. The Ketts, it must be admitted, had a better record of longevity than most of their contemporaries. Robert's father is believed to have reached the age of seventy-six, while four of Robert's five sons lived to sixty. His third son, Loye, probably died in 1614 when he would have been seventy-nine. Yet, even allowing for the exceptional longevity of the Ketts, Robert had reached an age when, if death were not imminent, bold new enterprises, certainly not the leadership of a great rebellion, would scarcely have been recommended.[5]

Kett's age was not the only factor that distinguished him from modern revolutionaries. Apparently without formal schooling, he cannot have had any great familiarity with the Christian radicalism and social criticism set forth by the commonwealth writers. Although he became the leader of the commons opposed to enclosing landlords, he was himself a prosperous landowner and an encloser. If he was greatly troubled by the spoliation of Wymondham Abbey, his conscience had not prevented him from purchasing former monastic property during the reign of Henry VIII.

Kett's qualifications as a rebel leader seem unusual by modern standards, but his pedigree was better suited to the world of the Tudors. Until 1547 Thomas Howard, third Duke of Norfolk was the leading figure in county politics. Norfolk served Henry VIII as Lord Treasurer and built a great mansion at Kenninghall. Henry charged Norfolk and his son, Henry, Earl of Surrey, with treason, but only Surrey was executed before the king's death. After the destruction of the Howards, fourteen families of upper gentry governed the county. A. H. Smith calculated that there were at least 424 gentlemen in the county in 1580, of whom about 300 were "mere gentlemen" who were generally excluded from the commission of the peace.[6] Kett belonged among a numerous class of prosperous yeoman freeholders, not with the gentry who dominated county society and politics. As a tanner and a farmer, he could not "live idly and without manual labor" or "bear the port, charge, and countenance of a gentleman," the qualities assigned to the genteel by Sir Thomas Smith in *De Republica Anglorum*. Kett lived and worked among the husbandmen, laborers, and artisans who had "no voice nor authority" in the Tudor commonwealth.[7] He was part of the class that provided some of the most important leaders of Tudor rebellions. Michael Joseph, the blacksmith, was a leader of the Cornish rebels in 1497, while Nicholas Melton, popularly known as Captain Cobbler, the shoemaker of Louth, was active in the Lincolnshire rebellion of 1536.[8] If Kett was too prosperous to experience the privation of the poor and the unemployed, he nevertheless was excluded from the Tudor establishment. His social standing provided the basic qualification for leadership of a revolt against the gentry.

The Kett family had lived in Norfolk for six centuries before the outbreak of the rebellion. Robert was born about 1492, the fourth son of Thomas and Margery Kett, who had small landholdings at Forncett. John, Sr., the eldest son, died in 1530, leaving his lands to William, the second son. The third son, John, Jr., died in 1549, and the fifth son, Thomas, in 1553. William, who joined Robert in the rebellion, combined the occupations of butcher and mercer. He was probably more of a grazier of cattle, selling livestock to other butchers, perhaps butchering only occasionally himself. It is likely that William worked closely with his brother, Robert, who needed hides for his tannery. William also kept a mercer's shop in Wymondham, a business that had little in common with the great mercers of London.[9] Far from being an entrepreneur of the cloth trade, William simply supplied a small local market with the cloth needed in the home for clothing and other household necessities.

Robert Kett married Alice Appleyard, daughter of Agnes Rokewood of Warham and Sir Nicholas Appleyard of Bracon Ash. Kett's father-in-law fought the Scots at the battle of Flodden and served as a justice of the peace.[10] The marriage linked Kett with a well-established family of lesser gentry and resulted in several interesting family connections. Alice Kett's brother, Roger Appleyard, married Elizabeth Scott, who, following Roger's death, was remarried to Sir John Robsart. Robsart and his wife were the parents of the famous Amy, first wife of Robert Dudley, Earl of Leicester, the Elizabethan courtier and statesman. The historian of the Kett family suggested that Robert Dudley may have met his future wife for the first time when he accompanied his father, the Earl of Warwick, to quell the Norfolk Rebellion. Many years later, after the mysterious death of Amy, John Appleyard, her half-brother, charged Leicester with murder. Robert Kett was himself acquainted with the Dudleys because he bought land from Warwick (then Lord Lisle) in 1546.

The family of Robert and Alice included five sons, William, James, Loye, George, and Richard. Loye Kett was probably named after the last Abbot of Wymondham, Loye Ferrers. Loye and his brothers, George and Richard, have been identified as yeomen farmers. Kett's sons obviously kept their heads down after the rebellion but continued to live in Norfolk very much as their ancestors before them had lived.

Kett provided for his family with income from the tanning trade and landholding. His landed income placed him among the very prosperous yeomanry. Three estimates have survived. According to the chroniclers John Stow and Charles Wriothesley, Kett's land was worth £50 annually.[11] When his property was granted to Thomas Audley in May 1550, the value was set at 40 marks [£26. 13s. 4d.].[12] A third, still lower estimate, based on the *inquisition post mortem*, gives a value of just over £18.[13] His major property, according to the *inquisition*, was Gunville's Manor, worth £13. 6s. 8d. annually. A second property, Wymondham Manor, formerly belonging to the Hospital of Burton Lazars, Leicestershire, was acquired from Lord Lisle and valued at £4.[14] Kett also owned at least one house in Wymondham, gardens, an orchard, and several small parcels of land. Other records indicate he bought and sold land between 1530 and 1548 and thereby built up a comfortable estate by thrift and careful investment.

Although no information about his tannery has survived, it is likely that Kett was the only tanner in Wymondham as well as one of the town's leading tradesmen. Tanning was an essential craft, serving shoemakers, farmers, and manufacturers. The leather industry of Tudor England was more important than the metal crafts and ranked second to the woolen cloth industry. A tanner's primary capital investment was in raw hides, which remained in pits for long periods before becoming salable leather. To secure a regular income a tanner "needed to have a large number of hides evenly spaced throughout the manufacturing process so that there was a steady supply of leather ready for the market."[15] Stow and Wriothesley both said Kett's movable property was worth 1,000 marks, a figure that must have included a substantial investment in hides. While his subsidy assessments are much lower, they reveal Kett's stature as a tanner and his standing in the community. The subsidy assessment of 1543 (34 and 35 Henry VIII) was for goods worth £60, a figure that placed him among the ten most affluent residents of Wymondham.[16] In April 1547, when Kett was assessed for the second payment of the subsidy of 1545, he was taxed on land rather than goods. His payment was well below that of Sir John Robsart, the wealthiest man in Wymondham, but the highest of the fourteen persons assessed in the township of Sutton. It is also interesting to learn that Kett's liability of forty shillings was only twenty shillings below that of John Flowerdew in neighboring Hethersett.[17] Two years later, when assessments were made for the relief on goods, a similar pattern prevailed.[18] Unfortunately, there are no sheep assessments for either Kett or his neighbors.

Tanners were often artisans of considerable standing in the local community. A tanner of Chipping Norton, Oxfordshire, who died in 1587, was richer than two butchers and a shoemaker living in the same village. Of forty-four Oxfordshire tradesmen for whom household inventories between 1580 and 1590 survive, only six left larger personal estates than the tanner of Chipping Norton. John Neall of Horncastle,

Lincolnshire, one of the most substantial provincial tanners of the sixteenth century, left a personal estate of over £1300 at the time of his death in 1567. An ambitious tanner, operating on a large scale, might produce enough profit to advance his family into the ranks of the gentry. At Myddle, Shropshire, for example, two of the most important families of resident gentry traced their origins to successful tanners. William Crugge, who operated a tannery on Exe Island, entered urban politics and served as mayor of Exeter four times beginning in 1505.[19]

Because of the limitations of surviving sources, we can only speculate about the reasons that caused Robert Kett to become leader of the Norfolk Rebellion. The combined income from tanning and agriculture should have allowed him to live comfortably and to provide for his family. Nothing in the family background suggests that the Ketts were troublemakers or that Robert was an angry or embittered man. Nor is it likely that he had an ideological commitment to social reform. If he entertained ambitions of advancing himself into the ranks of the gentry, no evidence of frustrated efforts has survived. He quarrelled with John Flowerdew when Wymondham Abbey was dissolved in 1539 and sought to protect the parish church, which was contained within the Abbey, but the dispute was a purely local affair and should have been settled short of a rebellion that inflamed a whole county.[20] Considering what is known of his life, Kett ought to have approached his sixtieth year a happy and contented family man.

One possible explanation for Kett's behavior — for which there is no corroborating evidence — is that he was annoyed by recent parliamentary legislation critical of tanners and the leather industry. The Act for the True Curing of Leather (2 and 3 Edward VI c. 9) called attention to "the covetousness of tanners in overhasting their work by divers subtle and crafty means." The statute further alleged that the king's subjects were "not only in their goods but also in the health of their bodies much endamaged by occasion of ill shoes and boots made of evil leather." Although leather was of poor quality, it had "grown . . . in such unreasonable price that the commons of this realm cannot now have for 12d. that they might in time past have had for 8d." The act's remedy was to increase the custom duty on all exported leather by three times. A second statute, an Act for the True Tanning of Leather (2 and 3 Edward VI c. 11), stated boldly that "there was never worse leather used or made within this realm" than that which was currently produced. In the past hides were left in the tanning fat for a year or more; through "sundry deceitful and crafty means," the time had been reduced to as little as three weeks. To correct the situation justices of the peace and searchers of leather were empowered to search tan pits and seize hides that were improperly tanned. Sheepskins were not to be tanned. A penalty of 6s. 8d. was authorized for each improperly tanned hide that was sold and for each sheepskin tanned.[21]

It is very difficult to determine whether Kett was motivated by general conditions within the tanning industry or whether the geographical, social, and economic realities of Tudor Norfolk created an environment that encouraged popular unrest to peak in the spring of 1549. Norfolk was a wealthy county in comparison with Devon and Cornwall, but its relative prosperity was declining in the sixteenth century. Southern and central Norfolk, the area where Wymondham was located, was a wood-pasture region where most farms were enclosed. Although sheep-farming was not unknown, most farmers were engaged in dairying and cattle-rearing. Large fields of grass and hay fed the cattle, while crops of barley, wheat, and rye were also produced. At Wymondham nonagricultural employment was available in the manufacture of wood products, and in other towns and villages cloth-making supplemented the income of the smaller farmers. Joan Thirsk has said that the average peasant living in the wood-pasture region was usually better off than his counterpart elsewhere in the county and that wealth tended to be more evenly distributed.[22]

To the north and west of Wymondham lay the lighter soils, the sands and loams where sheep-corn husbandry prevailed. Here the large-scale sheep-farmer was dominant. The dung of sheep was required to produce large crops of grain or corn. In order to achieve the necessary fertilization large farmers monopolized the right to graze sheep on the common fields and foldcourses. The system of folding placed irksome restraints on smaller farmers because the cultivation of their arable land "had to be ordered in such a way as to leave the land free at the seasons when it was grazed by the lord's flock."[23] The typical peasant lived in a nucleated village and subordinated himself to the rich farmers who dominated the manorial society. Although the gentry controlled the economic life of the sheep-corn region, the area also contained a large proportion of often individualistic and contentious freeholders.

Rural Norfolk was a center of popular discontent long before the days of Robert Kett. During the great Peasants' Revolt of 1381, the county rose with large bands of rebels wreaking havoc upon rich and unpopular gentry. Wymondham was one of the first towns from which violence was reported. Geoffrey Litster, a dyer of Felmingham near North Walsham, burst onto the scene as leader of the eastern Norfolk rebels as quickly as Kett did a century and a half later. Litster and Kett possessed leadership qualities that were strikingly similar although Litster's men were more given to pillaging and murder.[24]

Many years later, when Henry VIII was king, Norfolk experienced a wide variety of popular disturbances that the rebels of 1549 can hardly have forgotten. Enclosure raised tempers, ruined the poor, and provoked the protracted litigation for which Norfolk was famous. Local disputes were often fought out before the Court of Star Chamber; in fact J. A. Guy has shown that East Anglia was responsible for most of the enclosure cases in Star Chamber during the era of Cardinal Wolsey.[25] In 1525 the "decay of work," that is, unemployment, caused a rising of farm and cloth workers. Corn sellers were assaulted in Norwich two years later when sacks of grain were cut open for distribution to the poor. The next year irate women rose because of high corn prices as did a group of Yarmouth men, "not with intent to injure, but to hinder exportation."[26] After Henry VIII broke with Rome and began the dissolution of the monasteries, the county was divided religiously. The famous reformer, Thomas Bilney, was burned at Norwich in 1530. Later the city witnessed the burning of William Leyton, a monk of Eye, Suffolk, who was charged with denouncing religious images and favoring communion in both kinds. Opponents of the Reformation were no less active in Henrician Norfolk, because Sir Nicholas Mileham, sub-prior of Walsingham, attempted to "procure and make an insurrection" there in 1537. His supporters intended to fire beacons and raise the countryside in an effort to preserve the priory. After the rising was suppressed, fifteen persons were charged with treason, of whom five were executed at Norwich.[27]

An incident in 1540 serves as a reminder that antigentry sentiment was deeply rooted in the popular mind. One spring day John Walter delivered an astonishing harangue to the commons at Griston. He called for three or four brave men to ride through the countryside at night crying, "To Swaffham, to Swaffham!" By morning he thought ten thousand men could be assembled. The objective, according to depositions given to the government, was the destruction of the gentry. "You know," said Walter, "how all the gentlemen in manner be gone forth, and you know how little favor they bear to us poor men. Let us therefore go home to their houses, and there shall we have harness, substance, and victual." But Walter's design went beyond robbery and plunder. He urged the commons to kill all gentry who would not join them: "As many as will not turn to us, let us kill them, yes, even their children in the cradles, for it were a good thing if there were so many gentlemen in Norfolk as there be white bulls." Walter hoped for enough popular support to move on to King's Lynn. The first gentry to be attacked were the Southwells of Woodrising, the Bramptons, the Hogans of East Bradenham, and Sir Roger Townshend. John Walter may have been a lunatic or a man who suffered extraordinary injustice at the hands of the gentry. On the other hand, the details of his speech may have been embroidered by informers seeking payment from the government. Although we do not know how many commons rallied to Walter's side, his behavior offers a valuable insight into antigentry attitudes in Henrician Norfolk.[28]

After the accession of Edward VI in 1547, disputes over rights to common pasture and quarrels among the gentry continued to trouble the county. A controversy between tenants of Roughton, south of

Cromer, and the farmer of the manor, Robert Wigmore, Gent., concerning pasture rights on common land was brought before the Court of the Duchy of Lancaster. In Michaelmas term in 1547, the court proposed a compromise that allowed Wigmore rights of ingress and egress for his sheep and cattle across the common and also purported to guarantee the customary rights of the tenants. The settlement was far from satisfactory because it was subsequently alleged that Wigmore still usurped common rights with his livestock and took grass and hay belonging to the tenants from the common at Roughton.[29] A similar dispute arose at Erpingham, near Aylsham, where a commission appointed by the Duchy, including Sir William Paston, found that the king's tenants of Erpingham "proved their right to common of pasture with all kinds of beasts." This dispute also lingered on and came before the Duchy court for a second time in July 1549 when the common was divided by a ditch which was to be maintained by each of the hostile parties.[30] A court battle over common rights at Hindringham, near Fakenham, dragged on for eight years before the Duchy court managed to arrange a settlement. The king's tenants argued that the farmer of an adjoining manor could keep sheep or cattle on the common only during shack time (i.e. after the harvest) while the farmer, supported by the Dean and Chapter of Norwich Cathedral, claimed full rights over the disputed land.[31]

Quarrelsome gentry often stood behind disputes that affected the livelihood of tenants and poor commons. The Pastons, famous for the fifteenth-century family letters, remained powerful at the time of the Norfolk Rebellion. In September 1547 a disagreement arose between Sir William Paston and Thomas Woodhouse Esq., concerning debts owed by the latter. Paston and Woodhouse had extensive dealings in sheep, grain, and malt. A few years later Woodhouse countered with charges that Paston had ordered the digging of ditches that prevented the tenants from gaining access to pastureland. Paston also clashed with another leading Norfolk family in 1547 when the tenants of Sir John Clere at Winterton and Somerton sued him in the Court of Requests. The local residents contended that Paston and his bailiff, Anthony Brampton, enclosed six or seven acres of common, took land worth £5 per year from a copyholder, and stopped the people of Winterton from collecting wood and fuel. A man of sixty, claiming to have known the common land for forty years, stated that land near the sea enclosed by Paston was "parcel of the common of the town of Winterton." To the best of his knowledge Sir John Clere was "lord of the soil of all the said common and . . . the over-charging of the said common and wrong usage thereof hath been always punished in the said Sir John Clere's court."[32]

The Norfolk of Robert Kett clearly was suffering from potentially dangerous tensions. In the countryside the peasantry complained against encroachments on common land and enclosure while unemploy-

ment and high prices plagued those living in Norwich. With the Duke of
Norfolk under a sentence of death at the Tower of London, the gentry
scrambled for profit and position without sufficient concern for the
well-being of their tenants and neighbors. It is impossible to know
whether these conditions would have triggered a large popular rebellion
without the leadership of Kett. His attitude toward social and economic
problems is not documented, and we are left guessing about his
motivation. Nonetheless, contemporary accounts leave little doubt that
the rebels responded quickly to Kett's leadership. Infuriated by John
Flowerdew's offer of money to the rebels, Kett cast down his own
enclosures and led the men on to Hethersett. After accomplishing its
mission of destruction, the rebel force marched toward Norwich. Kett's
reasons for advancing to Norwich are unknown, but his decision
transformed a local disturbance into a major revolt of which the
ultimate consequences can scarcely have been foreseen.

The road to Norwich, now the A 11, led to Cringleford, across the
River Yare, to Eaton. Here the rebels turned northward to Bowthorpe,
where they cast down more hedges and then camped the evening of
Tuesday, July 9. The next day Sir Edmund Wyndham, the former sheriff
of Norfolk and Suffolk, proclaimed Kett's men rebels and commanded
them to return home in the name of the king. The rebels rejected the
proclamation and attempted to capture Wyndham, who barely managed
to escape to the safety of Norwich. At Bowthorpe Kett was within a mile
of the city. His army, swelled with eager recruits from Norwich and the
surrounding countryside and equipped with armor and artillery, was
ready to challenge the largest provincial city in England.[33]

Upon hearing of Kett's approach, a crowd of the poor and
unemployed in Norwich began to assemble. Some apparently had
participated in the festivities at Wymondham a few days earlier; others
merely joined in the heat of the moment. These men proceeded to the
common pastures of the city, called the town close, located near Kett's
camp at Eaton. The town close was an enclosed area where citizens of
Norwich pastured dairy cattle. A common herdsman was paid at the
weekly rate of a half-penny per animal by each citizen keeping cattle in
the close. The angry crowd, denounced as the scum of the city by
prosperous citizens, complained that the close was common property
and began to destroy the ditches and hedges enclosing it. After finishing
the work at hand, the Norwich men joined with Kett's forces located
nearby.

News of the disturbance quickly reached the mayor of Norwich,
Thomas Codd, who with a group of aldermen went to Kett's camp to
persuade the men to return home quietly. Codd first offered money and
then "fair promises," but his efforts were in vain. The whole body of
rebels, now firmly united under Kett's leadership, agreed to establish a
new camp on a hill called Mount Surrey, northeast of Norwich. The hill,

a place of pilgrimage for the sick, was also the site of a mansion built by Henry Howard, Earl of Surrey, the poet and courtier executed by Henry VIII in 1546. To the east of Mount Surrey lay Mousehold Heath, a vast common and mustering ground, stretching six miles in breadth. As the best route to Mount Surrey passed directly through Norwich, Kett requested the mayor's permission to conduct his forces through the city. The mayor refused to grant this favor, and, consequently, the rebels advanced by another route.

Marching to the north, the rebel force crossed the River Wensum at Hellesdon Bridge, about two miles from Norwich, and spent the night at Drayton. On the same day, Thursday, July 11, they had a curious encounter with Sir Roger Woodhouse. Holinshed is the only sixteenth-century writer giving a detailed account of the meeting: "Sir Roger Woodhouse with seven or eight of his household servants came to them bringing with him two carts laden with beer and one cart laden with other victuals. For a recompense whereof he was stripped out of his apparel, had his horses taken from him, and whatsoever else he had, the rebels accounting the same a good prey; he himself was cruelly tugged and cast into a ditch. . . ."[34] Having abused and imprisoned Woodhouse, they "spoiled" the goods and defaced a dovehouse of John Corbett of Sprowston en route to Mousehold Heath. If Kett's followers were less violent than the peasants of 1381, they were nonetheless angry men ready to rob and terrorize their opponents.

Kett occupied Mount Surrey, using it as a prison for Sir Roger Woodhouse and other captives, and established the great camp on Mousehold Heath. Among the first acts was the selection of Robert Watson, Canon of Norwich, to read morning and evening services from the newly authorized Book of Common Prayer.[35] Watson can hardly have been an enthusiastic supporter of Kett's cause, but he would have been derelict in his duty had he refused to read the English liturgy to the assembled rebels. Thomas Codd, mayor of Norwich, and Thomas Aldrich, a wealthy alderman and former mayor, joined Watson at the camp. None of the three openly supported the rebellion, but they collaborated with Kett and sought to moderate his actions. Their objective was to maintain as much order among the rebels as possible until Somerset's government could persuade them to disperse.

From the outset Kett's men regarded themselves as loyal subjects of Edward VI. Warrants such as the following were authorized to secure provisions:

> We, the king's friends and deputies, do grant license to all men to provide and bring into the camp at Mousehold all manner of cattle, and provision of victuals in what place soever they may find the same so that no violence or injury be done to any honest or poor man. Commanding all persons as they tender the king's honor and royal majesty and the relief of the commonwealth to be obedient to us governors and to those whose names insue.[36]

93

The warrants were signed by Robert Kett and the governors chosen from each of the hundreds that supported the rebellion. Other warrants authorized imprisonment of the gentry, destruction of enclosures, and acquisition of weapons.

Armed with spurious royal warrants, the rebels scoured the countryside for provisions. In some cases the outward forms of legality went by the board. "They ran into all places," Alexander Neville recounted, "and entered the houses of worshipful persons and gentlemen robbing them; and whatsoever cattle they found in the field, money in the houses, or corn in the barns, that ungodly and wickedly they took away (yes, the owners looking upon them) and carried it unto the camp."[37] Wine, taken from Katherine, Duchess of Suffolk, filled the stomachs of men unaccustomed to such luxury.[38] In addition to firearms obtained from confederates at Norwich, the rebels secured other ordnance from Paston Hall, Cromer, Yarmouth, and King's Lynn.

Enormous quantities of food were required to feed the vast numbers that flocked to Mousehold Heath. More than 20,000 sheep, 3,000 cattle, as well as swans, geese, hens, and ducks were obtained with Kett's warrants. The rebels paid nothing for these and then sold mutton at a penny a quarter to their comrades who roasted it on great open fires. The gentry were particularly infuriated as deer were taken from parks and similarly distributed.[39] Supporters of Kett in the township of North Elmham, on the other hand, sent twelve men as well as bread, beer, fish, onions, and garlic to Mousehold Heath.[40] Although we know nothing of Kett's commissariat, it was obviously vital to the success of the rebellion. Otherwise, without adequate food, rebels who had left their homes and families behind could have been held together for only a short time.

As the number of rebels on Mousehold Heath grew to 20,000, Kett had not only to provide food and arms but also rudimentary discipline for his supporters. The most famous scene from the rebellion is the commanding figure of Robert Kett dispensing justice beneath the great oak, called the Tree of Reformation. With him were governors representing twenty-four of Norfolk's thirty-two hundreds plus one Suffolk man. Idealistic admirers of Kett and writers with strong sympathies for the oppressed praised Kett as a wise lawgiver and humane righter of social wrongs. Contemporary narratives, written from the point of view of the Tudor establishment, were less charitable. Alexander Neville, the most hostile writer, flatly accused the rebels of robbing one another after spoiling the countryside. The earliest narrative account of the rebellion, written by Nicholas Sotherton, who, like Neville, had no love for Kett, conceded nonetheless that he and his fellow governors admonished the rebels "to beware of their robbing, spoiling, and other . . . evil demeanors."[41] Considering the size of the rebel camp as well as the traditional disorderliness of outraged, uneducated peasants, what is remarkable is not the lack of discipline, but rather Kett's remarkable genius for maintaining a high degree of order at the Tree of Reformation. Without his leadership, the rebel force might not have held together for seven weeks, and violent attacks on the gentry might have resulted.

The rebels brought captured gentlemen to the Tree of Reformation and shouted abuse at them. "Some cried, 'Hang him,' and some, 'Kill him,' and some that heard no word cried even as the rest even when themselves being demanded why they cried answered for that their fellows afore did the like." In other cases rebels pressed their weapons against the captives, attempting to kill or injure them. Master Wharton was pricked with "spears and other weapons on purpose to kill him." Several gentlemen were fettered with chains and locks to prevent escape.[42]

At the Tree of Reformation Kett, Codd, Aldrich, and other governors stood under an enclosure covered over with rough boards. Complaints were heard, and sentences meted out. The leaders, keenly sensitive to the collective outrage of the assembled hordes, "contended vehemently by all means possible . . . to restrain the needy and hungry common people from this importune liberty of rifling and robbing." To this end long speeches were made to calm the turbulent spirits among the rebels. Although prisoners suffered great personal indignity, loss of personal property, imprisonment, and occasionally personal injury, none received a sentence of flogging, mutilation, or death.[43] In the hierarchical society of Tudor England, it was outrageous for a gentleman to render account to social inferiors; merely to submit to Kett's authority at the Tree of Reformation was a humiliating affront. Yet every contemporary writer conceded that Kett exercised restraint in handling prisoners. The presence of Mayor Codd and Thomas Aldrich may have contributed to the rebels' moderation, but Kett, not Codd or Aldrich, commanded the men on Mousehold Heath.

Matthew Parker, later Archbishop of Canterbury under Queen Elizabeth, added his voice to the forces of moderation. A native of Norwich and vice-chancellor of Cambridge University, Parker made his way to Norwich "to do the office and duty of a good pastor, seeing all places environed with the flames of fury and mischief." Parker, accompanied by friends, visited the rebel camp. Finding the people "drowned in drink," he declined to speak but decided to return the following day when he hoped he would receive a better hearing. Early the next day he came back with his brother Thomas and found the rebels assembled under the Tree of Reformation hearing the English Litany read by Thomas Coniers, vicar of St. Martin's, Norwich. At the conclusion of the service Parker came forward to preach. The sermon was summarized by his secretary, Alexander Neville, writing during the reign of Elizabeth I:

> In the first he wisely admonisheth them that those things which for their sustentation they had brought into the camp being consumed and spent, they

would not spoil wickedly the fruits of the earth and the gifts of God. Next, that they should not defile their hands with blood following private and secret displeasures rashly carried with a desire of revenge, neither to punish them with imprisonment and bands whom they held as enemies, or take away any man's life wickedly or cruelly. Lastly, in regard of common profit to surcease from these enterprises and not distrust the king's herald or messenger, but to give unto the king due honor even in his young and tender age; whereby they might use him hereafter, when he came to more ripe and flourishing estate, (the valor and prowess of his ancestors being confirmed in him, and as it were deep rooted) with incredible delight and pleasure.[44]

Although Parker's sermon, on the basis of Neville's summary many years later, appears cautiously restrained, it did not produce the desired effect. Immediately at the conclusion one of the rebels denounced Parker as the hireling of the gentry. The crowd began to murmur and rage, threatening him with the points of their spears. Parker, like anyone of common sense, feared for his life. Incredible as it may seem, Parker was saved by the singing of the *Te Deum* in English. The vicar of St. Martin's, who had previously read the Litany, gathered together a few musicians, conveniently close at hand, to sing with "solemn music and distinct notes." Miraculously, the "sweetness" of the singing calmed the tumult. In the midst of the *Te Deum*, Parker and his brother fled toward Norwich. Before he reached the gates of the city, a crowd again engulfed him. This time, rather than risk further danger, Parker left his brother behind "to reason with them" and prudently made his way into Norwich.

The next day Parker preached against rebellion at St. Clement's, Norwich. As he left the church, rebels attempted to confiscate his horses. Ordered to hand over the horses immediately after dinner, Parker cleverly outsmarted his adversaries. He had the shoes removed from several horses and their hoofs pared to the quick. The others were annointed with a green medicine "as though they had been tired with overmuch travel." The rebels saw these led out to pasture and assumed they were of no use. Parker then left Norwich on foot, walking two miles to Cringleford, where he had arranged to rendezvous with another steed. Having deceived the rebels, he quickly made his way back to more hospitable surroundings at Cambridge.[45]

The attempted theft of Matthew Parker's horses at Norwich was one of several incidents revealing that Kett had substantial support within the city. Indeed, contemporary accounts of the Norfolk Rebellion emphasized the importance of Kett's urban allies. Edward VI wrote in his journal that the rebels had "the town confederate with them," while Nicholas Sotherton said that Norwich fell because of the "falsehood" of many of the citizens.[46] Sir John Cheke, in his tract *The Hurt of Sedition*, compared the Norwich citizenry unfavorably with the defenders of Exeter who withstood the rebel siege in the West: "Whose example if

Norwich had followed and had not rather given place to traitor Kett, than to keep their duty, and had not sought more safeguard than honesty, and private hope more than common quietness, they had ended their rebellion sooner and escaped themselves better."[47] Alexander Neville, writing in a like vein, complained that "many of the citizens had bound themselves to the fellowship" of Kett's villainy.[48] Antiquarians with a strong sense of loyalty to Norwich and apologists for the failures of East Anglian leaders were quick to blame what they termed the scum of the city[49] and to stress the agrarian character of the rebellion, but they could not deny the embarrassing truth that Norwich was the largest provincial city to fall into rebel hands during the sixteenth century.

Although usually portrayed as an agrarian revolt, the Commotion in Norfolk united various threads of popular discontent, including urban unrest. When the commonwealth writers spoke of social justice, they did not limit their concern to the countryside. Their complaints against the rich and denunciation of greed were directed as much against urban oligarchs as enclosing gentry. Nowhere in Tudor England was the inequality of wealth more visible than in the cities and towns. Rather than havens of opportunity and upward social mobility, the towns were rigidly controlled by the wealthy citizens. Merchants and craftsmen exercised as much control over their apprentices and employees as landlords had over their tenants. Urban courts protected the privileges of the rich in the same way that justices of the peace ruled the countryside in the interests of the gentry. Moreover, urban employment was subject to the vagaries of international relations, foreign competition, and general market conditions to a greater degree than agriculture. The problems of poverty and social inequality had urban dimensions that attracted the hostile criticism of reformers and aroused embittered discontent among the oppressed.

Norwich, after London "the largest and wealthiest town in England," had a population of about 13,000 in the early sixteenth century. In spite of its size and wealth, most of Norwich's inhabitants lived in poverty. It has been estimated that about 60 percent of the population was either poor or very poor. At the other end of the social scale, about 6 percent of the population owned 60 percent of the land and goods. This wealthy elite controlled the commerce, industry, and government of the city. Although there is little detailed information about the social and economic structure of Norwich between 1525 and 1575, it appears that important changes occurred during this half-century. Whereas the earlier prosperity of the city "depended on the activities of its textile workers, by the second decade of Elizabeth's reign it relied increasingly on the activities of its grocers and the demands of the surrounding gentry and countryfolk for its wealth." The mid-Tudor years were a period of depression which witnessed both the decline of the older textile industry and chronic unemployment. With declining industry and a static population, Norwich was obviously susceptible to disorder and radical agitation.[50]

While the preconditions for rebellion are readily apparent in Norwich, the immediate circumstances causing large numbers of citizens to join with Kett are highly obscure. In 1549 unemployment forced some tradesmen to leave the city and seek work elsewhere. The Common Council complained in May that "masons, carpenters, reeders, and tilers had left to find work in the country, the void created being filled by 'foreigners' and beggars."[51] It is possible that some of these journeyed to Wymondham where they met up with Kett and returned to the city as eager recruits in the rebel army. On the other hand, Kett apparently made no appeal to the citizens to enlist support of his cause. Those who joined Kett presumably did so not because he articulated a program of urban reform, but because they saw him as the effective leader of a growing rebellion committed to righting the wrongs of all oppressed men. As Kett's army approached Norwich, men from the city joined ranks, bringing with them supplies and weapons. The newly recruited supporters, drawn from the poorest classes, destroyed the ditches and hedges surrounding the town close where cattle of prosperous citizens were pastured.

Kett exercised great influence over Norwich before the rebel army actually occupied the city. By claiming to be an assembly loyal to the king, Kett and his supporters succeeded in obtaining the reluctant cooperation of the mayor, who was intimidated by the size of the rebel host and hesitant to resist Kett without the express authority of the crown. Although Mayor Codd refused Kett's demand to pass through Norwich, the mayor's policy was essentially vacillation and accommodation. His appearances with Kett at the Tree of Reformation gave rebel justice an appearance of legitimacy. Norwich was never fully closed to the rebels, and thus men and supplies moved freely from the city to Mousehold Heath.

Kett compelled Mayor Codd to provide money from the city treasury. Prisoners were kept at Norwich Prison, Norwich Castle, and Surrey Place. The rebels obtained munitions "by force out of the city and commanded every citizen to be to them assistant, setting their face to be the king's friends and to defend the king's laws." The citizens who resisted Kett "fell to prayer and holy life" despairing that they would never again see their city prosper, for the rebels threatened "to fire the city and to consume the substance and fainly if in every point they assented not to them." With Kett's authority city constables and other officers kept the gates so that "the citizens should not so fast range forth the city as also that no gentleman should escape."[52] Norwich remained under Kett's de facto control until the king's herald arrived on July 21.

The herald entered Norwich and then went to the camp at Mousehold Heath where he offered the king's pardon to all who would submit and depart quietly to their homes. Some of the rebels fell to their knees and accepted the royal pardon, but Kett refused, saying that he had offended no laws and required no pardon. Hearing his answer, the herald denounced Kett as a traitor in the king's name and ordered John Petibone, the mayor's sword-bearer, to arrest him. The rebels began to stir "on every side this way and that way striving with no less stout than dangerous contention."[53] Faced with growing resistance, the herald, Mayor Codd, Thomas Aldrich, and all who received the pardon returned to Norwich. The mayor immediately ordered the gates of Norwich closed and released all prisoners confined within his jurisdiction.

With the failure of the herald's offer of pardon, attitudes hardened, and the defense of Norwich began. Mayor Codd, acting with renewed confidence because of the herald's presence, convened Common Council to discuss the appropriate course of action. The council agreed that by defending the city the rebels might be forced to disperse because of weariness and want of supplies. No sooner had the council reached its decision than messengers arrived from the gates with news that many citizens of Norwich had joined Kett and were permitting rebels to enter the city. The mayor, faced with what can hardly have been a wholly unanticipated turn of events and perhaps fearing that the city could not be defended successfully, ordered the previously released prisoners back to prison. Alexander Neville explained this decision as follows:

> Request was made therefore (and it was easily obtained of the magistrates of the city) that the gentlemen should be shut up in the Castle as before, lest peradventure while they might be seen at liberty in the city and free from bonds, wherewith of late they had been holden, the minds of the rebels full of fury and rage should by that occasion be stirred up to murder and bloodshed.[54]

By returning the prisoners to jail, city leaders adopted a policy that cannot have inspired confidence among uncommitted citizens and may have contributed to Kett's victory.

In spite of the pessimism of city leaders, a serious effort was made to defend Norwich from the rebels. Norwich was easier to attack than Exeter because its walls were not completely intact and a great many men were required to defend those parts of the city not secured by masonry fortifications. To repel the rebel attack "ten of the greatet pieces of ordnance" were placed in the ditch at the Castle. Citizens fully harnessed for war guarded the walls. Others took up positions in the marketplace and in cross streets to be ready for any eventuality. Aldermen rode through the streets supervising the defenders. When it was seen that the artillery positioned near the Castle "did not much annoy the enemy," the guns were moved into the meadows along the river. Intense bombardment from both sides continued throughout the night.

The next day, Monday, July 22, Kett's men saw that their shots were passing over the city and relocated their guns below Mousehold Heath. Apparently because of a shortage of food and supplies, Kett agreed to a temporary truce. James Williams, a tailor, and Ralph Sutton, a hatter, entered Norwich under the flag of truce to negotiate with the mayor. The rebels proposed a truce of a few days in return for the privilege of securing supplies in the city as they had done before the appearance of the king's herald. If the demand was not immediately granted, Kett vowed to destroy Norwich "by fire and sword."[55] The mayor not only refused any succor to the rebels but also vowed utter defiance to traitors. Kett's men, hearing the mayor's reply, charged down the hill from Mousehold Heath and attempted to break into the city. The defenders of Norwich repulsed the first assault with pikes and arrows. Following the attack vagabond boys " 'brychles and bearars syde' came among the thicket of the arrows and gathered them up when some of the said arrows stuck fast in their legs and other parts and did therewith most shamefully turn up their bare tails against those which did shoot, which so dismayed the archers that it took their heart from them."[56]

The brazen determination of the unarmed, breechless boys turned the tide of battle. Although it is likely that sheer weight of numbers created more fear than the boys' nakedness, contemporary writers attached great importance to this bizarre episode. Neville identified the youthful attackers as beardless boys of the country, "the dregs of the people, men most filthy." Their obscene language offended all decent men, and Neville stressed the "odious and inhumane villainy" of one boy, who pulling down his hose, turned his bare buttocks to the defenders of the city "with an horrible noise and outcry, filling the air (all men beholding him) did that, which a chaste tongue shameth to speak, much more a sober man to write." But decency was avenged, for the boy was shot through the buttocks, giving him "as was meet, the punishment he deserved." Yet even the wounded continued the struggle and pulled arrows from "green wounds" with their own hands giving them, dripping with blood, to their comrades. If we are to believe the worthy Neville, Kett's attack on Norwich may be the only battle in history decided by such a timely, well-aimed outburst.[57]

Many of the citizens withdrew from positions along the city walls to resist another diversionary attack. Kett, seeing the opportunity for a massive assault against poorly defended positions, ordered his men forward to the river. About noon the intrepid boys, "a great company of country clowns" and "desperate vagabonds," some unarmed, others with clubs and spears, swam the river at Bishop's Gate bridge and broke into Norwich. The gunners fled in fear, abandoning six pieces of ordnance to the rebels. As a final, futile gesture, the king's herald, who had remained in Norwich, offered pardon to rebels who would lay down their arms and disperse. The victorious insurgents defiantly refused clemency and drove the herald away. Kett was now master of Norwich.

Following the occupation of the city, the rebels quickly apprehended and imprisoned Mayor Codd and several prominent citizens at Surrey Place. The prisoners included Thomas Aldrich and Robert Watson, both of whom had collaborated with Kett earlier; William Rogers, alderman; John Himerstone, alderman; and William Brampton, Gent. Except for the mayor and Aldrich, the captives remained in chains and fetters until the victory of the army of the Earl of Warwick. It was said that some of the prisoners died, but in the absence of a single name, the charges cannot be substantiated. Within a short time, perhaps a few days, the citizens appealed to Kett for the release of Codd and Aldrich. They protested against the indignity of imprisoning the mayor and feared that his life was in danger, especially after the rebels abused and berated him. One of Kett's men jested that those who would come to the rebel camp the next day could buy a cod's head for a penny.[58] The humor of this crude pun was altogether lost on the frightened citizenry, who had every reason to believe that Codd might be killed either by the order of Kett or by a rebel who bore the mayor a personal grudge. Thomas Aldrich, said to be "beloved of city and country" and obviously possessed of extraordinary personal influence with Kett, appealed directly to the rebel leader and secured the release of himself and the mayor.

Mayor Codd remained with the rebels at Mousehold Heath following his release. His freedom may have been conditional upon accepting limitations on his movements, or he may have believed that his presence in the rebel camp would serve to restrain the excesses of his former captors. Whatever the rationale, Codd appointed Augustine Steward, an alderman, as deputy mayor of Norwich. Steward and the two sheriffs, Henry Bacon and John Atkinson, did what they could to maintain order in the city in Codd's absence. Norwich, now fully at the mercy of Kett's forces, supplied the rebels with food and munitions. Loyal citizens lived in fear of their lives and property. Yet the rebels refrained from killing and widespread pillaging. Leonard Sotherton, the citizen who had brought the king's herald from London, was particularly hated and sought-after by the rebels. Nonetheless Sotherton managed to avoid capture by hiding with friends in the city. The surprising success of Sotherton in concealing himself under the most unfavorable circumstances raises serious doubts about the effectiveness of the rebel occupation.

Robert Kett was at the height of his power after the capture of Norwich. The largest provincial city in England had fallen, yet no revolutionary government — no commune of Norwich — was formed. His numerous allies in Norwich acquiesced in the release of the mayor and permitted an appointed deputy to exercise titular authority. At Mousehold Heath Codd and Aldrich openly collaborated with rebels whom the king's herald had formally condemned as traitors. This extraordinary situation may have been due to the leaders' ability to make the best of a hopeless position through negotiation and compromise. Perhaps Kett regarded Norwich of little military value and preferred to exploit its resources while keeping his headquarters on Mousehold Heath. Although no record of his goals survives, Kett's actions suggest that he never attempted to unite his agrarian supporters with the poor and unemployed of Norwich. Moreover, his willingness to associate with the mayor and aldermen indicates that he persisted in viewing himself as a loyal subject seeking redress of legitimate grievances. None of the sixteenth-century accounts of the Commotion in Norfolk mentions the existence of a command structure that would have been necessary for the implementation of a coherent political and military strategy. Kett's strength rested in numbers and in the unflinching determination to right the wrongs of all who rallied to his standard. In spite of impressive achievements, the tanner of Wymondham never molded his agrarian and urban supporters into an effective revolutionary force. The conquest of Norwich, in one sense symbolic of the high point of Kett's power, must be seen as a lost opportunity revealing Kett's limitations as an organizer and popular leader.

Kett's men attacked the port of Great Yarmouth shortly after the occupation of Norwich. In what must have been a commando-type surprise attack, a party of rebels seized the two town bailiffs and carried them off to Mousehold Heath. The bailiffs, however, soon escaped and returned to Great Yarmouth to warn the citizens to fortify the town against another attack. Kett continued to apply pressure to the town and hoped to exploit its wealth and resources for the benefit of the rebel camp. On August 5 he and Thomas Aldrich issued a commission in the king's name commanding Great Yarmouth to supply the rebels. The commission demanded the victualling of a force of 100 men sent to Great Yarmouth "for the maintenance of the king's town there against our enemies" and authorized the force to seize horses. Another commission, issued August 10 by Kett and Aldrich, ordered a compatriot, John of Great Yarmouth, to obtain a supply of beer for the rebel camp and threatened imprisonment of anyone who interfered with his efforts.[59]

The burgesses of Great Yarmouth not only refused to honor Kett's commissions but began to fortify the town. Fearing that they might suffer the same fate as Norwich, the citizens made elaborate preparations to protect all land and water approaches. A heavily armed force was dispatched into the surrounding countryside. The town and haven were to be guarded by a fleet of ships, while a pinnace with twenty-six men and four days supplies sailed up the River Bure toward Wey Bridge. The defense order also called for careful security measures within the town.

Constables were ordered to determine how many men had joined Kett on Mousehold Heath and how many wives had left to join their husbands. Kett obviously had supporters and sympathizers at Great Yarmouth, and authorities were properly concerned that the town should not be taken through internal subversion.

The second and more extensive attack on Great Yarmouth occurred about August 20. A large body of rebels occupied Gorleston, located to the west across the haven from Great Yarmouth. With six pieces of ordnance obtained at Lowestoft they began to bombard the town. Quickly sensing the danger posed by the guns, a party of defenders "set fire to a large stack of hay on the west side the haven, which being duly executed, raised a prodigious smoke, and the wind, being northerly, drove the said smoke directly upon the face of the enemy, which so blinded them, that they did not perceive the Yarmouth men coming upon them."[60] As a result of the successful counterattack, the rebels suffered heavy casualties and had thirty of their number taken prisoner. Moreover, the guns were also lost and taken to Great Yarmouth. But Kett's men, still determined to overwhelm the town, mounted another attack from the north "on the side of Norfolk to the very denes of Yarmouth."[61] The defenders fired on the rebels with demicannon as they approached the walls and succeeded in holding the town.

Although the rebels were thwarted at the gates of Great Yarmouth, they took their revenge by destroying the haven that was under construction about a quarter mile to the south. For centuries Great Yarmouth struggled against the forces of nature to keep a channel open to the sea so that ships would have safe and easy access to the town. Living entirely upon seaborne trade, Great Yarmouth depended on the haven for its prosperity. Early in 1549, after the town raised over £1800 and received a generous tax concession from the government of Protector Somerset, work began on what was called the sixth haven. For over six months 100 men worked every day to open a channel across the sand-covered denes to the sea, but their labor was in vain. The eighteenth-century historian Henry Swinden sadly recounted how the rebels

> wasted and spoiled the materials provided for the haven and in the night villainously ruined all their former work, which obliged the workmen to throw down their tools, fly to their arms, and with the magistrates of the town keep watch and ward not only to defend the town against the said rioters without but also against some of their adherents (who were more dangerous) within.

The destruction was so complete that it was impossible to resume work in 1549. Great Yarmouth successfully withstood the rebels' attack and denied Kett badly needed supplies but, as a result of the destruction of the haven, may have suffered more permanent harm at the hands of the insurgents than Norwich.[62]

The men who comprised Kett's army on Mousehold Heath, captured Norwich, and attacked Great Yarmouth, came from towns and villages scattered throughout the larger part of Norfolk. The names of representatives of twenty-four of the county's hundreds appear on the rebels' demands for redress of grievances.[63] The demands also give the name of one Suffolk man. The principal unrepresented region was the Breckland, a thinly settled, dry, and sandy area in southwestern Norfolk.[64] We must assume that laborers, husbandmen, and yeomen made up the majority of the army's rank and file. At Norwich young apprentices, the unemployed, and beggars rallied to Kett's standard, but peasants and the urban poor were not the only persons to assist the rebel cause. The Norwich clergy who read services from the Book of Common Prayer and preached must have joined Kett as ministers of the Gospel attending to the spiritual needs of the assembled hordes, not as favorers of rebellion. In addition to the clergy, artisans and tradesmen, including butchers, a tailor, a hatter, a shoemaker, a tanner, and a miller, flocked to Kett's army. Two tradesmen, James Williams, tailor, and Ralph Sutton, hatter, served as messengers for Kett. Robert Yysod, tanner, John Barker, butcher, and Echard, a miller of Heigham, led a band of eighty to the Guildhall and seized gunpowder, pellets, and morris pikes for the rebel army.[65]

Following Kett's defeat persons who suffered losses of property and money hurled accusations at others believed to be either participants or sympathizers. Although some charges were either baseless or exaggerated, it appears that Kett drew support from men of wealth and position. For example, Thomas Godsalve, Gent. of Thorpe, was accused in the Court of Star Chamber of being "a maintainer and a great setter forward" of the rebels. Godsalve naturally denied all charges against him, arguing that he was taken forcibly from his house, required to prepare bills for Kett, and imprisoned.[66] Sir Nicholas L'Estrange of Hunstanton, one of the leading Norfolk gentry, vehemently denied that he was "the beginner of the commotions in Norfolk," because he was in Hampshire when the rebellion began.[67] It is virtually impossible to determine the validity of such charges, but the bitter recrimination following Warwick's victory suggests that a number of collaborators from the upper classes lent their support to Kett.

Throughout the course of the Commotion in Norfolk it is easier to trace Kett's actions than to understand his objectives. That he perceived himself a loyal subject of Edward VI seeking redress of grievances against the gentry is abundantly clear. But a detailed statement of Kett's grievances appears only in a single, undated manuscript entitled "Kett's Demands Being in Rebellion" signed by him, Thomas Aldrich, Thomas Codd, and forty-five rebel deputies.[68] References to another document, probably compiled earlier and containing fewer grievances, indicate that it differed from "Kett's Demands" primarily in that it demanded a

KETT'S DEMANDS BEING IN REBELLION

1. We pray your grace that where it is enacted for enclosing that it be not hurtful to such as have enclosed saffron grounds for they be greatly chargeable to them, and that from henceforth no man shall enclose any more.

2. We certify your grace that whereas the lords of the manors have been charged with certain free rent, the same lords have sought means to charge the freeholders to pay the same rent, contrary to right.

3. We pray your grace that no lord of no manor shall common upon the common.

4. We pray that priests from henceforth shall purchase no lands neither free nor bond, and the lands that they have in possession may be letten to temporal men, as they were in the first year of the reign of King Henry VII.

5. We pray that reedground and meadowground may be at such price as they were in the first year of King Henry VII.

6. We pray that all the marshes that are held of the king's majesty by free rent or of any other, may be again at the price that they were in the first year of King Henry VII.

7. We pray that all bushels within your realm be of one stice, that is to say, to be in measure viii gallons.

8. We pray that priests or vicars that be not able to preach and set forth the word of God to his parishioners may be thereby put from his benefice, and the parishioners there to choose another or else the patron or lord of the town.

9. We pray that the payments of castleward rent, and blanch farm, and office lands, which hath been accustomed to be gathered of the tenements, whereas we suppose the lords ought to pay the same to their bailiffs for their rents gathering, and not the tenants.

10. We pray that no man under the degree of a knight or esquire keep a dove house, except it hath been of an old ancient custom.

11. We pray that all freeholders and copyholders may take the profits of all commons, and there to common, and the lords not to common nor take profits of the same.

12. We pray that no feodary within your shores shall be a counsellor to any man in his office making, whereby the king may be truly served, so that a man being of good conscience may be yearly chosen to the same office by the commons of the same shire.

13. We pray your grace to take all liberty of leet into your own hands whereby all men may quietly enjoy their commons with all profits.

14. We pray that copyhold land that is unreasonably rented may go as it did in the first year of King Henry VII and that at the death of a tenant or of a sale the same lands to be charged with an easy fine as a capon or a reasonable sum of money for a remembrance.

15. We pray that no priest [shall be a chaplain] nor no other officer to any man of honour or worship but only to be resident upon their benefices whereby their parishioners may be instructed with the laws of God.

16. We pray that all bond men may be made free for God made all free with his precious blood shedding.

17. We pray that rivers may be free and common to all men for fishing and passage.

18. We pray that no man shall be put by your escheator and feodary to find any office unless he holdeth of your grace in chief or capite above £10 a year.

19. We pray that the poor mariners and fishermen may have the whole profits of their fishings as porpoises, grampuses, whales, or any great fish so it be not prejudicial to your grace.

20. We pray that every proprietory parson or vicar having a benefice of £10 or more by year shall either by themselves or by some other person teach poor men's children of their parish the book called the catechism and the primer.

21. We pray that it be not lawful to the lords of any manor to purchase lands freely and to let them out again by copy of court roll to their great advantage and to the undoing of your poor subjects.

22. We pray that no proprietory parson or vicar in considera-tion of avoiding trouble and suit between them and their poor parishioners which they daily do proceed and attempt shall from henceforth take for the full contentation of all the tenths which now they do receive but viii d. of the noble in the full discharge of all other tithes.

23. [We pray that no man] under the degree of [esquire] shall keep any conies upon any of their own freehold or copyhold unless he pale them in so that it shall not be to the commons' nuisance.

24. We pray that no person of what estate, degree, or condition he be shall from henceforth sell the wardship of any child but that the same child if he live to his full age shall be at his own choosing concerning his marriage the king's wards only except.

25. We pray that no manner of person having a manor of his own shall be no other lord's bailiff but only his own.

26. We pray that no lord, knight, nor gentleman shall have or take in farm any spiritual promotion.

27. We pray your grace to give license and authority by your gracious commission under your great seal to such commissioners as your poor commons hath chosen, or to as many of them as your majesty and your council shall appoint and think meet, for to redress and reform all such good laws, statutes, proclamations, and all other your proceedings, which hath been bidden by your justices of your peace, sheriffs, escheators, and others your officers, from your poor commons, since the first year of the reign of your noble grandfather King Henry the seventh.

28. We pray that those your officers that hath offended your grace and your commons and so proved by the complaint of your poor commons do give unto these poor men so assembled iv d. every day so long as they have remained there.

29. We pray that no lord, knight, esquire, nor gentleman do graze nor feed any bullocks or sheep if he may spend £40 a year by his lands but only for the provision of his house.

reduction in the price of wool.[69] The references to a second document suggest that the rebels' grievances went through several stages of revision and elaboration, but without the document itself it is impossible to study the development of the rebels' political and social philosophy. "Kett's Demands" are themselves silent on a number of important questions. For example, we do not know at what stage in the rebellion the document was prepared, whether it was a preliminary draft, or a final, definitive text, or who was the principal author. Neither do we know whether the twenty-nine demands were ever presented to the government as the basis of a negotiated settlement. Yet, notwithstanding these important limitations on our knowledge, "Kett's Demands Being in Rebellion" stands alone as the only full statement of the men assembled on Mousehold Heath.

Although historians have studied Kett's demands and the rebels' behavior with great care, their conclusions are poles apart. S. T. Bindoff recognized the radical character of the rebel program while G. R. Elton saw the rebellion as "a definite attempt to enlist support from the center against the ruling class of a county which was particularly ill-administered by its traditional magistrates."[70] More recent accounts have stressed Kett's moderation and conservatism.[71] Roger B. Manning, influenced by E. J. Hobsbawn's study of archaic social movements in the nineteenth and twentieth centuries, argued that the rebels called on "the crown and gentry to exercise their paternalistic responsibilities and render traditional justice."[72] Julian Cornwall denied the existence of a "genuine egalitarian movement" and concluded that "Kett's people wanted to preserve, indeed, restore, traditional society."[73] In the fullest account of the Norfolk Rebellion since the nineteenth century work of F. W. Russell, Stephen K. Land stated unequivocally that the rising was "very conservative" and certainly not a revolt of "oppressed peasants."[74]

With one exception the twenty-nine demands refer to individual grievances rather than to theoretical constitutional rights. The document, taken as a whole, looks to the past, not the future. Its language resembles Magna Carta more than the Petition of Right or the Grand Remonstrance. The grievances were those of farmers and pastoralists looking backward to a golden age of prosperity and justice at the end of the fifteenth century before the onset of inflation. Although the demands were not utopian, they show little understanding of the realities of Tudor politics.

The only appeal to fundamental principles is the invocation of the Great Manumission of Calvary in article 16: "We pray that all bond men may be made free for God made all free with his precious blood shedding." Although few serfs remained in England at mid-century, article 16 reveals Kett's concern for the poorest and most oppressed persons in English society. It also hints at the rebels' familiarity with the German Peasants' War of 1525 where the abuses of serfdom constituted a major grievance. Article 16 stands apart from the other twenty-eight demands, but it emphasizes Kett's religious commitment, his idealism, and his vision of a Christian commonwealth of free men.[75]

About a third of Kett's demands refer to abuses of the nobility and gentry either as landlords or as officials of local government. Private wardship, a potentially lucrative source of income to landlords, was criticized in article 24.[76] Article 3 states that "no lord of no manor shall common upon the common," while article 29 demands that "no lord, knight, esquire, nor gentleman do graze nor feed any bullocks or sheep if he may spend £40 a year by his lands but only for the provision of his house." Radical demands such as those found in articles 3 and 29 would, as S. T. Bindoff aptly concluded, "have clipped the wings of rural capitalism."[77] The commons encountered the aristocracy not only as landlords but also as government officials. They were particularly critical of the two local officers of the Court of Wards, the feodary and escheator. "We pray," said the rebels, "that no feodary within your shores shall be a councillor to any man in his office making." An officer of the Court, who was also in the service of a local landowner, could easily assist his employer in the purchase of lucrative wardships and leases of wards' lands.[78] The voice of prosperous yeomen seeking immunity from wardship may be heard in article 18 where the rebels ask that "no man shall be put by your escheator and feodary to find any office unless he holdeth of your grace in chief or capite above £10 a year." It may not have been a coincidence that Kett's neighbor and adversary, John Flowerdew, was escheator for Norfolk the previous year. Perhaps the most extraordinary rebuke to local government was the demand that each officer who had offended the commons should pay 4d. for every day that the rebels were assembled.

The rebels' demands included no fewer than five complaints against the clergy, grievances embodying elements of medieval anticlericalism and anticipating the program of Elizabethan Puritans. Complaints about tithe payments, clerical landholding and rents, and the subordination of clergy to lay landowners were heard in the late medieval church. The rebels, on the other hand, proclaimed their Protestant commitment in articles 8 and 20. In the first Kett's men prayed "that priests or vicars that be not able to preach and set forth the word of God to his parishioners may be thereby put from his benefice, and the parishioners there to choose another or else the patron or lord of the town." The vigorous preaching of the Gospel was a central tenet of the Reformation, and the men of Mousehold Heath called preachers to their camp and recommended the same to the king. The suggestion that the parish laity should select suitable preachers reveals an early example of the spirit of congregationalism. The latter article, calling for religious instruction for children of the poor, draws attention to the failures of the beneficed clergy and reiterates the Protestant desire for the education of all Christians.

Inasmuch as the Commotion in Norfolk began as an enclosure riot, it is essential to determine what part opposition to enclosure played in the rebels' protests. Clearly, no comprehensive indictment of enclosure may be found among the twenty-nine articles. Article 1 seems to imply that enclosure of arable land had already been regulated by statute to the satisfaction of the ordinary Norfolk farmer. Indeed, recent agricultural historians are agreed that East Anglia was mainly an enclosed area with little open field farming.[79] The point of the rebels in the first article was not that further enclosure of arable land should be prohibited, but that "where it is enacted for enclosing that it be not hurtful to such as have enclosed saffron grounds. . . ." There can be little doubt that saffron growers, called "crokers" in the sixteenth century, were numbered among Kett's supporters.

Saffron was a highly valued money crop useful as a spice, a medicine, a dye, and as feed for cattle. William Harrison, the Elizabethan antiquarian, praised the medicinal value of saffron which, he said, was "very profitably mingled with those medicines which we take for the diseases of the breast, of the lungs, of the liver, and of the bladder." Its alleged curative properties were truly extraordinary. If mixed with the milk of a woman and applied to the eyes, it cured cataracts. Mixed with malmsey wine, saffron "will marvelously provoke urine, dissolve and expel gravel, and yield no small ease to them that make their water by dropmeals [drops]." The best saffron in England was grown at Saffron Walden and in Cambridgeshire, but "once in seven years" a crop was produced in Norfolk and Suffolk.[80] The choice of the cause of the crokers as the first of twenty-nine demands indicates that the rebels' complaints were directed not against lawful enclosure of arable land but against enclosure of pasture and loss of common rights.

Articles 3, 11, and 29 contain Kett's remedy for the commons' loss of pasture. In slightly different words articles 3 and 11 call for complete denial of common pasture rights to the lords and the establishment of an exclusive right reserved for freeholders and copyholders. Over the years the gentry placed more and more cattle and sheep on common land and encroached on the ill-defined customary rights of smaller farmers. But the rebel demands went beyond claiming a monopoly over the commons, for as we have seen, article 29 called for a prohibition of sheep-and cattle-keeping by wealthy landlords except for the small numbers required for household needs.

Although the rebel demands did not single out sheep raisers, the circumstances of the revolt hint at a conflict between sheep and cattle producers. For the poorer farmer a cow was "the most usual possession" supplying milk, cheese, and butter.[81] When we recall that the Kett brothers were engaged in tanning and butchering and find that many of the Norwich tradesmen supporting the rebels were also butchers, we see the possibility of a conflict over the use of common pasture. The likelihood that some of the prosperous yeomen supporting the revolt were wool-producers may explain why the articles did not include a specific attack on sheep grazing.

The rebel demands included complaints of special interests as well as general criticism of agrarian society. Rising prices hurt most farmers, but only fishermen of Great Yarmouth could have cared about whaling rights. Similarly, it is unlikely that many men on Mousehold Heath rose solely to protest against dove houses or coney keeping. The articles of the rebels constitute a curious patchwork quilt combining agrarian griev-ances with the individual interests of those who rallied to Kett's standard. There are also interesting omissions. For example, none of the articles reflect urban interests, either of artisans or of the poor and unemployed. If the articles were prepared early in the rebellion, the omission of urban complaints would be readily understandable. As so little is known about the circumstances that led to the preparation of the articles, our understanding of them is necessarily clouded with uncertainty.

Kett's twenty-nine demands required sweeping governmental ac-tion if they were to be implemented. In each instance the appropriate reforms call for parliamentary legislation, yet the rebels thought primarily in terms of local remedies. We find among the articles neither a denunciation of wicked councillors who had betrayed the king nor an appeal to Parliament. To assist the king in identifying the needs of his oppressed subjects, popular participation in local government was recommended. In article 8 the rebels proposed that parishioners should choose priests able to preach the word of God. Article 12 calls for the commons of each shire to select men of "good conscience" for the office of feodary. In article 27 Kett asked that the king with the advice of the Council appoint under the Great Seal commissioners nominated by the "poor commons" to reform all laws that had been enacted since 1485.

Implicit in Kett's demands was the establishment of more represen-tative local government. Whereas the countryside had formerly been governed by the gentry, Kett would transfer political power to the people — to yeomen, husbandmen, and artisans. No one would deny that the rebel demands embodied elements of traditionalism expressed in moderate and deferential language, but it is easy to be misled by the rebels' superficial conservatism. Whatever their shortcomings neither the Norfolk gentry nor the city fathers of Norwich thought of Kett as a respectable tanner humbly seeking the restoration of traditional good lordship. Kett and his men may have been ignorant of the institutional basis of Tudor government and indifferent to the realities of local politics in a hierarchical society, but they knew exactly what they wanted. As loyal subjects of the king, the rebels demanded popular government as the means for creating a just society based on historic English liberties and the tenets of the Christian religion.[82]

The rebels, missing their Captain Kett as God pleased, their hearts fainted, they being dispersed, slain, and a great number taken prisoners.

Nicholas Sotherton, "The Commoyson in Norfolk 1549"

5. THE PACIFICATION OF NORFOLK

English governments traditionally opposed negotiation with popular leaders. Various strategies might be used to buy time until armies could be raised, but the primary objective of the government was pacification. Edmund Dudley, writing shortly after the death of Henry VII, stated fundamental Tudor principles that were reaffirmed throughout the sixteenth century. The commons, said Dudley, "may not grudge nor murmur to live in labor and pain. Let not them presume above their own degree nor any of them pretend or counterfeit the state of his better."[1] During the Pilgrimage of Grace Henry VIII tricked the rebels with false promises that were withdrawn when his army gained the upper hand. Protestant reformers like Hugh Latimer denounced social injustice and exhorted the gentry to treat tenants charitably, but both churchmen and statesmen were agreed that change must come from above, not from below. Edward VI's government initially followed the pattern established in earlier disturbances. The rebels were commanded to abandon their leaders and return peacefully to their homes. Royal proclamations announced the government's policy, while from the pulpit preachers expounded Biblical texts that required the Christian subject to obey duly constituted authority. And simultaneously military preparations were begun to accomplish by force what could not be achieved through persuasion and threats. It was the government's willingness to negotiate with Kett that made the pacification of Norfolk an unusual episode in the history of popular rebellions.

Preaching before the king in April 1549, Hugh Latimer complained that he had never seen so little discipline in the country. "Men will be masters," he said; "they will be masters and no disciples. Alas, where is this discipline now in England? The people regard no discipline; they be without all order."[2] Latimer can scarcely have anticipated what followed, for the rebellions discredited the cause of the reformers and called into question the vigorous preaching with which he was identified. He later denounced the covetousness of the rebels and argued

113

that more good preachers would have prevented the rebellions, but during the critical summer months his voice was silent.

Major responsiblity for defending the Protestant religion fell to Thomas Cranmer, Archbishop of Canterbury, who as a privy councillor spoke for the government as well as the Church of England. Preaching at St. Paul's on July 21, Cranmer admonished the people of "the great plague of God" that reigned because of their sins and neglect of His word. He urged the people to give true obedience to the king and to put aside all pride and other sins and vices reigning among them. Later the same day Cranmer's chaplain, John Joseph, preached at Paul's Cross, repeating the substance of Cranmer's sermon "because all heard him not before." Cranmer preached again at St. Paul's on August 10 and gave thanks for Lord Russell's victory over the Western rebels. The pro-Catholic Grey Friars chronicler wrote that the archbishop emphasized the activities of "Popish priests" as the most important cause of the rebellion.[3]

Among Cranmer's surviving sermons only one could have been directed against the Norfolk Rebellion. Although the sermon cannot be dated with certainty, it was probably delivered during August. Cranmer denounced the pretensions of the poor and urged them to be humble in spirit. To those who believed the commons rose to relieve the oppression of the poor by the gentry, he replied that the "gentlemen were never poorer than they be at this present." The sermon contains no evidence that Cranmer had even the smallest amount of information about the situation in Norfolk, yet he was quite certain about the causes of the commotion. With the sublime confidence that comes only with profound ignorance, Cranmer was able to state that "the chief stirrers in these insurrections be ruffians and sturdy idle fellows, which be the causes of their own poverty, commonly resorting to tippling and to alehouses, much drinking and little working, much spending and little getting."[4]

Cranmer spoke directly to the charge that Protestants were responsible for acts of civil disobedience:

> It is reported that there be many among these unlawful assemblies that pretend knowledge of the gospel, and will needs be called gospellers; as though the gospel were the cause of disobedience, sedition, and carnal liberality, and the destruction of those policies, kingdoms, and common-weals, where it is received. But if they will be true gospellers, let them be obedient, meek, patient in adversity and long-suffering, and in no wise rebel against the laws and magistrates.

In Cranmer's judgment the false gospellers and idle ruffians were in league with the Pope, who stood to benefit from internal discord in England along with the country's traditional enemies, the French and the Scots.[5]

Cranmer's notes for a homily against rebellion have also survived. To support his views he drew on texts from the Old and New Testaments and noted the unwholesome results of previous rebellions in England and Germany. The example of the Ottoman Empire was used to show that the subject must obey the magistrate in all worldly things, "as the Christians do under the Turk, and ought so to do, so long as he commandeth them not do against God." He held that civil war was the "greatest scourge" that could befall society and saw its occurrence as evidence of God's indignation. The notes show more understanding of the Commotion in Norfolk, for they refer to the orders issued for levying men and the deliberate usurpation of the king's authority. Yet Cranmer retained his conviction that the Norfolk Rebellion was first incited by Papists who had come from the West of England.[6]

Besides his own preaching and writing, Cranmer encouraged the preparation of appropriate sermons for use in parish churches. When read by the curates, the sermons were intended to teach the commons obedience to the king and to preserve them from the sin of rebellion. The most prominent theologians responding to Cranmer's request were Peter Martyr and Martin Bucer, both of whom had come to England at his invitation. On August 31, immediately following Kett's defeat, Cranmer was to preach at St. Paul's once again, but on this occasion he sent John Joseph, who, like Cranmer, emphasized the well-worn argument that Popish priests were the chief instigators of sedition and rebellion.[7]

No other bishop undertook to preach against Kett. William Rugg, Bishop of Norwich since 1536, left no evidence of religious activity during the months that his diocese was affected by the rebellion; his apparent inertia helps explain why he was compelled to resign before the end of the year. The Bishop of London, Edmund Bonner, worked not to combat sedition, but to evade the intent of the Act of Uniformity by permitting the celebration of the Latin mass in private chapels. John Hooper, soon to be Bishop of Gloucester, wrote to Henry Bullinger that the people were "sorely oppressed by the marvellous tyranny of the nobility" but left no sermon in which he expounded these views to the public.[8] The courageous but fruitless sermon Matthew Parker delivered before the rebels on Mousehold Heath was easily the most heroic response of any clergyman. Parker journeyed to Norwich at great personal risk to exercise responsibilities that properly belonged to the inept Bishop Rugg and the clergy of the diocese of Norwich.

Royal proclamations, like sermons, were a public response to the rebellions and expressed the official attitude of the government. None of the royal proclamations, except those given by the king's heralds at Norwich, referred directly to Kett or the commotion in Norfolk. Offers of pardon were combined with threats of execution by martial law. Proclamations were directed against individual offenders such as rumor-mongers, rioters, and local officers raising unlawful assemblies rather than against the population as a whole. At the time of the Pilgrimage of Grace in 1536, a proclamation not only threatened death to the rebels, but also brutally vowed the destruction of women and children "with fire and sword to the most terrible example of such rebels and offenders." In 1549 language of this type was not repeated. In addition to offers of pardon, the proclamations called for price controls to limit the effects of rapidly rising food prices and for more rigorous enforcement of parliamentary statutes against enclosure. Referring to the work of the commission on enclosures, the proclamation of July 16 said that remedies were "part in execution and part ready to be executed and delayed only by the folly of the people seeking their own redress unlawfully." It added that surely "no subject can any more require of any prince than by his majesty, his said uncle, and Council hath been devised, ordered, and commanded." While such moderation encouraged the commons to expect more relief than the government could actually provide, the public response of the Protector's regime revealed a greater understanding of the plight of the common man than was characteristic of the early sixteenth century.[9]

The proclamations and sermons were public statements of policies agreed upon by Protector Somerset and the Council. The actual process by which these policies were evolved is very difficult to determine. If we assume that Somerset supported the commission on enclosures and sympathized with the poor, we can readily understand his reluctance to overreact to reports of insurrection from the provinces. During the previous summer John Hales had reported to Somerset that the people in areas where there had been minor disturbances were "tractable, obedient, and quiet."[10] If Somerset received similar reports during the spring and summer of 1549, they have not survived. By the time the Norfolk Rebellion attracted serious attention from the government, Lord Russell's army had already marched to the West to pacify insurgents in Devon and Cornwall. And as reports of disorder came in from Norfolk, the government learned of similar disturbances in the Midlands and the southern counties. Somerset also had to deal with the deteriorating military situation in Scotland and with French hostility on the continent. Each of these challenges taxed the already strained financial resources of the government.[11] It is therefore essential to appreciate the gravity and complexity of the problems facing Somerset before attempting to appraise the wisdom of his actions.

Officials at Norwich first appealed to the government for assistance on July 9, when they sent Edmund Pynchyn to London with letters to the Council telling about Kett's growing strength. The mayor hesitated to act on his own authority and received little assistance from the Norfolk gentry. Four days later a pursuivant named Grove arrived in Norwich with a commission under the great seal for Robert Watson, the preacher and Canon of Norwich, who had the confidence of both Kett and city officials. The councillors of Norwich deliberated over the newly arrived instructions at great length, requiring bread, drink, and candles for a meeting that lasted until after midnight. The nature of the commission brought by Grove is unknown, but it may have been similar to the royal proclamation of July 12, which granted the king's pardon to persons who assembled unlawfully and commanded those who had suffered "grief, damage, or loss" to refrain from any violence or force. Whatever the contents of the commission, Kett's men did not disperse, and the councillors of Norwich continued to lack authority for action against the rebels.[12]

During the first weeks of July, the Protector and his closest advisers received letters from prominent members of the Privy Council giving their reactions to the rapidly worsening crisis. The Earl of Warwick complained of his recent illness and pledged his complete devotion to Somerset "for the staying of the fury of this people" but offered no advice about what policies the government should pursue. The king's secretary and perhaps the most learned member of the Council, Sir Thomas Smith, did send advice. He wanted Somerset to authorize one or two men to execute proclamations against the rebels and recommended sending letters to "special men of trust" in each county empowering them to summon the gentry and "grave yeomen" so that order might be restored. Smith thought the gentry should discipline local watchmen who were spreading rumors throughout the countryside and contributing to greater unrest. He argued that Somerset's policy had been too lenient and urged greater severity. "If a great number of the boisterous were dispatched," said Smith, "the realm had no loss."[13]

Even sterner recommendations came from Sir William Paget, writing from Brussels where he was negotiating with the Emperor Charles V. Formerly Somerset's most trusted adviser, Paget gradually lost influence by criticizing the Protector's liberal policies. Paget favored the firmer stance of Henry VIII and stated emphatically that Somerset was courting disaster by seeking popularity with the commons. In a bold and unequivocal letter written on July 7, Paget urged Somerset to summon to his side all councillors in England and to levy all available military forces, including German mercenaries stationed at Calais. He told Somerset to go in person with the army through the countryside pacifying villages and towns and executing the chief rebels:

> Let your horsemen lie in such towns and villages as have been most busiest taking enough for their money that rebels may feel the surety of their villainies. Take the liberties of such towns as have offended into the king's majesty's hands; you may restore them again at pleasure afterward. If your grace send some of the doers a[t] warfare from their wives to the North or Boulogne to be soldiers or pioneers, it will do well.

Although Paget did not mention Kett by name, there can be no doubting his solution for the Commotion in Norfolk.[14]

Protector Somerset initially rejected the entreaties of Smith and Paget calling for repressive measures. He pushed ahead with a new commission on enclosures only to find that his goals were unattainable. On July 10 two of the commissioners, Sir Thomas Darcy and Sir John Gates, reported that they could not execute their commissions. "We are partly in fear," they said, "lest the people will think we do but only delay time with them, and thereby perchance they may be brought in more rage than before they were." They requested additional authority from the Protector and Council to summon persons who severed land from houses and kept excessive numbers of sheep and to make presentments against them. A few days later, Somerset, after learning of enclosure riots at Cambridge, stressed that the king "hath in his hands both mercy and justice" but continued to offer pardons to first offenders. Somerset's response to the disorder at Cambridge was identical to the terms of the royal proclamation of July 16 which offered pardon to those who would return to their homes and invoked martial law against future rioters.[15]

Somerset and the Council received information about Kett's demands by July 19. On that date the Imperial ambassador, Van der Delft, writing to Charles V, made direct reference to the demands and remarked that the Council was in great perplexity.[16] According to Sir John Hayward's life of Edward VI, the rebels "presented certain complaints to the king and desired that a herald or some other messenger of credit may be sent unto them to receive articles."[17] Neither Nicholas Sotherton nor Alexander Neville mentions these negotiations between the rebels and the government, but each gives an account of the meeting of Leonard Sotherton of Norwich with the Council in London. Sotherton, who had fled to London "for his own safe guard," was summoned before the Council to report on the situation in Norfolk. He asked for pardon for himself and "besought the king's majesty's grace for pardon to be offered" to the rebels "hoping that the office thereof would both glad a great number of hearts that would have remorse of their rebellion and to cause the same to revert and return to their habitations as faithful and true subjects are to do."[18]

Sotherton then departed with the York herald at arms, arriving at Norwich about noon on July 21. The herald received a hostile reception when he appeared before the rebel camp on Mousehold Heath. Dressed in a coat of armor, the herald offered pardon to those who submitted themselves and pledged to return quietly to their homes. While a few fell on their knees "giving God and the king's majesty great thanks for his gracious clemency and pity," Kett and the majority of his followers refused to accept pardon.[19]

Sir John Hayward gives details of important concessions offered by the Protector in addition to the pardon. The concessions, contained in a letter signed by Edward VI and Somerset, included a promise to summon Parliament in October to consider specific complaints of the rebels:

Touching their particular complaint for reducing farms and lands to their ancient rents, although it could not be done by his ordinary power without a Parliament, yet he would so far extend his authority, royal and absolute, as to give charge to his commissioners to travail with all persons within their counties to reduce lands to the same rents whereat they were farmed forty years before, and that rents should be paid at Michaelmas then next ensuing, according to that rate, and that such as would not presently yield to his commissioners for that redress should, at the Parliament which he would forthwith summon, be overruled.

Concerning their complaint for prices of wools, he would forthwith give order that his commissioners should cause clothiers to take wools, paying only two parts of the price whereat commonly they were sold the year next before; and for the other third part, the owner and the buyer should stand to such order as the Parliament should appoint. At which also he would give order that landed men, to a certain proportion, should be neither clothiers nor farmers. And further, that one man should not use divers occupations, nor have plurality of benefices nor of farms; and generally, that then he would give order for all the residue of their requests, in such sort as they should have good cause not only to remain quiet, but to pray for him, and to adventure their lives in his service.[20]

The government also promised to allow the rebels to appoint four or six representatives who would "present bills of their desires" to Parliament. This extraordinarily conciliatory response shows that the Council was informed of Kett's grievances and reveals that the surviving list of twenty-nine demands was not the only document prepared by the rebels inasmuch as that list made no reference to the price of wool. Kett's followers not only refused the generous terms offered them, but also drove the king's herald from Norwich and proceeded to occupy the city.

In view of the rebels' response, it is surprising that Somerset remained optimistic that a negotiated settlement would still be possible. His attitude may have been caused by an appreciation of the commons' grievances and by the feeling that the Norfolk Rebellion with its Protestant leadership posed a lesser threat than the Western rising. He also seems to have recognized Kett's disciplined leadership and the rebels' respect for human life and property. Nevertheless, Somerset and the Council sent an army of 1,500 to Norwich, commanded by the Marquis of Northampton. Northampton was instructed to avoid a direct confrontation with the rebels and to take up a position outside Norwich so that the rebels would be denied supplies and reinforcements. Shortly after Northampton departed for Norwich, Somerset wrote optimistically, "We trust there shall be no great matter, for presently are there come hither half a dozen chosen of their company who seek the king's majesty's mercy and redress of things and be returned to receive pardon by directions of the marquis. . . ." Somerset may have become a victim of wishful thinking, or possibly the six men seeking pardon did not represent the attitude of Kett and the vast force assembled on Mousehold

Heath.[21] Whatever his reasons, Somerset continued to reject the firm policies recommended by Sir William Paget.

The army dispatched to Norwich under the command of William Parr, Marquis of Northampton included leaders well-chosen to assert the king's authority and bring military pressure to bear on Kett's rebels. Although we do not know exactly why Northampton was appointed, it is significant that he was the highest-ranking privy councillor after Somerset. The only other English duke was Norfolk, then a prisoner in the Tower of London sentenced to death by Henry VIII. Northampton, like Somerset, was related to the late king by marriage, and he achieved prominence at court prior to the accession of Edward VI. He also had military experience, having served in France in 1544. While the Earl of Warwick had a better military record, Northampton was perhaps best suited, after the Protector himself, to be the personal emissary of the king.

Two other peers, Thomas, Lord Wentworth and Edmund, Lord Sheffield, accompanied Northampton. Lord Wentworth, who was a justice of the peace for Suffolk where he had extensive landholdings, had a long record of military service reaching back to 1523 when he went to France in the expedition of the Duke of Suffolk. Lord Sheffield, born in 1521, was a promising young noble formerly in the service of Thomas Cromwell. Sheffield fought in the vanguard of Henry VIII's invasion force of 1544 with 50 horsemen and 500 foot recruited from Lincolnshire and was remembered as a man of learning. Thomas Fuller, who ranked Sheffield among *The Worthies of England,* wrote, "Great was his skill in music" and noted that he wrote a book of sonnets "according to the Italian fashion," a work that no longer survives.[22] Neither Wentworth nor Sheffield were privy councillors although the former joined the Council before the end of 1549.

The Privy Council sent three other members in addition to Northampton: Sir Anthony Denny, Sir Ralph Sadler, and Sir Richard Southwell, all of whom were Henricians with long government service. Denny, best known for having courageously informed Henry VIII of his approaching death, had been knighted by the king for service at Boulogne in 1544. Sadler was a former Cromwellian administrator skilled in diplomacy and experienced in the financial aspects of warfare. At the battle of Pinkie in 1547 Sadler rallied the English cavalry to defeat the Scots. He was a close friend of Northampton and a colleague of Sir William Paget.[23] Sir Richard Southwell, like Denny, had been a prominent and favored courtier during the reign of Henry VIII and possessed extensive lands in Norfolk and Suffolk.

Many historians, basing their judgment on Northampton's subsequent failure, have erroneously assumed that the army was lacking in military competence.[24] Yet each of the peers had prior military experience as had Denny, Sadler, Southwell, and Sir John Gates. Another leader, Sir Richard Lee, was a military engineer who had worked on fortifications at Great Yarmouth, the Isle of Thanet, and in Scotland. Lee also served under Somerset and Warwick during the invasion of Scotland in 1547. Considering that the government was engaged in simultaneous military operations in Scotland, France, and the West of England, it is remarkable that so much talent was available for a small army instructed not to destroy the enemy, but to overawe it and cut off supplies.

Gentry from Norfolk and surrounding counties made up the remainder of the army's leadership. Sir Thomas Paston, Sir John Clere, Sir Henry Bedingfield, and Sir Richard Southwell were justices of the peace for Norfolk, while Sir Edward Warner and Sir John Sulyard were landowners with a vested interest in the county. Lord Wentworth, Sir William Walgrave, and Sir Thomas Cornwallis were justices in Suffolk. Two men, Sir Anthony Denny and Sir John Gates, were justices in Essex, while Sir Henry Parker and Sir Ralph Rowlet held the same office in Hertfordshire. Finally, the leadership was rounded out with Sir John Cutts, a Cambridgeshire man, Sir Gilbert Dethicke, Norroy king at arms, and an Italian named Malatesta, who commanded Italian mercenaries attached to the expedition.

Northampton advanced toward Norwich on July 31 and, reaching a point within a mile of the city, sent the herald forward to announce his presence and intention of entering the city. At this time Kett had relinquished direct control over Norwich, choosing to remain on Mousehold Heath where the mayor, Thomas Codd, was held with limited freedom to return to the city. Augustine Steward, who had been named the mayor's deputy, met the herald at St. Stephen's Gate and immediately sent a messenger to Codd with a request to receive the army in person. But, as Kett refused to permit Codd to leave Mousehold Heath, the mayor asked his deputy to take the sword of the city to Northampton and explain his absence. Steward then proceeded to Northampton's camp, handed over the sword, symbolizing the mayor's royal authority, and reported on the situation at Norwich. The army, headed by Sir Richard Southwell bearing the sword, entered the city and approached Guildhall, where the leaders refreshed themselves with wine, fruit, and meat. Northampton pledged to defend the city and repress the rebel host. He also appointed watches, supported by armed men, to guard the walls and gates. Up to this point it is difficult to fault Northampton's strategy, for, having met no resistance from the rebels either during the advance or within the city, he could now protect his men within the walls and give desperately needed moral support to the harassed citizenry.[25]

Before nightfall a party of Italian mercenaries skirmished with the rebels on Magdalen Hill to the north of Norwich. With superior numbers the rebels overwhelmed the Italians and forced them to withdraw into the city after both sides sustained heavy casualties. One of the Italians, a man named Cheauers, was captured. Although a ransom of £100 was offered for his life, the unfortunate mercenary was stripped naked and hanged in an oak tree at Mount Surrey. Nicholas Sotherton and Alexander Neville thought the man was killed primarily for his gorgeous apparel and armor, but a better explanation is that the rebels simply executed swift, country justice on a foreigner unlucky enough to be captured. If clothing and armor had been the sole objective, poor Cheauers could have been returned, and the £100 ransom duly collected.

To prevent a night attack soldiers were "appointed to guard the city in every part needful . . . , and especially in the market place was the chief number where were made bonfires and lights." Sir Edward Warner, the knight marshal, supervised security preparations while Sir Thomas Paston and four other knights guarded different sections of the city. Although the soldiers were exhausted after a three-day march in the summer heat, the leaders exercised great care in positioning the men for the night. Nevertheless, the rebels attacked about midnight. They sounded alarms throughout the city and began bombardment with artillery positioned on Mousehold Heath. Warner immediately awakened Northampton, who hastened to the marketplace and took personal charge of defense efforts. The commanders met together and ordered the rampiring of the wall and gates on the side of the city farthest from the rebel camp "for the better keeping of the city with fewer men." Laborers worked on the fortifications throughout the night, continuing until eight o'clock the following morning.[26]

The initial bombardment of Norwich did little damage, for the shots were aimed too high and passed harmlessly over the defenders' heads; but a second, more determined attack followed. Shortly after work on the fortifications was underway, the rebels "all at once as a violent stream came running from their dens with confused cries and beastly howlings" and broke into the city. Some burned and broke down the gates. Others climbed the walls and swam across the river, while still others entered through the breaches in the old dilapidated walls. Northampton's men fought back with pikes, arrows, swords, and firearms in a pitched battle of nearly three hours. Alexander Neville grudgingly acknowledged the fierce determination of Kett's men:

> For the minds of the rebels were so set on fire and incensed and the desire to fight so exceeding, as, although they were fallen down deadly wounded, yet would they not give over, but half dead, drowned in their own and other men's blood, even to the last gasp, furiously withstood our men. Yea, many also struck through the breasts with swords and the sinews of their thighs and hams cut asunder yet creeping on their knees were moved with such hellish fury, as they wounded the buttocks and thighs of our soldiers lying amongst the slain almost without life.[27]

But there was heroism on both sides, for the soldiers stood their ground. When the nighttime battle ended, 300 rebels were dead, according to Neville, and Northampton's force suffered many injuries but only a few dead.

The next morning Northampton, after having breakfast at the Maid's Head Inn, learned that four or five hundred persons were at Pockthorpe Gate seeking the king's pardon.[28] Northampton, the herald, and a trumpeter proceeded immediately to the gate where troops led by Sir John Clere and Sir Thomas Paston were stationed, but neither man, woman, nor child was to be found. The trumpet was sounded, and John Floateman of Beccles galloped forward with about twenty followers. When offered pardon, Floateman refused and defiantly denounced Northampton as a traitor. This meeting was apparently part of a diversionary feint devised by Kett, because in the midst of the fruitless negotiations, word came that a large group of rebels had entered Norwich near the Hospital of St. Giles. The herald rushed to the hospital over Whitefriars Bridge, while Northampton went to Tombland by a different route to see what was happening. Nearby in the plain before the bishop's palace, the decisive battle was fought.

Unfortunately, contemporary writers give fewer details of the battle of August 1 than of the engagement of the previous night. Sotherton, Neville, and Holinshed each saw the death of Lord Sheffield as the critical event of the battle, but it appears more likely that the rebels prevailed primarily on account of superior numbers. Neville estimated the rebel force at 20,000; and even if this figure is greatly exaggerated, Northampton's army of 1,500 was hopelessly outnumbered. The force led by Lord Sheffield undoubtedly bore the brunt of the initial rebel attack near the Hospital of St. Giles. "Having more regard to his honor than safety of life, desirous to show some proof of his noble 'valiancie,' " Sheffield "fell into a ditch as he was about to turn his horse." He was briefly held prisoner while he begged his captors to spare his life by offering money and stressing the importance of his nobility and family name.[29] Although Tudor society was highly materialistic and deferential with the common man paying proper respect to his betters, Lord Sheffield did not benefit by the customs of the age:

> As he pulled off his head piece that it might appear what he was, a butcherly knave named Fulks, who by occupation was both a carpenter and a butcher, slat him in the head with a club and so most wretchedly killed him. A lamentable case that so noble a young gentleman indued with so many commendable qualities, as were to be wished in a man of his calling, should thus miserably end his days by the hands of so vile a villain.[30]

Neville, in a slightly different version of this grizzly episode, has the rebels contending among themselves to decide which of them had actually dealt Sheffield the fatal blow. Eventually all agreed that the honor belonged to Fulks, who, Neville hastened to add, was himself killed shortly thereafter. Lord Sheffield was brutally beaten to death by desperate men who had no other way of expressing their hatred of the ruling aristocracy; he was not so much a military casualty as a victim of mob justice.[31]

Northampton's army never recovered from the loss of Lord Sheffield. The soldiers retreated in disarray to the marketplace where Northampton in effect ordered each man to shift for himself. The army was so overwhelmed and demoralized that no attempt was made to regroup or counterattack. The battle claimed over one hundred rebel lives and perhaps a similar number of gentry and soldiers.[32] The dead included Robert Woluaston, a man "appointed to keep the door of Christ's Church" (the cathedral), who was killed by the butcher Fulks. Woluaston's death was a case of mistaken identity, as he was taken for Sir Edmund Knyvett, whose men had successfully attacked an outpost of rebels several days earlier at Hingham, eleven miles from Norwich. The only important prisoner was Sir Thomas Cornwallis, who was not released until the victory of Warwick.[33] Accompanying the defeated army back to London were large numbers of refugees. Some of the wealthy brought their "plate, money, and stuff"; others, less fortunate, hid their possessions in wells, ponds, and privies hoping to preserve them from the rebels. Among the refugees were those who left Norwich with nothing but their lives: "In the which conflict there departed with them many that had wives and children, some that were with child, some that were sick and diseased, which were fain to leave them all, and some fled in their doublets and hose and some in their lightest garments best to escape and make haste away and also leaving their substance and other commodities."[34]

A worse fate befell those remaining behind in Norwich. The citizens who opened the city to Northampton's army were traitors in the eyes of Kett and his supporters. After the army retreated, the rebels set fire to large sections of the city. Houses on both sides of Holm Street were burned as were portions of the hospital for the poor. Bishop's Gate "with the lead thereof molten" and the gates and houses at Pockthorpe, Magdalen, St. Augustine's, Coslany, and Ber Street were also burned. A timely summer rain extinguished some of the fires, yet the damage was extensive. Augustine Steward, the mayor's deputy, unable to prevent the destruction, retired to his house where he watched the conflagration "out of his highest gallery." A band of rebels marching to a drum entered the city at St. Augustine's Gate and approached Steward's house. When they failed to break down his door, they set fire to the house. Fearing that he might be burned, he allowed the rebels to enter. "They came thrusting in and violently fell on the said deputy to pluck his cloak from him and called him traitor asking for the lord marquis and other that there were lodged." Although told that Northampton had fled, the rebels nonetheless ransacked the house and adjoining mercer's shop and took shirt cloths, doublet cloths, and money.[35] Leaving the Steward house, the rebels:

> under pretence of seeking for gentlemen . . . entered every man's house and spoiled all they could come by in so much that though the most part of the best of the city were departed . . . yet the servants of the said citizens to save the rest of their masters' goods devised to bake bread and to roast, bake pastry and give it unto them to save the rest notwithstanding great losses ensued to many.

The houses of the rich and those who had fled received the most severe damage. As the providential rain extinguished some of the fires, the rebels sought shelter in the cathedral and parish churches. Although these suffered damage, it does not appear that the rebels were motivated by any destructive religious impulse.[36]

The mayor's deputy commissioned Dr. John Barret and other preachers to speak to the rebels, but their words fell on deaf ears. Gripped in a veritable reign of terror, the citizens of Norwich had no way of resisting their adversaries. "Nothing was seen or heard, but lamentation and weeping." Women, according to Neville, seeing "the slaughter of harmless naked men, oft times offered themselves in the streets, entreating them to have compassion upon their country . . . their husbands and children." With the city wholly at their mercy, the rebels took charge of the gates and ordered the citizens "to watch their camp and gates in the night."[37] In the wake of Northampton's humiliating defeat, the city of Norwich suffered damage and a degree of mob rule unlike that of any other provincial capital during the Tudor period. Although none of the contemporary writers give details of the numbers killed, suggesting that the rebels had a greater respect for human life than for private property, the citizens of Norwich suffered losses that affected their livelihood for many years. The fires, pillaging, and the uncontrolled passions of the commons remained vivid in the memories of the upper classes long after the rebellion had been quelled.

Back in London the news of Northampton's defeat stunned Somerset and the Council. Although Somerset blamed Northampton for tactical blunders and inept leadership, the Protector had himself believed that the Norfolk Rebellion was a minor disturbance that could be ended quickly with a modest show of force. The government had no alternative plan of action, and for over a week the Council met continuously, trying to decide how to proceed. The Imperial ambassador, Van der Delft, tried to meet with Somerset, but his requests were refused "because of the continual consultations that are being held to prevent or remedy the peasants' evil, which is swelling daily."[38] If one thing was clear to the Protector, it was that substantial military force was required for the pacification of Norfolk. Sir William Paget and other members of the Council had already arrived at the same conclusion, and the whole Tudor political tradition was based on the rigorous maintenance of law and order. Somerset's sympathies for the poor and his commitment to a negotiated settlement were commendable in theory but unworkable in practice. Now the situation required all available manpower and strong leadership.

To obtain reinforcements from the North, Somerset and the Council wrote to the Earl of Shrewsbury at Doncaster on August 3. Shrewsbury, lord lieutenant of Yorkshire and five neighboring counties, was ordered to levy "as many able horsemen, and footmen within the king's majesty's commission, which you shall receive herewith, as may be conveniently furnished." The instructions, however, did not explain where and how the men were to be used. The force was to be held in readiness to march on an hour's notice "either towards the king's majesty or otherways, as by our next letters shall be signified unto you." Three days later a letter from the king and Somerset to officials at Yarmouth stated that "a main force . . . in the order of our said uncle" would be sent very shortly "to weed and try out our good subjects from the evil, to minister, aid, and comfort to the one, and contrarywise to extend the rigor and extremity of our sword to the other." The following day, August 7, came the first indication that the Earl of Warwick would also lead a military contingent against the Norfolk rebels. It had originally been intended that Warwick should take an army to Scotland; later another plan, also unexecuted, called for him to reinforce Lord Russell in the West. Warwick, who was suffering from ill health, remained in London until July 31, the day before Northampton's defeat at Norwich, when he left with 500 men on an undisclosed mission. His destination was probably Warwick, where riots also occurred, but the Imperial ambassador reported that he was en route to Wales.[39]

In the midst of these indecisive preparations for a counterattack came a bombshell from France. On August 8 the French king declared war on England. England's historic enemy could scarcely have chosen a more propitious moment to strike. The rebellions diverted troops and supplies badly needed in Scotland, while Charles V had only recently refused an English alliance and declined to guarantee the security of Boulogne. Following the war declaration Henry II led an attack on Boulogne which strained the already over-taxed English military resources. The Council also feared the possibility of a French attack on the Western ports and ordered Lord Russell to take appropriate precautions. The Earl of Warwick, upon hearing of the war declaration, reflected rather philosophically that open warfare was preferable to the "colored friendship" of the French and called upon his countrymen to pull up their hearts and put their confidence in the Lord, observations that may have strengthened sagging morale but served mainly to emphasize what desperate straits the country was in.[40]

An order on August 6 reaffirmed indications that Somerset would have supreme command of military operations against Kett. This order, probably one of several issued for raising troops, declared, "We have appointed our most entirely beloved uncle, the Duke of Somerset . . . with an army royal to go against them." The unnamed recipient of the proclamation was commanded to raise one hundred armed men and to have the force at Saffron Walden, Essex by August 17. The Earl of Warwick learned of his appointment to lead the shires of Cambridge, Bedford, Huntingdon, Northampton, Norfolk, and Suffolk about August 11. In response to the news, Warwick, in a letter to Sir William Cecil, expressed great concern about the discredited Marquis of Northampton and offered to serve under his command if Somerset desired. Warwick feared that Northampton might be so discouraged that he would be unwilling to offer further service to the country and added: "I wish that no man for one mischance or evil hap, to the which we be all subject that must serve, should be utterly abject, for if it should be so, it were almost a present discomfort to all men before they go to it, since those things lie in God's hand." Although Warwick's letter left no doubt of his sympathy for Northampton, it stands as further evidence that Somerset and the Council had not fully decided who should have supreme command. Warwick seemed unaware that he might be serving under Somerset, as in the Scottish campaign of 1547, and thought that Northampton's authority might be continued for the second attack on rebel positions in Norfolk. In other words, the earl knew that he was to lead the Midland and East Anglian shires, but not whether he would command all forces sent against Kett. It may have been as late as August 15, two weeks after Northampton's retreat from Norwich, before Somerset finally decided not to participate in the suppression of the Norfolk Rebellion. On that date a proclamation was issued ordering gentlemen from the counties of Essex, Suffolk, and Norfolk residing in London or at the court to serve under Warwick.[41]

It is not easy to explain Somerset's indecisive response to Kett's victory over Northampton, but several possible explanations have been offered. A. F. Pollard argued that the Protector could not in good conscience shed the blood of the poor commons for whom he had such sympathy. Somerset and his closest associates, inspired by the Christian idealism of the Commonwealth reformers, promised a Tudor equivalent of the New Deal to the commons, but, when their policies were resisted, succeeded only in raising the expectations of the poor. By refusing to crush the Norfolk rebels, Somerset chose principle over political expediency.[42] A second possibility is that Somerset's delay and ultimate decision not to lead the king's army resulted from a realistic political and military strategy. Somerset may have felt that the French war declaration, the still undecided rebellion in the West, the maintenance of order in London together with the security of the king, required attention and coordination which only he could provide. By assigning the Norfolk command to his friend and trusted colleague, Warwick, the Protector may have believed that the best interests of the country would be served.[43]

Although evidence for a conclusive answer no longer exists, a close examination of Somerset's leadership during the rebellions compels us to reject the first two explanations for a third. From the very beginning of the popular disturbances, Somerset misjudged the mood of the country. Catholic sympathies remained strong, particularly in the West of England, while the gentry opposed agrarian reforms which, in their judgment, would encourage disobedience among the commons. Sir William Paget, originally Somerset's most intimate political adviser, alerted him to potential dangers early enough to permit a change of course. After the full extent of the rebellions became apparent, Somerset readily discarded his idealism, which may never have been deeply held, but lacked the political skill to direct the country's foreign and domestic policies effectively. The challenges of the summer of 1549 were truly formidable and might well have destroyed any man required to provide leadership for the child king. Confused, overburdened by crisis heaped upon crisis, Somerset probably correctly calculated that the Earl of Warwick would have a better chance against the Norfolk rebels than he. Although an earlier decision to name Warwick would have been desirable, time was on the side of the government, not Kett's rebels, whose military power remained confined to East Anglia.

Warwick's army differed from Northampton's force primarily in numbers. Whereas Northampton had about 1,500 men in his command, Warwick had at least five times that number. Contemporary estimates vary widely from a low of 6,000 foot and 1,500 horse given by the journal of Edward VI to a high of 14,000 suggested by Alexander Neville.[44] Each was led by peers and local gentry, and each included mercenaries. As commander, Warwick drew on political and military experience reaching back to the reign of Henry VIII, when he served in France and Scotland. No available commander had significant experience with domestic insurrections, because the last major rebellion, the Pilgrimage of Grace, occurred thirteen years earlier in 1536 when the Duke of Norfolk had led the king's army. Besides his experience Warwick had a strong commitment to public service and a courageous determination to succeed. The presence of his two young sons, Ambrose and Robert, the future Elizabethan Earls of Warwick and Leicester, helped convince the officers and men that their commander was confident of his ability to defeat the rebels. The appointment of Northampton as second-in-command gave Warwick the benefit of the former's knowledge of conditions at Norwich and reaffirmed his judgment that the earlier debacle had not been entirely the result of Northampton's mismanagement.

Although Warwick and Northampton were the only two privy councillors, the army included three other peers, the Lords Bray, Grey of

Powis, and Willoughby of Parham, none of whom had served in the first campaign against Kett. Three of the gentry, Sir Thomas Gresham, Sir Andrew Flammock, and Sir Thomas Palmer, were trusted associates of the Earl of Warwick. Several leaders, including Sir Marmaduke Constable, Henry Willoughby, William Devereux, younger son of Lord Ferrers of Chartley, Giles Forster, and Flammock, came from the Midlands. Warwick must have had greater confidence in these men than the Norfolk gentry, whose record in resisting the rebels was extremely poor. The leaders who accompanied Warwick appear to have been no more distinguished for their military experience than those who previously served under Northampton, but they brought vigor and determination that was desperately needed.

The rank and file of Warwick's army came from East Anglia, the Midlands, and Wales. The Earl of Shrewsbury was ordered to bring men from the North, but neither Shrewsbury nor his men joined in the campaign. Lord Willoughby recruited 1,100 well-armed footmen in Lincolnshire and also led a force of 400 foot and 120 light horse drawn from King's Lynn and the surrounding area. Included among Willoughby's troops were thirty-seven men recruited and equipped by the town of Wisbech. Native Englishmen provided the great bulk of manpower, but they were reinforced by over 1,000 Swiss mercenaries, originally intended for service in Scotland. The English regularly employed foreign mercenaries as did other European powers, and therefore their use did not carry the stigma attached to such forces in later periods.[45]

The Earl of Warwick, advancing from Warwickshire, rendezvoused with Northampton, Grey of Powis, and Bray at Cambridge. Here Warwick met with a group of unarmed aldermen and citizens of Norwich, who had fled in panic to Cambridge seeking his assistance and pardon. He generously granted pardon in view of the great hardships the citizenry had suffered but also told them bluntly that the rebellion might have been stopped weeks earlier if only "a few valiant and wise men" had been willing to take decisive action. Warwick ordered the Norwich contingent to arm themselves and join the advancing army. These men were specially marked with "laces about their necks to be discerned from the rest."[46] While at Cambridge Warwick also met with the mayor and aldermen, who presented him with a gift valued at nineteen shillings. During the past month serious disturbances had taken place at Cambridge, and for this reason city officials were comforted by the army's presence. Although we cannot be certain, it is highly probable that Matthew Parker, vice-chancellor of Cambridge University and future Archbishop of Canterbury, heard Warwick grant pardon to the citizens of Norwich and perhaps even met privately with him to relate his own unsuccessful efforts to persuade Kett's followers to disperse.

Leaving Cambridge the army passed through Newmarket, where it was joined by troops from London, and reached Wymondham on

August 22. After spending the night at Wymondham, home of the Ketts, the army was further reinforced by Norfolk gentry and the force that Lord Willoughby recruited in Lincolnshire and King's Lynn. The enlarged army approached Norwich the next day, stopping two miles from the city at Intwood Hall, the house of Sir Thomas Gresham. At Intwood, Warwick and his men rested "not once putting off their armor but remaining still in a readiness, if the enemies should have made any sudden invasion against them."[47] By halting outside of Norwich, the army obtained rest and retained the freedom of maneuver that Northampton had denied himself when he entered the city at the end of a hard march. If Kett actually climbed into a tower to view the army from Norwich, as Sotherton tells us, the rebel leader must have been impressed by its size and discipline and realized that the young king, in whom he had placed his trust, had irrevocably betrayed the cause of the commons.[48]

Warwick, hoping to avoid bloodshed if possible, sent a herald forward "to summon the city either to open the gates that he might quietly enter, or else to look for war at his hands." As the herald approached, Kett appointed the mayor's deputy, Augustine Steward, and another alderman, Robert Rugg, to learn what terms would be proposed. The pair begged pardon for themselves, reassuring the herald that they had never consented to the rebellions, and asked that Warwick again offer the king's pardon to the assembled rebels rather than demand the opening of the gates to the whole army. Warwick wisely agreed to offer pardon one final time before attacking and sent the herald and a trumpeter through St. Stephen's Gate into the rebel-controlled city. Once within Norwich they were met by forty rebel horsemen, and this party along with Steward and Rugg proceeded across the city to Bishop's Gate opposite Kett's camp on Mousehold Heath. At the sound of the trumpet the rebels came forward and were commanded by the horsemen "to divide themselves and stand in order upon either side [of] the way." The rebels uncovering their heads, cried in unison, "God save King Edward; God save King Edward." The herald rode to the top of Mousehold Heath where he awaited the arrival of Robert Kett. He then condemned the rebels' disobedience and rebellion but said the king of his special mercy was giving them one last opportunity to accept pardon. Offended by the herald's speech, the rebels cursed and abused him, saying that the pardon was merely a trick. Others accused the herald of being nothing but the mouthpiece of the hated gentry. The herald nevertheless persevered and accompanied by Kett moved on to another part of the camp where the proclamation was repeated for the benefit of those who had been unable to hear the first time.[49]

At this critical moment a young boy, one of many who had rallied to Kett's standard, pulled down his breeches, "showed his bare buttocks, and did a filthy act." A party of Warwick's soldiers, who had come along the river to view the proceedings on Mousehold Heath, saw the boy and shot him dead. Immediately a dozen rebel horsemen appeared before Kett and the herald. They exclaimed that the king's representative had come to have them all destroyed and shouted, "Our men are killed by the water side, whereat they severed them like mad men." Apparently unmoved by the unexpected bloodshed, Kett rode on down the hill with the herald intending to go with him to meet Warwick. But the rebels persuaded their leader to stay with them, saying, "Wither away, whither away, Master Kett; if you go, we will go with you, and with you will live and die!" The herald saw the multitude accompanying Kett and urged him to remain behind and pacify them. Accompanied by the trumpeter and aldermen, the herald then returned to Warwick and reported that pardon had been refused.[50]

Kett's desire to meet face-to-face with Warwick is one of the most puzzling and intriguing aspects of the Norfolk Rebellion. What can the rebel leader's objectives have been? A major difficulty in understanding his motivation lies in the fact that two different versions of the pardon have survived. One version, given by Neville and Holinshed, states that the pardon included all of the rebels; the other, contained in Sotherton's narrative, explicitly excluded Kett from the king's mercy. Another question is whether Kett and Warwick knew each other. There is a possibility that they were acquainted, because Kett acquired land from him at Wymondham. If we assume that Kett was excluded from the pardon and that he knew Warwick, it is possible that Kett intended to negotiate the surrender of the rebel army in return for his own life. By appealing to Warwick's good lordship, Kett may have hoped that he could save both himself and his devoted followers. But Kett's trust and optimism were not shared by his men, whose doubts were confirmed by the senseless killing of the boy, who could scarcely have chosen a worse time for obscene exhibitionism. At this point Kett became the prisoner of his overwrought supporters. Recognizing the strength of the king's army, knowing Warwick's determination to crush the rebels if pardon were refused, and at the same time sensing that his own authority was diminishing, Robert Kett decided that a meeting with Warwick would be fruitless. No longer confident that he could persuade his followers to accept terms of capitulation, he chose to remain with his comrades, whose hopes for redress of grievance and justice in any case were unattainable.

Military operations followed the rebels' refusal to accept pardon. Warwick's first objective was to reoccupy Norwich. The army approached St. Stephen's Gate, the main entrance into Norwich, which the rebels blocked by lowering the portcullis. While the king's master gunner began to bombard St. Stephen's, Augustine Steward informed Warwick that entrance into the city might be more quickly achieved through the smaller Brazen Doors. This gate, secured only with beams, pieces of timber, and rampired with stones and earth, was opened by a force of pioneers who entered the city in the face of stiff resistance. Shortly thereafter the gunners demolished the portcullis at St. Stephen's, permitting troops led by Northampton and Captain Thomas Drury to fight their way inside. A third entrance was secured through Westwick (or St. Benedict's) Gate, which Steward caused "to be set open." Warwick entered with little opposition and advanced to the market-place. By three o'clock in the afternoon most of the army accompanied by supply carts took up positions around the marketplace.[51]

The first phase of military operations was completed with only a few casualties among the army and moderate damage to St. Stephen's Gate, but Warwick, like Northampton, quickly learned that it was easier to enter Norwich than to hold it against the rebels. After occupying the marketplace, Warwick ordered the execution of forty-nine rebels on a pair of timber gallows erected at the expense of the city. These men, having already refused pardon, were subject to the death penalty according to martial law. Scores of citizens, who came out of hiding to seek pardon, also diverted the commanders' attention. Warwick granted the pardons and sent the citizens home with orders that no rebels were to be harbored on the premises.

While the army was preoccupied, the rebels regrouped for a counterattack at Tombland near the cathedral. Assuming that War-wick's commanders were unfamiliar with the narrow streets and lanes, the rebels divided themselves into three companies. Sotherton recalled that one group was in St. Michael's Street, another in Wymer Street, and the third at St. Simon's and St. Peter Hungate "by the elm and about the hill next corner late the Blackfriars." The rebels, eager for battle, killed several gentlemen near Blackfriars. When Warwick heard the fighting, he quickly moved his main force from the marketplace through St. John's Street to a point near St. Andrew's Church where rebel bowmen fired "a mighty force of arrows." Captain Drury and his band of hackbutters fought their way forward and managed to put the rebels to flight with heavy volleys of shot. The retreating rebels were pursued with such zeal that many were forced to hide in churchyards, under walls, and in alleys. The survivors fled to the safety of their camp on Mousehold Heath. Sotherton estimated that 100 rebels died in the fighting, while Neville put the losses at 330. After the fighting ended, Warwick fortified Norwich with soldiers stationed on the walls and in every street. All gates to the city were closed and rampired except Bishop's Gate, where supplies and artillery were concentrated for an attack on Mousehold Heath.[52]

Two rebel attacks on the army's supplies accompanied the bitter street fighting around St. Andrew's Church. The first occurred under curious — indeed incredible — circumstances. In the late afternoon heavily loaded carts and carriages were brought into Norwich through Westwick Gate. Because of the "rashness and folly of the keepers of the carriages," the vehicles went not to the marketplace where the army was assembled, but proceeded across the entire breadth of Norwich and exited through Bishop's Gate opposite the rebel camp. Kett's men could scarcely believe their eyes. Sweeping down from the hillside, they seized the undefended carts loaded with guns, gunpowder, and "all kind of instruments of war" and began carrying their booty back to camp. Captain Drury, making another timely appearance, succeeded in retrieving a few of the carts but not without losses to his men. This catastrophe may have been due to the carters' ignorance of Norwich or to poorly executed orders to transport supplies to Bishop's Gate for the advance on Mousehold Heath. It appears that a worse incident happened several hours later when artillery were again placed at Bishop's Gate and defended only by a small force of Welshmen. Rebels led by the chief gunner, Miles, seeing the guns lacked powder and were poorly guarded, attacked once again. Miles shot the king's master gunner, and his comrades, "some of them naked and unarmed, some armed with staves, bills, and pitchforks," advanced quickly and captured the artillery. The indefatigable Drury reinforced the hapless Welsh and managed to recover part of the guns and munitions.[53]

To prevent further losses Warwick stationed a large force of soldiers under the command of Lord Willoughby at Bishop's Gate and ordered the destruction of Whitefriars Bridge. Nevertheless the damage had already been done, as the rebels now possessed guns with which to bombard the city from Mousehold Heath. Gunners demolished the tower at Bishop's Gate, damaged the walls, and provoked panic among the citizenry. Fortunately for the army and the townspeople many of the shots were aimed too high and passed harmlessly over the tops of the houses; with better aim Neville speculated that the "greatest part" of Norwich would have been "beaten down and made even with the ground." Warwick and Northampton, enduring the bombardment with their men, lodged during the night at the house of Augustine Steward, the deputy mayor. The leaders found time for a quarter hour's caudle drinking with Steward but cannot have had much opportunity for sleep considering the gunfire from Mousehold Heath and a new rebel attack that began in the early hours of Sunday morning.[54]

Kett's men attempted to enter the city at Conesford Gate and also crossed the river into South Conesford ward where they burned "a whole parish or two" before being driven out. A warehouse called the Common Staithe where merchants stored merchandise from Great Yarmouth was destroyed and with it great stores of grain and "other commodities of many honest merchants." The rebels intended either to burn the entire city or draw soldiers and townspeople to South Conesford while they attacked in another quarter. Warwick, anticipating the rebels' strategy, allowed the fires to burn themselves out although city records show that two men were paid four pence for demolishing the Common Staithe with the city crome, which was a long hook used for pulling down burning buildings. The rebels mounted a second attack from the northern part of Norwich where they tried to fight their way into the heart of the city by crossing the bridges over the River Wensum. Warwick initially ordered all bridges demolished but later modified the order with the result that only Whitefriars Bridge was destroyed. The other bridges were heavily defended by soldiers who, in spite of heavy losses, succeeded in holding the attackers north of the river.[55]

In the midst of the heavy fighting on Sunday, a deputation of Norwich citizens came to Warwick and advised him to withdraw the army. The citizens, probably the same persons who vacillated before the rebels from the very beginning of the revolt and failed to defend the city with local manpower, argued that Warwick's army was too small, that the rebel hordes were too large, and that Norwich had already suffered heavy damage from the fighting, fires, and bombardment. Holinshed's *Chronicle* gives another interesting argument that withdrawal of the army was necessary because "the whole appointed numbers as yet were not come, neither of strangers nor Englishmen." Warwick refused to be persuaded. In indignation he replied to the citizens:

> Why and do your hearts fail you so soon? Or are you so mad withall to think that so long as any life resteth in me that I will consent to such dishonor? Should I leave the city heaping up to myself and likewise to you such shame and reproof as worthily might be reputed an infamy to us for ever? I will rather suffer whatsoever either fire or sword can work against me.

Drawing his sword, he commanded each of his men to kiss the others' swords thereby pledging a solemn oath that none should depart from Norwich until they had either "vanquished the enemies or lost their lives in manful defense of the king's honor."[56]

By sundown on Sunday, the second day of fighting, the king's army gained the upper hand within the city although Kett's camp on Mousehold Heath had not been attacked. In spite of the fires and bombardment, Warwick's troops managed to hold defensive positions around the perimeter of Norwich. The army sustained its share of fatalities and injuries, but these were within limits acceptable to the commanders. However, many of the soldiers were exhausted after continuous fighting for over twenty-four hours. To provide the men with rest and food every householder was ordered to receive a contingent of soldiers and "make them hearty." Those not needed to man the defenses during the night went "to their beds and had victuals furnished, which encouraged them much." Warwick, who had established his headquarters at the house of Augustine Steward, displayed his arms, the bear and ragged staff, on the gate. The squires and gentlemen "took each man's house as their own til their departure when . . . for joy of victory every man set up the ragged staff upon their gates and doors in the lord lieutenant's honor."[57] The appearance of Warwick's arms symbolized growing optimism that the king's army would prevail, an attitude deliberately encouraged by Warwick's brave speech to the nervous citizens. He undoubtedly sensed that his men could hold Norwich in face of the rebel attacks, but more important, he probably knew that reinforcements were coming the next day.

The following day, Monday, August 26, a thousand Swiss mercenaries arrived from London. They announced their approach by firing into the air. Warwick's men received the reinforcements enthusiastically and fired volleys of shot to welcome them to Norwich. The citizens received the Swiss joyfully, quartered them and their wives as commodiously as the English, and entertained them "liberally and courteously." The arrival of the mercenaries had the opposite effect on Kett and his men. The rebels, after failing to drive the army from Norwich, despaired and debated among themselves about what course to follow. When a snake leapt from a rotten tree into the bosom of Kett's wife, the rebel leader had to comfort an understandably hysterical woman and also determine what hidden meaning this strange incident had for his cause. Kett saw in the event an omen of doom that made him increasingly receptive to prophecies that were "phantastically devised" and openly proclaimed among his men.

There is no evidence that prophecies inspired the Norfolk Rebellion, but Keith Thomas has discussed those associated with Lollard, Catholic, and antigovernment movements during the fifteenth and sixteenth centuries. Scorned by sophisticated writers, prophecies remained highly influential among the classes supporting Kett's Rebellion. The rebels' dependence on prophecy probably increased as prospects for the success of their cause diminished. In fact Kett's final military strategy was ultimately based on an interpretation of two ambiguous prophecies.[58] The first is recorded by Neville and included in Holinshed's *Chronicle*:

> The country gnoffes [i.e. knaves], Hob, Dick, and Hick,
> With clubs and clouted shoon
> Shall fill up Dussindale
> With slaughtered bodies soon.

Sotherton gives a second, but similar prophecy: "And that in Dussens dale there should the [sic] perish both great and small." Dussindale, said to be within a mile of Mousehold Heath, cannot be located with certainty, but it has been identified with a nearby valley called Ossian's Vale.

An earlier prophecy, dating from 1537, predicted momentous events at Mousehold Heath rather than Dussindale: "There should land at Walborne Hope the proudest prince in all Christendom and so shall come to Mousehold Heath, and there should meet with other two kings and shall fight and shall be put down; and the white lion should obtain [mastery]." According to local legend the Danes landed at Weybourne Hope before the Norman Conquest. The prophecy may have been a protest against the oppressive Norman yoke, but whatever it was it was rejected in favor of the prophecies directing the rebel army to Dussindale. Although prophecies lead into the murky waters of folklore and traditional religion, Kett's response was unambiguous, for his men burned their huts on Mousehold Heath and during the night of August 26 moved their guns, munitions, and all supplies to Dussindale.[59]

A more rational explanation for Kett's puzzling strategy is found in Edward VI's journal, where the king says that the rebels left Mousehold Heath because Warwick's soldiers operating in the surrounding countryside cut off food supplies. Faced with the threat of starvation the rebels seized the initiative and engaged the army in a desperate battle where the victor would take all. S. T. Bindoff preferred the king's explanation to the prophecies, but an eyewitness serving with Warwick was astounded when he saw Kett withdraw to the "open valley." John Hornyold, who ought to have known if the army had cut off the rebels' supplies, wrote that he could not imagine what desperation had driven Kett to abandon Mousehold Heath for Dussindale.[60]

Kett's men, taking up positions at Dussindale, "devised trenches and stakes wherein they and theirs were entrenched and set up great bulwarks of defense before and about and placed their ordnance all about them." The gentry who had been held prisoner at Surrey Place were brought to Dussindale and chained together in front of the hastily erected fortifications so that they would protect the rebels behind them. Observers located in the steeple of Norwich Cathedral watched the rebels' movements and reported to Warwick. On Tuesday, August 27, Warwick, accompanied by English horsemen and a thousand Swiss mercenaries, marched through St. Martin's Gate toward the enemy. The leadership included Northampton, Willoughby, Bray, Powis, and Lord Ambrose Dudley. Before attacking, Warwick sent Sir Thomas Palmer and Sir Edmund Knyvett forward to offer pardon, but it was stoutly refused. Warwick, urging his men to regard the rebels not as men, but brutish beasts, ordered the army to advance. Miles, Kett's master gunner, fired at the standard-bearer, wounding him and killing his horse. The army returned the fire and charged forward to rescue as many of the prisoners as possible. Although a few were slain by the Swiss who "knew not what they were," most of the prisoners managed to "shrink aside and escape the danger." The rebels broke ranks and running in all directions were slaughtered by Warwick's pursuing horsemen. At least two thousand rebels were killed and a great many wounded. Warwick's losses were put at only forty, but among the mercenaries the casualties were higher. Kett and a few of his closest comrades fled the battlefield and rode toward Swannington, northwest of Norwich.[61]

Deserted by their captain and pursued by Warwick's horsemen, the rebels had no hope of victory, yet the die-hards rallied and vowed to fight to the last man. They collected swords, spears, and javelins, some of which were scattered among the corpses of fallen comrades, and surrounded themselves with carts and carriages. Warwick took pity on the courageous men and sent a herald to offer pardon. But a determined remnant of Kett's once-mighty army refused because they doubted the sincerity of the offer and preferred to die fighting rather than at the end of a rope. John Hornyold recounted that many were so "blinded with desperation" that "I myself in that their imminent misery presented to my said lord two or three that utterly refusing the king's pardon chose only to try the quarrel with the extremity of the sword." Finally, in a humanitarian gesture Warwick sent the herald forward once again to ask whether the rebels would lay down their arms if he came in person to guarantee the pardon. The rebels agreed, and Warwick advanced into their midst. After the herald read the pardon, the rebels laid down their weapons and cried, "God save King Edward, God save King Edward." And thus, wrote Holinshed, "through the prudent policy and favorable mercy of the Earl of Warwick, a great number of those offenders were preserved from the gates of death into the which they were ready to enter."[62]

Robert Kett fled from the battlefield at Dussindale and made his way to Swannington, about eight miles from Norwich, where his horse tired. He took refuge in a barn belonging to Robert Richers but was seen by two farm laborers who took him to the house and notified Richers' wife, who was away at church. Too tired and hungry to resume his flight, Kett remained unguarded at the house with a small child until Mrs. Richers returned. For Kett the long, desperate struggle was over; he craved only food and an opportunity to rest. The next day, August 28, an armed guard brought Kett to Norwich where he remained in prison until he was moved to London to be tried with his brother, William, for high treason.[63]

A service of thanksgiving took place on August 29 at St. Peter's Mancroft Church with Warwick, the military commanders, gentry, and prominent citizens in attendance. Warwick was hailed as the savior of Norwich, and his deeds were long remembered. The city government paid to erect and maintain Warwick's coat of arms, the bear and ragged staff, at each of the gates. As late as the mid-nineteenth century, four centuries after the Norfolk Rebellion, an inn in Fisher's Lane, St. Giles, displayed Warwick's arms. The city also decreed that on each anniversary of August 27 all inhabitants should close their shops and attend a divine service "to give humble thanks to God and pray for the preservation of the king's majesty heartily for the deliverance of this city from the great peril and danger it was in." The commemoration continued at least until 1667 when records indicate that instructions were given for services at St. Peter's Mancroft and the cathedral.[64]

When the thanksgiving service and the rejoicing of the wealthy citizens and gentry ended, the people of Norwich turned to the task of cleaning and rebuilding the battered city. Warwick's army left behind tons of litter as well as a legend of valor. City walls, gates, and bridges were damaged by fire and the rebel bombardment, while countless private shops and houses sustained heavy damage. Two laborers, Henry Woodrof and Andrew Robynson, worked for twenty-four days after the army's departure removing rubbish from the marketplace. A third worker, John Angell, employed for twelve days, assisted Woodrof and Robynson in the cleaning and loaded carts to carry away refuse. Robert Rogers spent eleven days cleaning the Guildhall, which had been used by the rebels as a prison and left in a foul and unwholesome condition. Across the city lay the burned out Common Staithe, the warehouse where large quantities of grain were destroyed. Here two laborers worked for twenty-seven days between Michaelmas and Christmas cleaning the streets, carrying bricks and stones, and removing ashes, cinders and burned grain. The cleanup operations were done by common laborers paid at the rate of five pence a day, but the rebuilding required skilled carpenters, masons, and locksmiths employed at higher rates.[65]

Most of the city gates were damaged either by the rebels or the attacking army. At St. Stephen's Gate, where Warwick's army forced its way into the city, new timber was required as well as hinges and iron work. John Elye received a shilling for mending the lock and making a key. Similar repairs were required at Pockthorpe, Bishop's and St. Augustine's Gates. John Ronhale paid seven shillings for over a hundred pounds of iron work salvaged from Fye Bridge Gate, which had been badly burned. The city walls also suffered heavy damage. A mason and his helper closed holes in the walls between St. Stephen's and St. Giles' Gates broken open "at my lord of Warwick's coming." Whitefriars Bridge, demolished on Warwick's orders as the rebels attacked, was rebuilt with the expense shared by the city and residents who lived nearby. William Spratte replanked the bridge and was paid six shillings eight pence for planks, nails, and labor. The Hospital of St. Giles, located between Bishop's Gate and the cathedral, sustained extensive damage, and like the gates and walls was repaired at the expense of the city. If we add private losses to the cost borne by the city and recorded in the City Chamberlain's account, it is clear that Kett's Rebellion imposed a heavy financial burden on Norwich and its citizens.[66]

The countryside, like Norwich, suffered during the weeks that Kett's army camped on Mousehold Heath. To feed the hungry rebels, enormous quantities of food were commandeered from surrounding farms. At Thorpe Wood outside the city, the rebels cut a large number of trees and thereby reduced the supply of firewood available to the commons. Sir Thomas Woodhouse, who complained bitterly that the ordnance and spoil left in the rebel camp were confiscated for the crown, claimed to have lost 2,000 sheep, all of his bullocks and horses, and "the most part" of his corn. While the gentry — the target of the rebels' anger and hatred — lost crops and livestock, smaller farmers willingly supplied Kett's men with food and supplies. Harry Ruston, church warden in the township of Elmham, paid for bread, beer, butter, and fish supplied to the township's contingent of twelve who joined Kett at Mousehold Heath. The weeks passed, and the people of Norwich and the towns and villages of rural Norwich returned to their former lives fully conscious that the gentry had triumphed but perhaps relieved that the rebellion had finally come to its inevitable conclusion.[67]

*The xviii day of July, whereas there was a book made and sent up
to the commons of Cornwall and Devonshire with all other parts of
all the realm for because of their rising and pulling down of
enclosures, the which was some time common unto the poor men,
and great men took them in and enclosed it to them and made parks
in divers places, and at this time the commons for the most part
within the realm rised and pulled up hedges and pales and set it
open again.*

Chronicle of the Grey Friars of London

6. ALL OTHER PARTS OF THE REALM

Although Kett's Rebellion in Norfolk and the Western
Rebellion were the most important popular disturbances of Edward VI's
reign, it does not follow that the remainder of the country remained
quiet and orderly. The early years of the reign saw rebellion, riot, and
popular unrest throughout England. The countryside seethed with
disorder from Kent to Hampshire in the south. Popular protest was
heard in the Midlands and extended as far to the north as Yorkshire and
Lancashire. Tudor chroniclers knew about these disturbances and
carefully recorded all but a very few. Later historians, especially
antiquarians and local historians, added significant details, but no one
has attempted to study the disturbances from a national perspective, to
relate them to the major rebellions, and to assess their impact on
government and society. Popular protests affecting over twenty-five
counties and culminating in destruction of property, personal injury,
and loss of life may not be dismisssed as "lesser stirs."[1] On the contrary,
an investigation of disorder outside Norfolk and the West is essential for
an understanding of the popular unrest that troubled Edwardian
England.

Disorder resulted from complex social, economic, and religious
grievances the origins of which often reached back into the early decades
of the sixteenth century. Rising prices and rents irritated a peasantry that
had enjoyed relative prosperity and an improved standard of living
during the fifteenth century. For the first time since the Black Death the
countryside felt the pressure of over-population and a shortage of
pastureland. Although open fields were enclosed only in select areas,
particularly in the Midlands, the gentry enclosed the commons that were
vital to the well-being of tenants and small landholders and established
deer parks as private hunting preserves. The standing of copyhold

tenancies at common law was in doubt as late as 1550, and consequently, complaints festered in local communities and led to protracted litigation in the conciliar courts.[2] The government of Protector Somerset, encouraged by Protestant reformers and proponents of the Commonwealth ideal, helped awaken the commons to their plight and seemed to assure them that the king understood their needs. Religion was another ingredient contributing to popular discontent. While some clergy favored the outright restoration of the Latin mass as in Devon and Cornwall, the objectives of others were less clear. In each instance local circumstances aroused unrest and set one neighbor against another.

Paradoxically, the localized disorders created a national crisis of unparalleled proportions. If the disturbances were confined to local communities, the threat to the gentry, private property, and Protestant reform was nationwide. Occurring in the midst of costly military operations in Scotland, the rebellions and riots forced the government to reorder its priorities. In theory Somerset's domestic program should have guaranteed peace throughout the countryside and permitted the government to concentrate on foreign policy and financial reform, but it had exactly the opposite effect. While it is easy to fault the Protector's government for its failure to cope with the disturbances, no Tudor regime had the competence or resources to deal with such an extensive breakdown of law and order. Somerset and the Council initially had poor intelligence about the nature, location, and extent of the risings. Reports from justices of the peace and gentry were either inadequate and confused or entirely lacking. Without accurate information about the insurrections, Somerset and his colleagues were the prisoners of rumor and uncertainty. Later the government's action was limited by shortages of manpower and arms. Somerset, confronted with disorder from one end of the country to the other — in addition to war with Scotland and France — struggled to restore stability. The localized character of the disturbances and the disunity of the commons made the government's task less difficult.

In East Anglia popular discontent was not limited to Kett and his followers at Norwich. Serious disturbances took place in other parts of Norfolk as well as in Cambridgeshire and Suffolk. Although commons from many Norfolk villages made their way to Mousehold Heath to join Kett, another camp was established in the neighborhood of Castle Rising near King's Lynn. Rebels led by Robert Bunting and Sir John Chaundeler, a priest, tried unsuccessfully to seize King's Lynn but were repulsed by the townsmen. Bunting, who was later pardoned, apparently had a change of heart and surrendered himself to the magistrates of Lynn, but the bolder Chaundeler, making his way southward into Suffolk and Essex, incited the commons with stories of atrocities committed by the gentry around Lynn. He alleged that the gentry sent their servants into the countryside to kill pregnant women and poor men working in the fields.[3] There were smaller camps at Brandon Ferry, Downham Market, and Watton, and a larger assembly at Thetford that drafted formal demands which Thomas Gawdy, justice of the peace, forwarded to the Council. The Thetford rebels opposed the grant of the manor of Thetford to the Duke of Somerset, objected to tolls charged either at the market or at the bridge across the Little Ouse, and demanded changes in the commission on enclosures. The Council agreed to have the manor repossessed by the crown and to permit "the tolls by lease in farm as ye had it before." To deal with complaints against the enclosure commission, the Council sent a herald to Thetford with a list of new names to be included.[4]

From Thetford and Brandon Ferry roads led southward to Bury St. Edmunds, the major center of discontent in Suffolk. In June 1548, a riot broke out at Great Livermere, five miles northeast of Bury, when tenants, armed with spades and shovels, pulled down a hedge enclosing a common. The tenants claimed to have enjoyed ancient common rights for twenty-eight years prior to enclosure.[5] A year later Robert Bell of Gazeley, laborer, John Fuller of Canon, collarmaker, Robert Capp also of Canon, laborer, Thomas Kynge of Gazeley, smith, and John Stephenson of Bury, also a smith, were arrested and imprisoned for complaining to the king about the destruction of their corn and for other illegal activities. They denied participating in any riots but admitted paying four marks to Thomas Roughte of Bury, said to be learned in canon law, for preparing a formal supplication and promising to get a commission from the Council. John Stephenson was accused of saying that if Bell were sentenced to be executed, a hundred men would fetch him away. All five Suffolk men were held at the Tower of London in October 1549, but only Robert Bell was tried and executed on a charge of compassing and imagining the king's death. Numerous other alleged rebels from Suffolk were brought to London and examined although Richard Wade, accused as a "stirrer of sedition," cleared himself and was released after paying a fine.[6]

The only estimate of the size of the rebel camp at Bury St. Edmunds comes from a highly prejudiced source, Sir John Chaundeler, the peripatetic Norfolk priest, who claimed that seven thousand gathered there from the towns of Lavenham, Hadleigh, and Brent Eleigh. The Suffolk rebels submitted a list of articles to the king and Council protesting unlawful enclosures and received a reply in mid-July. The rebel demands have not survived, but the Council's response promised action against illegal enclosures so far as the law permitted and pledged to recall Parliament a month earlier than planned to consider reforms that could not be enacted by the king and Council. Following the approach used in negotiating with Kett, the Council expressed satisfaction that the worst disorders were over and offered generous pardon to everyone who would return to his home peaceably. We know that the

Council was either unduly optimistic about conditions in Suffolk or exceedingly misinformed, because disorder continued into August. Sir John Chaundeler undoubtedly harangued the commons, inciting them to resist the hated gentry, but left no evidence of his religious views. In East Suffolk the rebels established a camp at Ipswich and then, numbering about a thousand, moved to Melton, a small village near Woodbridge. The rebels seized livestock, imprisoned gentry, and held courts to right the wrongs of the commons. One of the rebel leaders was John Harbottle, a small businessman and former town official at Ipswich. It would appear that the Suffolk commotion differed from the Norfolk Rebellion mainly in that it attracted fewer yeomen, tenants, and artisans. Although the rebel leaders achieved very little, the Chaundelers, Harbottles, and Bells took their place in the folklore of the Suffolk countryside where they were remembered not for what they accomplished but for their audacity and bravery.[7]

The best-documented rebellions in East Anglia outside Norfolk were in Cambridgeshire. Serious disorder erupted at Cambridge when the poorer townspeople rose against their more affluent neighbors. They compiled a list of thirty-two complaints directed mainly against unlawful enclosures and the decay of arable husbandry. Prominent among the offenders were four colleges of Cambridge University:

> We find that the master and fellows of Jesus College have let their farm wholly with all commodities together, and the farmer thereof hath let the land to certain persons and severed the dwelling house and the sheepgate from the land so that the house and sheepgate be in divers men's hands and likewise the closes be let from the house, and the whole is let for £10 10s. by the year.
>
> We find that Trinity College hath enclosed a common land, which was a common course both for cart, horse, and man leading to the river unto a common green, and no recompense made therefore.
>
> We find that the said college doth commonly use to lay their muck and manure on their back side upon the foresaid green where they will suffer no man else to do the like and have builded a common jakes [privy] upon part of the same.
>
> We find that the King's College hath taken in and enclosed St. Augustine's lane leading from the High Street unto the waterside without recompense.
>
> We find that the Queen's College have taken in a piece of common ground commonly called Gosling Green without recompense.[8]

The Cambridge colleges for all their lofty devotion to religious reform and humanistic idealism were, to those who knew them best, merely improving landlords.

The colleges were not alone in exploiting the poor. The former town bailiff enclosed part of the Cambridge common for his own benefit, the ex-mayor unlawfully pastured six or seven hundred sheep on the common "to the undoing of the farmers and great hinderance of all the inhabitants of Cambridge," and Master Braken "demised" (conveyed by will or lease) Fisher's lane and "enclosed the same which of late lay open and was common." One offender was a woman, Mistress Lacys, who severed the land and the sheepgate (pasturage or right of pasturage for sheep) of her farms. In another part of the town, houses and shops had been built on land that had previously been common arable fields.[9] The whole tenor of the complaints suggests rapid population growth and the resulting loss of common land to the poor inhabitants of the town. In Cambridge urban growth and improvement both by the townspeople and the colleges worked to the disadvantage of the less fortunate. Although there was a tradition of town and gown rivalry, both parties stood together in favoring the kind of progress that advanced their common vested interests.

Formal complaint gave way to direct action on July 10, 1549, when several hundred malcontents assembled to the beat of a drum, marched to the site of Barnwell priory, now leased to a former town official, and pulled down recently erected fences. Faced with a serious revolt and the destruction of private property, the mayor joined with his traditional enemy, the vice-chancellor of the university, to restore order. The serious rioting lasted only a few days, for Protector Somerset wrote the mayor and vice-chancellor on July 13 praising them for pacifying the unruly mob. Somerset also promised redress of legitimate grievances. He pledged that the commission on enclosures would deal with unlawful acts and empowered the mayor and vice-chancellor to take immediate action "if there be any manifest unlawful enclosures of late made." It is doubtful whether Cambridge authorities fully agreed with Somerset's policy of appeasement, for local records show expenditures for erecting the town gallows and for the purchase of a new rope. Futhermore, William Cecil, the Protector's private secretary, personally intervened to obtain pardon for the rebels. Three days after writing to the mayor and vice-chancellor, Somerset, in response to Cecil's request, sent the king's pardon to offenders in Cambridgeshire together with the hope that in the future they would behave themselves as "faithful subjects not committing the like offences." Unfortunately the names or number of persons executed or pardoned have not survived. The commotion in Cambridge produced positive results in that the poorer inhabitants, even those with no plowland, received the right to use the town commons.[10]

Another disturbance occurred at the open-field village of Landbeach located on the edge of the fen a few miles away. Landbeach consisted of two manors, one of which, Chamberlains, was acquired by Corpus Christi College, Cambridge, in the fourteenth century. The college also held the advowson of the parish church, and it became the regular practice for a senior fellow, often the master himself, to hold the living. The other landlord in the village was Richard Kirby, lord of the manor of Brays, whose family had originally come from London. As resident squire, Kirby became the scourge of the poorer villagers, who looked to Corpus Christi College for the protection of their rights. The college tenants complained that Kirby overstocked the commons with cattle from neighboring villages and deliberately depopulated the village. The college tenants made the following charges:

1. He and all his predecessors hath letten all his tenements fall down to the number of fourteen of which divers were standing within the mind of man and some of very late days decayed.
2. Likely, he intendeth the destruction of the rest of the town, for he wishes that there were no more houses in the town but his own and no more.

Indeed, village records showed that in 1549 there were tenants on only four of Richard Kirby's properties.

When violence erupted in May 1549, relations between the villagers and Kirby were already poisoned. The two sides accused each other of using armed men to seize and impound cattle and sheep. Kirby charged that a dozen men "in riotous manner arrayed, having upon them divers and sundry weapons, arrayed after the fashions and manner of war, that is to say, with bills, bows, arrows, swords, daggers, and other kinds of weapons" went into the fens and unlawfully impounded livestock belonging to him and his tenants. The accused men replied that they were only six in number and had acted on instructions from Corpus Christi College and that they had used only small rods for driving the cattle. While the villagers did not deny Kirby the right to keep livestock on common land, they charged that he had pastured twelve hundred sheep belonging to strangers and had taken sixty cattle in agistment (in feeding at a fixed rate) in additon to eighty of his own. They protested that Kirby went about armed with a sword and dagger and hired armed men to seize cattle in the fen. To dramatize the oppression of Kirby as vividly as possible the villagers emphasized the plight of a poor man named Thomas Mytton, "lately coming out of the king's majesty's wars." Mytton, "having no cattle of his own, hired a poor nag for his meat, the said poor nag grazing upon the common, the said Kirby seized him to his pound treyce [three times] in two years, and at one time he took for the harm that the said nag had done (which indeed was none) 4d., and at another time 4d." These exorbitant charges were levied at a time when the justices of the peace had told Kirby that a single penny for four or five lawfully impounded cattle was a just fine. The controversy was more than a war of words and four-penny fines, because the villagers charged that poor women, including one who was pregnant, had been assaulted and beaten. As J. R. Ravensdale has said, "Rival bands seizing each other's cattle is the very stuff of melodramatic violence and could quickly build up dangerously into local civil war."[11] The conflict in Landbeach was in microcosm the kind of dispute that led to Kett's Rebellion in Norfolk.

The timely intervention of Matthew Parker, master of Corpus Christi College, prevented further violence and loss of life. The college joining with its tenants in Landbeach brought pressure to bear on Richard Kirby. In the autumn a new field book was prepared under the supervison of Parker clarifying the rights of all of the villagers. Until the village was enclosed in the nineteenth century, Parker's field book served as a Domesday survey for resolving local disputes. Kirby, perhaps frightened by the intense hatred directed against the gentry throughout East Anglia, retired to a smaller house in the village and leased the rest of his manor to his son-in-law. Although Parker failed in persuading the rebels on Mousehold Heath to disperse, the future Archbishop of Canterbury, backed by the influence of his college and university, succeeded in restoring some semblance of the rule of law in tiny Landbeach.[12]

Rebels were also active in the counties adjoining East Anglia. Essex, a prosperous enclosed county with a large number of copyholders, appears to have been the scene of greatest turmoil.[13] Information about disturbances in Saffron Walden comes from a native son, Sir Thomas Smith, secretary to Edward VI. When Saffron Walden was incorporated in February 1549, Smith's elder brother became treasurer and his father and uncle were joint keepers of the borough's almshouse.[14] Smith was at Eton in July when he wrote of an "uproar" at Saffron Walden, but he must have had reliable information supplied by his family. The uproar, according to Smith, was the work of seditious watchmen who did all the mischief "themselves being for the most part of that number that hath nothing, and in the night then do they consult how they may invent some mischief; and by reason of them, from town to town, they spread their news faster than any post can." Smith wrote, "If any gentleman come through, he is straight stayed, if they think themselves strong."[15] The wealthier and more influential citizens managed to avoid serving as watchmen, leaving the important responsibility of protecting the town during the night to those likely to be sympathetic to rebels and willing to spread new and rumors. The solution to the problem, as Smith clearly recognized, was to have the justices of the peace prevent unauthorized watchmen from moving about at nighttime. Implementation, however, was more difficult since the better sort of men, the class to which Smith himself belonged, preferred to lie in their beds.

About the same time that the watchmen of Saffron Walden were doing their nocturnal mischief, the Council in London received a list of grievances signed by William Essex in the name of the commons. The "writings," as they were called, have apparently disappeared, but the Council in a condescending tone praised the rebels for the knowledge of the Holy Gospels revealed in their use of Biblical texts and reminded them that true believers obeyed the commandments of the king. That the commons of Essex were protesting against enclosure of pasture is indicated by the Council's disclosure that two enclosure commissioners, Sir Thomas Darcy and Sir John Gates, had received the commons' grievances.[16] Although we know nothing more about the activities of William Essex, both he and another rebel, Nicholas More, an unscrupulous scrivener, were prisoners at the Tower of London in September 1549.[17] Lord Rich, the lord chancellor, ordered the two returned to Brentwood for trial along with Essex's "boy," who was expected to give incriminating evidence against his master. Confidently anticipating the verdict, Rich arranged in advance that Essex should be executed at Malden and More at Braintree.[18]

In August the irrepressible priest, Sir John Chaundeler, traveling southward from Norfolk through Suffolk, arrived at Colchester where he dined at the house of William Browne, a draper and tailor.[19] Sir Roger Peerson, a Colchester priest, and two Suffolk men were also present and heard Chaundeler rave about the revolts in East Anglia. He denounced the gentry of King's Lynn, accusing them of killing poor men and pregnant women, criticized the Privy Council for refusing to hear the commons' complaints, and described in glowing terms the great rebel camps at Bury St. Edmunds and Norwich. The bailiffs of Colchester apprehended Browne, Peerson, and the two Suffolk men, but their interrogation implicated only Chaundeler, who predictably had vanished.[20] Spreading seditious rumors was a capital offense as another Essex man, the bailiff of Romford, learned to his sorrow. The bailiff, arriving in London, had the misfortune of talking with the curate of St. Katherine Christ's Church. The curate inquired curiously, "What news in the country?"

The bailiff's only words were, "It is said that many men be up in Essex, but, thanks be to God, all is in good quiet about us." The zealous curate reported the conversation to City authorities with the result that the "very well-beloved" bailiff of Romford was tried by court martial and hanged.[21]

In Lincolnshire to the north an enclosure riot took place at Kirby Underwood. While John Hassilwood, Esq., was fighting with the Earl of Warwick against Kett, twenty armed men entered his twenty-eight-acre close and destroyed the hedge. Herdsmen from two neighboring towns then brought more than 160 "cattle and beasts" to the close. When Hassilwood attempted to repair the hedge, the commons destroyed it for a second time. The opposing parties argued about the legality of the enclosure before the Court of Star Chamber. Hassilwood contended that the disputed land had been enclosed for ten years without any question or opposition. His neighbors, the defendants, disagreed, saying that the land had been wrongfully enclosed only seven years before. John Drury, a husbandman, stated that Lord Willoughby and other enclosure commissioners ordered constables to open gaps in the hedge in March 1549. The commissioners subsequently declared that the defendants had the right of common. Although the outcome of this dispute is unknown, it appears that the commissioners on enclosure encouraged the commons to challenge the legality of Hassilwood's enclosure, a challenge that led to a riot and destruction of private property.[22]

To the south there was serious popular unrest in Hertfordshire. The county had a long tradition of disorder reaching back to 1381 when the men of Watford, Cheshunt, and Northaw joined the Peasants' Revolt. In 1548, before the enclosure commissioners began their work, the commons rose at Cheshunt and Northaw, adjacent parishes lying near the Middlesex border.[23] Rebels gathered in July of the following year near St. Albans and threatened to "dispark and unclose" land belonging to Sir Richard Lee.[24] A native of Hertfordshire and an expert on military fortifications, Lee was generously rewarded for his services to the crown with land grants throughout the county. In 1544 Henry VIII granted Lee the manors of Hexton and Newland Squillers and monastic property from the nunnery of Sopewell and the abbey of St. Albans. But Lee was also a minor benefactor of St. Albans, for he presented the abbey church with a massive brazen font which he removed from the chapel of Holyrood while campaigning in Scotland.[25] The Hertfordshire commons saw Sir Richard as a rising courtier who was rewarded by the crown at the expense of the local community. Although he may not have been a large-scale encloser, Lee provoked a violent reaction from his less fortunate neighbors. The Council warned the St. Albans rebels to avoid direct action and to seek redress of legitimate grievances from the enclosure commissioners.

The Hertfordshire rising intensified a bitter personal dispute between two Watford men, Henry Heydon and John Warren. The controversy, beginning in 1546 and continuing until 1551 when litigation was begun in the Courts of Star Chamber and Requests, affords a rare insight into the individual grievances that often aggravated popular unrest. The conflict began in 1546 when Heydon, a justice of the peace, asked Warren to vacate a farm that he had leased. Warren's departure was delayed, but the two remained friendly until Warren "did earnestly set forth the king's proceedings concerning the plucking down of images." At this point Warren complained to Sir William Paget and others of the Privy Council that Heydon would not allow the images to be removed from the parish church. The church-warden, a fifty-five-year-old warrener, recalled, however, that before the issuance of the Edwardian injunctions, Warren had been more a favorer of images than Heydon. When asked by Paget what images had been pulled down, Warren answered that they had plucked down four tabernacles (a recess in a wall to contain an image). "Yea," replied Heydon, "and the Trinity [a symbolical figure representing the persons of the Godhead] also." Paget answered that it was the "chiefest thing that ought to be plucked down." Next, one of Heydon's servants repossessed the house and land occupied by Warren. The quarrel intensified as Warren berated Heydon as an "extortioner" and "false justice" and accused him of retaining his (Warren's) goods. These were put into a chamber of the house in the presence of constables and other "honest" people of Watford. The wives also got into the act. Mrs. Heydon would not allow the goods to be removed, and Mrs. Warren retaliated by protesting to no lesser personage than Protector Somerset, who promptly sent a bill of complaint ordering Heydon to return the disputed goods.

The dispute between Henry Heydon and John Warren dragged on until 1549. "At the time of the rising of the people," Warren came forward as a "great favorer" of the commons and was allegedly so troublesome that no one dared meddle with him. Supported by the rebels, Warren brought a bill of particulars to the parish church listing the goods still held by Heydon. Heydon admitted holding certain brewing vessels and a hutch "for to put corn in" but eventually got the upper hand and had his enemy committed to jail. The final battles between the two were fought out in court in 1551. By then John Warren had left Watford, but Heydon was able to assemble a long list of deponents who said that Warren was a troublemaker and would not live peacefully with his neighbors. Warren countered with a suit in the Court of Requests backed by testimonials contending that he had always lived quietly and troubled no one.[26]

Contemporaries saw the disturbances in Oxfordshire and Buckinghamshire as the work of seditious Roman Catholic clergy. "During this hurly-burly amongst the Popish rebels in Cornwall and Devon," wrote John Foxe, "the like commotion at the same time, by such Popish priests as Homes and his fellows began to gender in the parts of Oxford and Buckingham."[27] Upon closer investigation, however, it is clear that social and economic grievances were also important in the eyes of the rebels. Between 1440 and 1520 the region suffered from enclosure and depopulation.[28] In 1549 the Oxfordshire commons first attacked Thame Park, an ancient preserve said to have been enclosed in the Anglo-Saxon period, and killed all the deer. They next proceeded to Rycote, which was imparked in 1539, three miles away, again disparking the land and killing the deer. Deer parks were highly favored by the aristocracy in the early sixteenth century. To the commons these recreational grounds were a symbol of social privilege as well as a waste of valuable pastureland. Both Thame and Rycote were properties of Sir John Williams, treasurer of the Court of Augmentations and M.P. for Oxfordshire.[29]

After destroying Williams's parks, the rebels entered his house at Rycote, "drank their fill of wine, ale, and beer, slew many sheep and ate them." The rebels moved on to Woodstock but, hearing of the advance of a strong military force led by Lord Grey of Wilton, abandoned it for Chipping Norton, located high in the Cotswolds. At Chipping Norton they established a camp large enough to create extreme anxiety among the councillors in London, because it was almost certainly this assembly of the commons that the Council offered pardon and redress of grievance on July 7. It must be presumed that the rebels rejected the Council's terms, since Lord Grey's army attacked the camp successfully and took 200 prisoners.[30]

When Buckinghamshire peasants threatened to demolish enclosures in 1548, Protector Somerset ordered John Hales to return to towns already visited to reassure the inhabitants that enclosure violations would be corrected in a lawful and peaceful manner. Hales was skeptical about the extent of the disorder when he replied: "The like bruits were also declared to my Lord of Warwick at his being in Buckinghamshire, before, at the time, and after our sitting there, which being true I think surely that his lordship would either have committed the parties to ward or else advertised your grace thereof, so much he loveth quietness."[31] The next year rebels appeared at the house of Sir Robert Dormer at Eythrope, near Aylesbury. Left alone to protect the house, Lady Dormer offered hospitality to the rebels, but at the same time shrewdly fortified the place against attack. "Many of all sorts" flocked to Eythrope, but the rebels promised Lady Dormer no harm because of her charity and good works. Although the parks and lands of neighboring gentry suffered severe damage, bands of rebels only passed through Lady Dormer's grounds and trampled the grass.[32]

The opinion of John Foxe that disorder in the two counties was instigated by Catholics is supported by orders for the execution of four Oxfordshire priests: Richard Tomson, vicar of Duns Tew, Henry Joyce, vicar of Chipping Norton, John Wade, curate of Bloxham, and Henry Mathew, a priest from Deddington. Tomson and Wade were eventually pardoned, but a fifth priest, James Webbe, vicar of Barford St. Michael, was tried in London as a rebel captain and executed at Aylesbury.[33] On the other hand, there is no corroborating contemporary testimony that the commons rejected the new prayer book and demanded the restoration of the Latin mass. The vicar of Chipping Norton joined the revolt because four chantry priests in the parish church had been pensioned off under the chantries act, leaving him to minister to 800 parishioners.[34] The tendency of reformers to blame Catholics for all opposition is also noteworthy, for as early as August 1548 John Hales predicted that Papists might attempt to subvert the work of the enclosure commission.[35] The attacks against the gentry and the destruction of deer parks leave little doubt that social and economic grievances contributed to disorder in Oxfordshire and Buckinghamshire. In addition to the five priests, references to eleven other rebels have survived, none of whom were clergymen. Two of the men, Thomas Bowldrey of Haseley and William Bowlar of Watlington, were "captains at the breaking up [of] the parks." Bowldrey was hanged, drawn, and quartered at Oxford, while Bowlar was eventually pardoned. The occupations of three others,

John Brokyns, a craftsman of Islip, Richard Whyttington, a weaver of Deddington, and William Hychecocke, a Buckinghamshire carpenter, testify to the role of artisans in popular disturbances.[36] Lord Grey crushed the rebels of 1549, but Oxfordshire experienced enclosure riots again in 1550 and the 1590s.[37]

Elsewhere in the Midlands unrest was reported in Northamptonshire, Warwickshire, Leicestershire, Rutland, Derbyshire, Staffordshire, Herefordshire,[38] Bedfordshire,[39] and Worcestershire.[40] The disturbances in several of these counties were so minor that information about rebels was not reported. Discontent in Northamptonshire began in 1548 when there was "a foolishness about the mass and sacraments" at Glapthorne. Commons led by John Broughton, John Desborowe, and Richard Trusse created such "great disturbance and disorder" at Glapthorne that the bailiff was reported to be "in much unsurety by the lewdness" of the population.[41] A surprisingly well-informed London butcher protested against enclosures in the county before Protector Somerset and the Council. Speaking directly to Sir William Paget, the butcher allegedly said, "It is notorious the number of commons you have taken in Northamptonshire and the poor people complain that there is no place where they can pasture their stock." Except for a pardon granted at the end of July, nothing is known about rebel activity in the county the following year.[42] From Warwickshire came reports in July 1549 that the commons, aided by servants of the gentry, "began to stir" and planned to "spoil the town of Warwick."[43] The Marquis of Dorset and the Earl of Huntingdon thwarted rebels in Rutland and Leicestershire before a serious commotion could be organized. Huntingdon reported in September that "there have already divers in the county of Rutland been condemned and have suffered for the same."[44] Early in the reign of Edward VI, tenants at Ashbourne, Derbyshire destroyed enclosures surrounding a common where they fed cattle. Matthew Knyveton, Esq. claimed the disputed land was his by right of inheritance and freehold. The controversy reached the Court of the Duchy of Lancaster where Sir William Paget judiciously ordered that the land be divided in the middle by a ditch so that Knyveton and the tenants would each have a share.[45]

There is evidence of both urban and agrarian disorder in Staffordshire. An enclosure riot in May 1549 attracted one hundred persons at Lichfield. The city bellman read a proclamation calling for the destruction of ditches enclosing common land near the city and urged everyone to bring their cattle there. To incite the populace further Robert Plummer rode a white horse through the streets and boasted that he was captain of the commons. Later passions cooled, and Plummer, according to Star Chamber records, suddenly abandoned his agitation to attend a wedding![46] About the same time a mob assembled on Pensnett Chase, a vast expanse extending into the counties of Staffordshire, Worcestershire, and Shropshire. The chase was a possession of the Earl of Warwick and had been enclosed for eight years. The mob, led by a yeoman farmer and the parson of Swinford, destroyed a hedge "to the great hurt and hindrance of the young springs [lambs] growing upon the chase."[47] At Keele in north Staffordshire trouble arose as Sir William Sneyde summoned his servants and tenants for service against Kett in Norfolk. Traditionally, copyholders joined the lord of the manor, but Edward Brett, Gent., and four others refused. They berated Sneyde with "arrogant and terrible words . . . and assembled themselves together arrayed in manner of war to resist." Faced with such overwhelming opposition in what he called "perilous and tumultuous" times, the sensible Sneyde simply abandoned his efforts and went home.[48]

Each of the southern counties with exception of Dorset experienced disorder of one kind or another during the summer months. From Kent to Somerset came reports of illegal assemblies, hostility toward the gentry, and destruction of parks and enclosures. Kent had a tradition of popular discontent reaching back to 1381 when the commons, led by Wat Tyler and inspired by the eloquent preaching of John Ball, captured Maidstone, Rochester, and Canterbury. Terence R. Murphy has calculated that there was at least one insurrection in every generation from the last quarter of the fourteenth century until the mid-sixteenth century.[49] The county literally seethed with unrest throughout the reign of Edward VI, beginning with the protest of radical Commonwealth men and culminating in widespread Anabaptist activity. One Commonwealth activist, George Fletcher, a married man with eight children, was apprehended and charged in September 1549 with speaking seditious words. It was alleged that Fletcher practiced mischief under the pretense of simplicity and poverty, but Sir Anthony Aucher nonetheless recommended that he be treated leniently.[50] The most interesting figure, however, was a man named Latimer, usually incorrectly identified as Hugh Latimer, the court preacher and former bishop, who traveled up and down the countryside speaking at inns and tippling houses. In every town and village he accepted bills of complaint and boasted that he had Protector Somerset "in his sleeve." As Somerset's appointed or self-appointed spokesman, Latimer enraged the gentry by arranging pardons for some of his followers. Whereas Aucher had favored mercy for George Fletcher, he wanted the "lusty knave" Latimer cuffed and beaten.[51]

Although it is difficult to establish the exact circumstances and chronology of the rebellion in Kent, a number of areas were affected. In July 1549 rebels advanced to Eltham, according to the Imperial ambassador, and pulled down one of the king's parks. The ambassador also heard rumors that the rebels threatened to come to London to release prisoners in the Tower and feared the worst because the city was "over full of people who asked for nothing better than an opportunity of sacking it."[52] About the same time rebels began to gather outside

Canterbury. They abused the king of arms sent to negotiate with them, demanded payments of money for the poor, and prepared a set of articles for Protector Somerset, which regrettably have not survived. Canterbury officials were also alarmed by the circulation of seditious letters within the city. The Protestant reformer, Richard Turner, preached twice before the camp and, like Matthew Parker at Norwich, bravely faced angry men who threatened his life. To restore order officials employed several expedients. A messenger was dispatched to London to obtain artillery, pardons were offered, and money was drawn from the Canterbury mint to buy off some of the rebels. It is not known which approach was most successful, but the camp dispersed in August with little destruction of property and minimal loss of human life.[53]

Other disturbances occurred in the Maidstone area, and in Sheppey when 500 villagers demolished fences and opened pastureland belonging to Sir Thomas Cheyney. An East Malling man was accused of sedition in the spring of 1549, while rebels destroyed enclosures in the parish of Boxley. Many years later, when Elizabeth was queen, old John Fletcher, yeoman, of Maidstone, possibly one of George Fletcher's eight children, remembered the great "rebellion of the commonwealth." He recalled which enclosures had been cast down by the rioters and added that he had helped enclose a portion of woods while employed by Sir Thomas Wyatt. In attempting to explain the motivation of the rebels, Peter Clark concluded that "the cumulative pressure of economic distress and seigneurial abuse drove the Kentish peasantry to collective, and, as far as class terminology can be said to have any meaning in this period, to class action — in self-defence."[54]

Complaints against the Sussex gentry "chiefly for enclosures, where cause in truth was found" prompted the dramatic intervention of the Earl of Arundel. Although well-armed and supported by the gentry together with their household servants, the earl decided to avoid a military confrontation and met the rebels face-to-face at Arundel Castle. The men, trusting Arundel as their "ancient and chiefest lord" according to a rather uncritical biography written in 1580, came into his presence, dined at great tables placed in the courtyard of the castle, and discussed their grievances. When Arundel found the gentry to be at fault, he ordered them to mend their ways: "Where again it was found that some of their ringleaders, as mutinying varlets, had animated the people upon false suggestion, such did his lordship set by the heels in the marketplaces of Arundel and Chichester several market days, in open show of the country, for example to the residue." The earl's even-handed feudal justice reminded Lawrence Stone of the great French king, Louis IX, who three centuries earlier heard the complaints of his subjects under an oak tree. This remarkable drama, appropriately acted out at one of the great medieval castles of Sussex, was wholly out of character with the bitter class hatred evoked in other areas, but it did reveal, as

Stone has shown, the "cohesive psychological bond" that held society together.[55]

Compared with the Earl of Arundel's apparently successful reconciliation of the commons and gentry, other evidence concerning disorder in Sussex is fragmentary and inconclusive. It is clear, however, that Tudor Sussex was not a feudal paradise where all men lived as brothers tilling the soil under the watchful eye of a judicious and paternalistic nobility. In the latter years of Henry VIII there had been armed riots around Waldron, Laughton, Hoathly, and Lordington in which enclosures were destroyed, hedges burned, and livestock taken out of pound. About the same time a complaint was made against engrossing and overgrazing of sheep at farms in Preston and Patcham. During the summer of 1549 Protector Somerset examined and pardoned rebels from the Chichester area. Other Sussex men were less fortunate. Richard Tomson, a tilemaker of Harting, was arrested by Sir Anthony Windsor on July 29 and charged with saying that the king would have trouble again before November. John Patchyn, a yeoman of Horsham, was found guilty of compassing and imagining the king's death and executed at Tyburn notwithstanding his plea of innocence.[56]

Tudor Middlesex was still a rural county although its proximity to London resulted in rapid growth of population and wealth. In May 1548 complaints to the Council about the royal chase at Hampton Court led to a decision to remove the deer to the forest of Windsor. The chase had been built for Henry VIII so that the aged and infirm king might have easy access to hunting. The Council's action was a clear victory for local residents who recovered the land at the old rents. Whether it was a consequence of lobbying by Commonwealth reformers must remain an open question. An enclosure controversy at Enfield was not so amicably resolved. In the autumn of 1547 Robert Wood, Gent., and other tenants of Durants manor, Enfield made a complaint to the Court of the Duchy of Lancaster against Sir Thomas Wroth. The issue was some twenty-four acres of common pasture that had been enclosed in 1546. The court ordered Wroth to pay 6d. per acre to the inhabitants of the town "to be employed and bestowed in such deeds of charity" as the townspeople thought appropriate. This apparently generous settlement was a failure, because in July 1549 over twenty armed men rioted and destroyed ditches as well as grass. The Privy Council considered the matter in August and committed the ringleaders to prison.[57]

Compared to Kent, Sussex and Middlesex, the commons of Surrey left behind very little evidence of discontent. Surviving estate records for the Carews of Beddington and Mores of Loseley give no indication of trouble.[58] Nor do there appear to have been any executions in the county. Yet on June 29 the Earl of Arundel, who was justice of the peace for Surrey as well as Sussex, wrote to Sir William Petre from Guildford, "You shall understand that these parts remain as well as may be, in a quavering quiet." The following day the Council ordered Sir Christopher More, one of the most influential gentry in the Guildford area, to assemble and arm as many men as possible. This force of horse and foot, drawn from More's friends, favorers, servants, and tenants, was to be held in readiness for service at a moment's notice. Two months later, when the crisis had passed, another justice, Henry Polsted, complained that "the 'partyes' of Guildford, Farnham, Godalming, Chertsey and the other parishes thereabout" lacked sufficient numbers of reliable gentry owing primarily to the death of Sir Christopher More. Polsted also complained about the absence of a common jail in either Sussex or Surrey. He spoke vaguely of "stirs" around Guildford; and another source, dating from the reign of Elizabeth, states that rebels pulled down the pale or fence surrounding the park at Witley, located south of Godalming.[59] Both Guildford and Godalming were centers of the Surrey cloth industry, but we find no protests against overgrazing sheep or conversion of arable land to pasture.

Among several serious disturbances in Hampshire, the most intriguing was a non-event, a bizarre conspiracy at Winchester that never materialized. Mid-Tudor Winchester was a stagnant cathedral city where the bishop, Stephen Gardiner, exercised great influence. An opponent of the Edwardian Reformation, Gardiner was charged with encouraging religious contention in Winchester and Hampshire and imprisoned in 1548. A year later Hampshire justices of the peace examined Andrew Blakman, yeoman, of Horwell and Richard Sylver, a servant of the king, of Clatford. The pair confessed to conversations with John Garnham, a Winchester carpenter and would-be rebel. Meeting at the sign of the Crown, Garnham revealed his bold plan to Blakman.

"Thou art a good fellow," he said. "We have ten thousand men in readiness, for Flynte he will bring a great sight of them out of Sussex. And we shall have all the bishop's tenants full and whole, and all the country round about will repair unto us, for I know there is not one of the bishop's servants but if he have 12d. we shall have 6d. of it, for Bishop's Waltham and Botley look every day when we shall begin. And we do but tarry for an answer of Flynte, and we shall begin our first meeting at Ports Down."

With these vague but highly suggestive words Garnham implied that a rising of ten thousand men drawn from the tenants of Stephen Gardiner, Bishop of Winchester, and from West Sussex would begin at Ports Down, a few miles north of Portsmouth. He then invited Blakman and Sylver to accompany him to Botley, where they would meet Flynte and learn "all the whole matter." Botley, a village located between Southampton and Portsmouth, had been the center of disorder the previous year. In December 1548 pardons were granted to a group of laborers, husbandmen, a beer brewer, and a horse gelder from Botley, Hamble, and other places for unspecified treasons, conspiracies, and riots.

Andrew Blakman, obviously a cautious and skeptical yeoman, hesitated and asked, "Yea, but is not this a feigned matter?"

"No, by God's blood," replied Garnham, "it is no feigned matter. Stick therefore to it, for we shall have a fair day."

Blakman demanded more information, particularly about how the rebellion would be financed. Garnham answered, "Tush, hold thy peace, for we shall have all the aid of the priests in the close, and we shall have money enough." When pressed for more details, Garnham mentioned the chancellor of the diocese; John White, the warden of Winchester College; and Peter Langryge, formerly prebendary of Winchester, as financial supporters of the conspiracy.

Blakman, still skeptical, inquired, "Did you ever ask them this question?"

"Yea, twice," Garnham replied.

Next Blakman wanted to know whether the clergy would "depart with any by and by."

"Nay," said Garnham, "not till we be together. And then when we be come together to Longwood we must send to them for two barrels of beer and let as we would take them from them forslie [forcibly]. And then we shall have therein all the money which the same priests have." He went on to explain that the rebel force, equipped with carts supplied by local farmers and ordnance brought from Selsey, would proceed to Salisbury where they would "strike off the mayor's head."

"Why will you do so?" asked Blakman.

"Mary, then will all the villains which be gone against the western men flee," said Garnham, "and then will the western men come over with speed, and we shall come over their backs and destroy them all and in especial the villain Herbert."

Blakman and Sylver, after hearing of the plan to destroy Sir William Herbert and his army, agreed to go to Botley. When they arrived, the people welcomed Garnham "as though he had been a very honest man." Then Garnham and the son of a farmer from Waltham began to make "a banner of the five wounds and with a chalice and a host and a priest kneeling to it upon the same banner." However, the archconspirator Flynte, upon whom the success of the conspiracy depended, failed to appear, forcing Garnham to return to Winchester to await further developments. Here the account breaks off, leaving the distinct impression that nothing more ever materialized. Possibly Flynte was captured, for he was a prisoner in the Fleet in 1551. This strange tale is as important for what it says as for what it does not say. The alleged complicity of the clergy together with the banner of the five wounds of Christ, chalice, and host reveal the strong Catholic sentiments of the conspirators. On the other hand, the absence of complaints against either the gentry or enclosures suggests a social milieu very different from Kett's Norfolk. Nowhere did Garnham say how the men of Hampshire would benefit from the rising. In fact, it appears that the conspiracy had as its only purpose the assistance of the Western rebels who faced defeat at the hands of Lord Russell and Sir William Herbert.[60]

Another troublemaker causing concern to the authorities at Winchester was a mysterious Friar Wigg who "used language there of the limitation of the king's majesty's reign nothing unlike a traitor." Wigg probably questioned King Edward's authority to introduce Protestant reforms during his minority, following a line of argument popular among pro-Catholic clergy. Protector Somerset called for Wigg's apprehension and imprisonment in July, but the friar promptly left the city after receiving a warning from his servant. The mayor of Winchester, embarrassed by his failure to capture Wigg, wrote to officials at Southampton asking them to capture Wigg if he appeared there.[61]

Southampton unfortunately had problems of its own, because of a dispute over pasture rights in the salt-marsh east of the town. A source of friction since 1500, the salt-marsh was the cause of a riot in 1517 involving 300 persons. In 1549 the townspeople protested that Thomas Bettes, Gent., of Northam kept too many sheep on the salt-marsh. Bettes, a rich and enterprising farmer who was the son of the former collector of customs at Southampton, wished to use public pasture for private gain. The Court Leet, in response to complaints against Bettes, held that he "of right ought to have no common . . . but only for that he is a burgess he may common as a burgess may according to the ordinances of the town." The Court Leet further declared that each burgess was entitled to keep only two beasts at a time on the salt-marsh. On June 14, a month later, the mayor and council ignored the presentment of the Court Leet and gave Bettes the right to pasture 200 sheep on the salt-marsh until August 1. Although the officials of Southampton were able to control the angry populace, it was necessary to order two watchmen to keep the walls and four to walk the streets during the night.[62]

Overton, King's Somborne, and Odiham were other centers of popular unrest in Hampshire. The "misorder and disobedience" at Overton may have been connected with enclosures, because the town was located in an area of large-scale capitalist farming where sheep were kept in large numbers.[63] At King's Somborne rioters destroyed the deer park and its pale. Sir John Thynne inquired into disorder at Odiham, a town with a large park and a decayed castle that once sheltered King John. In June a large number of rebels, many of whom were strangers unknown in Odiham, spoiled, killed, and took away cattle and sheep belonging to John Norton, Esq., a justice of the peace. The rebels dispersed when Thynne offered the king's pardon, but later Norton aroused more hostility when he forced his neighbors to pay him for his losses. Some peasants were fined £3 and others £5 or more. The dispute was brought before the Court of Star Chamber by George Rithe, Esq. of Lyss, who championed the cause of the commons primarily because of a personal quarrel with Norton. Rithe contended that Norton had collected £200 in fines whereas the damage resulting from the riot had amounted only to £40 to £50. John Norton wholly denied Rithe's allegations and said that he collected only £30, a sum far below losses which he put at £300. Although the gentry at times instigated small riots to advance their own interests, it is unlikely that George Rithe's role went beyond assisting the peasants in Star Chamber. The Norton's park affair emerged again when Sir John Thynne followed his patron Somerset into political oblivion. In November 1549 the Privy Council asked Thynne whether he had encouraged the rebels to pluck down Norton's park or spoil his house. Thynne, of course, denied all, maintaining that he had done everything in his power to pacify the unruly commons.[64]

The picture of popular discontent that emerges in Hampshire is a mosaic of religious and social unrest. John Garnham's elaborate plans for a massive rising to assist the Western rebels came to naught, and the Catholic clergy of Winchester lost their champion when Stephen Gardiner was deprived of his bishopric. The commons protested vigorously against the loss of pasture rights and highhandedness of the gentry but failed to organize a rising that reached beyond the boundaries of a town or parish.[65]

A few miles to the north in Berkshire small disturbances occurred which seem to have been related to the risings in Oxfordshire and Buckinghamshire. But the trouble in Berkshire continued into the autumn, for two weavers of Newbury and a shoemaker of Reading were arrested in November for "machinating and compassing the king's death." Although the three protested of their innocence, they were found guilty and executed at Reading.[66] Unrest in Wiltshire resulted from the enclosure of parks and common land and followed the pattern already seen in East Anglia and the Midlands. Peasants at Wilton near Salisbury "plucked down Sir William Herbert's park . . . about his new house and divers other parks and commons" that were enclosed in the area. The Wiltshire commons, like Kett's men in Norfolk, confined their anger to attacks on property and harmed no one. "They say they will obey the king and Protector," a correspondent in London wrote, "but will not have commons and grounds enclosed and taken from them."[67]

Popular disorder at Bristol, one of the country's largest provincial capitals, closely paralleled what took place at Southampton. In May 1549 young men broke down hedges and thrust down ditches near the city and organized an insurrection against the mayor. Unpaid soldiers also contributed to urban unrest. Discharged and sent home without traveling money, "excepting that their captain was appointed to give them some money from his own purse," the soldiers sold their coats and harnesses and grumbled about their shabby treatment. The mayor and city officials managed to restore order without inflicting capital punishment. One benevolent official, William Chester, took special pains to obtain pardons for unruly persons who were guilty of rioting. To protect the city the walls and castle were armed with men and guns. The gates were rebuilt, and watchmen policed the streets both day and night. Outside assistance came from Lord Grey, who stopped at Bristol en route to Devon. His presence assisted the mayor, and he almost certainly recruited any unpaid soldiers wishing to join the army.[68]

Somerset was the scene of two separate risings. The first took place in May when 200 "weavers, tinkers and other artificers" assembled at Frome and pulled down hedges and fences. The men saw themselves as acting within the law of the land and echoed the cry of the Commonwealth reformers when they asked, "Why should one man have all and another nothing?" At the height of the rebellion the leaders boasted that if any of their number were imprisoned, they would be released by a force of a thousand men. There was also a "lewd uproar of the people" in the southwestern part of the county that forced Sir Hugh Paulet to remain at his house at Hinton St. George until mid-June.[69] The second rising came in the aftermath of the rebels' defeat in Devon. John Bury of Devon, one of the leaders of the Western rebellion, raised a force said to number fifteen hundred at Kingweston. Lord Russell's victorious army overtook the rebels and dealt them a crushing defeat. John Bury was tried for treason with Robert Kett and executed at Tyburn.[70]

The Yorkshire rebellion, although geographically separate from the other centers of disorder, fits into the general pattern seen in East Anglia, the Midlands, and the South. The major difference lay in the brutal murder of four persons. The rebellion, which began late in July 1549, affected an area of about eighty square miles to the south and west of Scarborough. Formerly dominated by the powerful Percy family, the district was part of the Vale of Pickering where common field agriculture was rapidly giving way to the newer "up and down husbandry." The new husbandry — described as "the backbone of the agricultural revolution" — was the conversion of permanent tillage and grassland to alternating tillage and grass. "In up-and-down husbandry," wrote Eric Kerridge, "everything hinged on the arable fields, known as 'pastures,' being laid down to grass for a few years and then ploughed up and tilled for a time, all the farmland, saving some pieces of wet meadow and permanent grass being subject to the same treatment." In good years the Vale of Pickering produced an abundance of butter, cattle, sheep, bacon, and oats. As a farming region it resembled the Midlands and East Anglia more than upland areas of northern England.[71]

The rebellion resulted from a combination of religious and economic grievances.[72] John Foxe, the primary authority for the details of the revolt, held that the commons' "traitorous hearts grudging at the king's most godly proceedings in advancing and reforming the true honor of God and his religion" was the principal cause of disaffection. Yorkshire was an extremely conservative county and showed little enthusiasm for the Protestantism of the Edwardian reformers. Opposition to the dissolution of chantries was heard in Hull, and Pontefract; and Seamer, the center of the rebellion, was the site of two of the many chantries that dotted the countryside. As a second cause of the rising, Foxe spoke of a "blind and a phantastical prophecy" that motivated the poorest of the commons to seek vengeance against the gentry:

> The tenor of which prophecy and purpose together of the traitors was, that there should no king reign in England, that the noblemen and gentlemen should be destroyed, and the realm should be ruled by four governors, to be elected and appointed by the commons, holding a parliament in commotion [sic] to begin at the south and north seas of England, etc. Supposing that this their rebellion in the North, and the other of the Devonshiremen in the West, meeting (as they intended) at one place, should be the mean how to compass this their traitorous devilish devise.[73]

The prophecy revealed the desperate and unattainable aspirations of a superstitious society. Through the destruction of the old order the Yorkshire commons hoped that a new community of free men might be born. But in Yorkshire — as elsewhere — a vast gulf separated the dream and its realization. Whether the Yorkshire rebels were more committed to restoring Roman Catholicism or to the destruction of the nobility and gentry must remain a moot question. Although it is possible to view either objective with sympathy, the rebels' efforts to achieve their goals through brutal and senseless killing remind us of the savage barbarism that lurked on the fringe of Tudor society.

Three men organized the rebellion: William Ombler of East Heslerton, yeoman; Thomas Dale, parish clerk of Seamer; and a man named Stevenson, a neighbor of Dale and nephew of Ombler. Stevenson served as an intermediary bringing together Dale and Ombler, who lived seven miles apart. The trio, moved by their hatred of religious reform and their belief in the prophecy, met together on St. James Day, July 25. After arousing the commons in the parishes of Seamer and Wintringham, they, "beginning with the rudest and poorest sort," planned to assemble their followers at Seamer and East Heslerton by burning beacons during the night. "To the intent they would give more terror to the gentlemen at their first rising, lest they should be resisted, they devised that some should be murdered in churches, some in their houses, some in serving the king in commission, and others as they could be caught; and to pick quarrels with them for alteration of service on the holy days." Before this bold plan could be carried out, one of the conspirators, Calverd, under the influence of drink, revealed some of the details at an alehouse in Wintringham. The idle talk and boasting of the drunk aroused the suspicions of the gentry, who notified Archbishop Holgate, Lord President of the Council in the North, and took appropriate precautionary measures.[74] The rebels, however, merely shifted the center of their operations to Staxton, a few miles south of Seamer, where they lighted the beacon and assembled a large company of supporters.

The rebel force led by Ombler and Dale proceeded to the house of Matthew White, a chantry commissioner for Yorkshire, who was hated as an agent of the government's religious reforms. The rebels seized White and three others: Clopton, his brother-in-law; Savage, a merchant from York; and Berry, a servant of Sir Walter Mildmay, general surveyor of the Court of Augmentations. The victims were taken from Seamer toward the wold, where they were murdered. The corpses, stripped of clothes and purses, were left behind for the crows to feed on until the widows of White and Savage could arrange burial. Afterwards rebel bands ranged at will throughout the countryside increasing their numbers to as many as three thousand. Following the policy used in other areas of disorder, the government offered pardon to all who would lay down their arms and return home before August 21. Ombler, like Kett, refused pardon and continued to incite the commons. He moved on toward Hunmanby in the East Riding, traveling from town to town before the gentry captured him and brought him to York. Within a short time all of the ringleaders were apprehended, and the rebellion subsequently collapsed. Ombler, Dale, and six of their closest associates were tried and executed at York on September 21.

The Yorkshire rebellion had many puzzling and unexplained features. Although Ombler and Dale were committed to the restoration of Catholicism, they apparently had little support from the clergy. Nor is there any evidence that they restored the Latin mass in areas under their control. Matthew White and Berry were murdered presumably as a protest against the government's dissolution of the chantries, but Clopton and Savage were innocent victims of the rebels' rage. In spite of the rebels' avowed destruction of the gentry, no prominent Yorkshire family sustained harm. The Vale of Pickering, of which Seamer, Wintringham, and East Heslerton were part, was in the process of enclosure and conversion to up-and-down husbandry; yet the rebels destroyed no hedges or other property. Many of the unanswered questions may be attributed to inadequate sources, for John Foxe was better informed about events in southern England than in the distant north. Curiously, the major Yorkshire chronicler, Robert Parkyn, knew even less about the rebellion than Foxe.[75]

The outbreak of disorder in what the Grey Friars chronicler called "all other parts of all the realm" constituted a massive challenge to Protector Somerset's government.[76] With the advantage of hindsight, we can see that many of the disturbances never developed beyond vigorous local protests,[77] but under only slightly different circumstances the rebels might have rivalled the success of their counterparts who besieged Exeter and camped with Kett on Mousehold Heath. In Hampshire and

Oxfordshire, where religion was a leading issue, local clergy assumed leadership roles or worked actively behind the scenes. Opposition to the enclosure of commons and controversy over land use were most pronounced in Suffolk, Cambridgeshire, Hertfordshire, and Kent. Often a combination of religious and economic grievances interacted to produce popular discontent. In most areas of unrest, angry commons opposed the gentry and town officials. The rebels found no leaders of the stature of Robert Kett or Humphrey Arundell, and they failed to coordinate their efforts to right the wrongs that they felt so deeply.

Although the disorders had different causes, each threatened the authority of central and local government. Somerset and the Council, like all Tudor governments, relied heavily on local officials to enforce social, economic, and religious policies. If for any reason central and local government failed to cooperate, the potential for rebellion and riot increased. Shortly after the accession of Edward VI, Somerset and the Council sent circular letters to each county reappointing the justices of the peace because all commissions expired on the death of Henry VIII. The Council exhorted the justices to do their duty to preserve the peace and ordered them to remain in close communication with the government in London. The Council directed the justices to write once every six weeks indicating "in what state that shire standeth and whether any notable things have happened or were like to happen." These instructions, coming at a time when the influence of the cautious Sir William Paget was at its height, suggests that the Council anticipated the possibility of trouble as a consequence of the boy king's succession to the throne of his powerful father. The absence of reports from the provinces indicates that negligent justices may have been responsible for the sudden and widespread outbreak of popular disturbances.[78]

Further evidence that Somerset's government was alert to the danger of rebellion may be seen in an "order to be taken for repressing of commotions and uproars if any such shall happen in the counties of Oxfordshire, Berkshire, and Buckinghamshire." This undated plan to head off disorder before it became a serious menace was probably prepared in the early summer of 1549. The directive recognized that law and order in the countryside depended on the vigilance and close cooperation of the gentry and local officials. The gentry were ordered to "put their tenants in readiness" and inform them that their lands would be forfeited if they failed to serve their lord. If any gentleman left his house, he was to leave word of his whereabouts; if it was necessary for him to leave the county, he was ordered to "leave behind such men and furniture as he shall condescend unto for the aid of the shire." The Oxfordshire gentry were required to confer with their counterparts in the neighboring counties of Buckinghamshire and Berkshire and join with them if necessary. In market towns mayors, constables, bailiffs, and head officers were expected to make special efforts to preserve the peace and be ready to attend on the justices of the peace with loyal servants. Town constables were to "take a view of harness within the same [town], . . . take it into their hands," and bring it to the justice appointed for the hundred where the town was located. Town officials were required to appoint honest men to the watch. At the center of this elaborate scheme stood the justices of the peace. If popular disturbances erupted, each justice was to report to an assigned hundred and from there coordinate military efforts of the gentry.

The order for repressing "commotions and uproars" included a provision for trials by martial law. Four gentry from each county were to be named marshals "to see execution done upon mutineers or rebels." Suspected offenders were to be brought before a commission of two justices and two gentry for examination and "so being found guilty, their persons together with their examination shall be sent to the marshal . . . for execution to be done immediately" at the nearest market town on the next market day.[79] The executions in Oxfordshire leave no doubt that the procedures for martial law were implemented.[80] It is not known how fully other aspects of the plan were put into operation or whether similar schemes were devised for other parts of the country.

Although the government's plan failed to prevent riot and rebellion, the gentry and nobility successfully restored law and order in Yorkshire, East Anglia (except for Norfolk), the Midlands, and the South. The Earl of Arundel, assuming the role of a paternalistic overlord, pacified the commons in West Sussex, while the Marquis of Dorset and the Earl of Huntingdon pacified the Midlands. Despite the intense class hatred that infected many rebels, the Edwardian aristocracy still managed to draw on the old traditions of rural England, and the commons continued to practice loyalty, obedience, and deference to their betters, even when the good lordship of the aristocracy was more myth than reality. Urban officials at Cambridge, Colchester, Southampton, Winchester, and Bristol acted vigorously and cooperated with the central government. Norwich was the only city where local authorities were unable to maintain control. The fact that outside military force was required only in Oxfordshire and Somerset is persuasive evidence that the propertied classes were fully capable of ruling the countryside and towns. The rebel leaders — priests, yeomen, and artisans — opposed Protestant reforms, resisted the gentry, and challenged the authority of local government but failed to achieve their objectives.

 *Andrew Woodcock, one of the bridgemasters, was straightly commanded by the court to provide with all speed timber to make a false drawbridge of, to be used for a season in case need should require by reason of the stirring of the people (which God defend) to cast down the other.*

Repertory 12 (1), fol. 104v. July 11, 1549.

7. LONDON

London stood as a pivot in a country engulfed by rebellion. News and rumors of rebel activity came from all corners of the kingdom, and throughout July and August 1549 the City was exposed to attack by rebels from the surrounding counties as well as from Devon and Norfolk. Couriers returning from the West reported on Lord Russell's advance toward Exeter, while refugees from Norwich must have told exaggerated tales of Robert Kett. The City swarmed with soldiers who disrupted business and the normal routine of urban life. Anxiety was further heightened by the City's proximity to Westminster, where Protector Somerset and the Council worked to organize the government's counteroffensive. In retrospect we know well enough that rebel leaders failed to launch an attack on London and that the City remained secure, but the mayor and aldermen, who struggled feverishly to maintain law and order, were not privileged to foresee how the unfolding drama of popular rebellion would end.

The threat to London was not merely an external one arising from disorder in the provinces, because the country's largest urban center had a long tradition of internal unrest. "Food riots, often led by apprentices, recurred throughout the sixteenth century and were a constant cause of government concern."[1] Early in the reign of Henry VIII, inhabitants of the surrounding towns of Islington, Hoxton, and Shoreditch enclosed common fields with hedges and ditches that interfered with the shooting and recreational walks of Londoners. Citizens were so infuriated that an angry mob armed with spades and shovels boldly destroyed the enclosures and filled the ditches.[2] The Evil May Day riots of 1517 were the most striking example of popular discontent in London. Grievances were directed against foreign merchants and artisans and as such were primarily economic although the privileges granted to foreigners represented government policy. Military forces led by the Earls of Shrewsbury and Surrey quickly restored order. Over four hundred persons were arrested and fourteen executed, including John Lincoln, the principal agitator. The City aroused itself again in 1525 to resist Cardinal Wolsey's Amicable Grant, an income tax not sanctioned by Parliament. The outcry was so loud that the king and cardinal were obliged to back down. Wolsey was greatly offended and is reported to have said that the whole of London were traitors to the king. The City's opposition to Wolsey sprang from its historic anticlericalism as well as from its dislike of his financial policies. Earlier, as a result of the Hunne case, London anticlericalism had assumed massive proportions, and after the fall of Wolsey in 1529, it was to assist the king and Thomas Cromwell in legislating the break with Rome.

A small merchant oligarchy, led by the mayor and aldermen, governed early Tudor London. The Court of Aldermen, whose members represented each of the City's twenty-five wards, exercised great executive and judicial power. The larger Common Council, made up of company liverymen, served as the City's legislature but was subordinate to the Court of Aldermen. The two sheriffs were chosen from the aldermen and carried out important police and judicial duties. Throughout the century the Twelve Great Companies — Mercers, Grocers, Drapers, Fishmongers, Goldsmiths, Skinners, Taylors, Haberdashers, Salters, Ironmongers, Vintners, and Cloth-workers — dominated politics, often at the expense of the lesser companies. G. D. Ramsay has written that "London owed its economic ebullience and its aldermen their wealth to virtually one thing only — the English woollen cloth traffic." The Company of Merchants Adventurers, whose members were officially listed among the larger companies, controlled the cloth trade and by the mid-sixteenth century became "the effective masters of London."[3]

The wealth, the prestige, and the favored location of London attracted peers, gentry, and aspiring courtiers who spent lavishly and sometimes recklessly. John Stow recalled the construction of Thomas Cromwell's house in Throgmorton Street. Small tenements were cleared away to make room for the imposing edifice. When the house was finished, Cromwell enlarged his garden at the expense of Stow's father and other less privileged Londoners:

> He caused the pales of the gardens adjoining to the north part thereof on a sudden to be taken down; twenty-two feet to be measured forth right into the north of every man's ground; a line there to be drawn, a trench to be cast, a foundation laid, and a high brick wall to be built. My father had a garden there, and a house standing close his south pale; this house they loosed from the ground, and bare upon rollers into my father's garden twenty-two feet, ere my father heard thereof. No warning was given him, nor other answer, when he spake to the surveyors of that work, but that their master Sir Thomas commanded them so to do. No man durst go to argue the matter, but each man lost his land, and my father paid his whole rent, which was 6s. 6d. the year for that half which was left.[4]

About the same time Henry VIII's brother-in-law, Charles Brandon, Duke of Suffolk built a "large and most sumptuous house" in Southwark which was later converted to a royal mint. The Earl of Warwick and Sir William Paget secured London residences by acquiring former bishops' houses, while Protector Somerset demolished a former priory church to build Somerset House. Lawrence Stone estimated that by 1560 about half the peerage had a London town house.[5]

Life for the great majority of Londoners was very different from that of the courtiers and rich merchants. The ranks of the poor and unemployed swelled as the population rose from 60,000 in 1520 to 200,000 at the end of the century, when London had nearly fifteen times the population of its nearest rival, Norwich. Most of the population increase came from immigration, because overcrowding, squalid living conditions, and the persistence of the plague limited the natural increase. J. F. D. Shrewsbury argued that London was the "chief focus and principal disseminating center" of the plague in England and found "strong evidence that London was the scene of local outbreaks of the disease in the interval between national outbreaks." The city was infected every few years throughout the 1520s and 1530s and again in 1543. The first two years of the reign of Edward VI were plague years, and the pestilence lingered into the autumn of 1548 before it was extinguished by cold weather. Stow documented vividly the extremes of wealth and poverty within the City. In contrast to the fine houses of the wealthy, he saw in Bishopsgate ward small houses "built with alleys backward, of late time too much pestered with people" and "filthy cottages" near the church in Whitechapel. At Shoreditch he observed the "continual building of small and base tenements." Social stratification created a potential for conflict that required the continuous vigilance of City authorities.[6]

The Henrician Reformation contributed to unrest as radical Protestants attacked the Church and demanded more rapid change. The authorized English Bible nourished enthusiasts whose appetites were already whetted on illegal Lutheran writings smuggled into the city. A bricklayer, John Harrydaunce, preaching from the window of his house, drew crowds of listeners. A group of Londoners, including the landlord of the Saracen's Head in Friday Street and Thomas Gardiner and his three apprentices, "had to answer the accusation that they had gathered together secretly in the evening and introduced ill preachers among the people." Hugh Eton, a hosier, was another troublemaker, who disguised himself in "fond fashion" and walked up and down in St. Bride's Church disturbing the priests before mass. For his misbehavior Eton was placed in a cage in Fleet Street with a paper on his head setting forth his offenses against the Church.[7]

At the beginning of the reign of Edward VI, religious discontent was one of the most vexing problems facing City authorities. "Violent discussion and controversy, especially regarding the mass," said W. K. Jordan, "could not be stilled by fiat, and even the licensed clergy declined to be restrained by guidelines laid down somewhat naively by the Council. There was disorder in St. Paul's every Sunday, inspired by a now almost fanatical demand that the mass be disowned."[8] On May 3, 1548 a bill declaring the misdemeanors of certain unnamed persons against the priest of St. Botoloph without Aldgate was read before the Court of Aldermen by Henry Goodyere who then delivered it to the mayor for presentation to the Lord Chancellor. Two days later the mayor with a deputation of aldermen appeared before Protector Somerset and the Council to explain the behavior of rash preachers.[9] In September Charles Tylby, a youthful troublemaker of only twelve or thirteen, cast his cap at the sacrament of the mass at St. Mary Woolnoth and was sentenced to be whipped naked.[10] The lenience of Protector Somerset toward radicals is revealed in a letter in behalf of John Armstrong sent to the aldermen. Armstrong and several accomplices had pulled down altars in the parish church of St. Leonard's, East Cheap. The Court of Aldermen, agreeing to obey Somerset's request, took sureties of the offenders and allowed them to rebuild the altars at their own expense.[11]

The new service contained in the Book of Common Prayer obviously went a long way toward satisfying the objections of Tylby, Armstrong, and critics of the mass in general, but authorities continued to be troubled by the more extreme Anabaptists. Although the Anabaptists were primarily a thorn in the side of the bishops, their role in urban disturbances at Deventer, Leyden, Amsterdam, and especially Münster made them highly suspect to the mayor and aldermen of London.[12] The case of one alleged Anabaptist preacher, Thomas Putto, suggests some connection between religious radicalism and insurrection. On May 5, 1549 Putto, a tanner from Colchester, bore a fagot at St. Paul's Cross for denying that Christ descended into Hell.

Two weeks later Putto was again in trouble. Charles Wriothesley recorded that

> Putto, which bare a fagot the second Sunday after Easter at Paul's Cross because he stood that time with his cap on his head all sermon time, to the people's estimation unpenitent for his offense, was sent for to my Lord of Canterbury, who further joined him in penance to stand this day again at Paul's Cross with a fagot on his shoulder bareheaded, which he did; and after confessed his error showing himself to be penitent for his offense, which the audience well accepted, praying for his reconciliation.[13]

Putto's "lewd preaching" was brought to the attention of the Privy Council in 1550 and 1551. While there is no evidence connecting him with the rebellions of 1549, Putto was accused "of gathering on

November 10, 1554, twenty or more other people, with force of arms and swords, at Mile End within Colchester Liberty, and elsewhere in unlawful conventicles."[14] Putto's religious dissent may have been nonviolent in 1549, yet as his later activities demonstrated, he was the kind of activist who caused apprehension among London officials.

Performances of interludes constituted another potential source of disorder. This popular form of drama was, as T. W. Craik has shown, "readily adaptable to subjects of topical interest," especially controversial political and religious matters which were presented with "a blend of grim invective and hearty ridicule." The interludes, usually staged indoors, encouraged close contact between the actors and spectators, who were often coaxed to join in; and it was not uncommon for great excitement to be whipped up.[15] The Court of Aldermen first attempted to prevent attendance at interludes and on May 27, 1549 ordered all servants and youths to be kept at home between the hours of 10 P.M. and 4 A.M. until Michaelmas. The wardens of the companies were specifically warned not to allow servants and youths "to make any May games, or to resort to any such unlawful assemblies and gatherings of people together at any interludes or other unlawful games upon the holy day."[16] The action of the aldermen was probably prompted by the activities of John Wylkynson, a currier, who "commonly suffreth and maintaineth interludes and plays to be made and kept within his dwelling house." On the same day that the Court of Aldermen prohibited attendance at interludes, it also commanded Wylkynson to stop further performances at his house upon pain of imprisonment.[17]

Although there is no subsequent evidence of dramatic performances at Wylkynson's house or elsewhere, the Court of Aldermen repeated its prohibition on July 4. It was agreed that the mayor should at his next meeting with the Lord Chancellor "desire his lordship's aid and advice for the staying of all common interludes and plays within the City and suburbs thereof."[18] Protector Somerset and the Privy Council responded to the City's initiative, for on August 6, a royal proclamation was issued prohibiting plays and interludes. Such plays, according to the proclamation, contained "matter tending to sedition, and contemning of sundry good orders and laws; whereupon are grown, and are daily like to grow and ensure much disquiet, division, tumults, and uproars in this realm." The proclamation extended to all of England and was to remain in force until November 1.[19] Shortly after the proclamation expired, the aldermen established procedures for regulating dramatic performances. Two officials, Mr. Atkyns and Mr. Burnell, secondaries of the compters, were instructed to "peruse" interludes and report their findings to the mayor before performances could take place.[20]

The most important person involved in a disturbance in the City was Sir William Pickering. Educated in the New Learning at Cambridge, he was knighted at the accession of Edward VI and then elected

M.P. for Warwick.[21] In May, 1549 Pickering, a gentleman named Foster,[22] and several others had an altercation with the London constables. Pickering was accused of "light and evil demeanor" toward constables making the king's watches in the streets of the City about midnight. Geoffrey Walkerderne, skinner, one of the constables, was so fearful of reprisals that he asked for and received the "surety of the king's peace" for himself against Pickering. Moreover, two aldermen were named to meet with Protector Somerset and the Council to discuss the matter.[23] The records unfortunately do not give further details about this episode; the incident, however, was neither the first nor last time that Pickering was in serious trouble. In 1543 he and Henry Howard, Earl of Surrey had been brought before the Council, charged with walking in the streets of London at night and "breaking the windows of the houses with stone shot from cross-bows." For this Pickering was briefly committed to the Tower and released on recognizances of £200.[24] His nocturnal activities in May, 1549 may have been nothing more than another drunken brawl like the earlier escapade with Surrey, but later events reveal that he was capable of sedition and rebellion. After the accession of Mary, Pickering was implicated in Wyatt's Rebellion and indicted for treason.[25] Given the tensions of the summer of 1549, irresponsible behavior by one of Pickering's standing could scarcely be regarded as trivial.

Servants of Sir Thomas Smith, principal secretary of state and influential adviser to Somerset, committed offenses similar to those of Pickering. Two constables of the ward of Farringdon Within, Gilbert Penyngton and Thomas Tailler, "stayed" Smith's servants in July as they were "passing out of the City in the night season with his harness and weapons." During the course of the confrontation two handguns belonging to Smith were lost.[26] Smith reacted to the constables' action by ordering them committed to Marshalsea prison. The aldermen, taking the position that the constables were merely doing their duty in performing the night watch, sent a letter of complaint to Smith. The aldermen argued that "the other constables of the City hearing the punishment of the said two constables do much murmur and grudge and say that they will no more watch."[27] The constables were released before the end of July, and the aldermen authorized each to be paid twenty shillings in recompense of charges sustained while in prision.[28] Again, surviving evidence is fragmentary, but it does seem clear that the servants behaved suspiciously and that Smith was scarcely sympathetic toward the City's security measures.[29]

Sir Thomas Smith's men may have been from a contingent of twenty recruited by him for service in Scotland.[30] If so, they were part of a larger group of undisciplined soldiers who were responsible for disorder in the City. The unwelcome presence of these soldiers brought forth a series of royal proclamations, beginning in January, 1548, requiring them to return to their posts.[31] The issuance of successive proclamations suggests not only poor discipline among the English forces, but also the complete ineffectiveness of the proclamations themselves. On April 29, 1549, the fourth in a series of similar proclamations was issued, threatening to hang every man at large in the London area without a "special license in writing" from his captain.[32] That this proclamation was no more effective than its predecessors is evidenced by the presence in July of soldiers serving under Captain Thomas Drury.

On July 18, Robert Hartor, goldsmith and deputy to Alderman Robert Chertsey, complained to the Court of Aldermen of the "evil behavior of certain persons" in Drury's command. Upon hearing Hartor's complaint, the aldermen ordered him "to make suit to the Earl of Warwick to whom the said Drury doth belong that the said persons may be removed out of the City."[33] Further details about the men and the action taken against them are not known, but a few weeks later Captain Drury with a band of 180 men served with distinction under Warwick in his successful campaign against Robert Kett in Norfolk.[34] Drury's forces, according to Warwick, sustained sixty fatalities during two months of service.[35] Unfortunately, the survivors were paid only after Warwick's intervention;[36] and when a group returned to London in October, it received anything but a hearty welcome for services rendered to the country. Rather, the aldermen again acted to rid the City of what they regarded as a common nuisance. They agreed on October 3 that "if any of Captain Drury's men depart from him and return hither, . . . they shall be apprehended and punished."[37]

Although each of the incidents examined up to this point disturbed the normal routine of London, none revealed the kind of religious and social discontent found in the West and in Norfolk. Two persons, Anthony Roberts and John Wheatley, were, however, accused of complicity in the rebellions. Roberts, of Tonbridge, Kent, was apprehended by the City watch in July as one "vehemently suspected" of being a party "of this rebellion" and committed to ward.[38] Although the exact nature of Roberts's activities is unknown, the offense was important enough to be brought to the attention of Protector Somerset.[39] Wheatley, identified only as a saddler and rebel, was also arrested by the watch and committed to ward in Newgate "for that he enticed men's servants and apprentices . . . to repair and go with him to the rebels at Norwich." He was ordered to remain in ward until the Court of Aldermen directed otherwise, but no evidence of subsequent action against him has survived.[40]

These events indicate that the City of London was not a haven of quiet during the rebellions. Unrest and extreme tension resulted from rapidly rising prices as well as from the revolts in the countryside.[41] Although the disturbances were relatively minor and apparently unco-ordinated, officials could not regard them with indifference. Under only slightly different circumstances the actions of Thomas Putto, John

Wylkynson, Sir William Pickering, or John Wheatley could have sparked a large-scale urban rising. For this reason the mayor and aldermen can scarcely be accused of acting rashly when they prepared London to meet any challenge either from within or without the City.

Early Tudor London was a city without a professional police force. Law enforcement in each ward was the responsibility of the beadle, constables, and watchmen. The beadle set the watch for each ward, while constables supervised and kept suspicious people under observation. The system of watches, according to Stow, dated back to 1253 when Henry III commanded them to be kept for "the better observing of peace and quietness amongst his people."[42] Constables and watchmen were minor officials, and their work was often dangerous. Neither position attracted men of the highest rank. In times of danger or emergency, it was necessary to reinforce the watch.[43]

Although it was not until 1549 that London made elaborate preparations for defense, the aldermen acted during the previous year to upgrade the usual watch. On May 25, 1548, the Aldermen ordered that good watches be kept from ten to three at night and required one man in each parish to assist the constable.[44] The most spectacular event of the year, however, came in June with the resumption of the midsummer marching watch. The midsummer watch, Stow wrote, had taken place yearly "time out of mind" until 1539 when Henry VIII forbade it for the year, "which being once laid down, was not raised till the year 1548," when it was revived by the mayor, Sir John Gresham.[45] Contemporary writers were enthusiastic in their praise of the colorful pageant. Stow recounted that the watch took place on the evenings of St. John the Baptist (June 23) and St. Peter the Apostle (June 28) and that it was "beautified by the number of more than three hundred demilances and light horsemen, prepared by the citizens to be sent into Scotland for the rescue of the town of Haddington and others kept by the Englishmen." Charles Wriothesley described, in addition to the horsemen for Scotland,

> seven hundred gunners and Morris pikes all in one livery with drums and standards and thirteen hundred armed men of the lord mayor's watch, the king's trumpeters blowing afore him both nights, and he had sixteen gentlemen of the mercers riding in velvet and chains of gold afore him, every man having three in a livery to wait on them, which was at their own charges, the sheriff's watch following after my lord mayor.

Stow would certainly have agreed with Wriothesley that the whole affair was "the goodliest sight."[46]

In 1549 the City of London's preparations for defense were closely related to the violent outbreaks in the West and in Norfolk, but the City's action was by no means a simple matter of responses to outside stimuli. Although discontent in Cornwall dated back to 1547, the revolt began in Devon only after the new Book of Common Prayer was introduced on Whitsunday, June 10, 1549.[47] Two weeks earlier, on May 27, the City had begun its program of repression, for it was on that date that John Wylkynson was ordered to stop performing interludes and the wardens of the companies were warned to keep their servants and youths off the streets and at home between the hours of 10 P.M. and 4 A.M. until Michaelmas (September 29). This action by the Court of Aldermen marked the beginning of a long and difficult summer in the City.[48]

During the month of June the mayor issued two proclamations to improve the efficiency of the watch. The first, issued on June 5 — five days before the introduction of the Prayer Book — was authorized by the king, and required a "good watch" to be kept in each ward from 10 P.M. to 4 A.M. until Michaelmas. It further stated that all gates by land and water were to be closed.[49] The second proclamation, dated June 17, was also issued on the king's behalf and reiterated the need to keep a good watch during the vigils of St. John the Baptist and St. Peter and Paul. Men making the watch were to be "well and convenably harnessed," and every constable "arrayed with decent jornettes and furnished with cresset light" to pass through the streets during the vigils. The watches were to begin two hours earlier at eight o'clock and continue to three in the morning. All taverns and alehouses were ordered closed at nine o'clock and not to reopen until four the following morning.[50]

More intense preparations followed during July and August. In the West of England the situation became more acute as the rebels made camp at Clyst St. Mary and then on July 2 advanced upon Exeter. The West had not risen since 1497 when the Cornish camped at Blackheath outside London before they were defeated by Henry VII. In 1549 there were probably few if any who witnessed the rebellion of a half century earlier; yet in spite of the absence of references to the rising of 1497, Londoners may well have sensed the parallel with the past and pondered the grim reality that their king was not the victor of Bosworth but a child. London was safe as long as Exeter withstood the rebels' siege. If, however, Exeter were to fall, the rebels might advance as rapidly on the capital as they had done in 1497. And, to make matters worse, news began to arrive in London about Kett's Rebellion in Norfolk.

Further action to restrict movement within the City was taken on July 2 when the mayor ordered the company wardens to command all householders to see that none of their families or servants "go abroad" from nine in the evening until five the following morning. This order was to remain in force until the "time of unquietness" passed and the wardens were duly advised. At the same time the Court of Aldermen agreed that the mayor and aldermen or their deputies should ride nightly through the streets to survey all the watches.[51] Wriothesley, corroborating the action of the aldermen, reported on July 3 that Sir Henry Amcottes, the lord mayor, "began to watch at night, riding about the city to peruse the constables with their watches . . . for the preservation of the city because of the rebellion in divers places of this realm."[52]

Judging from what followed, the appearance of the mayor in the streets of the City served as a powerful stimulant for bolstering the defenses. As we have already seen, interludes and buckler playing were prohibited.[53] The mayor, obviously unimpressed by the quality of the watch, ordered that in the future watches should be made up of discreet persons from substantial households and "not of boys and naked men as they are now commonly made and kept."[54] The chamberlain and bridge masters were ordered immediately to inspect the gates of the City and London Bridge and to see that repairs were made.[55] On July 11, Andrew Woodcock, one of the bridge masters, was commanded to "provide with all speed timber to make a false drawbridge of, to be used for a season in case need should require by reason of the stirring of the people (which God defend) to cast down the other."[56] To protect the City further from attack along the Thames, watermen were ordered to leave their boats at "Queenhithe, Westminster, Bridge, and London side." Rebels advancing upon the City from Surrey would then be denied transport across the river.[57]

Another aspect of London's defense preparations is seen in the surveys of weapons and armament. Two aldermen and the chamberlain took "a true note of all the guns, and gunpowder, harness, weapons, and habilment of war belonging to the city" on July 5.[58] A few days later the Court of Aldermen requested that a Privy Council warrant be sent to the Tower of London "for the delivery at all times, if need shall so require, the twelve pieces of ordnance that they [the Council] have granted for the safeguard of the city."[59] On July 15 the aldermen directed each constable to search his ward for harness and weapons with a member of Common Council. Furthermore, each householder was required to provide harness for himself and every manservant in his house. A list of those householders able to bear arms was to be given to the mayor.[60]

The seriousness of the situation in early July was emphasized by the fact that the mayor and aldermen took personal charge of defense preparations. In normal times the constables and watchmen might go their own way with little or no supervision; if they did their jobs badly, little harm could come of it. In the summer of 1549, however, normal times were but a fond memory. Several aldermen, including William Roche and Augustine Hynde, who were away from London, were asked to return "with all speed for the safe custody of the city in the time of this stirring of the people."[61] Steps were also taken for procuring assistance from the king's government. Accordingly, the mayor and an impressive delegation of eight aldermen joined together to ask Protector Somerset and the Privy Council to loan the City 200 pikes and 200 hackbutters "with the condition to pay for them if they shall occupy them."[62] The Court of Aldermen was also bold enough to send the common sergeant to the Lord Chancellor asking him to command the benchers of the four houses of court and the principals of the houses of Chancery "to see their companies honestly and quietly governed."[63] Nonetheless, the City notified the Lord Chancellor that because of defense expenditures it could not grant money "toward the finding of the men of war called Albonyes that are lately come hither to serve the king's majesty."[64] In time of crisis the City fathers assumed that the interests of London should take priority over the national interest.

Somerset's government attempted to assist magistrates in London and throughout the country by issuing royal proclamations which authorized the use of martial law. The proclamation receiving the most attention in London appeared on July 18.[65] Wriothesley described the event in the following manner:

> The eighteenth day of July was a proclamation made in the city of London for martial law, both the sheriffs riding and the knight marshal with them in the middle with the trumpet and the common crier afore them with one of the clerks of the papers with him, which proclamation was made within the city in divers places in the forenoon, and at afternoon without the gates of the city, which proclamation was for rebels and upstirrers without any indictment or arraignment [to be apprehended].[66]

This action is difficult to interpret for two reasons. First, the whole question of martial law in Tudor England is a highly obscure subject. Holdsworth contended that martial law was illegal in England, but conceded that its use "did not excite much public feeling during the Tudor period." Normally martial law governed only men in arms under the jurisdiction of the Constable and Marshal's court, but this court's jurisdiction was extended to ordinary citizens when the crown deemed it necessary for the welfare of the state.[67] In Holdsworth's judgment "the chequered history of the law which has governed the discipline of the army sufficiently accounts for the vagueness of the term 'martial law' and the uncertainty as to the legal force of a proclamation of martial law."[68] Unfortunately there is nothing in the records of the City of London for this period which removes the ambiguity found so puzzling by Holdsworth.

The second problem is whether the proclamation applied to London or whether it was intended for areas suffering enclosure riots. The proclamation specifically included offenses against enclosures, but also referred to "any other unlawful act, which is forbidden." A magistrate "upon the knowledge of any offender against the tenor of this proclamation" was to commit the culprit to jail and "certify the Lord Protector and the rest of the Council, or any of them, to the intent most speedy order may be given for the execution of the offender with such haste and expedition as is above mentioned."[69] The chronicle accounts do little to clarify the text of the proclamation. Wriothesley's account seems to imply that London was under martial law or at the very least that martial law would be used against rioters apprehended within the City. The Grey Friars chronicler, on the other hand, referred to the proclamation as a "book made and sent up to the commons of Cornwall and Devonshire with all other parts of all the realm for because of their rising and pulling down of the enclosures"; this emphasis, quite different from that of Wriothesley, suggests that the proclamation was not in the first instance designed for maintaining law and order in London.[70]

A fascinating anecdote related by John Stow in the *Survey of London* reveals that martial law was used in the City. He gives an eyewitness account of the execution of the bailiff of Romford, Essex, who had been condemned by the sheriffs of London and the knight-marshal. Standing on the ladder of the gibbet, the bailiff spoke the following to the crowd assembled at Aldgate:

> "Good people, I am come hither to die, but know not for what offence, except, for words by me spoken yesternight to Sir Stephen, curate and preacher of this parish, which were these: He asked me, 'What news in the country?' I answered, 'Heavy news.' 'Why?' quoth he. 'It is said,' quoth I, 'that many men be up in Essex, but, thanks be to God, all is in good quiet about us,' and this was all, as God be my judge."
>
> Upon these words of the prisoner, Sir Stephen, to avoid reproach of the people, left the city, and was never heard of since amongst them to my knowledge.[71]

This man was apparently executed under the provision of the proclamation of martial law forbidding the circulation of news or rumors. Whether he was innocent as he claimed or rather a dangerous agitator must remain an open question. Although others were executed by martial law in London, none can be positively identified as residents punished for crimes committed within the City.

Only two days after the proclamation of martial law, a watch was instituted during the daytime hours for the first time. Five men from each company assembled at 5 A.M. on July 20 at Cripplegate under orders "to remain until eight o'clock at night watching and having continually during all the said season a vigilant eye." They were empowered to detain any suspicious persons until given orders for their release. John Sendall was appointed master gunner of the City with responsibility for all ordnance and gunners.[72] Wriothesley, obviously impressed by the defense preparations, wrote that "divers great pieces of ordnance of brass of the king's was had from the Tower and set at every gate of the city, all the walls of the City from Cripplegate to Bevis Marks, by Christ Church, were set with ordnance on the walls, which was the City's ordnance, and gunners appointed to every gate and for the walls, having wages at the City's charges."[73]

The first sign that tension was lessening came at an unusual time. On July 30 steps were taken to reduce the day watch. The company of curriers, for example, was permitted to reduce its commitment of manpower from three to two.[74] The mayor made similar concessions to other companies with the result that the number assigned to watch each gate during the day was cut to five.[75] The timing of this modest reduction is puzzling inasmuch as Norwich had fallen to Robert Kett only a week earlier. City authorities undoubtedly assumed that the large army commanded by the Marquis of Northampton, advancing on Norwich, would quickly put an end to Kett. If London had predicated its reduction of the day watch on the assumption of an easy victory over Kett, the rebels' dramatic defeat of Northampton removed any false optimism that peace would soon be restored in Norfolk. On the other hand, news from the West was better. Forces led by Lord Russell began to advance on Exeter on July 28 although they did not reach the walls of the city until August 6.[76] The defeat of Northampton overshadowed the successes in the West, and, therefore, the reduction of the day watch on July 30 proved to be a false start.

Early in August steps were taken to prepare London to withstand a siege. The most ambitious measure was a project to clean and reopen the ditch outside the walls of the City. Originally two hundred feet in breadth, the ditch was constructed to protect London from attack. The ditch was last cleaned in 1540, and during the intervening nine years it had become clogged and of little use for defense.[77] On August 2, the mayor ordered the ditch reopened and requested the Company of Mercers to employ at its own expense twelve men for a period of a month.[78] Others joined the work force with the result that a total of 140 laborers began to pull down the gardens that lined the ditch between Aldersgate and Newgate.[79] The work unfortunately did not proceed as rapidly as had been hoped. Consequently, the mayor requested the companies to provide wages for yet another month's work.[80]

Further precautions against a possible siege are seen in the City's efforts to ensure adequate supplies of food. Before Kett's defeat of Northampton at Norwich, the country was troubled by rising prices and food shortages. By a royal proclamation of July 2, the Protector's government attempted to stabilize prices charged for cattle, sheep, and butter.[81] The situation in London was exceptionally critical as large numbers of nobles, gentry, and soldiers concentrated in the area.[82] The mayor and aldermen drew up a list of twelve butchers on July 20 who were given "full power and authority to take oxen, sheep, and other cattle at the prices appointed by the king's majesty's last proclamation ... for the provision and victualling of this said city and of the king's majesty and his nobles and subjects repairing to the same in this time of this rebellion of the people."[83] Later, on August 5, the London beer brewers were ordered to purchase enough malt to last for an entire month. If necessary, the Court of Aldermen was willing to provide the brewers with financial assistance.[84] Furthermore, each household in the City was asked to supply itself with victuals of a type that would remain wholesome for a month.[85] Inevitably in such a period of crisis there were households that went to excessive lengths in acquiring provisions, and the resulting reports of hoarding forced the aldermen to add a plea for moderation.[86]

The extreme anxiety in London resulting from the successes of Kett and the fear of an urban insurrection readily explain the prohibition of wrestling at Bartholomew Fair. Since the reign of Henry I, Bartholomew Fair held at Clerkenwell had been one of London's greatest festivities. Traditionally people came from far and wide to buy and sell and enjoy the varied entertainments, including exhibitions of wrestling. The fair was precisely the type of event that might have sparked violence during the tense month of August 1549.[87] On August 20, four days before St. Bartholomew's Day, the Court of Aldermen ordered the cancellation of wrestling and further required all watches doubled "for the even, the day, and the morrow."[88] It would appear that with the exception of the wrestling the fair proceeded almost as usual. The Grey Friars chronicler related that "this year was no cheeses in Bartholomew Fair but such as came out of divers men's houses within London that was not good, and the cause was for them that rose in Essex at that time."[89] The fact that the fair was permitted to take place with only one restriction may indeed be interpreted as evidence that City authorities as well as the Protector and Council felt confident that they were in control and that no serious disturbances were likely to occur.

Three days after Bartholomew Fair, on August 27, the army of John Dudley, Earl of Warwick, entered Norwich, crushed the rebels, and captured Robert Kett. Although the greatest danger had passed, City officials reacted with prudence and caution. It was not until September 10 that the day watch was ended and the king's ordnance placed before the gates of the City was returned to the Tower of London. Nearly another week passed before the aldermen who were overseeing the constables during the night watch were discharged of their duties.[90] As the country was pacified by force of arms, executions took place in and around London. Men were executed at Tyburn, Aldgate, Southwark, Tottenham, Tower Hill, and Bishopsgate. Only one, the bailiff of Romford, committed his crime within the City.[91] Since the City's preparations for defense and security were never fully tested, we shall never know whether London could have withstood a prolonged siege or put down a major insurrection. Yet the surviving evidence suggests that City officials reacted to the crisis with a high sense of responsibility and determination. There was neither panic nor hysteria, and as a result, London survived as a source of strength in a country badly shaken by rebellion.

After the rebellions had been put down, the City of London played an important role in the overthrow of the Protector. Somerset, faced with growing opposition within the Council, withdrew to Hampton Court accompanied by Edward VI and a small group of supporters. Tensions mounted, and Somerset moved the king to Windsor Castle, where he planned to make a stand against the councillors remaining behind in London. The Council's opposition to Somerset resulted from his authoritarian leadership, his program of social reform, and his inept response to the rebellions. While the peerage and gentry, both at court and throughout the country, had a host of grievances against Somerset, the reasons for London's opposition remain obscure.

R. R. Sharpe, who made a careful study of manuscript sources at Guildhall, suggested that the citizens of London hated Somerset "not for his favouring the reformers, but for the injury he had caused to trade and for his having debased the coinage still further than it had been debased by Henry VIII."[92] W. K. Jordan, on the other hand, concluded that the mayor, aldermen, and Common Council were "under direct and overweening pressure" from the councillors who assembled in London.[93] Unfortunately neither Sharpe nor Jordan gave the documentation upon which their judgments were based. The surviving evidence, sparse though it is, indicates that Sharpe was closer to the truth by arguing that there was genuine opposition to Somerset and his government in the City. London, traditionally reluctant to play an active role where its direct interests were not involved, declined to contribute towards the payment of foreign mercenaries recruited to pacify the countryside, but expected Somerset's government to aid in the defense of the City. When the mayor asked Somerset and the Council for military assistance in July, it does not appear that help was provided. The London oligarchs may have held Somerset responsible for the policies that led to the revolts and for failing to provide for the City's defense. By the end of the summer, it was clear that London had been spared through its own efforts and the successes of Lord Russell in the West and the Earl of Warwick in Norfolk, not as a result of any vigorous action by Somerset.

Further friction between the City and Somerset may have occurred in negotiations over a loan to the king. On July 2, the Court of Aldermen agreed to ask Somerset, the Lord Chancellor (Rich), the Lord Great Master (St. John), the Earl of Warwick, the Earl of Shrewsbury, the Earl of Arundel, the Earl of Southampton, Sir William Paget, Sir Thomas Cheyney, Sir John Baker, Sir Anthony Denny, Sir Edward North, Sir William Petre, and Sir Thomas Smith "to be bound by obligation to the chamberlain of London for the repayment of such money as the City at this time shall lend to the king's majesty."[94] It was also decided that a delegation of aldermen, including the mayor, should discuss the matter with the lord great master. This issue was apparently not settled on this occasion, for two months later, on September 3, the mayor again arranged to see the Protector and Council "for answering of their request concerning the borrowing of certain money of this city."[95] A week later there was another hint of disagreement. The Repertory entry states tersely that at the request of the Protector and Council the mayor and all of the aldermen will begin "to travail" with the inhabitants of every ward being assessed at £20 or more "toward the first payment of the relief" granted by Parliament.[96]

The most intriguing incident suggesting tension between the City and Somerset prior to October was Somerset's unsuccessful attempt to have John York dismissed from the office of sheriff.[97] The Court of Aldermen received a letter to this effect on August 2 and ordered the recorder, Robert Brook, to inform Somerset that the laws of the City did not permit one to be discharged from the office of sheriff without the consent of Common Council or without the oath of the man himself.[98] John York was not removed from office and, indeed, played a leading role in negotiations between the City and Privy Council leading to the Protector's downfall.

The City of London learned officially of the conflict between the Protector and the Council on Sunday morning, October 6, when the mayor and aldermen were summoned to the Earl of Warwick's residence at Ely Place in Holborn. The Mayor and Aldermen were almost certainly receptive to the proposals put to them, for they agreed to meet at Guildhall in the afternoon at which time requests for military assistance both from the Protector and the Council were considered. While no decision was taken to offer military assistance to either party, the aldermen did agree to strengthen the day and night watches at the gates of the City.[99] Later the same day Warwick moved from Holborn into the City and took lodgings with John York. The fact that Warwick took up residence within London would seem to indicate that he and his supporters were confident that the City would commit itself to their cause. The same conclusion is suggested by the meeting of the Privy Council at the Mercers' Hall on October 7 and the dinner that evening with the mayor. According to Wriothesley, "all the lords of the Council sat in the forenoon at the Mercers' Hall and dined at my lord mayor's and sat there in council till night."[100]

Common Council also met on October 7 in the presence of the mayor, recorder, and aldermen. Letters from Somerset and the Privy Council were "plainly and distinctly read and the whole contents and effects of either of them by the commons in the said Common Council assembled ripely and deliberately debated and pondered." Afterwards Common Council agreed "with one assent and consent" to join with the privy councillors "for the defense, safeguard, and maintenance of the king's majesty's person and of this his grace's City of London and to aid the said Lords therein *within* the said City according to the tenor of their said letters."[101] By this action Common Council committed itself to those opposed to Somerset, but significantly limited its action to the

City. Thus, on October 7, Common Council declined to provide armed forces for removing Edward VI from Somerset's custody at Windsor.

Common Council convened again the following day, but the proceedings were not recorded in the Journal. The leaders of the Privy Council were present at this meeting at Guildhall, and, according to Wriothesley, Rich, the Lord Chancellor, and "other of the lords" declared "the great abuses of the said Lord Protector, desiring all the citizens to be aiding and assisting with the lords for the preservation of the king's majesty's person, which they greatly feared being in his adversaries' hands." After the mayor, aldermen, and Common Council heard these remarks, all that is known is that they "promised their aid and help to the uttermost of their lives and goods."[102] There was apparently no commitment to provide the armed forces previously requested.

It is possible that this meeting of Common Council on October 8 was the occasion of George Stadlow's moving oration against supplying troops for use against Somerset. Stadlow spoke in response to a strong plea by Robert Brook, the recorder, that Common Council should support the leaders of the Privy Council on the grounds that Somerset "had abused both the king's majesty and the whole realm." The response of Stadlow, which cannot be dated, recalled how London had lost its liberties for supporting the baronial opposition to Henry III in the thirteenth century and proposed that a petition be sent to the king detailing grievances against Somerset's rule.[103] The fact that minutes of this session of Common Council were not preserved may be an indication that there was heated controversy, prolonged debate, and strong resistance to committing London to military operations that might possibly have led to open warfare between the Privy Councillors in London and the supporters of Somerset.

Common Council decided to provide armed men on October 9, the third consecutive day on which it met. Pressure was undoubtedly applied by the aldermen, who sat earlier the same day and warned Common Council to meet at one o'clock in the afternoon "for the answering of the Lord's request opened by Mr. York, sheriff, to this city for 1,000 men to be set forth out of hand by this city for the accomplishment of their enterprise for the speedy safeguard and conveying of the king's majesty out of the hands of the late Lord Protector."[104] Common Council agreed to provide 500 men, or if necessary 1,000 on the ninth,[105] and then assembled on the next day when it "finally assented" to a commitment of 500 men of whom 100 should be horsemen. On this occasion a list was drawn up with the numbers of men to be provided by each of the companies.[106] This military force actually mustered in Moorfields on October 11, but by that day the Protector's supporters had dwindled to the point where the troops were not required. Somerset was taken into custody by Sir Anthony Wingfield, captain of the Guard, and on the fourteenth the former Protector was lodged in the Tower of London.[107]

Throughout the complex proceedings John York played an important role in negotiations between the Council and City authorities. Although the exact nature of the business transacted at York's house in Walbrook is unknown, the meetings on the critical days of October 8 and 9 obviously suggest that York was the chief intermediary between the Council and the mayor and aldermen.[108] York received his reward for services rendered on October 17, when Edward VI rode through London and dined at Suffolk House, Southwark, site of the mint of which York was master. After the dinner the king knighted York, who was the only City officer to receive this honor.[109]

Events in London, the country's major urban center, constitute an important chapter in the history of the rebellions of 1548-49. While the City suffered no insurrection, enough discontent was present to cause alarm among the ruling oligarchs. The elaborate security preparations were a response to conditions within the City as well as a reaction to the tumult throughout the countryside. In retrospect it may appear that London went to inordinate lengths to prepare for perils that never materialized, but the mayor and aldermen could not have foreseen how quickly peace would be restored and, therefore, were wiser to err on the side of excessive preparedness. The necessity of upholding law and order was recognized by all Tudor politicians and writers, and for this reason City officials acted in the best tradition of the century. Protector Somerset, on the other hand, was the obvious scapegoat after the revolts had been quelled. By joining with the Councillors opposed to Somerset's policies and leadership, London, with its great wealth and growing population, made the Protector's position almost untenable.

We heartily pray thee to send thy Holy Spirit into the hearts of them that possess the grounds, pastures, and dwelling places of the earth, that they, remembering themselves to be thy tenants, may not rack and stretch out the rents of their houses and land, nor yet take unreasonable fines and incomes after the manner of covetous worldlings.

Authorized Prayer, 1553, *Tudor Economic Documents*

8.   THE STRUGGLE FOR STABILITY

The commons suffered crushing military defeat in every part of the country, and the fall of Protector Somerset ended any hopes that he would champion parliamentary legislation to remedy the rebels' grievances. The grim determination of small groups of rebels to fight on against overwhelming odds at Norwich and in the West revealed a realistic assessment of the price of failure. In Tudor England rebellion was a crime against God and the king. The government might promise pardon and redress of grievance as a tactical maneuver to buy time, but when order was finally restored, the rebels' lives and property were solely dependent on the king's mercy. The commons, of course, had no assurance that the king and his ministers would consider their claims to mercy, because the frightened and embittered gentry, supported by the army, were in a position to hand out rough and ready justice on the spot with little regard to the niceties of legal procedure. Even in the best of times the majority of Englishmen lived under the arbitrary rule of landlords and local officials, and the death penalty was invoked for what the twentieth century would regard as minor crimes. The law-abiding commoner had to accept arbitrary increases in rent, the loss of arable land and grazing rights, and the always-present risk of starvation. Considering the harshness of life both in the towns and countryside, the terrible consequences of rebellion inevitably lost their sting.

1. The Price of Defeat

Repression was most severe in the West, because of the government's determination to eradicate Catholicism and the gentry's humiliation by the rebel army. No one bothered to make a careful accounting of the dead, but John Hooker put the number at 4,000. The casualties fell into three categories. First, there were those who died in battle. Second, priests who rejected the Book of Common Prayer and aided the rebels were singled out; third, the surviving leaders were tried and executed.

Although the principal ringleaders were tried in London, the secondary figures were dealt with locally. Most of the rank and file escaped with their lives, but they undoubtedly suffered unrecorded punishment and persecution at the hands of landlords and neighbors in the weeks and months that followed the end of the rebellion. The military casualties were heavier in Devon where most of the fighting took place. Cornwall, on the other hand, quickly fell to the rebels but was later dealt with more harshly than any other county.[1]

Throughout the length and breadth of Cornwall, Sir Anthony Kingston, who was appointed provost-marshal, instituted a reign of white terror. Among at least eight priests executed was Simon Morton, vicar of Poundstock, whose traitorous deeds inspired a popular Protestant ballad:

> The vicar of Poundstock with his congregation
> Commanded them to stick to their idolatry;
> They had much provision and great preparation,
> Yet God hath given our king the victory.

Nicholas Boyer, either mayor or deputy of Bodmin, entertained Kingston at dinner only to learn that he was to be the first hanged on newly erected gallows. The contemporary chronicler, Richard Grafton, wrote that when Boyer showed Kingston how strong the gallows were, the latter said, "Well, then, get you even up to them for they are provided for you." Boyer replied, "I trust you mean no such thing to me." But Kingston was adament: "Sir, there is no remedy, you have been a busy rebel, and therefore this is appointed for your reward."

Kingston's contempt for due process of law and grotesque sense of humor were repeated as he hanged a simple but innocent miller's servant. The miller, knowing that he was likely to be executed as a rebel, slipped away before Kingston arrived, leaving the mill in the keeping of his trusty servant. "I must go forth," said the miller, "if there come any to ask for me say that thou art the owner of the mill, and that thou hast kept the same this four years, and in no wise name not me." When Kingston questioned the servant, he did as he was told and was promptly carried off to be hanged on the nearest tree. Finally coming to his wits, the servant revealed his true identity. But Kingston said to him, "You are a false knave to be in two tales, therefore hang him up." After the servant was hanged, a man passed by and said to Kingston, "Surely this was but the miller's man." To which Kingston replied, "What then could he ever have done his master better service than to hang for him."[2]

Executions by martial law, confiscation of property, and unrestrained plundering were also the order of the day in Devon and Somerset. To prevent future risings and to compensate the government for the cost of pacification, the Council ordered Lord Russell to remove the bells from all parish churches in Devon and Cornwall, leaving only one to summon parishioners to divine service. At Exeter Robert Welsh, the rebel priest who helped prevent the burning of the city, received the death penalty as his reward for an act of brotherly love. Another Exeter man, Robert Paget, was probably saved by his connections at court. Protector Somerset, having heard that Paget was a "captain of rebellion," ordered his execution despite the fact that his brother was a privy councillor. Somerset was acutely sensitive about granting pardons to persons with family in high places, because he had refused only a few months earlier to save his brother, Thomas, Lord Seymour. The absence of any mention of Paget's execution suggests that he was eventually pardoned. Most of the rebel leaders had no influential family or friends and felt the full brunt of the government's repressive policy.[3]

Hangings took place throughout Somerset, where the Western rebels made a futile last stand after the collapse of their army surrounding Exeter. One hundred four prisoners taken at Kingweston were conducted to Wells at the end of August. Although some received pardon, executions occurred at Wells, Bath, Frome, Milverton, Wiveliscombe, Exford, and other towns. Payments to Sir John Thynne, Sheriff of Somerset, tell a grim tale of suffering. Fees were paid for cords to tie the prisoners, a poor man earned a handsome fee of two shillings for serving as executioner, and twelve pence was expended for wood to burn the entrails of the victims. The total cost of the executions came to over £26.[4]

The defeated rebels in Norfolk received much the same punishment as their counterparts in the West. After the Earl of Warwick entered Norwich for the first time, forty-nine rebels who had refused the king's pardon were hanged at the market cross. Robert Kett was captured after the battle of Dussindale and imprisoned at Norwich until he and his brother, William, were transported to London where they were tried for high treason. Other rebels received immediate punishment at the hands of Warwick. Many were tried and executed at Norwich Castle, according to Alexander Neville. Nine ringleaders, including the expert gunner, Miles, and two prophets who recommended abandonment of the camp at Mousehold Heath, were hanged at the Oak of Reformation where Kett only a few days earlier conducted his court. Explaining the execution process for the edification of his readers, Neville wrote that the men were first hanged and then cut down alive. "Their privy parts are cut off, then their bowels pulled out alive, and cast into the fire; then their head is cut off, and their bodies quartered, the head set upon a pole and fixed on the tops of the towers of the city, the rest of the body bestowed upon several places and set up to the terror of others." Neville concluded, "These are the judgments of traitors in our country."[5]

Warwick's strategy for pacification called for exemplary sentences for the leaders and pardons for the smaller fry who merely rallied to Kett's standard. Accordingly, John Bothom, surgeon of Ispwich, and George Houghton, yeoman of Docking, were pardoned of all treasons and unlawful speeches and had confiscated property and goods restored.

The gentry, however, opposed anything savoring of leniency and urged Warwick to allow indiscriminate executions of the kind carried out by Sir Anthony Kingston in Cornwall. Warwick calmed the hotheads and stressed that restraint was essential if lasting peace was to be restored. He reminded the angry gentry that if too many were killed they would have to plow and harrow the fields themselves. Warwick's arguments had the desired effect, for many who "burned wholly with cruelty" were "far more courteous towards the miserable common people."[6]

Outside Norfolk and the West rebels also paid the supreme price for insurrection. The names of the unhappy victims at Cambridge have not survived, but the town spent ten pence for erecting the gallows, buying new rope, and finally, when the hangings were finished, returning the gallows to storage. Not all of the Cambridgemen kept their rendezvous with the hangman, because the town also had to pay out twelve pence for mending a lock and grate at the prison after the inmates escaped.[7] Two Essex rebels, William Essex and Nicholas More, were first imprisoned at the Tower, removed to Brentwood for trial, and executed at Malden and Braintree, respectively. The government's policy of scheduling executions at towns scattered throughout a rebellious county may be seen clearly in Oxfordshire. In July Lord Grey ordered executions at Oxford, Banbury, Deddington, Islip, Watlington, Thame, Bicester, Chipping Norton, and Bloxham. The vicar of Chipping Norton suffered the indignity of being hanged on the steeple of the parish church, but other rebels were sentenced to die away from their homes, presumably to intimidate communities that failed to produce a rebel worthy of execution. Sir Henry Mathew of Deddington, a priest, was ordered hanged in that town, but a weaver, Richard Whyttington, also of Deddington, was sent to Bicester for execution.[8] From the Midlands the Earl of Huntingdon reported, "There have already diverse in the county of Rutland been condemned and have suffered." Rebels from Leicestershire were arraigned before Huntingdon and the king's justices of assize, and it is likely that there were executions. The ringleaders of the Yorkshire Rebellion, William Ombler, Thomas Dale, Henry Barton, and five other "busy stirrers" were captured, taken to York for trial, and executed on September 21, 1549.[9]

Although many important rebel leaders were tried and executed locally, a select few received the dubious privilege of coming to London to stand trial. On August 21, the Council directed Lord Russell to send up Humphrey Arundell, Maunder, the mayor of Bodmin, and "two or three of the most rankest traitors and ringleaders." The prisoners were to be heavily guarded during the long journey from Exeter, and the Council sent explicit orders that the soldiers accompanying them should kill any attempting to escape.[10] The following list of eleven names are those actually sent by Russell from the West:

Humphrey Arundell, Esq.
John Bury, Gent.
John Castell
Coffin, Gent.
William Fortescue
William Harris
Thomas Holmes, Yeoman
Sir Thomas Pomeroy
John Wise
John Winslade, Esq.
William Winslade, Esq.

Only four of the leaders were brought to trial. Pomeroy, William Winslade, Fortescue, Wise, and Harris were released by order of the Council on November 2. Coffin disappeared from the records without a trace, while Castell, who served as secretary to Humphrey Arundell, was sent to London not as a prisoner, but as an informer who surrendered voluntarily to give evidence against his master and Coffin.[11]

Joining the Western rebel leaders for trial were Robert and William Kett. A correspondent writing from Westminster on September 9 reported, "The arch-traitor Kett of Norfolk and his brother came hither to the court yesterday, pinned by the arms in permy [or penny] halters, according to their degrees and so were returned to the Tower where presently they remain. The chief traitors of the West parts be likewise arrived here this day." Each of the leaders was subjected to intensive interrogation. Under examination the Western men contended that they joined the rebellion only after intimidation. Arundell said that he fled into a woods near Helland for fear of the rebels and remained there for two days. He returned to his house when his wife "being great with child desired him." While visiting his wife, he was seized by rebels and taken to Bodmin. But he remained wary and continued with the rebels on the advice of Sir Hugh Trevanion; later he feigned illness and returned home only to be apprehended once again. John Winslade allegedly joined the rebels when they threatened to burn his house and never left Bodmin during the whole course of the rebellion, while Holmes claimed that he merely accompanied the parishioners of Bliston to Bodmin where rebels forced him to join their ranks. John Bury of Silverton, the sole Devon man among the Western rebel leaders, alleged that he went to Exeter to attend upon Sir Thomas Denys, returned home, and was then taken by five hundred rebels. The responses of the Ketts were not recorded, but it is likely that they perceived themselves as law-abiding subjects attempting to enforce the government's agrarian policies.[12]

The six men remained at the Tower for two-and-a-half months awaiting trial. There is some indication that William Kett was considered for a pardon, and he was permitted greater freedom at the Tower than the others. If such favor raised hope of mercy, it was to no avail because each was tried for treason under a special commission of oyer and terminer at Westminster on November 26. Each man entered a plea of guilty, and was sentenced to die at Tyburn. The penalty for treason included forfeiture of property and goods. Arrangements for the execution of the Ketts were changed, and Sir Edmund Wyndham conveyed them to Norwich on November 29. Robert remained in prison at the Guildhall for about a week before his execution on December 7. On the appointed day he was drawn on a hurdle to Norwich Castle and hanged in chains over the wall. The method of execution, hanging alive in chains until dead with the body remaining in public view until consumed by decay, was the most cruel penalty known in Tudor England. Although there is a possibility that the executioner mercifully allowed Kett to be strangled as he was hoisted onto the wall, such favor was contrary to the letter of the law. Shortly after Robert's execution, his brother was transported to Wymondham where he was hanged in chains from the church tower.[13]

Arundell, Winslade, Bury, and Holmes lingered at the Tower of London awaiting execution until January 27, 1550. Like the Ketts, they were dragged through the dusty streets on a horsedrawn hurdle. Leaving London on a wintery morning by way of Holborn Bars, the condemned men probably received the customary bowl of ale at St. Giles in the Fields before beginning the remainder of the journey along Oxford Road to Tyburn. At the place of execution they were hanged, drawn, and quartered. The procedure required that the victim be cut down alive and then castrated and disembowelled. The entrails were burned before the dying man's eyes. Finally the head was cut off and the body hacked into quarters. When the executions were completed, the heads and quarters of the four rebels were set on the gates of London to serve as a reminder of the price one paid for making war against the king.[14]

The leaders of the Western Rebellion and the Ketts were the most important figures in the rebellions of 1549, but they were not the only men brought to London for trial and execution. As early as July 22, the bailiff of Romford, Essex died at Aldgate, and an unnamed man from Kent was hanged at "the bridge foot" into Southwark. John Stow referred to the execution of four persons on August 16, one of whom was a man named Payne, a Suffolk rebel, sentenced to die at Waltham. On the same day four others were tried at Guildhall for treasonable activities in Norfolk, Suffolk, and Oxfordshire. Three of these, John Allen, a Southwark peddler, Roger Baker, falconer of Southfield, Suffolk, and William Gates, shepherd of Hampton, Wiltshire, died at Tyburn, Tower Hill and Tottenham, respectively, while the fourth, James Webbe, vicar of Barford, Oxfordshire, was executed at Aylesbury. Yet another group of rebels to die were three from the Westcountry executed at Tyburn on August 27.[15]

By October 22, nine more rebels were imprisoned at the Tower of London. Five were Suffolk men, while the others came from Buckinghamshire, Sussex, and Hampshire:

Robert Bell, laborer, Gazeley, Suffolk
John Fuller, collarmaker, Canon, Suffolk
Robert Capp, laborer, Canon, Suffolk
John Stephenson, smith, Bury St. Edmunds, Suffolk
Thomas Kynge, smith, Gazeley, Suffolk
William Hychecocke, carpenter, Buckinghamshire
Richard Tomson, tilemaker, Harting, Sussex
Thomas Richardson, clerk, Plaitford, Hampshire
John Unthanke, parson, Headley, Hampshire

All presumably were interrogated at length, and beside the name of each prisoner, except Unthanke, the letter *J* was inscribed. The mark would seem to imply that each man was indicted, tried, and perhaps executed, but evidence of trial and execution survives for only one, Robert Bell.[16]

Bell was brought to Westminster on December 1 along with Fuller, Capp, Stephenson, and Kynge; only Bell was indicted. The next day he and John Patchyn, yeoman from Horsham, Sussex, were tried for treason. Both were sentenced to die at Tyburn. Some two months later, on February 10, 1550, a man named Bell, apparently Robert, was hanged, drawn, and quartered at Tyburn. As for Patchyn, a Privy Council letter to his wife allowing her to inherit forfeited copyhold land suggests that he too died. Fuller, Capp, Stephenson, and Kynge, however, were released from the Tower in April 1550. Three Berkshire men were tried on December 10 for crimes that were probably related to the summer risings. Two Newbury weavers, Thomas Wattes and William Turner, and a Reading shoemaker, Thomas Bonam, were charged with machinating and compassing the king's death on November 20. Each pleaded not guilty but was convicted and sentenced to die at Reading. While it is impossible to determine with any confidence exactly how many relel leaders suffered imprisonment, trial, and execution in London, it is clear that the vengeance of the government extended far beyond the destruction of the best-known leaders of the rebellions in Norfolk and the West.[17]

Although the rebellions of 1549 have been called a revolt of the peasantry, an occupational and social analysis of the leadership and rank and file reveals that the risings were much more complex. If we begin with the six leaders tried in London, the Ketts, Arundell, Bury, Holmes, and Wynslade, we find that half of the leadership was drawn from the gentry: Arundell and John Winslade were esquires, while Bury was a gentleman. As lesser country gentry living in remote Western counties, those provincials had never enjoyed the social, economic, and political benefits associated with the Tudor court. It must be assumed that they mistrusted the court politicians, the Seymours, Russells, and

Pagets, more than their tenants and poor neighbors. Whereas Paget feared social upheaval, Arundell and his companions feared political centralization and court-inspired reforms. Of the three nongentry leaders, Holmes was a yeoman, while the Ketts were artisans. These rebels had enough wealth to be free from privation or poverty, but at the same time their political loyalties lay more with the commons than with the gentry.

Difficulties increase as we attempt to analyze the social status of the rebels on a regional basis. Names of rebels occur in narrative accounts, chronicles, lists of prisoners, trial records, references to executions, and pardons. Unfortunately the documents do not always give the class or occupation of the individual rebel. Some social and occupational categories were more carefully recorded than others; for example, members of the clergy were regularly identified as were knights, esquires, and gentlemen. Tudor record keepers were always less meticulous when dealing with the lower ranks of society. Another problem is that many of the most resourceful rebels were never caught; hence their names do not appear in records. Among the rank and file besieging Exeter and encamped on Mousehold Heath, large numbers apparently accepted royal pardons and returned home without having their names recorded. It is possible to learn the social status only of the rebels who were important enough or unfortunate enough to have their names and occupations included in surviving records.

Tables 1, 2, and 3 give the results of a social and occupational analysis of the 1549 rebels. The small numbers listed require that any conclusions be highly tentative. As might be suspected, clergy were the most numerous social class implicated in the Western Rebellion. Nonetheless gentry, citizens, urban officials, and yeomen make up half of the total. In Norfolk artisans constitute the largest occupational category. Even in the West there were more artisans than the combined total of yeomen, husbandmen, and laborers. In the counties outside Norfolk and the West artisans were the largest single category although the combined total of yeomen, husbandmen, and laborers was larger (unless the figure of 200 tinkers, weavers, artificers at Frome, Somerset is used to distort the small numbers in other categories). The occupations appearing most frequently among the artisans include butcher, tailor, weaver, and shoemaker. Artisans employed full-time in a trade were likely to have greater freedom from landlords than copyholders and leaseholders. They might have considerable social mobility and, as in the case of Robert Kett, substantial wealth. It must be emphasized, however, that the working people of Tudor England often combined more than one occupation. Most artisans outside London and the provincial capitals were part-time agriculturalists and often pursued their trades on a seasonal basis. William Kett, for example, is referred to both as a mercer and butcher, while his brother was a tanner as well as a farmer. Although artisans played significant roles in popular risings of the middle ages, their contribution to Tudor rebellions has been greatly underestimated. The data presented in Tables 1, 2, and 3 cannot stand as an occupational census representative of the entire rank and file, but the evidence contained there draws attention to the importance of artisans and indicates the social diversity of the rebels of 1549.[18]

2. Government Strategy, 1549-53

After pacifying the countryside and executing rebel leaders, the government pursued policies intended to prevent new outbreaks of popular disorder. A vigorous propaganda offensive was a prominent feature of the government's strategy. Royal proclamations and official replies to the rebels' articles reaffirmed traditional Tudor doctrines of obedience to the magistrate. From the pulpit clergy of all ranks from the Archbishop of Canterbury downward denounced the evils of sedition. Preachers placed great emphasis on Catholic agitators as the most insidious enemies of the commonwealth. When John Joseph, chaplain to Archbishop Cranmer, preached against the rebels at St. Paul's on August 31, he stressed that "the occasion came by Popish priests."[19] The Protestant reformers were determined to dissociate their teachings from the rebel protests and readily invoked the popish menace without giving careful consideration to the true causes of discontent. Faced with a powerful challenge to the reformed religion as well as to political stability, the clergy did not hesitate to abandon their compassion for the plight of the poor. Archbishop Cranmer took the lead when he said, "They to whom God hath sent poverty in goods, let them also be poor and humble in spirit, and then be they blessed in heaven, howsoever they be here in earth." He added, "If they will be true gospellers, let them then be obedient, meek, patient in adversity, and long-suffering, and in no wise rebel against the laws and magistrates."[20]

Two learned treatises on the evils of rebellion appeared before the end of 1549. In "An Answer to the Articles of the Commoners of Devonshire and Cornwall," Nicholas Udall, a canon of Windsor, refuted the Western rebels' sixteen articles in a lengthy tract of forty folio pages. Inasmuch as Udall's work was not published, it is unclear how highly the government regarded his efforts.[21] *The Hurt of Sedition* by John Cheke, on the other hand, appeared in two printed editions during the year. Whereas Udall directed his arguments toward the Western rebels, Cheke engaged the rebellious commons in both Norfolk and the West: "And yet ye pretend that partly for God's cause and partly for the commonwealth's sake, ye do arise, when as yourselves cannot deny, but ye that seek in word God's cause, do break indeed God's commandments, and ye that seek the commonwealth have destroyed the common-wealth." He berated the commons who sought greater social equality, for "if there should be such equality, then ye take away all hope from

Table 1

Status of Persons Implicated in Western Rebellion

Gentry	8
Urban official or citizen	10
Clergy	14
Yeoman	3
Husbandman	1
Laborer	1
Artisan	5
Fishdriver	
Smith	
Shoemaker	
Tailor	
Miller	

This table is based primarily on the "List of Insurgents" printed in Rose-Troup, pp. 497-502. It includes persons pardoned, imprisoned, indicted, tried, and executed, as well as persons alleged to be supporters or favorers of the rebellion.

yours to come to any better estate than you now leave them." He asked the commons to remember the "daily benefits" they received from the gentry and insisted that King Edward intended "a just reformation of all such things as poor men could truly show themselves oppressed with."[22] Cheke, a humanistic scholar anxious to advance in government service, was rewarded before the king's death with appointment to the Council and the office of secretary.

Although the propaganda campaign was important in restoring social and political stability, words alone were not enough. The rebellions had weakened the government and divided the ruling elite to a greater degree than any conflict since the Tudor dynasty secured the throne in 1485. In the past a strong monarch had asserted royal authority and rescued the country from crisis, but in 1549 the king was a child whose government was headed by his discredited uncle, the Duke of Somerset. By charging Somerset with misgovernance and removing him from office, the Council followed the traditonal political strategy of freeing the blameless monarchy from the grip of a wicked councillor. The overthrow of Protector Somerset — irrespective of its fairness to Somerset himself — was an essential step toward restoring the integrity of the king's government.

But the problems of the government did not end with the bloodless deposition of Somerset. The costly war with France continued, and plans for the subjugation of Scotland lay in ruins. By September 1552 military expenditures for the reign reached £1,356,687. The direct cost of

Table 2

Status of Persons Implicated in Norfolk Rebellion

Gentry	Nicholas LeStrange and Thomas Godsalve accused	
Urban official or citizen	Mayor Codd and other officials collaborated with Kett	
Clergy		4
Yeoman		1
Husbandman		13
Laborer		2
Artisan		28
Mason	1	
Tanner	4	
Tailor	4	
Shoemaker	1	
Miller	2	
Mercer	2	
Butcher	8	
Hatter	1	
Fisherman	1	
Cooper	1	
Other	3	

This table is based on persons mentioned in Sotherton, Neville, Holinshed, pardons listed in the *Calendar of Patent Rolls,* and scattered references in manuscript and printed sources.

the rebellions in Norfolk, Devon, and Cornwall was put at £27,330.[23] The financial difficulties, which were serious at the beginning of 1549, had grown steadily worse. The poor harvest of 1549 and the continuing inflationary spiral created conditions favorable to renewed social unrest. Although the Council was determined not to repudiate the religious reforms of the Protectorate, conservative clergy and gentry favored a return to the policies of Henry VIII. The most urgent problem facing the Council was the need to formulate policies that would heal the wounds dividing the court and country. If the government could regain the confidence of the landed gentry, who had opposed Somerset's agrarian program and suffered humiliation at the hands of the rebels, it could view the future with confidence and attend to all other problems in an orderly and deliberate fashion.

The unanticipated outbreak of rebellion forced the government to issue royal proclamations against enclosure rioters and unlawful assembly, but after the fall of Somerset proclamations were used less frequently. Parliament reassembled on November 4, 1549 and passed

Table 3

Status of Persons Implicated in Other Rebellions and Riots of 1549

	Berkshire	Buckinghamshire	Essex	Hampshire	Hertfordshire	Kent	Lancashire	Lincolnshire	London and Middlesex	Oxfordshire	Somerset	Staffordshire	Suffolk	Surrey	Sussex	Warwickshire	Wiltshire	Yorkshire
Gentry												1				1		
Urban Official or citizen		1						1				2						
Clergy		1	5		1					5		1	2					1
Yeoman				1	1						2	1			1			1
Husbandman								7		2		2	7					
Laborer												7	8					
Tinker, weaver, artificer											200							
Carpenter		1	1									1						
Cobbler			1															
Collarmaker												1						
Cooper			1									1						
Craftsman										1								
Draper			1															
Falconer												1						
Nailor												3						
Peddler														1				
Shepherd																1		
Shoemaker	1		3			1				1								
Smith												2						
Surgeon												1						
Tailor												1						
Thatcher												2						
Tilemaker														1				
Weaver	2											1						

This table is based on persons mentioned in chronicles, pardons listed in the *Calendar of Patent Rolls*, and scattered references in manuscript and printed sources.

legislation that permitted the government to use statutory authority in repressing popular unrest. The Act for the Punishment of Unlawful Assemblies and Rising of the King's Subjects (3 and 4 Edward VI c. 5) was intended to promote "tranquility and peace" throughout the commonwealth and contained elaborate provisions for repressing disorder. If twelve or more persons assembled to kill or imprison a privy councillor or to alter existing laws were commanded to disperse by a sheriff, justice of the peace, mayor, or other official and refused to obey, they were to be charged with high treason after one hour had elapsed. If twelve or more attempted to destroy enclosures, parks, deer, pull down houses or barns, or burn stacks of grain, they were to be charged with felony if they failed to disperse within one hour after receiving an official order. Groups of forty or more assembled for the same purpose could be charged with treason after two hours. Smaller assemblies of two to eleven that intended to kill one of the king's subjects or destroy enclosures and refused to disperse were subject to one year's imprisonment and fines amounting to three times the damage caused to private property. The act granted pardon to those who in response to an official order killed or maimed rioters. Copyholders, husbandmen, and yeomen between the ages of 16 and 60 would forfeit their property if they refused to serve against offenders. The statute contained the specific words of a proclamation to be read before the penalties could be imposed. Although the act was undeniably harsh, it was a logical response to the rebellions and was partially mitigated by the provision that it would continue only until the end of the next Parliament.

Three other statutes passed before Parliament was prorogued on February 1, 1550, gave the government authority to uphold law and order. An Act for the Abolishing and Putting Away of Divers Books and Images (3 and 4 Edward VI c. 10) was directed against Catholics. The prophesies that inspired rebels in Norfolk and Yorkshire undoubtedly prompted passage of An Act Against Fond and Fantastical Prophecies (3 and 4 Edward VI c. 15) which prescribed fines and imprisonment for persons inciting rebellion. An Act Concerning Retaining of Journeymen by Divers Persons (3 and 4 Edward VI c. 22) attempted to remedy a major source of disorder in cities and towns. Clothmakers, fullers, shearmen, weavers, and shoemakers, the statute alleged, lived idly and at their pleasure fled and resorted from place to place. By terms of the legislation such artisans could not be hired for a period of less than three months. Long terms of employment, while potentially expensive to employers, would reduce the number of vagrants and masterless men roaming the streets and troubling urban officials.

The astonishing successes of rebel forces in Norfolk and the West served as a grim reminder of the country's military weakness. Since the reign of Henry VIII there had been a growing awareness of the shortage of trained soldiers and the absence of an efficient military organization, but the problem was more easily diagnosed than remedied. Before the end of 1549 Sir Thomas Wyatt submitted to Somerset a proposal to organize in every county a reserve of trained soldiers who would serve under a professional commander. As Wyatt maintained close ties with the Earl of Warwick and other privy councillors, it is likely that his ideas for military reform were discussed by the government after Somerset's removal as Protector. Although Wyatt's program was never implemented, the government took several less costly steps toward improving its military posture. In place of the professional commanders recommended by Wyatt, lords lieutenant were sent into the counties to supervise the levying of shire musters. One of the most successful appointments was John Russell, Earl of Bedford, who gave the West more efficient leadership than it had had since the fall of the Courtenays.[24]

The decision of the Council to allow its members to retain substantial numbers of men was another initiative intended to strengthen the military. In February 1551 the Council debated establishing men at arms, including horsemen, to serve the king and preserve order. The force mustered on several occasions before being disbanded. To remedy the country's manpower shortage and lessen dependence on expensive mercenaries, the Council advised the lords lieutenant in October 1549 to recruit "idle persons" who would not labor, including the "greatest doers and ringleaders in the late sedition and commotion." Recruitment remained difficult and the quality of recruits low, because soldiers levied from the ranks of the unemployed and seditious were scarcely the basis of a reliable military force. All efforts to improve the military were hindered by the government's financial difficulties and decades of neglect. The notion that the reign of Edward witnessed "a menacing revival of aristocratic military power" conflicts with the country's severe military weakness. As Jeremy Goring has emphasized, significant progress toward improvement of the military did not occur until the passage of the Militia Act of 1558.[25]

As the government worked to repair damage caused by the rebellions and maintain order, Commonwealth writers renewed their demands for reform. They agreed with the government on the evils of rebellion but argued that the causes of social unrest still remained. Their main contention was that the reform of society must begin with the moral improvement of individual men and women. Hugh Latimer, preaching before the king during Lent 1550, condemned "great men and men of power" who oppressed the poor. Thomas Becon's *Jewel of Joy*, dedicated to Princess Elizabeth in 1550, berated avaricious sheep-mongers and nobles who delighted in building gorgeous houses. Although Becon served as chaplain to Someset, his objection to extravagant building can have referred only to the duke's construction of Somerset House in the Strand. In *The Fortress of the Faithful*, also published in 1550, Becon accused the gentry of "making common pasture several to themselves" and of "inclosing more ground to their own use than heretofore hath been accustomed and by this means [taking] away the necessary food from the poor men's cattle." Another target was the "new preachers" whose zeal caused the commons "to aspire and breach unto carnal liberty." Becon recognized that there were both good and bad preachers and gentlemen, and he exhorted them to serve the commonwealth. Becon and Latimer were highly moralistic and stressed repeatedly that human covetousness lay at the root of all social malaise.[26]

Thomas Lever, fellow of St. John's, Cambridge, following in the footsteps of Latimer, preached powerful sermons before the king and Council calling for reform. Early in 1550 he courageously praised the work of the discredited enclosure commissions in easing the plight of the rural poor. Lever flattered the councillors as honorable, wise, and godly men but also called on them to amend their faults. The gentry and officers of the crown, said Lever, built "many fair houses and keep few good houses, have plenty of eloquence to tell fair tales, but use little faithful diligence in doing their duties." On another occasion Lever reproached "ungodly, shameful [and] wicked" officials for failing to enforce good laws.[27]

The most energetic Commonwealth propagandist in the years immediately following the rebellions was the writer and printer, Robert Crowley. In his view social unrest was a disease that could be cured "by cherishing the humours natural and by quickening again of the spirits vital, which, in the commonwealth are the subjects true." Crowley accepted a hierarchical society and implored the poor to obey their masters. "If God have laid his hand on thee and made thee low in all men's sight," he said, "content thyself with that degree." Nevertheless he reserved heaviest condemnation for the rich and powerful and left little doubt that they had the most important role to play in restoring the health of the commonwealth. Crowley urged the gentry not to raise rents or enclose land to increase their income. He called on magistrates to avoid tyranny, execute all statutes, and help the poor and needy. A critic of the government's Scottish policy, Crowley implored the king's ministers to avoid aggression against "strange nations" because there was charge enough "to answer for thine own commons." Although he condemned all who rebelled, he argued that the lower classes learned disrespect for the law from their betters when they disobeyed the proclamations against enclosures. Speaking directly to the gentry in *The Way to Wealth, wherein is plainly taught a most present remedy for Sedition* (1550) Crowley charged, "You have been the only cause of their offence."[28]

The writings and sermons of Crowley, Becon, Latimer, and Lever are persuasive evidence that demands for reform were not halted by the rebellions and the overthrow of Protector Somerset. As spokesmen of the Church of England, they showed that the state church championed the cause of the poor against the propertied classes. The church's potential for social reform must have been a powerful attraction for Crowley, because he abandoned printing and received ordination as a deacon in 1551. Although the clerical reformers have been criticized for trafficking in moralistic platitudes laced with effusive rhetoric, they held that political leaders influenced by Christian values could easily devise policies that would restore the health of the commonwealth. Political programs, parliamentary legislation, and administrative procedures were secondary to a sound understanding of the Gospel. When the "graziers, rich butchers, the men of law, the merchants, the gentlemen, the knights, the lords" — in short, all of the privileged classes condemned by Crowley — abandoned their old ways and began to practice Christian charity, practicable solutions to the country's ills would be quickly forthcoming. The reformers' moral philosophy may have looked to the past, but their belief that the commonwealth could never be any better than the individuals comprising it was hardly unrealistic. Motivated by such principles, Crowley called on the Lord to "work in the hearts of the rich,"[29] and his fellow reformers prepared a prayer for landlords that was authorized by the king in 1553:

> We heartily pray thee to send thy Holy Spirit into the hearts of them that possess the grounds, pastures, and dwelling places of the earth, that they, remembering themselves to be thy tenants, may not rack and stretch out the rents of their houses and land, nor yet take unreasonable fines and incomes after the manner of covetous worldings, but so let them out to other, that the inhabitants thereof may both be able to pay the rents, and also honestly to live, to nourish their families, and to relieve the poor.[30]

A Discourse of the Commonweal of This Realm of England, written in 1549 but not published until the reign of Elizabeth, is generally regarded as the most brilliant and enduring contribution to the reform literature of the mid-sixteenth century. For many years it was believed to be the work of John Hales, but Mary Dewar has argued persuasively that the author was Sir Thomas Smith, secretary to the king under Protector Somerset. In contrast to Latimer, Lever, Becon, and Crowley, Smith examined social and economic problems with a secular lens. He did not deny that men were wicked and avaricious, but asked, "Can we devise that all covetousness may be taken from men?" He replied, "No, no more than we can make men to be without ire, without gladness, without fear, and without all affections. What then? We must take away from men the occasion of their covetousness in this part." He argued that the four major economic problems were inflation (termed dearth by sixteenth-century writers), "the exhaustion of the treasure of this realm," enclosure of arable land, and the decay of towns and villages. An authority on coinage, Smith contended that debasement was "the first original cause" of inflation and recommended minting coins with higher silver content. Enclosure of arable land could be limited by allowing farmers to make larger profits through overseas grain sales. To revive decaying towns Smith urged the government to encourage the export of manufactured goods and to develop "new crafts" including the making of swords, tools, paper, and parchment. Although Smith was out of favor after the fall of Somerset, his proposals influenced government policy to a greater extent than the moralistic precepts of clerical writers.[31]

Until recently historians believed that the government headed by John Dudley, Earl of Warwick and Duke of Northumberland, was a corrupt and despotic regime that turned its back on all demands for reform except religion. That the new ordinal, the revised *Book of Common Prayer* of 1552, and the Forty-Two Articles of Religion completed the Protestant reforms begun after the accession of Edward VI has never been doubted, but it is quite clear that the government initiated and supported reforms covering a far wider spectrum. "It really took hold of England's government and tackled the crying needs of the day," wrote G. R. Elton, "and it did so with a thoroughness and competence that approached (at a distance) those customary in the 1530's." Northumberland, governing through a carefully managed Council, drew upon the talents of Sir William Cecil, Sir Thomas Gresham, William Paulet, Marquis of Winchester, and Sir Walter Mildmay. Responding to Sir Thomas Smith's criticism of debasement, the government undertook a bold reform of the coinage. The Royal Commission of 1552 proposed improved financial management and reform of the Exchequer. The king's untimely death in 1553 left some of the government's work incomplete, but its initial achievements and wide-ranging objectives are impressive.[32]

The Northumberland regime, headed by a duke and supported by other peers and gentry, pursued social and economic policies that reflected the interests of the landed classes to a greater degree than the needs of the commons. Nonetheless a healthy commonwealth required law and order, sound finances, and the well-being of men and women of all ranks and degrees. While the government, striving to avoid the mistakes of Somerset's Protectorate, worked to maintain unity among the landed classes, it dared not ignore the social and economic conditions that drove the commons to rebellion. Inflation and poor harvests in 1549, 1550 and 1551 forced the government to assign a high priority to price control. Inflation adversely affected all classes, but the poor, especially day laborers and tenants-at-will, were the most vulnerable. There can be no doubt that the government sought price stability, for it issued royal proclamations fixing food prices, restricting middlemen who bought foods and held them until prices rose, and prohibiting the export of grain, wool, leather and other commodities. The Council made a determined effort to enforce the proclamations, but the economic realities of the age — like those of later eras — worked against the government's best efforts.[33]

As the Northumberland government sought to control prices, it also supported agrarian reform. No other area of policy-making was more vexed and fraught with political danger. Memories were all too vivid of Protector Somerset's enclosure commissions that raised false hopes among the commons and antagonized the gentry. The government's caution may be seen in its primary reliance on parliamentary statutes whereas Somerset had ridden roughshod over the gentry by formulating agrarian policy through royal proclamations. The first statute to address the question of enclosure, An Act Concerning the Improvement of Commons and Waste Grounds (3 and 4 Edward VI c. 3), was passed in 1550. As the title indicates, the act deliberately avoided enclosure of arable lands; however, peasant rights in woodland, commons, and waste were issues no less contentious. The act first confirmed thirteenth-century legislation giving lords of the manor rights over these lands as long as their tenants had "sufficient pasture" and rights of ingress and egress. The vagueness of the word "sufficient" prompted Hugh Latimer to criticize the statute for its partiality to landlords, but the act merely restated rights which they had enjoyed for centuries. It is the second part of the statute that reveals the government's commitment to reform. Here Parliament recognized a squatter's right by restricting the landlord's manorial rights over commons and waste. The restriction applied to houses built on less than three acres and to gardens and orchards of less than two acres, "which doth no hurt and yet is much commodity to the owner thereof." While the act offered nothing to the yeoman or husbandman, it granted protection to the rural poor who had built homes in the woods or in wasteland or enclosed a small garden in order to feed their families.[34]

Before Parliament was prorogued on February 1, 1550, the controversial sheep tax was repealed on the grounds that it was cumbersome to clothiers, harmful to the poor, and objectionable to the commissioners who were required to implement its complex provisions. The government's determination to appease the peerage and gentry appears in the Act... Touching the Taking of Wildfowl at Certain Times in the Year (3 and 4 Edward VI c. 7). It repealed more permissive legislation from the reign of Henry VIII and restricted the taking of fowl by tenants to the period May 31 to August 31, when, according to the statute, other food was in short supply.

When Parliament was recalled in 1552, it turned to the question of maintenance of tillage and enclosure of arable land. New legislation was undoubtedly prompted by the ineffectiveness of a proclamation issued the previous year denouncing sheep masters, engrossers, and enclosers in language similar to the Commonwealth literature. Despite its high-sounding rhetoric, the proclamation of May 11, 1551, imposed no specific punishment. The Act of 1552 (5 and 6 Edward VI c. 5), the only agrarian reform of the session to win passage, dealt with the traditional need to maintain tillage and increase grain production. The objective of the statute was to have as much land under cultivation by March 1553 as in any one year since 1509. Commissioners appointed by the king under the great seal were to enforce the legislation. Although the commissioners could enquire, search, and convene a jury of freeholders to identify offenders, there is no evidence commissioners were appointed during the short period that remained before the king's death. The agrarian legislation of the Northumberland regime was at best a partial solution to an almost impossible problem. As Joan Thirsk has said, the Acts of 1550 and 1552, while hardly forceful enough, "at least made a show of defending the poor against the powerful."[35]

The continuing problem of unemployment, vagrancy, and poverty forced the government and Parliament to find legislative remedies. The Vagrancy Act of 1547 containing provisions for enslavement was promptly repealed in 1550 in a statute that revived a more lenient act from the reign of Henry VIII. The Henrician policy of relieving the impotent poor — that is, sick and aged persons — on the parish level, was improved in 1552. The new poor law (5 and 6 Edward VI c. 2) constituted an important step toward establishing a compulsory parish tax for poor relief. Parish officials were empowered to appoint two collectors of alms. The law provided that when the people were at church and had heard "God's Holy Word," the collectors should "gently ask and demand of every man and woman what they of their charity will be contented to give weekly towards the relief of the poor." After receiving pledges from the parishioners, the collectors of alms were to record them in a book. The collectors were also responsible for distributing the alms among the impotent poor. The poor law of 1552 was an improvement on the policies of Henry VIII and the Protectorate and pointed the way toward the Elizabethan poor law.[36]

The Northumberland government was not alone in devising programs of poor relief, because urban governments were also active. As early as 1547, the City of London imposed a compulsory tax for supporting the poor at St. Bartholomew's Hospital. Four years later City authorities took charge of St. Thomas' Hospital in Southwark. At St. Bartholomew's 100 beds were maintained, while St. Thomas' relieved 260 "aged, sore, and impotent persons." In 1552 buildings of the dissolved Grey Friars were remodeled into a school for fatherless children. The new school became known as Christ's Hospital and accommodated 400 children. Before the king's death, Nicholas Ridley, Bishop of London, managed to obtain the former royal palace of Bridewell for the training, correction, and relief of the able-bodied poor. The work of the inmates was to include making caps, feather bed ticks, and drawing wire.[37] The larger provincial cities followed the example of London in providing for the poor. At Lincoln four aldermen proposed to employ both young and old in fulling and dyeing woolen cloth for terms of eight to nine years. Persons refusing to work were to be given a month's notice to leave the city. Officials at Norwich imposed compulsory contributions for the poor in 1549, only two years after London introduced the same policy. Although the mid-Tudor response to poverty bears little resemblance to modern concepts of job training and social security, the Edwardians proceeded along lines that changed very little over the next hundred years.[38]

3. Popular Disorder 1550-53

In spite of the combined efforts of Parliament, the Privy Council, and local governments, popular unrest continued after 1549. The commons produced no leaders of the stature of Robert Kett, but conspiracy, riot, and small-scale rebellion persisted. Disorder resulted in part from the failure of government policy, because the Northumberland regime, notwithstanding its reforming efforts, governed in behalf of the landed and moneyed classes. Neither Northumberland, his fellow councillors nor their predecessors regarded the well-being of the commons as highly as the prosperity of the gentry. Government at all levels was prisoner of a tradition that never questioned the virtue of an ordered society, a society where the rich, the well-born, and the fortunate flourished at the expense of ordinary men and women.

The government lacked the financial resources as well as the will to undertake more ambitious social reforms. From the accession of Edward VI until his death in 1553, the government wrestled with crippling financial problems. A government that could scarcely pay its debts was in no position to initiate costly social programs. As important as the failures of government were economic conditions that eroded the commons' standard of living. Inflation, poor harvests, increasing population, and shortages of arable and pasture land were the real villains of mid-Tudor England. Social and economic malaise contributed to the rebellions of 1549 and to the recurrence of disorder in 1550, 1551, and 1552.

In 1550 the most serious disturbances took place in Essex, Kent, and Oxfordshire, three counties that experienced rebellion the previous year. In March 1550 the Council ordered the arrest and examination of "certain light fellows" that came from Sussex to Witham, Essex where they drank all day and read books at night. At the end of June rebels were arrested for a conspiracy in the Romford area. A puzzling episode occurred at Christmas when a group of Kentishmen lodged with Robert Cook, a clothier, in Bocking. The visitors, including a schoolmaster from Maidstone, moved to the house of Thomas Upcharde when Cook's wife gave birth to a baby. The next day being Sunday, sixty townspeople assembled at Upcharde's house and fell into an argument "of things of the Scripture, specially whether it were necessary to stand or kneel barehead or covered at prayer, which at length was concluded in ceremony not to be material, but the hearts before God was it that imported [sic] and nothing else." Upcharde's confession led to the arrest of a dozen men from Essex and Kent who admitted under examination by the Council that "the cause of their assembly [was] for talk of Scriptures not denying but they had refused the Communion above two years upon very superstitious and erroneous purposes." The Christmas gathering would appear to have been an assembly of religious radicals with separatist leanings.[39]

Kent was the scene of an unsuccessful rebellion in April 1550 that led to the execution of two men at Ashford and one at Canterbury. Edward VI's journal suggests that the rising had religious overtones: "Certain were taken that went about to have an insurrection in Kent . . ., and the priest, who was the chief worker, ran away into Essex where he was laid for." The Imperial ambassador heard rumors that 10,000 commons gathered at Sittingbourne early in June, but it is doubtful whether such a multitude ever assembled.[40] An enclosure riot at Banbury, Oxfordshire, in December confirmed earlier indications that popular unrest in the county was not limited to opponents of the Protestant Reformation. Commons led by George Danvers of Calthorpe "riotously digged [sic] down the ditches enclosing the demesnes lying about Banbury Castle. . . ." Danvers and his men claimed right of commons and were ordered to appear before the Council. Trouble persisted at least until August 1552 when the Council instructed the surveyor for Oxfordshire in the Court of Augmentations to determine the common rights of the inhabitants of Calthorpe.[41]

Elsewhere we find restlessness among the commons revealed by agrarian disputes, charges for speaking "seditious words," and above all a flood of wild and often unsubstantiated rumors. The government's policy of rewarding informers may have encouraged Thomas Lovett to come forward with a report that constables in Nottinghamshire were attempting to raise the commons in the king's name, even though the royal proclamation offering informers £20 was issued two days after Lovett's appearance before the Council. He also accused two men from Thame, Oxfordshire, who, after proving their innocence, were released on recognizances of £5.[42]

In July the Duke of Somerset, deprived of his authority as protector but restored to the Council, journeyed to Oxfordshire, Hampshire, Wiltshire, and Sussex attempting to maintain law and order. Unrest continued at King's Somborne, Hampshire as Richard Gifforde, Esq., farmer of the demesne, sued local tenants in the court of the Duchy of Lancaster. The controversy concerned pasture rights. The tenants claimed ancient rights, but the records showed that they "had not sufficiently proved themselves to have any such right or title to have common pasture or feeding." Gifforde proved that the common belonged to the demesne of the manor, and the court ordered him to possess the disputed land quietly and peacefully.[43] At Southampton the mayor inquired about a man spreading rumors that there would be a greater stir before Michaelmas than occurred the previous year. From Sussex came reports of "a conspiracy among the commons" planned for Whit Monday at Heathfield. The disclosures led to a search throughout the county for "vagabonds, gypsies, conspirators, prophesiers, all players and such like." Somerset's role in law enforcement is not documented, but the former protector's presence helped convince the commons that he supported the government's policies.[44]

Vagabonds, undisciplined soldiers, and radical preachers troubled officials in London. The unlicensed Essex cleric, Thomas Putto, was in trouble once again for preaching "as lewdly as he had done before." In June the king noted that the mayor "caused the watches to be increased every night, because of the great frays, and also one alderman to see good rule kept every night."[45] Outside the City a mysterious Captain Redde Cappe attracted enthusiastic crowds throughout Middlesex. The captain was a former rebel released from prison in Westminster. After hearing that "the commons had feasted him," the Council unsuccessfully tried to determine who had authorized his release.[46] Farther afield came rumblings of discontent in Wales and the West country. Sir William Herbert was dispatched to Wales in April to inquire into the "inconstant disposition of the commons," while the Earl of Bedford returned to Exeter. At Bristol the mayor discovered seditious bills and was advised by the Council in London to determine the authors "by comparison of writings" and to examine all "idle and suspect persons."[47]

Norwich remained quiet after Kett's defeat, but many artisans fondly remembered their fallen leader and spoke against the triumphant gentry. Their bitterness is revealed in testimony before the mayor and aldermen, who busily ferreted out every potential dissident. A laborer, Edmund Johnson, was charged in September 1549 for allegedly saying that if Kett was executed, "it should cost a thousand men's lives." In February 1550, John Redhedde, a worsted weaver, called for the removal of Warwick's insignia, the bear and ragged staff, from the gates of the city. He also boasted that Kett's body would "be plucked down from the top of the castle" before Lammas Day (August 1). An unemployed weaver, William Whyte, boldly proclaimed, "By the mass, we shall have as hot a summer as ever was." Robert Burnam, parish clerk of St. Gregory, damned the Norfolk gentry as thieves saying, "There are too many gentlemen in England by 500." Roger Woodhouse, he charged, had "moated his house about double" out of fear of the commons. In June informers listening from a window at five o'clock in the morning heard a fisherman in the street below recall the camp on Mousehold Heath and exclaim, "It was a merry world when we were yonder eating of mutton." Perhaps the most zealous informer was an eighteen-year-old shoemaker's apprentice who overheard his master berate the gentry. The shoemaker, John Warde, muttered that the gentry would need "to watch all the days of their lives" because they would have "such plague as they have not had before." The youthful informer lived in his master's house and shared his bedroom.[48]

Record has survived of a few other brave souls in East Anglia who foolishly spoke to the wrong people at the wrong time. William Whitered was set on the pillory at Whissonsett, Norfolk, for seditious words and had an ear cut off. In April 1550, the Suffolk justices of the peace sent the Council the confession of an informer against Giles Stanton "touching words and matter of rebellion." Not long afterwards the Council issued a warrant to bring both Stanton and the informer to London for further examination. The following September the Council learned of an alleged conspiracy at East Dereham, Norfolk, and still later in the midst of winter the commons reportedly assembled at Thetford and cut down trees along the highway.[49]

Echoes of Kett's Rebellion continued into 1551. In that year the Court of Requests heard a case between John Spencer, Esq., and Dame Anne Paston, widow of Sir Thomas Paston, concerning Mousehold Heath, site of the great rebel camp. The dispute had to do with a hedge built three or four years earlier by Paston separating the heath from an adjoining area, Thorpe Wood. The hedge enclosed part of the woods and affected the commons' use of both the heath and the woods. John Spencer, farmer of a fold course for sheep at Thorpe, complained that he had previously fed sheep on "plain ground" adjacent to Thorpe Wood. It was alleged that until four or five years previously the mayor of Norwich, the aldermen, and citizens came annually in a procession to Thorpe Wood and heard a sermon preached there. A man of fifty-six stated that the poor folks of Norwich and Thorpe had previously been free to collect "dry and sapwood" without any interference. The wood was regularly replenished until the rebels of 1549 cut part of it; later the servants of Paston felled what remained. Another witness, Christopher Grape, aged sixty, said that the tenants of Thorpe pastured cattle on Mousehold Heath and in Thorpe Wood prior to Paston's erection of the hedge. Several conflicting issues were clearly involved. The Pastons claimed the right to enclose Thorpe Wood, while Spencer wanted a right-of-way through the woods and pasture for his sheep. Caught in the middle were the unfortunate commons who stood to lose pasture as well as firewood.[50]

As the dispute over Thorpe Wood simmered, the last of the Norfolk rebels, John Wythe of Aylsham, suffered execution. Wythe remained at large after the fiasco at Dussindale and was specifically excluded from the parliamentary pardon of 1550. His identity and role in the Norfolk Rebellion remain something of a mystery. Described as "a great rich man" by the Grey Friars chronicler, Wythe was actually a prosperous copyholder. He served as one of twelve headboroughs for the court leet in 1546 and demonstrated his literacy by signing a complaint against the local curate. Wythe remained at large until February 1550 when he was returned to Norfolk and condemned to be hanged at his own door. The execution, however, was delayed for over a year. In July 1551, the Council asked the Earl of Warwick to decide whether the execution should take place. Warwick gave his approval. A month later the Council denounced Wythe as "the notablest offender that was in the time of rebellion" and ordered his execution.[51]

Although John Wythe was finally silenced, new voices of protest were heard in 1551. Richard Greneway, gentleman usher to the king and justice of the peace for Buckinghamshire, was brought before the Council in March and charged with destruction of enclosures. Greneway contended that his neighbor, Ralph Lee, had enclosed a common meadow "contrary to right." After taking legal advice, Greneway had two of his men break down Lee's hedges and then pastured cattle on the land. The Council rebuked Greneway and ordered him to repair the hedge at his own expense. Because of long service to the crown, he received no further punishment, and his collaborators were released. A few weeks later the king learned of an attempted conspiracy in Essex where the culprits denounced the arrival of aliens at Chelmsford and tried to "spoil the rich men's houses." Before the end of the year, the Council heard of yet another riot in Essex.[52]

The spring of 1551 saw rumblings of discontent in London. Although the exact causes are difficult to determine, rising food prices, the reform of the coinage, and hostility to foreigners contributed to unrest. City officials reinforced the night watch early in April and arrested suspicious persons. A Southwark man was questioned for disobeying a sheriff's officer, and seventeen vagabonds were whipped. The constable of Farringdon apprehended John Storye, a gentleman's servingman, about midnight on April 16. Captured with a "naked sword all bloody" in his hands, Storye said that he had been in a fight at Holborn Bridge. There were rumors of a large rising on May Day, but nothing serious materialized. Butchers, angered by government price regulations, grumbled openly; and the Court of Aldermen ordered the company warden to question those who had spoken slanderous and seditious words. Tempers gradually cooled and by July London was suffering more from an epidemic called the sweating sickness than from sedition.[53]

The Duke of Somerset, supported by an armed force, went to Wokingham, Berkshire in August to pacify commons who organized a conspiracy for "the destruction of the gentlemen." Edward VI recorded in his journal that Somerset promptly executed several offenders. Another troublemaker, Isaac Herne of Beaconsfield, Buckinghamshire, helped organize the rising at Wokingham but was eventually pardoned. Herne demanded a reduction in rents and prices and reportedly said to his followers, "If you will you may now assemble a good company together, for I know where to set a great many, and they may help to get more; and then we will have the rents of farms and prices of victuals to be brought lower again as they were in King Richard's time." After six decades of Tudor rule, memories of the good old days of Yorkist rule lingered in the popular mind. A few months after order was restored at Wokingham, the Council appointed a commission of oyer and terminer to inquire about "treason or commotion" in another Berkshire town, Abingdon.[54]

Early in September Lord Clinton reported widespread unrest in the Midlands. "Stirrers of commotion" were active in Lincolnshire, and the justices of the peace were alerted to apprehend suspicious persons. Sir John Harrington learned that the commons of Leicestershire, Northamptonshire, and Rutland planned a rebellion. Harrington went to Uppingham, Rutland, where he captured the leading conspirator at his house. Three brothers were arrested at Morcott, but a fourth escaped. It was rumored that 400 commons intended to assemble near Uppingham and then visit certain unnamed gentlemen. When authorities arrived at the designated meeting place, no one was there. Details unfortunately are lacking, but Harrington was convinced that the troublemakers were "light knaves, horse corsers [traders], and craftsmen." Throughout the region gentry and local officials were urged to see that strong watches were kept in every town and to have horses ready for themselves and their servants. In the absence of more complete information it is impossible to determine whether the Midland gentry overreacted and fell prey to malicious rumormongers or whether the authorities' vigilance and prompt action prevented a serious rebellion.[55]

From 1552 until the king's death in July 1553 the commons aroused themselves less often than during the early years of the reign. A measure of credit must be given to the government for successfully enforcing its policies. Government officials at all levels learned the bitter lessons of 1549, and history did not repeat itself. The Council inquired into conspiracies, examined suspicious persons, and maintained close contact with justices of the peace. But the government was more than a law-and-order regime. It freed bondmen in Norfolk and investigated the condition of others in Lincolnshire.[56] In February 1553 the Court of the Duchy of Lancaster ordered its officers to meet with all parties involved in a dispute over pasture in Yorkshire and Lancashire, arrange an equitable division of the land, and set reasonable rents.[57] An encloser of waste ground at Newby and Clapham, Yorkshire was ordered to appear before the duchy chancellor at Westminster and threatened with a fine of

£200.[58] Duchy officers surveying land at Haslingden, Lancashire were directed to leave sufficient common land for all tenants.[59] The government's commission for a survey of church goods led to the confiscation of silver chalices and other valuables. Although the commissioners were required to implement an unpopular policy, the government specifically instructed them to "go forward with as much quiet and as little occasion of trouble and disquiet of the multitude as may be."[60]

Local officials in the towns and countryside worked as energetically as the central government to maintain peace and quiet. The bailiffs and aldermen of Colchester attempted to supervise tavernkeepers and limit the hours of business in order to prevent unlawful assemblies. Youths, maidens, and apprentices were specifically forbidden to visit taverns and ale houses on Sundays during either "divine service or preaching time."[61] While credulous officials often exaggerated the significance of seditious rumors and idle gossip, they were undoubtedly wise to err on the side of excessive caution. It is difficult to measure the contribution of the church, but the appointment of new bishops of Exeter and Norwich was clearly intended to provide stronger leadership in two important cities. Although Protestant reformers complained constantly about the shortage of able preachers, long lists of new clerical appointments and preaching licenses suggest that a serious effort was made to improve the quality of parish clergy.[62] In the final analysis an improvement in economic conditions may have been of greater importance than the best efforts of government and the church. The harvest of 1552, rated as average to good, made life less difficult for the commons. Prices fell during the last years of Edward's reign. According to the Phelps Brown-Hopkins scale the decline was 3 percent in 1552 and 6 percent in 1553. The Bowden price indices show similar and in some instances larger declines.[63] The temporary halt in the inflationary spiral lessened tension among all social classes and improved the living standard of tenants, wage laborers, and the poor.

Despite a better harvest and lower prices, isolated examples of disorder may be found in both urban and rural areas. In May 1552 the Council ordered the imprisonment of a man charged with beginning a "fray" at Exeter. Soon afterwards the Council wrote to the mayor of London about unrest in the parish of St. Gregory, a poor district south of St. Paul's that was, according to Stow, defaced by the sheds of cutlers and leather bag makers.[64] William Lowe, a Southwark tailor, was pilloried in September for saying, "The king of England is a cuckold's son and a bastard born."[65] From Oxford came news of a dispute over pasture rights that required the Council's intervention. The mayor and burgesses were ordered to remove their sheep from two pastures and to stop digging and raising banks around the pastures until an investigation was completed. At Chichester three men who offended the mayor were taken into custody in February 1553 on orders of the Council.[66]

Agrarian problems persisted in the countryside, but the government's vigilance prevented a major rising. The Council directed the Lord Chancellor to issue a commission of oyer and terminer in May 1552 for the examination of conspirators in Hampshire. A year later a widow from the same county, Avys Cowdrey, and her son Francis, sued Richard Puttenham, Esq., in the Court of Requests over a land dispute at Sherfield-upon-Loden, near Basingstoke. The plaintiffs alleged that the property in question should have descended to Francis Cowdrey after his father's death. According to the deceased man's will, a brother was to occupy the land until Francis came of age. When the brother attempted to take possession, he was "riotously and with force expulsed out" by Puttenham and his armed men. The Hampshire justices of the peace subsequently indicted Puttenham, who responded by asserting his own rights. The Puttenhams were major landholders whose estates included forty cottages, sixty houses, four water mills, and over fifteen hundred acres of land. The Court of Requests, true to its reputation as the poor man's court, ordered Puttenham not to molest Cowdrey until the former could prove his claim by "due order of the law."[67]

Disputes over pasture rights resulted in litigation in Norfolk and Wiltshire. The Court of the Duchy of Lancaster heard a complaint against William Day, a farmer of the manor of Feltwell, Norfolk, in 1552. It was alleged that Day overcharged the pasture and common at Methwold with sheep contrary to an order of the manorial court. In response the Duchy Court called for a full inquiry.[68] The next year four freeholders of Tysbury, Wiltshire — Thomas Sangar, Maude Davis, Robert Gerrard, and Thomas Benet — charged Sir John Marvin in the Court of Requests with unlawful occupation of a pasture for cattle, sheep, and swine. The irate freeholders claimed a right of common from time "out of memory of man." Marvin, unable to prove his claim, acted with "delay, slackness, and negligence." The Court ordered the plaintiffs to enjoy their common rights without any interference until such time as Marvin could produce better evidence.[69] If, as the fragmentary evidence suggests, the commons of Tysbury and other communities successfully protected their customary rights against the encroachment of the gentry, others suffering from similar grievances may have been more inclined to choose the courts in favor of violent and often counterproductive riots.

The trial of the Duke of Somerset in December 1551 and his execution the following month attracted great interest as the former protector had a considerable following among the commons, but those most affected were the gentry and ambitious careerists who found themselves on the losing side of court politics. A Wiltshire justice of the peace who was closely allied to Somerset, Matthew Colthurst, misunderstood the verdict and arranged a great celebration at Bath on December 3. Ringing bells summoned a crowd that feasted on food and drink provided by Colthurst on the false assumption that Somerset had been acquitted on all charges. The exuberant justice's only reward was to be reported to the Council by an informer.[70] From Somerset's execution on January 22, 1552 until the king's death, men and women, both brave and foolish, denounced the Duke of Northumberland for real and imagined crimes. Other agitators, enraged by the deflationary effects of the reform of the coinage, criticized the financial policies of the government. The Council shrewdly dealt with such persons on an individual basis often showing moderation and restraint.[71] As a result the defeated supporters of Somerset failed to organize a significant movement of popular protest.

Another threat that failed to materialize was that of the Anabaptists. The progress of religious reform under Edward VI inevitably encouraged a wide range of radical Protestants, but the structure and doctrines of the Church of England failed to satisfy many extremists. To uphold religious uniformity as established by Parliament, Archbishop Cranmer, supported by Nicholas Ridley, John Knox, and other clergy, worked tirelessly to repress the Anabaptists and other radical nonconformist sects. The clergy and the government saw the Anabaptists as a threat to religious unity and, by association with continental extremists, a danger to the social and political stability of the commonwealth. Religious persecution claimed George van Paris, a Dutch surgeon who was a Unitarian, and Joan Bocher, who denied that Christ was incarnate of the Virgin Mary. Other Protestant radicals, although attacked by church leaders, remained active in London, Kent, and Essex. Highly individualistic and passionately committed to their beliefs, the radicals posed a serious danger to religious uniformity, but there is little evidence that they sought to incite the commons to violence or revolutionary change.[72]

The failure of substantial numbers of commons to risk the dangers of rebellion and riot allowed the government to win the struggle for stability. Although there were determined religious, political, and social protests, the last years of Edward VI were relatively peaceful. As historians traditionally commend governments that successfully uphold law and order, it is appropriate that the Northumberland regime should receive praise for its achievements. Northumberland's government supported reforms intended to improve the well-being of the commonwealth and worked to see that laws — both old and new — were enforced. But repression was the other arm of government policy. Local officials enforced the law not only because they were loyal and obedient to the central government, but also because they were determined to protect their own interests. The rebellions of 1549 left a legacy of anxiety and fear among the aristocracy that was not quickly forgotten. Memories of the Norfolk Rebellion were revived by the publication of Alexander Neville's narrative in 1575, and as late as 1607 officials associated the name of Robert Kett with agrarian disturbances.[73] It is easier to explain the role of the aristocracy and government in achieving social stability than to account for the commons' quiescence. Better harvests and more stable prices obviously helped. The humiliation of military defeat in 1549 and the heavy hand of repression that followed may have been of even greater importance. The commons of mid-Tudor England lacked the resources, organization, leadership, and vision necessary to achieve their objectives, and having failed once, they were not eager to relive the horrors of Clyst Heath, Sampford Courtenay, and Dussindale.

CONCLUSION

The rebellions and riots of the reign of Edward VI were not isolated episodes unique to England, because the continent experienced similar popular protests. Everywhere adverse economic conditions contributed to discontent. In his classic study of the Mediterranean world, Fernand Braudel found that the movement of upward social mobility characteristic of the early sixteenth century was checked between 1550 and 1560. Better times followed 1560 "only to come to another standstill, perhaps as early as 1587 in Burgundy or in about 1595 as, all over the world, the secular trend was being reversed." Successive phases of revival and stagnation culminated in the "short-lived triumph of the aristocracy and the partial freezing of society at the very end of the century."[1] In this European environment increasing population outdistanced production of food and manufactured goods. Prices rose, but wages lagged behind the inflationary spiral with the result that the common man's standard of living tended to stagnate or decline. The great majority of mankind lived in fear of malnutrition and starvation. Throughout Europe from England to the Mediterranean there were shortages of food, housing, and work. The demand for poor relief increased rapidly. As it was never "very difficult anywhere to start a riot," the crowned heads of Europe, their ministers, and the aristocracy governed in an atmosphere of uneasiness and anxiety.[2]

While popular protests in England represented a direct response to social and economic conditions prevailing thoughout Europe, each disturbance had its own peculiarities. Moreover, politics and religion played important roles in the rebellions of 1548-49 and in subsequent risings. The government of Protector Somerset failed politically because it could not implement programs intended to ease the plight of the commons. Somerset's desire to restrict enclosure of pasture and common land was a bold response to the agrarian crisis, but leaders of the gentry and peerage who controlled Parliament refused to pass the necessary legislation. Somerset's determination to proceed in the face of opposition and implement his program through royal proclamations alienated the aristocracy and raised false hopes among the commons. The disenchantment of the gentry and urban leaders led to a breakdown in the close cooperation between central and local governments that was fundamental to the efficient operation of the Tudor state. Although the county and urban elites did not support the rebellions, their misgivings about government policy and their lack of vigor allowed small localized protests to grow into major rebellions. In Cornwall support for the government was almost entirely lacking, while the Devon and Norfolk gentry also failed to restore order. The leaders of Exeter successfully defended the city against the rebel siege, but their counterparts at Norwich were confused and bewildered when challenged by the forces of Robert Kett. The success of the Earl of Arundel in Sussex, on the other hand, is dramatic evidence that energetic leaders invoking traditional concepts of good lordship could stem the tide of popular protest. Stronger political leadership from the Council and in the provinces would not have restored prosperity in a year of poor harvests, but it would have reduced or eliminated the need for large armies to pacify Norfolk and the West during the summer of 1549.

There can be little doubt that religious grievances contributed to unrest at all levels of society. Conservative Henrician clergy, particularly in Cornwall and Devon, misunderstood and disliked the flood of Protestant reforms legislated by Parliament after 1547. The rapid pace of religious change angered traditionalists, who were already unhappy with the slower and more cautious reforms of Henry VIII. The clerical opposition defended the Henrician settlement against the innovations of what they perceived to be a heretical court party. Lay persons of all ranks listened to the misgivings of the clergy, and some fell prey to irresponsible rumors and exaggerated fears of what would result from the new Protestant teachings, because the sixteenth century was an age of clerical influence and intellectual deference to learned authorities. The complex conspiracy unravelled at Winchester was an unusual example of religious discontent, but from Cornwall to Yorkshire opponents of Edwardian Protestantism contemplated or participated in acts of violence. By contrast, the Protestant sympathies of Kett's followers in Norfolk sustained the conviction that the king sympathized with the commons and that irresponsible local authorities were the real enemies of the commonwealth. The decline of religious protests after 1549 may be explained by the overwhelming defeat of the rebels, the deprivation of Henrician bishops, and the growing acceptance of the government's religious program. If liturgical innovation may be said to symbolize the stages of the Edwardian Reformation, it is likely that the introduction of the second Prayer Book in 1552 disturbed fewer clergy and lay persons than the abolition of the Latin Mass in 1549.

In *The Anatomy of Popular Rebellion in the Middle Ages,* Guy Fourquin argued that rebellions were often linked to crisis situations.[3] The rebellions and popular disturbances of the reign of Edward VI are a vivid example of this phenomenon. The accession of the nine-year-old king in 1547 created political problems never before encountered by the Tudors. Rising prices, a poor harvest, and the ill-fated sheep tax coincided with radical religious change. And to make matters still worse the fall of the Courtenays in Devon and the Howards in Norfolk weakened local leadership in two important areas at the very moment when it was most needed. While it may be conceded that the Edwardian governments, led first by Somerset and then by Northumberland, suffered from many shortcomings, they had the misfortune of governing a country engulfed in the worst crises of the sixteenth century.

Expressions of popular discontent were heard from one end of the country to the other. Major rebellions in Cornwall, Devon, and Norfolk contrast with riots, conspiracies, and smaller disturbances elsewhere. Since over half the counties in England suffered from disorder in 1549, the traditional idea of two separate and distinct rebellions must be rejected. Common social, economic, and political grievances linked rebellious commons throughout the country. It is, of course, quite clear that religion was more important in Cornwall, Devon, and Oxfordshire than in East Anglia and the Midlands, but, as the preceding chapters have shown, none of the rebellions may be attributed to a single cause. Opposition to the enclosure of common land and waste was of paramount importance in Norfolk, where Kett's men destroyed fences and hedges, yet the rebels also protested against the clergy, high rents, and local government. While it is tempting to seek an explanation based exclusively on geography or agrarian change, especially in East Anglia, it is safer to conclude that unrest resulted from complex causes of which some were so localized and obscure that surviving records give only an imperfect indication of the full depth of human conflict. The nation-wide scope of popular disorder shows that the relative wealth of Essex and Norfolk did not guarantee peace in those counties and that the poverty of remote Cornwall did not prevent the commons from arming themselves and resisting the government's religious reforms. Future local studies focusing on individual villages may one day reveal demographic conditions and patterns of discontent that are now difficult to document.[4]

Previous accounts of the Edwardian rebellions have either ignored or minimized the extent of urban discontent.[5] This study has shown the importance of townspeople to the success of Kett's Rebellion and has examined urban unrest in London, Exeter, Southampton, and other towns. Rebel forces included butchers, weavers, and other artisans as well as yeomen, husbandmen, and farm laborers. Urban authorities were generally more successful than the gentry in maintaining order primarily because they were better organized and more experienced in managing poverty and social unrest. The gentry lost control of the populace in East Anglia and the West, but only in Norwich were urban officials unequal to the challenge. In both urban and rural areas popular unrest fed on older traditions of dissent dating in a few instances as far back as the Peasants' Revolt of 1381. A few signs of religious radicalism may also be detected, but Edwardian popular discontent — whether in the towns or countryside — provides no convincing evidence of significant unrest based on either millenarianism or anabaptism.

The objectives of the Edwardian rebels and rioters threatened the established social order. The formal articles and demands produced in 1549 are worth more careful study than they are usually accorded because they not only recite important grievances but also reflect something of the passion of popular protest. Prepared by articulate spokesmen for the rebels, the formal grievances call for sweeping changes in social, economic and religious policy. But it would be a mistake to judge the rebels solely on the basis of these complaints. Further insight into the objectives of the rebellious commons may be gained from studying their actual behavior, from testimony contained in court records, and from the correspondence of government military and political leaders. The rebellions and most lesser disturbances had distinct antigentry and antiestablishment characteristics, and hatred of the gentry and aristocracy continued long after the rebels of 1549 had been defeated. The rebels killed Lord Sheffield, William Hellyons, and Sir William Francis, and abused captured gentry, but the great weight of their wrath fell upon private property. Enclosures were demolished, sheep and cattle stolen, and houses ransacked. Lawrence Stone saw "clear class-war overtones" in the rebellions, and it is difficult to refute his argument.[6] Although the rebels pledged their loyalty to the king, often humbly begged for redress of grievance, and like Protestant reformers, cast their demands in conservative language, the politicians, military commanders, and clerical writers, who knew the rebels best, regarded them as dangerous radicals.

With a few exceptions rebel leaders came from the ranks of the commons. Conservative Henrician bishops hostile to Edwardian Protestantism such as Stephen Gardiner and Edmund Bonner kept their heads down as did peers and prominent gentry. On the other hand, popular disturbances usually had respectable leadership. Prosperous yeomen, artisans, town officials, and parochial clergy (sometimes unbeneficed) were typical organizers and spokesmen of the poor and oppressed. The gentry active in the Western Rebellion stood outside the county elite and apart from the king's court at Westminster. Elsewhere gentlemen occasionally instigated lawsuits in behalf of the commons, lurked behind the scenes in riots, or collaborated reluctantly with rebels as a result of intimidation. But for the most part the rebellions and riots of Edwardian England had a distinct popular flavor. The rebel leaders understood and inspired their supporters but lacked the strength required to topple the government. Because of their leadership, the rebellions of 1549 stood apart from elitist rebellions of the Middle Ages and ended very differently from the Great Rebellion of 1642.[7]

The process of pacification included both repression and reform. The government was initially poorly prepared to meet the challenge of popular rebellion and unrest throughout the length and breadth of the country. Offers to negotiate with the rebels, whether genuine or feigned, bought valuable time for the government but sowed seeds of uncertainty in the minds of gentry and urban leaders. After a period of vacillation and delay, the government adopted the traditional Tudor policy toward rebels — military repression. Large armies were dispatched to Norfolk and the West, and after the rebels' defeat the survivors received rough and ready justice. The tale of the hapless miller's man who was unjustly hanged in 1549 was perhaps the most sordid example of mid-Tudor justice. It was, of course, unthinkable that the principal rebel leaders such as the Ketts and Humphrey Arundell should have received pardon from the king. The gentry and townspeople who suffered personal injury and property losses at the hands of the rebels reacted more violently than Protector Somerset and the privy councillors. Somerset's leniency toward the rebels damaged his reputation, but Warwick and Russell also urged restraint during the period of pacification.

Opponents of Protector Somerset held him responsible for policies that led to social disorder and rebellion.[8] While we may legitimately question the extent of his commitment to the poor, the majority of the Council, supported by the leaders of London, demanded new leadership. It is significant that Somerset was the only major Tudor politician whose fall from power was hastened by popular rebellion. Although unrest continued until the death of Edward VI in 1553, the vigorous efforts of the Council and the gentry successfully maintained order. The cautious reforms implemented after 1549 helped restore the commonwealth even if government policies fell far short of the commons' needs. Throughout the sixteenth century Tudor monarchs, parliaments, and ministers ruled in the interest of the gentry and men of property, and those who governed after the fall of Somerset in no way departed from established tradition.

ABBREVIATIONS USED IN NOTES

APC	*Acts of the Privy Council of England*
BL	British Library
CLRO	Corporation of London Records Office
CPR	*Calendar of the Patent Rolls*
Holinshed	*Holinshed's Chronicles of England, Scotland, and Ireland*, Vol. 3
Hooker	John Vowell alias Hoker, *The Description of the Citie of Excester*
L & P	*Letters and Papers, Foreign and Domestic of the Reign of Henry VIII*
Neville	Alexander Neville, *Norfolkes Furies or a View of Ketts Campe*, trans. Richard Woods
Pocock	Nicholas Pocock, ed., *Troubles Connected with the Prayer Book of 1549*
PRO	Public Record Office
Russell	F. W. Russell, *Kett's Rebellion in Norfolk*
Sotherton	Nicholas Sotherton, "The Commoyson in Norfolk 1549," ed. B. L. Beer
STC	*A Short-Title Catalogue of Books Printed in England, Scotland, and Ireland and of English Books Printed Abroad, 1475 - 1640*, compiled by A. W. Pollard et al.
TRP	P. L. Hughes and J. F. Larkin, eds. *Tudor Royal Proclamations*, Vol. 1
VCH	*Victoria History of the Counties of England*
Wriothesley	Charles Wriothesley, *A Chronicle of England*

NOTES

Chapter 1

1. An important departure form the view that the king's law prevailed in Tudor England may be found in G. R. Elton, *Policy and Police* (Cambridge, 1972), p. 4: "Henry VIII's England was not an easy country to govern. On the contrary, breaches of the peace were distinctly commonplace and could arise from the most trivial of causes." On the other hand, the author's interest is in law enforcement rather than popular disorder.

2. The best introductions to the subject are Anthony Fletcher, *Tudor Rebellions*, 2nd ed. (London, 1973) and Penry Williams, *The Tudor Regime* (Oxford, 1979). For the medieval background see R. H. Hilton, *Bond Men Made Free* (London, 1973) and *The English Peasantry in the Late Middle Ages* (Oxford, 1975), Michel Mollat and Philippe Wolff, *The Popular Revolutions of the Late Middle Ages* (London, 1973), and Guy Fourquin, *The Anatomy of Popular Rebellion in the Middle Ages* (New York, 1978).

3. The older standard works on the 1549 risings are F. W. Russell, *Kett's Rebellion in Norfolk* (London, 1859) and Frances Rose-Troup, *The Western Rebellion of 1549* (London, 1913). More recent studies include Julian Cornwall, *Revolt of the Peasantry 1549* (London, 1977) and Stephen K. Land, *Kett's Rebellion* (Ipswich, 1977).

4. D. M. Loades, *Two Tudor Conspiracies* (Cambridge, 1965).

5. Joel Hurstfield, *Elizabeth I and the Unity of England* (London, 1960), p. 190, wrote that England was within sight of civil war. He added, p. 192, "His revolt was the first big attack on the Elizabethan system, against which it broke in vain."

6. Keith Thomas, *Religion and the Decline of Magic* (Harmondsworth, Middlesex, 1973), p. 472.

7. Lawrence Stone, *The Crisis of the Aristocracy* (Oxford, 1965), p. 51.

8. W. G. Hoskins, *The Age of Plunder: King Henry's England 1500 - 1547* (London, 1976), pp. 57-59.

9. Alan Everitt, "Farm Labourers," in *The Agrarian History of England and Wales*, vol. 4, ed. Joan Thirsk (Cambridge, 1967), p. 398.

10. John Pound, *Poverty and Vagrancy in Tudor England* (London, 1971), p. 25.

11. Christopher Hill, *The World Turned Upside Down: Radical Ideas during the English Revolution* (New York, 1973). Emmanuel LeRoy Ladurie, *The Peasants of Languedoc* (Urbana, Ill., 1974), p. 208, argues that "to turn the world upside down is not the same as to revolutionize it, or even to transform it in a true sense. It is, nevertheless, in an elementary way, to contest, to deny, to proclaim one's disaccord with the world as it is."

217

12. *The First Tome or Volume of the Paraphrase of Erasmus upon the Newe Testamente (1548)*, ed. John N. Wall, Jr. (New York, 1975). The King James version also differs from the translations of Wycliffe, Tyndale, and the Geneva *Bible:*
"And whanne thei founden hem not, thei drowen Jason and summe bretheren to the princes of the city, criynge, for these it ben, that mouen the world, and hidir thei camen whom Jason receyuede." *The Holy Bible containing the Old and New Testaments with the Apocryphal Books in the Earliest English Versions Made from the Latin Vulgate by John Wycliffe and his Followers*, ed. J. Forshall and F. Madden (Oxford, 1850), vol. 4.
"These that trouble the worlde are come hyder also which Jason hath receaved prevely." William Tyndale, *New Testament* (Antwerp, 1534).
"These are they which have subverted the state of the world, and here they are." Geneva *Bible*, 1583.
13. J. A. Guy, *The Cardinal's Court: The Impact of Thomas Wolsey in Star Chamber* (Totowa, N.J., 1977), p. 58, n. 33. Sir Thomas Smith preferred a more general definition of a riot: "where any number is assembled with force to doe any thing." *De Republica Anglorum* (London, 1583), p. 94.
14. Elton, p. 4.
15. Guy, p. 52.
16. Roger B. Manning, "Patterns of Violence in Early Tudor Enclosure Riots," *Albion* 6 (1974).
17. John Cordy Jeaffreson, ed., *Middlesex County Records* (London, 1887), 2: 245.
18. Peter Clark, "Popular Protest and Disturbance in Kent, 1558-1640," *Economic History Review*, 2nd ser. 29 (1976). Cf. Buchanan Sharp, *In Contempt of All Authority, Rural Artisans and Riot in the West of England 1586-1660* (Berkeley, 1980).
19. Manning, "Patterns of Violence," p. 121.
20. Clark, "Popular Protest," p. 378.
21. Marc Bloch, *French Rural History* (Berkeley, 1966), p. 170.
22. Bloch, p. 170.
23. Natalie Z. Davis, *Society and Culture in Early Modern France* (Stanford, 1975), p. 166.
24. Davis, p. 167.
25. LeRoy Ladurie, *The Peasants of Languedoc*, pp. 192-97. The author gives a fuller account in *Carnival in Romans* (New York, 1979).
26. Hajo Holborn, *A History of Modern Germany* (New York, 1959), 1: 170-74.
27. For an introduction to the historiographical debate see Janos Bak, ed., *The German Peasant War of 1525* (London, 1976) and Bob Scribner and Gerhard Benecke, eds., *The German Peasant War of 1525 — New Viewpoints* (London, 1979).
28. Max Steinmetz, "Theses on the Early Bourgeois Revolution in Germany, 1476-1535," in *The German Peasant War of 1525 — New Viewpoints*, p. 9.
29. John C. Stalnaker, "Towards a Social Interpretation of the German Peasant War," in *The German Peasant War of 1525 — New Viewpoints*.
30. Northamptonshire Record Office, Fitzwilliam of Milton Manuscripts, Paget Letter Book. Paget to Somerset, July 7, 1549. Paget wrote, "In Germanie when the very lyke tumult to this beganne fyrst yt might haue bene appeased with the losse of twenty men, and after that with the losse of a hundred or two hundred, but it was thought nothinge and might be easely appeased."

Chapter 2

1. The controversy surrounding Southampton's fall and readmission to the Council may be studied in W. K. Jordan, *Edward VI, The Young King* (London, 1968), pp. 69-72; D. E. Hoak, *The King's Council in the Reign of Edward VI* (London, 1976), pp. 43-45, 48-50; A. J. Slavin, "The Fall of Lord Chancellor Wriothesley: A Study in the Politics of Conspiracy," *Albion*, 7 (1975), 265-86; B. L. Beer, *Albion*, 10 (1978), 91; and "Northumberland: The Legend of the Wicked Duke and the Historical John Dudley," *Albion*, 11 (1979), 1-14.

2. 31 Henry VIII, c. 14.

3. Jasper Ridley, *Thomas Cranmer* (London, 1962), p. 235.

4. J. J. Scarisbrick, *Henry VIII* (London, 1968), p. 480, quoting John Foxe.

5. *Select Works of John Bale*, ed. H. Christmas (Cambridge, 1840), p. 220.

6. James K. McConica, *English Humanists and Reformation Politics under Henry VIII and Edward VI* (Oxford, 1965), pp. 200-234.

7. L. B. Smith, "Henry VIII and the Protestant Triumph," *American Historical Review*, 71 (1966), 1237-64, but also see B. L. Beer, "A Study of John Dudley," Ph.D. diss., Northwestern, 1965, pp. 153-58. S. T. Bindoff, *Tudor England* (Harmondsworth, Middlesex, 1950), pp. 149-50.

8. *L & P*, 19-2-726.

9. J. Cornwall, "English Population in the Early Sixteenth Century," *Economic History Review*, 23 (1970), 32-44. See also J. C. Russell, *British Medieval Population*, (Albuquerque, 1948), and John Hatcher, *Plague, Population, and the English Economy, 1348-1530*, (London, 1977), pp. 63-67.

10. E. H. Phelps Brown and S. V. Hopkins, "Seven Centuries of the Prices of Consumables, Compared with Builder's Wage Rates" in *The Price Revolution in Sixteenth-Century England*, ed. Peter H. Ramsey (London, 1971). Peter Bowden, "Agricultural Prices, Farm Profits, and Rents," in *The Agrarian History of England and Wales*, vol. 4, ed. Joan Thirsk (Cambridge, 1967). J. D. Gould, *The Great Debasement* (Oxford, 1970), p. 9. C. E. Challis, *The Tudor Coinage* (Manchester, 1978).

11. Peter Ramsey, *Tudor Economic Problems* (London, 1963), pp. 51-53.

12. Gould, *The Great Debasment*, pp. 122-37; C. E. Challis, "Currency and the Economy in Mid-Tudor England," *Economic History Review*, 2d ser., 25 (1972), 313-22.

13. Thomas Smith, *De Republica Anglorum* (London, 1583), p. 35.

14. A. R. Bridbury, "Sixteenth Century Farming," *Economic History Review*, 2d ser., 27 (1974), 538-56.

15. Whitney R. D. Jones, *The Mid-Tudor Crisis 1539-1563* (London, 1973), p. 135; W. G. Hoskins, "Harvest Fluctuations and English Economic History, 1480-1619," *Ag. H. R.*, 12 (1964), 28-46; C. J. Harrison, "Grain Price Analysis and Harvest Qualities, 1465-1634," *Ag. H. R.*, 19 (1971), 135-55.

16. Ian Blanchard, "Population Change, Enclosure, and the Early Tudor Economy," *Economic History Review*, 2d ser., 23 (1970), 441. Bridbury, "Sixteenth Century Farming." W. G. Hoskins, "Harvest Fluctuations." E. Kerridge, *The Agricultural Revolution* (New York, 1967).

17. For analysis of Henry VIII's foreign policy see R. B. Wernham, *Before the Armada* (London, 1966), pp. 136-78; Scarisbrick, *Henry VIII*, pp. 424-97; L. B. Smith, *Henry VIII, The Mask of Royalty* (London, 1971), pp. 168-223.

18. W. K. Jordan, *Edward VI, The Young King* (London, 1968), pp. 230-304, M. L. Bush, *The Government Policy of Protector Somerset* (Montreal, 1975), pp. 7-39. B. L. Beer

and S. M. Jack, eds., *The Letters of William, Lord Paget of Beaudesert, 1547-1563, Camden Miscellany XXV*, (London, 1974), p. 31.

19. G. R. Elton, *Reform and Renewal* (Cambridge, 1973), pp. 159-60.

20. Bush, *The Government Policy of Protector Somerset*, p. 83. Cf. J. G. A. Pocock, *The Machiavellian Moment* (Princeton, 1975), pp. 347-48.

21. Ridley, *Thomas Cranmer*, p. 259.

22. On the subject of preaching see G. R. Owst, *Literature and Pulpit in Medieval England*, 2nd. ed. (Cambridge, 1961) and J. W. Blench, *Preaching in England in the Late Fifteenth and Sixteenth Centuries* (New York, 1964).

23. Public preaching in London is discussed by John Stow, *Survey of London* (London, 1956), p. 151. *The Works of Hugh Latimer*, ed. G. E. Corrie (Cambridge, 1844), vol. 1. There is a listing of court preachers in *The Literary Remains of King Edward the Sixth*, ed. J. G. Nichols (London, 1857), 1: ci-cviii. References to other sermons are found in the chronicles and the king's journal, which is printed in vol. 2 of *The Literary Remains*.

24. Wriothesley, 2: 1.

25. For Smith's recantation on May 15, 1547, see accounts in Wriothesley, Stow, and Edward VI's Journal. The sermons of Peren or Peru are mentioned in John Stow, *The Annales of England* (London, 1605), p. 1001 and G. Burnet, *History of the Reformation*, (London, 1841), 1: 306.

26. The best accounts of Latimer are Allan G. Chester, *Hugh Latimer* (Philadelphia, 1954) and Harold S. Darby, *Hugh Latimer* (London, 1953). See also B. L. Beer, "Hugh Latimer and the Lusty Knave of Kent: The Commonwealth Movement of 1549," *Bulletin of the Institute of Historical Research*, 52 (1979), 175-78.

27. Latimer, *Works*, 1: 67.

28. Latimer, *Works*, 1: 64, 69, 94.

29. J. G. Nichols, *Narratives of the Days of the Reformation* (London, 1859), pp. 71-80. Cf. A. G. Dickens, "Robert Parkyn's Narrative of the Reformation," *English Historical Review*, 62 (1947), 58-83, and Christopher Haigh, *Reformation and Resistance in Tudor Lancashire* (Cambridge, 1975), pp. 168-71.

30. The best study of the Commonwealth writings is Whitney R. D. Jones, *The Tudor Commonwealth* (London, 1970). See also G. R. Elton, *Reformation and Reform* (London, 1977), pp. 319-27, and "Reform and the Commonwealth-Men of Edward VI's Reign," in *The English Commonwealth, 1547-1640*, ed. P. Clark et al. (New York, 1979) for a critical view of the reform movement.

31. G. R. Elton, *England under the Tudors*, 2nd ed. (London, 1974), p. 10, n. 1.

32. H. S. Bennett, *English Books and Readers 1475 to 1557* (Cambridge, 1952), pp. 19-29. R. S. Schofield, "The Measurement of Literacy in Pre-Industrial England," in *Literacy in Traditional Societies*, ed. J. Goody (Cambridge, 1968), pp. 311-25; Peter Clark, "The Ownership of Books in England, 1560-1640; The Example of Some Kentish Townsfolk," in *Schooling and Society*, ed. L. Stone (Baltimore, 1976); David Cressy, *Literacy and the Social Order* (Cambridge, 1980), pp. 44, 176.

33. R. H. Tawney and E. Power, *Tudor Economic Documents* (London, 1924) 3: 311-45.

34. *England in the Reign of King Henry the Eighth*, ed. S. J. Herrtage (London, 1878), pt. 1, lxxix-xcix.

35. *STC* 6086 [1548]. *The Select Works of Robert Crowley* (London, 1872), pp. 151-76.

36. *Tudor Economic Documents*, 3: 312.

37. Other Commonwealth treatises printed before the rebellion include: *The Prayse and Commendacion of Such as Sought Comonwelthes* [c. 1548] *STC* 20182, *Certayne Causes Gathered Together wherein is Shewed the Decaye of England* [c. 1548] *STC* 9980;

D. M. Loades, *Politics and the Nation, 1450-1660* (London, 1974), p. 210 did not consider the dating of the Commonwealth works and assumed that the commons were the author's primary audience. *Certayne Causes*, for example, was addressed specifically to the Council and Parliament.

38. Paget Letter Book, July 7, 1549.

39. A. G. Dickens, *The English Reformation* (London, 1964), pp. 205, 218. Alan Kreider, *English Chantries, The Road to Dissolution* (Cambridge, Mass., 1979), pp. 186-208.

40. Philip Hughes, *The Reformation in England* (London, 1963), 2: 106-7.

41. Mary Dewar, *Sir Thomas Smith* (London, 1964); F. G. Emmison, *Tudor Secretary, Sir William Petre at Court and Home* (London, 1961); Mary Coyle, "Sir Richard Rich, First Baron Rich (1496-1567) A Political Biography," Ph.D. diss., Harvard, 1967.

42. Bush, *The Government Policy of Protector Somerset*, pp. 40-83, is more concerned with the objectives of social reform than the process by which the programs were formulated. See also D. E. Hoak, *The King's Council in the Reign of Edward VI* (London, 1976), pp. 260-62.

43. W. K. Jordan, *Edward VI: The Young King* (London, 1969), p. 172.

44. C. S. L. Davies, "Slavery and Protector Somerset: The Vagrancy Act of 1547," *Economic History Review*, 2d ser., 19 (1966), 533-49.

45. Jordan, *Edward VI: The Young King*, p. 179. See also C. G. Ericson, "Parliament as a Legislative Institution in the Reigns of Edward VI & Mary," Ph.D. thesis, London, 1973, pp. 30, 176.

46. *TRP*, pp. 427-29. PRO, SP 10/8 nos. 24 and 25, give insight into the implementation of Somerset's policy.

47. Jones, *The Mid-Tudor Crisis, 1539-1563*, pp. 114-18; E. Kerridge, *Agrarian Problems in the Sixteenth Century and After* (New York, 1969), pp. 94-133; R. H. Tawney, *The Agrarian Problem in the Sixteenth Century* (London, 1912), pp. 401-9; Joan Thirsk, "Enclosing and Engrossing," in *The Agrarian History of England and Wales*, ed. Thirsk (Cambridge, 1967), 4: 200-255.

48. E. Lamond, ed., *A Discourse on the Commonweal of this Realm of England* (Cambridge, 1929), p. lxiii; for Warwick's position see BL, Lansd. MS 238, fol. 321 v. and PRO, SP 10/7 no. 35.

49. M. W. Beresford, "The Poll Tax and Census of Sheep, 1549," *Agricultural History Review, 1* (1953), 9-15 and 2 (1954), 15-29; B. L. Beer, "A Critique of the Protectorate: An Unpublished Letter of Sir William Paget to the Duke of Somerset," *Huntington Library Quarterly*, 34 (1971), 277-83.

50. M. L. Bush, "Protector Somerset and Requests," *Historical Journal*, 17 (1974), 451-64.

Chapter 3

1. The preceding paragraph is based on A. L. Rowse, *Tudor Cornwall* (London, 1969), esp. pp. 20-27.

2. Richard Carew, *The Survey of Cornwall* (London, 1602), fol. 66.

3. Joan Thirsk, ed., *The Agrarian History of England and Wales* (Cambridge, 1967), 4: 72.

4. For contemporary accounts of mining in Cornwall see J. Norden, *Speculi Britanniae pars, A Topographical and Historical Description of Cornwall* (London, 1728) and

Carew. The principal secondary authorities are Rowse, G. R. Lewis, *The Stannaries* (Boston, 1908), and J. Hatcher, *English Tin Production and Trade before 1550* (Oxford, 1973).

5. Carew, fol. 64.

6. Rowse, p. 77.

7. Lewis, pp. 126-28.

8. Rowse, pp. 114-26; Anthony Fletcher, *Tudor Rebellions*, 2nd ed., (London, 1973), pp. 13-16.

9. Rowse, p. 140.

10. Evidence connected with the dispute between the prior and town of Bodmin may be found in *Lake's Parochial History of the County of Cornwall* (Truro, 1867, reprint, 1974), 1: 94-97. The dissolution is discussed in Rowse, p. 229.

11. *L & P* 12-1-1001; G. R. Elton, *Policy and Police*, (Cambridge, 1972), pp. 295-96.

12. *L & P* 13-1-1106.

13. R. S. Schofield, "The Geographical Distribution of Wealth in England, 1334-1649," *Economic History Review* 2d ser., 18 (1965), 483-510.

14. Thirsk, p. 72.

15. Joyce Youings, "The Economic History of Devon, 1300-1700," in *Exeter and Its Region*, ed. Frank Barlow (Exeter, 1969), pp. 165-73; W. G. Hoskins, *Old Devon* (Newton Abbot, 1966), p. 186; Thirsk, pp. 72-73, 687.

16. Youings, p. 169.

17. BL, Harl. MS 352, fols. 57v-58r; *APC*, 2: 535-36; W. K. Jordan, *Edward VI: The Young King* (London, 1969), pp. 161-64. Rowse, p. 253, implies that Body acted in connection with the new chantries act. Frances Rose-Troup, *The Western Rebellion of 1548* (London, 1913), p. 71, states that the tumult occurred at Penryn.

18. The fullest account of Body's career is in Rose-Troup, pp. 47-69. See also Rowse, pp. 148-51 and G. R. Elton, *The Tudor Revolution in Government* (Cambridge, 1953), p. 304.

19. Rose-Troup, p. 80.

20. PRO, KB 8/15; *Fourth Report of the Deputy Keeper of Public Records* (London, 1843), App. 2, pp. 217-19. Rose-Troup, pp. 81-82; Rowse, p. 258; R. N. Worth, *Calendar of the Plymouth Municipal Records* (Plymouth, 1893), p. 115.

21. Cf. the near contemporary accounts of Carew, fol. 98; Norden, p. 47; and John Hayward, *The Life and Raigne of King Edward the Sixth* (London, 1630), p. 53. The French ambassador heard that the removal of a crucifix had excited the mob; Rose-Troup, p. 93.

22. The initial pardons in *TRP*, 427. Additional pardons are given in *CPR*. The pardons of William Kilter and Pascoe Trevian are in *CPR*, 2: 68. PRO, SP 46/58 fol. 5; SP 46/1 fol. 162r.

23. PRO, KB 8/15; Wriothesley, 2: 4; *Chronicle of the Grey Friars of London*, ed. J. G. Nichols (London, 1852) p. 56.

24. Charles Henderson, *History of the Parish of Constantine in Cornwall* (Truro, 1937), pp. 149, 162; *Lake's Parochial History*, 2: 177, 339-48; W. J. Blake, "The Rebellion of Cornwall and Devon in 1549," *Journal of the Royal Institution of Cornwall*, 18 (1910), 160-69.

25. Rowse, p. 88; Carew, fols. 123-24; Norden, p. 72.

26. John Carion, *The Thre Bokes of Cronicles*, ed. Gwalter Lynne (London, 1550), fol. 274v. [STC 4626]; Carew, fol. 124.

27. There are biographical accounts of the rebel leaders in Rose-Troup. Holmes is identified as a yeoman in PRO, SP 10/9/48. Humphrey Arundell's early leadership is discussed in Rose-Troup, p. 124 and Davies Gilbert [Giddy], *The Parochial History of*

Cornwall (London, 1838), 1: 88; 2: 191-93. The account of the rebels' capture of St. Michael's Mount is based on Carew, fol. 155v.

28. Gilbert, 2: 194; Rose-Troup, p. 127.

29. Carew, fols. 99v., 111-12. Cawsand Bay is Plymouth Sound on modern maps. Grenville's role is discussed in A. L. Rowse, *Sir Richard Grenville of the Revenge* (Boston, 1937), pp. 41-44. The Early Chancery Proceedings provide evidence of another gentleman who was robbed at Trematon Castle, C 1/1321/27, and of a priest of Saltash who suffered losses for supporting the government's religious policies, C 1/1273/55.

30. R. N. Worth, *History of Plymouth* (Plymouth, 1890), p. 389.

31. Inner Temple, Petyt MS No. 538, vol. 46, fol. 442v. Worth, *Plymouth*, p. 38. Worth, *Plymouth Municipal Records*, pp. 17, 115, 151. I gratefully acknowledge the assistance of Mr. R. W. Chell, Area County Archivist, Devon Record Office, Plymouth, who generously responded to my queries.

32. *L & P* 16, p. 241. Three cases that came before the Court of Requests show no evidence of enclosure disputes at Sampford Courtenay: PRO, REQ 2, 2/121, 12/189, 16/59.

33. Holinshed, p. 940. The Rev. David Bickerton, Rector of Sampford Courtenay, informed me that Harper was instituted to the parish on October 16, 1546. Although parish records begin only in 1558, there is no evidence that Harper suffered for his role in the rebellion. Although it is difficult to document the favorable reception of the new liturgy, it appears that the new service was accepted without disorder at Ashburton. See Alison Hanham, ed., *Churchwarden's Accounts of Ashburton, 1479-1580* (Torquay, Devon, 1970), pp. 121-24.

34. Hooker, 2: 93; Blake, p. 326; Jordan, p. 456. A William Hillinges of Northam, Devon is mentioned in *CPR*, 3: 139.

35. Pocock, pp. 15-19. Inner Temple, Petyt MS No. 538, vol. 46, fols. 432-34.

36. John Hooker, "The Discourse and Discovery of the Life of Sir Peter Carew," in *Calendar of the Carew Manuscripts at Lambeth*, ed. J. S. Brewer (London, 1867), 1: lxxxvi. Rose-Troup, p. 143.

37. Holinshed, p. 941.

38. Longleat, Thynne MS, vol. 2, fol. 123v.

39. Hooker, "Carew," p. lxxxvii; Holinshed, p. 953.

40. Holinshed, p. 942; cf. Rowse, p. 267.

41. Holinshed, pp. 943-44.

42. Exeter City Archives, Act Book 2, p. 179; hereafter cited as ECA. *APC* 2: 534.

43. ECA, Act Book 2, p. 206.

44. On Dr. Tonge's preaching see ECA, Book 51, fol. 348r. The best account of Exeter for the period is W. T. MacCaffrey, *Exeter, 1540-1640*, 2nd ed., (Cambridge, Mass., 1975). On matters concerning the church see R. J. E. Boggis, *A History of the Diocese of Exeter* (Exeter, 1922).

45. Holinshed, pp. 946-47.

46. Ibid.

47. Hooker, 2: 73; Holinshed, p. 948. The meetings of the twenty-four are not recorded for the period of the siege. Entries in the Act Book end June 10 and do not resume until September 11.

48. Holinshed, p. 948.

49. ECA, Act Book 2, p. 209. MacCaffrey, p. 82 identified this man as Nicholas Rowe. See also M. M. Rowe, ed., *Tudor Exeter, Tax Assessments 1489-1595 including the Military Survey 1522* (Torquay, Devon and Cornwall Record Society, 1977), NS, vol. 22, 48.

50. MacCaffrey, p. 9.

51. Holinshed, pp. 951-52; MacCaffrey, p. 192. B. F. Cresswell, *The Edwardian Inventories of the City and County of Exeter* (London, 1916), lists parishes that sold plate to relieve the poor.

52. Hooker, 2: 92; Holinshed, pp. 958-59.

53. Holinshed, pp. 948, 950; Hooker, 2: 77-78.

54. For a discussion of the rebels' military potential see Julian Cornwall, *Revolt of the Peasantry 1549* (London, 1977), pp. 59, 94-97. My review of Cornwall's book, in *American Historical Review*, 84 (1979), 147, and Roger B. Manning's review essay "The Rebellions of 1549 in England," *Sixteenth Century Journal*, 10 (1979), 92-99 should be consulted before using this work.

55. Hooker, 2: 56.

56. A. F. Pollard, *England under Protector Somerset* (London, 1900), p. 239.

57. W. J. Blake's "The Rebellion of Cornwall and Devon in 1549," appeared three years before Rose-Troup's study and criticized Pollard's emphasis on agrarian discontent, p. 196. More recently Rose-Troup's interpretation has been supported by Cornwall, *Revolt of the Peasantry 1549* and challenged by Anthony Fletcher, *Tudor Rebellions.*

58. Nicholas Udall quotes the 16 Articles in his reply to the Western rebels, and internal evidence suggests that the articles were prepared while the rebel army was encamped outside Exeter. Udall's *Answer* is printed in Pocock, pp. 141-93. There is a detailed discussion of the articles in Rose-Troup, pp. 211-31.

59. Cf. Gregory Dix, *The Shape of the Liturgy* (London, 1960), pp. 597-626.

60. J. J. Scarisbrick, *Henry VIII* (London, 1968), pp. 346-47.

61. Rose-Troup has brief biographies of Crispin and Moreman in her study of the Western Rebellion. See also MacCaffrey, p. 187 and Herbert Reynolds, *A Short History of the Ancient Diocese of Exeter* (Exeter, 1895).

62. M. H. and R. Dodds, *The Pilgrimage of Grace 1536-1537 and the Exeter Conspiracy, 1538* (Cambridge, 1915), 2: 277-327; Mortimer Levine, *Tudor Dynastic Problems, 1460-1571* (London, 1973), pp. 70-71.

63. Rose-Troup, p. 127.

64. G. S. Thomson, *Two Centuries of Family History* (London, 1930), pp. 199-200; Diane Willen, "The Career of John, Lord Russell, First Earl of Bedford: A Study in Tudor Politics," Ph.D. diss., Tufts University, 1972, p. 251.

65. The letter of "R.L." is contained in a rare tract of which only three copies are known to have survived. The copy in the Lambeth Palace Library is printed in Rose-Troup, pp. 485-96.

66. On the general question of good lordship see L. Stone, *The Crisis of the Aristocracy 1558-1641* (Oxford, 1965), pp. 42-49 and Mervyn James, *Family, Lineage, and Civil Society* (Oxford, 1974), pp. 32-35.

67. *Original Letters Relative to the English Reformation*, ed. H. Robinson (Cambridge, 1846), 1: 66.

68. *Calendar of State Papers, Spanish*, 9: 397.

69. Thomas Cranmer, *Miscellaneous Writings and Letters* (Cambridge, 1846), p. 194.

70. Pocock, p. 146.

71. John Stow, *The Annales of England* (London, 1605), p. 1005; John Foxe, *Acts and Monuments* (London, 1684), 3, ix, 14.

72. Holinshed, p. 917; Richard Grafton, *A Chronicle at Large* (London, 1569), pp. 1301-02; Pocock, p. 17.

73. PRO, SP 10/8/6, printed in Rose-Troup, pp. 433-40. Cf. M. L. Bush, *The*

Government Policy of Protector Somerset (Montreal, 1975), pp. 52-53 and M. W. Beresford, "The Poll Tax and Census on Sheep, 1549," *Agricultural History Review, 1* (1953), 9-15 and 2 (1954), 15-29.

74. PRO, SP 10/8/6.

75. Pocock, p. 67.

76. Pocock, p. 16.

77. Holinshed, p. 924.

78. PRO, SP 10/8/6.

79. Although A. F. Pollard's interpretation of Somerset has been severely challenged, no consensus has emerged. For recent views see Bush, pp. 160-61; D. E. Hoak, *The King's Council in the Reign of Edward VI* (Cambridge, 1976), pp. 176-81; and B. L. Beer, "A Critique of the Protectorate," *Huntington Library Quarterly,* 34 (1971), 277-83.

80. PRO, SP 10/8/4. Paget to Somerset, July 7, 1549.

81. Bush's distinction between spring and summer rebellions, pp. 89-91, is neither clear nor useful in understanding government policy. The risings outside Norfolk and the West are discussed in Chapter 6.

82. PRO, SP 10/7/37; Pocock, pp. 4-6.

83. Hooker, 2: 81; Hooker, "Carew," lxxxviii.

84. The preceding paragraph is based on Diane Willen, "The Career of John, Lord Russell."

85. PRO, SP 10/7/40 and 42.

86. Inner Temple, Petyt MS No. 538, vol. 46, fols. 432-34.

87. PRO, SP 10/7/41. No date, but MS is marked in pencil, "? June 24." Pocock, p. 11.

88. R. W. Heinze, *The Proclamations of the Tudor Kings* (Cambridge, 1976), p. 217.

89. *TRP,* 473-74. Pocock, p. 24.

90. Pocock, p. 41; Beer, "A Critique of the Protectorate," 277-83; P. F. Tytler, *England under the Reigns of Edward VI and Mary* (London, 1839), 1: 189.

91. Rowse, p. 273; Jordan, pp. 462-69; Bush, pp. 91-93. Diane Willen, "Lord Russell and the Western Counties," *Journal of British Studies,* 15 (1975), 35-39. Rose-Troup, pp. 153-55, 253-54.

92. The replies of Somerset and the Council to Russell's requests are printed in Pocock. Russell's letters have not survived. On the military buildup see Cornwall, pp. 132-36, 176-81, but this account lacks adequate documentation.

93. Pocock, p. 44. On July 14 the Council ordered Sir Anthony Kingston to muster horsemen and footmen for service in Devon. PRO, SP 42/2 fol. 21r.

94. Inner Temple, Petyt MS No. 538, vol. 46, fol. 4r; Pocock, p. 20. PRO, SP 10/8/30. Tytler, 1: 185. BL, Add. MS 27, 402, fol. 40r.

95. Holinshed, p. 954. MacCaffrey, p. 206.

96. Contemporary authorities do not agree on the details of the advance. Cf. Hooker, 2: 82f., journal of Edward VI, and Hayward, p. 61, who apparently combined the accounts of Hooker and the king. Material from the Thynne Manuscripts at Longleat, never before used in the study of the Western Rebellion, has been used in the succeeding paragraphs.

97. Gregory Carye acquired the manor of Grendon and Salterton in the large parish of Woodbury in 1546. *L&P* 21-1 g. 1537 (35). Hooker, 2: 86-87. John Fry located the windmill five miles from Exeter. Longleat, Thynne MS 2, fols. 123-25. Rose-Troup, pp. 263-65, also discusses the location of the windmill.

98. Hooker 2: 87. Holinshed, p. 956. Estimates of men killed are from Fry; Sir Hugh Paulet's figures are higher. Thynne MS 2, fol. 127. Paulet also gives figures for injured archers.

99. Hooker, 2: 88; Holinshed, pp. 956-57.
100. Longleat, Thynne MS 2, fol. 127. Holinshed, p. 957.
101. Hooker, 2: 88. Longleat, Thynne MS 2, fols. 121-22.
102. Hooker, 2: 94-95. Holinshed, p. 960. Longleat, Thynne MS 2, fols. 123-25.
103. BL, Cotton MS Galba B 12, fols. 113-14; Harl. MS 523, fols. 50-53.

Chapter 4

1. Holinshed is the only sixteenth-century authority giving an account of this episode. According to Holinshed, 3: 963, the disturbances were "done before Midsummer."
2. Holinshed, p. 964. Master Hobart was possibly Henry Hobart, Sr. of Hales Hall, Loddon, a justice of the peace. See Francis Blomefield, *An Essay towards a Topographical History of the County of Norfolk* (London, 1805-10), 2: 480, 482. *CPR*, 2: 154. A. H. Smith, *County and Court* (Oxford, 1974), p. 353.
3. For an account of the later history of the family see A. H. Smith, p. 192.
4. Neville, B3r.
5. L. M. Kett, *The Ketts of Norfolk, A Yeoman Family* (London, 1921), pp. 53-59.
6. A. H. Smith, pp. 52-53.
7. Thomas Smith, *De Republica Anglorum* (London, 1583), pp. 27, 33.
8. Anthony Fletcher, *Tudor Rebellions*, 2d ed. (London, 1973), p. 15. M. H. and R. Dodds, *The Pilgrimage of Grace 1536-1537 and the Exeter Conspiracy, 1538* (Cambridge, 1915), 1: 92.
9. Kett, pp. 53-59.
10. This and the succeeding paragraph are based on Kett, loc. cit.
11. John Stow, *The Annales of England* (London, 1605), p. 1007; Wriothesley, 2: 21-22.
12. *CPR*, 3: 190-91.
13. The Latin inquistion is printed and translated by Russell, pp. 228-35.
14. *L&P*, 21-1 p. 251. March, 1546.
15. L. A. Clarkson, "The Organization of the English Leather Industry in the Late Sixteenth and Seventeenth Centuries," *Economic History Review* 2d ser., 13 (1960-61), 245-56.
16. PRO, E 179/151/314. Cf. E 179/151/340.
17. PRO, E 179/151/346.
18. PRO, E 179/151/362.
19. M. A. Havinden, ed., *Household and Farm Inventories in Oxfordshire 1550-1590* (London, 1965), pp. 1-13, 237-38. Clarkson, "The Organization of the English Leather Industry." David G. Hey, *An English Rural Community, Myddle under the Tudors and Stuarts* (Leicester, 1974), p. 86. E. M. Carus-Wilson, *The Expansion of Exeter at the Close of the Middle Ages* (Exeter, 1963), p. 23.
20. I find no evidence that conflict over the dissolution of Wymondham Abbey contributed to the Norfolk Rebellion. See H. F. Westlake, *The Parish Gilds of Medieval England* (London, 1919), pp. 14, 50, 217. Blomefield, 2: 509-21. William Dugdale, *Monasticon Anglicanum* (London, 1821), 3: 323-29. Two more recent accounts are R. P. Mander, "Wymondham Abbey and the Robert Kett Rebellion of 1549," *East Anglian Magazine*, 6 (1947), 605-10 and J. G. Tansley Thomas, "A Brief History of Wymondham Abbey" in *The Abbey Church of St. Mary and St. Thomas of Canterbury in Wymondham* (Wymondham, 1957).
21. L. A. Clarkson, "English Economic Policy in the Sixteenth and Seventeenth

Centuries: The Case of the Leather Industry," *Bulletin of the Institute of Historical Research*, 38 (1965), 149-62.

22. R. S. Schofield, "The Geographical Distribution of Wealth in England, 1334-1649," *Economic History Review*, 2d ser., 18 (1965), 483-510. A. H. Smith, pp. 3-16. Joan Thirsk, ed., *The Agrarian History of England and Wales* (Cambridge, 1967), 4: 46-49.

23. Thirsk, p. 42.

24. C. W. C. Oman, *The Great Revolt of 1381* (Oxford, 1906), pp. 111-14.

25. J. A. Guy, *The Cardinal's Court: The Impact of Thomas Wolsey in Star Chamber* (Totowa, N.J., 1977), p. 110.

26. Blomefield, 3: 197-98, 210. *Complete History of Norwich* (Norwich, 1728), p. 44.

27. Russell, pp. 4-5.

28. Russell, pp. 8-9. Thirsk, p. 441. *L&P*, 15 nos. 682, 748, 755. PRO, SP 1/160, fol. 157.

29. PRO, DL 1/27 p. 15. DL 5/8 fols. 122, 288r. In 1550 the Court concluded that Wigmore had been treated unfairly and remitted all amercements against him. All charges were dismissed. This case suggests that the Duchy under Sir William Paget was more sympathetic to the commons while Somerset was Protector than after he was removed by the Privy Council.

30. PRO, DL 5/8 fols. 89v, 222v.

31. PRO, DL 5/8 fols. 151-153.

32. BL, Add. MS 27,447 fols. 78-91. PRO, REQ 2/14/171.

33. The dating of these events varies. Sotherton gives the date July 9; Neville, July 10. Holinshed's account is undated. Sir Nicholas L'Estrange was sheriff in 1548-49.

34. Holinshed, p. 965.

35. Watson was granted a prebend in Norwich Cathedral on May 26, 1549. The grant stated that although "he is not a priest and is married and even twice married, he may take the fruits as if he were a clerk unmarried." *CPR*, 2: 178. By May 1551 he had resigned. BL, Royal MS 18C 24 fol. 92v. See also G. R. Elton, *Policy and Police* (Cambridge, 1972), pp. 138-39. Thomas Coniers, vicar of St. Martin's also preached before the rebels. Holinshed, p. 966. After the rebellion Coniers was presented to the rectory of Westwick. *CPR* 2: 375.

36. Holinshed, p. 966.

37. Neville, C3r.

38. PRO, SP 10/10/39.

39. Neville, D3. Sotherton, fol. 253r.

40. Russell, pp. 181-84. G. A. Carthew, *The Hundred of Launditch and Deanery of Brisley* (Norwich, 1877), 2: 592-95.

41. Neville, C3r. Sotherton, fol. 252v.

42. Sotherton, fol. 253r. D. MacCulloch, "Kett's Rebellion in Context," *Past and Present*, No. 84 (1979), 57, has identified Wharton as Richard Wharton of Bungay.

43. Neville, C3v. One gentleman later charged a former rebel with extortion, but the defendant denied supporting the rebellion. PRO, C 1/1206/15, 16.

44. Neville, C4v.

45. Neville, D2r. Sotherton's narrative does not mention Parker's appearance before the rebels.

46. Journal of Edward VI, printed in Gilbert Burnet, *History of the Reformation* (London, 1841), 2: clix. Sotherton, fols. 252v, 253v.

47. *The Hurt of Sedition*, printed in Holinshed, p. 997.

48. Neville, E2v.

49. Blomefield, 2: 229.

50. John Pound, "The Social and Trade Structure of Norwich 1525-1575," *Past and*

Present, no. 34 (1966), 49-64. See also J. Patten, *English Towns, 1500-1700* (Folkestone, Kent, 1978), pp. 247-70.

51. Pound, p. 52.

52. Sotherton, fols. 252-53.

53. Neville, E2r.

54. Neville, E2v.

55. Neville, E3v.

56. Sotherton, fol. 254r.

57. Neville, E4r.

58. Neville, Flv.

59. Henry Swinden, *The History and Antiquities of the Ancient Burgh of Great Yarmouth* (Norwich, 1772), pp. 934-41. See also Henry Manship, *The History of Great Yarmouth* (Great Yarmouth, 1854), pp. 145-57.

60. Swinden, p. 939.

61. Manship, p. 153.

62. Swinden, pp. 397-402. Manship, pp. 287-94. Blomefield, 2: 260-68.

63. BL, Harl. MS 304 fols. 75r-77r. Twenty-four hundreds are listed in the rebel demands. Holinshed, p. 966, however, states that twenty-six hundreds supported the rebellion. Tudor Norfolk was divided into thirty-two hundreds plus the city of Norwich.

64. Eric Kerridge, *The Agricultural Revolution* (New York, 1967), pp. 75-77. M. R. Postgate, "The Field Systems of Breckland," *Agricultural History Review*, 10 (1962), 80-101.

65. Russell, p. 82. *CPR*, 3: 328. See also chapter 8.

66. PRO, STAC 3/1/74.

67. PRO, SP 10/8/60. Russell, pp. 209-13.

68. BL, Harl. MS 304, fols. 75r-77r.

69. BL, Add. MS 48018, fol. 388. Quoted by Hayward, p. 70. See also fols. 388v-389v.

70. S. T. Bindoff, *Ket's Rebellion, 1549* (London, 1949), p. 9. G. R. Elton, *England under the Tudors*, 2nd ed., (London, 1975), p. 207.

71. E.g., C. S. L. Davies, *Peace, Print, and Protestantism* (St. Albans, Herts., 1977), p. 279.

72. Roger B. Manning, "Violence and Social Conflict in Mid-Tudor Rebellions," *Journal of British Studies*, 16 (1977), 39.

73. Julian Cornwall, *Revolt of the Peasantry, 1549* (London, 1977), pp. 146, 239.

74. Stephen K. Land, *Kett's Rebellion, The Norfolk Rising of 1549* (Ipswich, 1977), pp. 62, 72.

75. It has been suggested that article 16 was directed against the Duke of Norfolk whose estates included bondmen. As Norfolk was attainted and his lands forfeited, it is unlikely that the rebels would have regarded him as their primary target and omitted his name from the articles. Cf. D. MacCulloch, "Kett's Rebellion in Context," 55. There is a petition of bondsmen on former Howard lands addressed to Somerset in PRO, C 1/1187/9.

76. Joel Hurstfield, *The Queen's Wards* (Cambridge, Mass., 1958), pp. 96-97.

77. Bindoff, p. 9.

78. H. E. Bell, *An Introduction to the History of the Court of Wards and Liveries* (Cambridge, 1953), p. 133. Flowerdew's appointment is listed in *CPR* 4: 327.

79. Thirsk, p. 247.

80. William Harrison, *The Description of England*, ed. G. Edelen (Ithaca, N. Y., 1968), pp. 352-54. Cf. D. MacCulloch, "Kett's Rebellion in Context," 52.

81. Thirsk, p. 185.

82. C. S. L. Davies stressed moderation in "Peasant Revolt in France and England: A Comparison," *Agricultural History Review*, 21 (1973), 132-33. A different and in my judgment sounder view may be found in C. Hill, "The Many-Headed Monster in Late Tudor and Early Stuart Political Thinking," in C. H. Carter, ed., *From the Renaissance to the Counter-Reformation* (New York, 1965), pp. 296-317. For an earlier study that recognizes the radical character of Kett's Rebellion see W. Gordon Zeeveld, "Social Equalitarianism in a Tudor Crisis," *Journal of the History of Ideas*, 7 (1946), 35-55.

Chapter 5

1. Edmund Dudley, *The Tree of Commonwealth*, ed. D. M. Brodie, (Cambridge, 1948), pp. 45-46.
2. *The Works of Hugh Latimer*, ed. G. E. Corrie, (Cambridge, 1844), 1: 230.
3. Wriothesley, 2: 17, 20. *Chronicle of the Grey Friars of London*, ed. J. G. Nichols (London, 1852), p. 61.
4. *The Works of Thomas Cranmer*, ed. J. E. Cox, (Cambridge, 1846), 2: 193-94. John Strype, *Memorials of Thomas Cranmer* (London, 1853), 1: 270 attributes this sermon to Peter Martyr.
5. Cranmer, *Works*, 2: 195.
6. Cranmer, *Works*, 2: 188.
7. Strype, *Memorials of Thomas Cranmer*, 1: 269-71. *Chronicle of the Grey Friars of London*, p. 62.
8. W. K. Jordan, *Edward VI, The Young King* (London, 1968), p. 245. *Original Letters Relative to the English Reformation*, ed. H. Robinson, (Cambridge, 1846), 1: 66.
9. *TRP*, pp. 245, 475.
10. PRO, SP 10/4/33.
11. *Calendar of State Papers, Foreign*, ed. W. B. Turnbull, (London, 1861), 1: 45. Adverse rumors about the rebellions made it difficult to borrow money at Antwerp. At the end of July it was impossible to borrow £100,000 at 13 percent.
12. Russell, pp. 32, 39. Sotherton, fol. 252r. *TRP*, p. 474.
13. B. L. Beer, *Northumberland* (Kent, 1973), pp. 78-85. Tytler, 1: 185-89.
14. PRO, SP 10/8/4.
15. PRO, SP 10/8/24. Russell, pp. 197-99. *TRP*, pp. 475-76.
16. *Calendar of State Papers, Spanish*, 9: 405. BL, Add. MS 48018, fols. 388v-389r.
17. John Hayward, *Life and Reigne of King Edward the Sixth* (London, 1636), p. 68.
18. Sotherton, fol. 253r. Leonard Sotherton may also have presented the Council with complaints of the rebels mentioned by Hayward. On the other hand, this information may have arrived earlier, conveyed by the pursuivant who was in Norwich on July 13, or perhaps brought by a personal representative of Robert Kett, whose meeting with the Council is not mentioned in surviving sources. If Leonard served as a spokesman for Kett, Nicholas, who was related to him, may have been reluctant to mention this embarrassing fact in his narrative account of the rebellion. If Neville derived his information on this point from Sotherton, we can readily understand why the accounts of the two earlier writers differ from Hayward.
19. Sotherton, fol. 253v.
20. Hayward, p. 70. Cf. BL, Add. MS 48018, fol. 388 and Pocock, p. 32.
21. Pocock, pp. 27-28, 32, 58.
22. Thomas Fuller, *The Worthies of England* (London, 1952), p. 333.

23. A. J. Slavin, *Politics and Profit* (Cambridge, 1966), pp. 152-53.

24. J. Cornwall, *Revolt of the Peasantry 1549* (London, 1977), p. 168. D. M. Loades, *Politics and the Nation, 1450-1660* (London, 1974), p. 211. Jordan, p. 487.

25. Accounts of Northampton's arrival at Norwich may be found in Sotherton, Neville, and Holinshed. Cf. Russell, p. 90.

26. Sotherton, fol. 255v.

27. Neville, Glv-G2r.

28. Sotherton, fol. 255v. Neville and Holinshed have multiplied the number by 100.

29. Neville, G3v-G4r. Holinshed, p. 974.

30. Holinshed, p. 974.

31. Only Sotherton, fol. 256r., states that Sheffield was killed "about the hospital corner," but both he and Neville mention contention about who actually killed Sheffield and remark that Fulks (or Fulk) was later hanged.

32. Estimates vary: Neville, 140; Edward VI's journal, 100; Sotherton, 40. Lord Sheffield and thirty-five others were buried at the church of St. Martin's at the Palace. Russell, p. 98. Pocock, p. 59.

33. Holinshed, p. 974. Edmund Lodge, *Illustrations of British History* (London, 1838), 1: 133. Pocock, p. 59.

34. Sotherton, fol. 256r.

35. Sotherton, fol. 256v. Holm Street is now called Bishopgate Street.

36. Ibid.

37. Barret was appointed to the rectory of St. Michael at the Pleas on November 16, 1550. *CPR*, 3: 237. Neville, Hlr. Sotherton, fol. 256v.

38. Lodge, 1: 133. *Calendar of State Papers, Spanish*, 9: 423.

39. Henry Swinden, *History of Great Yarmouth* (Norwich, 1772), p. 938. *A.P.C.*, 2: 309. PRO, SP 46/124 fol. 73.

40. R. B. Wernham, *Before the Armada* (London, 1966), pp. 176-77. Tytler, 1: 193.

41. *TRP*, p. 481.

42. A. F. Pollard, *England under Protector Somerset* (London, 1900), p. 241.

43. See M. L. Bush, *The Government Policy of Protector Somerset* (Montreal, 1975), pp. 95-99.

44. For details of the compostion of the army see Cornwall, pp. 212-14.

45. Russell, p. 120. Cornwall, pp. 209-11. Bush, pp. 94-95.

46. Neville, H3r.

47. Holinshed, p. 977.

48. Sotherton, fol. 257r.

49. Holinshed, p. 977.

50. Neville, Ilv. Sotherton, fol. 257v.

51. Sotherton, fol. 257v.

52. Sotherton, fol. 258r. Neville, 12v.

53. Sotherton does not mention the first incident; Neville and Holinshed have essentially the same account.

54. Holinshed, p. 980. Neville, I3v.

55. Neville, I4r.

56. Holinshed, p. 981.

57. Sotherton, fol. 258v.

58. Neville, I4v-Klr. Sotherton, fol. 258v. Keith Thomas, *Religion and the Decline of Magic* (Harmondsworth, 1973), pp. 389-404. Russell, pp. 4-6.

59. Sotherton locates Dussindale within a mile of Norwich; the indictment against Kett

places it within the parishes of Thorpe and Sprowston. See Russell, pp. 143, 159. For the prophesy of Walborne Hope see Russell, p. 6 and *L&P* 12-1-1212.

60. S. T. Bindoff, *Ket's Rebellion, 1549* (London, 1949), p. 6. Longleat, Thynne MS 2, fol. 148. Hornyold also states that he saw rebels moving on the afternoon of Tuesday, August 27, an observation that indicates that Kett's move was not completed the previous night.

61. Holinshed, p. 982. Hornyold estimated the rebels dead at 2,000, Edward VI, 2,000, and Neville, 3,500.

62. Longleat, Thynne MS 2, fol. 148. Holinshed, p. 983.

63. Neville, K3v. Sotherton, fol. 259r. Francis Blomefield, *An Essay towards a Topographical History of the County of Norfolk* (London, 1805-10), 8: 262-65. Cf. *CPR* 1: 337; 3: 52, 57; 4: 73.

64. Neville, K4r. Russell, pp. 155-56.

65. The rebuilding and repair is documented in the City Chamberlain Accounts printed in Russell, Appendix 1, pp. 184-96. Neville reports that there was conflict between the army and the citizens of Norwich after Kett's defeat:

> The battle being ended, all the prey the same day was given to the soldiers and openly sold in Norwich market. Moreover, this thing is in record that many gentlemen and some of the chief of the city were slain in this tumult and heat of the fight although they gave money and great rewards to the soldiers to spare their lives. K3v.

66. Russell, pp. 131-32, 134, 140, 187.

67. PRO, SP 10/8/55, printed in Russell, pp. 151-53. G. A. Carthew, *The Hundred of Launditch and Deanery of Brisley* (Norwich, 1877), 2: 602-3.

Chapter 6

1. W. K. Jordan, *Edward VI: The Young King* (London, 1968), p. 439.

2. C. M. Gray, *Copyhold, Equity, and the Common Law* (Cambridge, Mass., 1963), pp. 61, 65.

3. Russell, pp. 40-41, 113, 120. John Strype, *Ecclesiastical Memorials* (Oxford, 1822), 2, pt. 1, 275. *Calendar of State Papers, Domestic*, ed. M. A. E. Green (London, 1856-72), 6 Addenda, 401. *CPR*, 3: 27. Castle Rising was formerly held by the Duke of Norfolk. In February 1550, John Robsart and Lord Robert Dudley were appointed stewards of the manor. BL, Royal MS 18C24, fol. 21v.

4. BL, Add. MS 48018, fol. 389v. *CPR*, 2: 29.

5. PRO, REQ 2/17/73. The tenants of the manor of Great Livermere included a number of bondmen.

6. PRO, SP 10/9/48. *APC*, 3: 308-17.

7. BL, Lansd. MS 2, fol. 60r.; printed in Russell, p. 113. BL, Add. MS 48, 018, fols. 189v-190r. PRO, SP 10/9/48. For an account of the rebel camps in East Suffolk see D. MacCulloch, "Kett's Rebellion in Context," *Past and Present*, no. 84 (1979), 36-59.

8. John Lamb, *A Collection of Letters, Statutes and Other Documents from the MS Library of Corpus Christi College* (London, 1838), pp. 157-60.

9. C. H. Cooper, *Annals of Cambridge* (Cambridge, 1843), 2: 36-44.

10. *VCH, Cambridgeshire*, 3: 14-5 Cf. *APC*, 2: 303.

11. J. R. Ravensdale, "Landbeach in 1549: Kett's Rebellion in Miniature," *East Anglian Studies*, ed. L. M. Munby, (Cambridge, 1968), pp. 94-116.

12. The preceding paragraphs are based on Ravensdale's excellent study, "Landbeach in 1549." See also by the same author, *Liable to Floods: Village Landscape on the Edge of*

the Fens AD 450-1850 (New York, 1974), pp. 133-34.

13. Felix Hull, "Agriculture and Rural Society in Essex, 1560-1640," Ph.D. thesis, London, 1950, pp. 333, 518, 521.

14. Mary Dewar, *Sir Thomas Smith, A Tudor Intellectual in Office* (London, 1964), p. 34.

15. Tytler, 1: 185-90. For a dispute over grazing rights at Saffron Walden, see PRO, C 1/1187/15, 16, 17.

16. BL, Add. MS 48018, fol. 391.

17. For additional information on More see W. Gurney Benham, *The Red Paper Book of Colchester* (Colchester, 1902), pp. 132-34 and *The Oath Book or Red Parchment Book of Colchester* (Colchester, 1907), pp. 164-166.

18. PRO, SP 10/8/61, printed in Tytler, 11 199-200.

19. For additional information on Browne see Benham, *Oath Book*, pp. 165, 179. The will of a William Browne of St. Runwald, Colchester, proved 1566, may be found at the Essex Record Office, Chelmsford, D/ACR 6, no. 20.

20. BL, Lansd. MS 2, fol. 60r.; printed by Russell, p. 113.

21. Strype, *Ecclesiastical Memorials*, 2, pt. 1, 274, 320-21. *Stow's Survey of London* (London, 1965), p. 131. I am pleased to acknowledge the assistance of Professor Marjorie McIntosh in attempting to identify the bailiff of Romford. It is her opinion that he was not the official bailiff of Havering but a local manorial bailiff, elected by the court, who served as the functional offical for the court.

22. Roger B. Manning, "Violence and Social Conflict in Mid-Tudor Rebellions," *Journal of British Studies*, 16 (1977), 29. Gerald A. J. Hodgett, *Tudor Lincolnshire* (Lincoln, 1975). Wriothesley, 2: 13. PRO, STAC 3/1/85. DL 42/96 fol. 28v.

23. Strype, 2, pt. 1, 259 believed the Edwardian rebellions first began in Hertfordshire. PRO, STAC 3/1/49. *VCH, Hertfordshire*, 2: 357; 3: 441; 4: 215-16. Henry Chauncy, *Historical Antiquities of Hertfordshire* (Bishop's Stortford, 1826), 1: 578 E. Lamond, ed., *A Discourse on the Commonweal of This Realm of England* (Cambridge, 1893), p. lviii.

24. BL, Add. MS 48,016, fol. 390v. *VCH, Hertfordshire*, 3: 198f.

25. *DNB*.

26. Manning, "Violence and Social Conflict," 35. *VCH, Hertfordshire*, 2: 451, 462-66. PRO, STAC 3/7/53, REQ 2/15/93, E 315/391. In the Star Chamber proceedings there were thirty-three depositions; of these only seven were able to sign their names. They were Heydon's wife, aged thirty-eight; a gentleman of thirty-six; a clothier also thirty-six; a man aged forty; a butcher aged forty-two; gentleman aged twenty-two; and a yeoman aged thirty-nine.

27. John Foxe, *Acts and Monuments* (London, 1684), 2, book 9, p. 17.

28. J. A. Yelling, *Common Field and Enclosure in England 1450-1850* (Hamden, Conn., 1977), p. 23.

29. *VCH, Oxfordshire*, 1: 444-45; 7: 160, 170-71, 217. C. L. Kingsford, *Two London Chronicles, Camden Miscellany XII* (London, 1910), p. 18. Joan Thirsk, *The Agrarian History of England and Wales* (Cambridge, 1967), 4: 195, 239, 452.

30. BL, Add. MS 48,018, fol. 389v. Pocock, p. 29.

31. BL, Lansd. MS 238, fols. 318v-321v.

32. Henry Clifford, *The Life of Jane Dormer, Duchess of Feria* (London, 1887), pp. 44-46. This account is undated, but it appears more likely that the events occurred in 1549 than the previous year. Cf. *VCH, Buckinghamshire*, 1: 309. *APC, 2: 307*.

33. PRO, SP 10/8/32. A. Vere Woodman, "The Buckinghamshire and Oxfordshire Rising of 1549," *Oxoniensia*, 22 (1957), 78-84. *VCH, Oxfordshire*, 4: 74. It appears that

Mathew was not a beneficed clergyman; H. M. Colvin, *A History of Deddington* (London, 1963), p. 97.

34. Joan Simon, *Education and Society in Tudor England* (Cambridge, 1966), p. 219.

35. BL, Lansd. MS 238, fols. 319v-321v.

36. PRO, SP 10/8/32.

37. *Calendar of State Papers, Domestic,* ed. M. A. E. Green (London, 1869), 4: 342-45.

38. John Higgins was indicted for his role in an enclosure riot at Hereford. Manning, "Violence and Social Conflict," p. 29.

39. Kingsford,*Two London Chronicles,* p. 18.

40. Strype, 2, pt. 1, 259-60.

41. PRO, SP 46/5, fol. 268. SP 46/1, fol. 171.

42. *Chronicle of Henry VIII of England,* ed. M. A. S. Hume (London, 1889), p. 171. This episode appears to have been in 1549.

43. Longleat, Thynne MS 2, fols. 24-25. For evidence of a dispute over enclosure of common land at Dunchurch see PRO, 46/2, fol. 68. Cf. SP 10/7/35.

44. E. Lodge, ed., *Illustrations of British History* (London, 1791), 1: 163. PRO, SP 10/7/31; SP 10/8/46.

45. PRO, DL 5/8 fols. 119v., 142v., 211r-212r. DL 6/3.

46. Manning, "Violence and Social Conflict," p. 32. PRO, STAC 2/2 fols. 197-203.

47. PRO, STAC 2/2 fol. 158.

48. PRO, STAC 3/3/35. In 1548 there was dissatisfaction at Tamworth when the collegiate church was suppressed and church goods were seized. As a result of the intervention of Somerset, vestments and plate were restored to the church. *VCH, Staffordshire,* 3: 45.

49. Terence R. Murphy, "The Maintenance of Order in Early Tudor Kent, 1509-1558," Ph.D. diss., Northwestern, 1975, pp. 120-21.

50. Francis Godwin, *Annales of England* (London, 1630), p. 219, characterized Kent as "the fountain of this general uproar." PRO, SP 10/8/56.

51. B. L. Beer and R. J. Nash, "Hugh Latimer and the Lusty Knave of Kent: The Commonwealth Movement of 1549," *Bulletin of the Institute of Historical Research,* 52 (1979), 175-78.

52. *Calendar of State Papers, Spanish,* 9: 405-16.

53. BL Microfilm, M485/39, vol. 150, fol. 117 [MSS of Marquess of Salisbury]. *Historical Manuscripts Commission, Salisbury,* 1:52-54. PRO, SP 10/8/50 and 56. *Chronicle of Henry VIII,* p. 171. *The Works of Thomas Cranmer,* ed. J. E. Cox (Cambridge, 1846), 2: 439. Thomas Wright, "On the Municipal Archives of the City of Canterbury," *Archaeologia,* 31 (1846), 211.

54. Peter Clark, *English Provincial Society from the Reformation to the Revolution: Religion, Politics, and Society in Kent 1500-1640* (Hassocks, Sussex, 1977), p. 81. *APC,* 2: 303, 308, 314, 358. PRO, E 133/6/815. Cf. I. B. Horst, *The Radical Brethren* (The Hague, 1972), pp. 97-140.

55. Lawrence Stone, "Patriarchy and Paternalism in Tudor England: The Earl of Arundel and the Peasants' Revolt of 1549," *Journal of British Studies,* 13, no. 2 (1974), 19-23.

56. PRO, SP 10/9/48. *Fourth Report of the Deputy Keeper of the Public Records* (London, 1843), App. 2, 223. *HMC, Bath, Seymour Papers,* 4: 111. *VCH, Sussex,* 2: 190. For evidence of a dispute over pasture rights at Willingdon, see PRO, DL 1/27, p. 71.

57. *APC,* 2: 190-92, 219. PRO, DL 1/27 p. 59. DL 5/8 fols. 113-15.

58. The larger part of the Carew Manuscripts is at the Surrey Record Office, Kingston,

but there is also material at the Wallington Public Library. I have examined the Loseley Manuscripts at the Museum and Muniment Room, Guildford, but was unable to gain access to those manuscripts retained at Loseley House. A third part of the Loseley Manuscripts is at the Folger Library, Washington, D. C.

59. PRO, SP 10/7/44. *Historical Manuscripts Commission, 7th Report*, p. 605. SP 10/8/48. *VCH, Surrey*, 3: 61. Some or all of the troops raised by More may have been for service at Boulogne; see Guildford Museum and Muniment Room, BR/OC/1/5, p. 144.

60. PRO, SP 10/8/41. For Gardiner's role see J. A. Muller, *Stephen Gardiner and the Tudor Reaction* (New York, 1926), pp. 171-81 and *APC*, 2: 550-51. Cf. *The History and Antiquities of Winchester* (Winchester, 1773), 2: 97. One Flynte, "seditious stirrer . . . [and] doer among the rebels" was in the Fleet in October 1551; *APC*, 3: 383-84.

61. R. C. Anderson, ed., *Letters of the Fifteenth and Sixteenth Centuries from the Archives of Southampton* (Southampton, 1921), pp. 71-72.

62. Colin Platt, *Medieval Southampton* (London, 1973), pp. 50-51, 218. A. L. Merson, *The 3rd Book of Remembrance of Southampton 1514-1602* (Southampton, 1955), 2: 20, 98. F. J. C. Hearnshaw, *Court Leet Records 1550-1577* (Southampton, 1905), pp. xviii, 2-4, 21.

63. Thirsk, *The Agrarian History of England and Wales*, 4: 65.

64. *VCH, Hampshire*, 4: 88-90. *Historical Manuscripts Commission, Bath, Seymour Papers*, 4: 111-12. PRO, STAC 3/1/76. Anderson, ed., *Letters of . . . Southampton*, pp. 68-69. For further details on the dispute at King's Somborne see PRO, DL 42/96, fols. 10-12 and BL, Royal MS 18C 24, fols. 252-53.

65. There is an undated letter from the Council to rebels in Hampshire promising those accepting pardon immunity from molestation by the gentry. BL, Add. MS 48018, fol. 391r. Two other Hampshire men held at the Tower of London were Thomas Richardson, clerk, of Plaitford, and John Unthanke, parson, of Headley. Richardson allegedly said, "God speed the Western men well for if they do not well, I know not how we shall do." Unthanke was examined by Somerset in connection with a vision, the nature of which is not disclosed. PRO, SP 10/9/48.

66. *Fourth Report of the Deputy Keeper of the Public Records* (London, 1843), App. 2, 224. Cf. Manning, "Violence and Social Conflict," p. 34.

67. *Historical Manuscripts Commission, Rutland*, 1: 36. Rose-Troup, p. 238. R. C. Hoare, *Modern History of Wiltshire* (London, 1845), 6: 261. *VCH, Wiltshire*, 4: 3, 49.

68. Samuel Seyer, *Memoirs Historical and Topographical of Bristol* (Bristol, 1823), 2: 231. *Historical Manuscripts Commission, Bath, Seymour Papers*, 4: 110. *VCH, Gloucestershire*, 2: pp. 164-65. *APC*, 2: 318.

69. *Historical Manuscripts Commission, Bath, Seymour Papers*, 4: 109-110. Longleat, Thynne MS 2, fol. 70. Wriothesley, 2: 13. Anderson, ed., *Letters of . . . Southampton*, p. 66. PRO, SP 38/1 fol. lv.

70. *Fourth Report of the Deputy Keeper of the Public Records*, App. 2, 222. Rose-Troup, pp. 305, 318. John Collinson, *History and Antiquities of the County of Somerset* (Bath, 1791), 2: 80-81.

71. Eric Kerridge, *The Agricultural Revolution* (New York, 1967), pp. 181, 215. Thirsk, *The Agrarian History of England and Wales*, 4: 33.

72. Much of what follows is based on the excellent study of A. G. Dickens, "Some Popular Reactions to the Edwardian Reformation in Yorkshire," *Yorkshire Archaeological Journal*, 34 (1939), 151-69. See also Holinshed, pp. 985-87 and *VCH, Yorkshire, North Riding*, 2: 485; 3: 415.

73. John Foxe, *Acts and Monuments* (London, 1684), 2, book 9, p. 17.

74. A. G. Dickens, *Robert Holgate, Archbishop of York and President of the King's*

Council in the North (London, 1955), p. 13. Foxe, 2, book 9, p. 18.

75. A. G. Dickens, ed., "Robert Parkyn's Narrative of the Reformation," *English Historical Review*, 62 (1947), 58-83.

76. J. G. Nichols, ed., *Chronicle of the Grey Friars of London* (London, 1852), p. 59.

77. A "great riot and unlawful assembly" at Wigan, Lancashire on June 1, 1549 is a good example of a localized disturbance. A mob led by a blacksmith and two yeomen allegedly assaulted the sheriff. PRO, DL 1/27 p. 60. For a complaint against enclosure in Lancashire see DL 5/8 fol. 236r.

78. BL, Cotton MS Titus BII, fols. 45r-46r; cf. fol. 90r.

79. PRO, SP 10/8/9.

80. PRO, SP 10/8/32.

Chapter 7

1. Peter Clark and Paul Slack, *English Towns in Transition 1500-1700* (London, 1976), p. 69.

2. *Stow's Survey of London* (London, 1965), p. 381. *Hall's Chronicle* (London, 1809), p. 568.

3. G. D. Ramsay, *The City of London in International Politics at the Accession of Elizabeth Tudor* (Manchester, 1975), pp. 37, 41. Cf. Valerie Pearl, *London and the Outbreak of the Puritan Revolution* (Oxford, 1961), pp. 53-55. After 1550 there were twenty-six aldermen in London.

4. *Stow's Survey*, p. 161.

5. Lawrence Stone, *The Crisis of the Aristocracy, 1558-1641* (Oxford, 1965), pp. 365, 387, 395.

6. J. F. D. Shrewsbury, *A History of Bubonic Plague in the British Isles* (London, 1970), p. 157. Clark and Slack, p. 69. *Stow's Survey*, pp. 149, 376, 378.

7. Claire Cross, *Church and People, 1450-1660, The Triumph of the Laity in the English Church* (Hassocks, Sussex, 1976), pp. 72-73. R. R. Sharpe, *London and the Kingdom* (London, 1894), 1: 422.

8. W. K. Jordan, *Edward VI: The Young King* (London, 1968), p. 188; see also pp. 146-49.

9. CLRO, Repertory 11, fols. 432v., 456v.

10. CLRO, Rep. 11, fol. 373v. Sharpe, *London and the Kingdom*, 1: 423.

11. CLRO, Rep. 12 (1), fol. 2.

12. G. R. Elton, ed., *The New Cambridge Modern History, Vol. II, The Reformation, 1520-1559* (Cambridge, 1958), pp. 127-28.

13. Wriothesley, 2: 12-13.

14. J. E. Oxley, *The Reformation in Essex* (Manchester, 1965), pp. 167, 225.

15. T. W. Craik, "The Political Interpretation of Two Tudor Interludes: Temperance and Humility and Wealth and Health," *Review of English Studies*, N.S. 4 (1953), 98-108; and *The Tudor Interlude* (Leicester, 1958), p. 24. See also E. K. Chambers, *The Medieval Stage* (Oxford, 1903), 2: 189.

16. CLRO, Rep. 12 (1), fol. 91v.

17. CLRO, Rep. 12 (1), fol. 92.

18. CLRO, Rep. 12 (1), fol. 100. E. K. Chambers, *The Elizabethan Stage* (Oxford, 1923), 4: 261.

19. *TRP*, p. 478.

20. CLRO, Rep. 12 (1), fol. 162v. Chambers, *The Elizabethan Stage*, 4: 261. The compters, located in Bread Street and in the Poultry, were prisons under the authority of the Sheriff.

21. *Return of the Name of Every Member of the Lower House of the Parliaments of England, Scotland, and Ireland* (London, 1878) pt. 1; *DNB*.

22. Possibly John Foster of Loughborough; see D. M. Loades, *Two Tudor Conspiracies* (Cambridge, 1965), p. 33.

23. CLRO, Rep. 12 (1), fol. 93.

24. *DNB*.

25. Loades, *Two Tudor Conspiracies*, p. 96.

26. CLRO, Rep. 12 (1), fol. 104.

27. CLRO, Rep. 12 (1), fol. 103.

28. CLRO, Rep. 12 (1), fol. 119.

29. Smith remained loyal to Protector Somerset during the crisis of October, 1549. For further details see Mary Dewar, *Sir Thomas Smith* (London, 1964), p. 56-66; this account, however, does not mention Smith's conflict with the City of London.

30. Robert Lemon (ed.), *Calendar of State Papers, Domestic* (London, 1856), 1: 16-18.

31. *TRP*, pp. 415-16.

32. Ibid., pp. 456-57.

33. CLRO, Rep. 12 (1), fol. 110v.

34. Russell, pp. 118-49; Neville, I2-I3v.

35. P. F. Tytler, *England under the Reigns of Edward VI and Mary* (London, 1839), 1: 198.

36. *APC*, 2: 308, 311, 347; Russell, p. 157.

37. CLRO, Rep. 12 (1), fol. 148. Bands of soldiers had complained earlier about the high cost of meals in London; Journal 16, fol. 28v.

38. CLRO, Rep. 12 (1), fol. 110.

39. CLRO, Journal 16, fols. 28v-29.

40. CLRO, Rep 12 (1), fol. 122.

41. See Peter Ramsey, *Tudor Economic Problems* (London, 1968), pp. 114-18.

42. *Stow's Survey of London* (London, 1965), p. 92.

43. For further details on constables and watchmen see William Lambard, *The Duties of Constables* (London, 1587), p. 11; *Stow's Survey*, pp. 91-96; W. L. M. Lee, *A History of Police in England* (London, 1901), pp. 30-31, 53-55; and F. F. Foster, *The Politics of Stability, A Portrait of the Rulers in Elizabethan London* (London, 1977), pp. 30-33, 48 n. 3.

44. CLRO, Rep. 11, fol. 440. Jordan's statement on p. 439 of *Edward VI* that "no watch was mounted in London until rather late in the summer" is in conflict with the Repertory entry.

45. *Stow's Survey*, p. 94; Wriothesley, 1: 100; *L & P*, 14-1-1144. Cf. J. G. Nichols, ed., *Chronicle of the Grey Friars of London* (London, 1852), p. 56, which states that in 1548 "the watch at midsummer was begun again, that was left from M. Dodmer unto this time." This account is in error since Dodmer was Sheriff in 1524 and Mayor in 1529.

46. Wriothesley, 2: 3.

47. Anthony Fletcher, *Tudor Rebellions* (London, 1973), pp. 48-49.

48. CLRO, Rep. 12 (1), fols. 91v, 92.

49. CLRO, Journal 16, fol. 15v., Letter Book R, fols. 8v-9. On the previous day the Court of Aldermen agreed that precepts for keeping the watch should be directed to every Alderman; see Rep. 12 (1), fol. 95.

50. CLRO, Journal 16, fol. 15v. A jornette is a large coat or cloak; a cresset is a vessel

made to hold grease or oil to be burned for light.

51. CLRO, Journal 16, fol. 17v., Rep. 12 (1), fol. 98v.

52. Wriothesley, 2: 15. On July 18 the mayor and aldermen were to keep a "privy watch" throughout the City; see Rep. 12 (1), fol. 111.

53. CLRO, Rep. 12 (1), fol. 100.

54. CLRO, Journal 16, fol. 17v., Rep. 12 (1), fol. 102v., Letter Book R, fol. 11v.

55. CLRO, Rep. 12 (1), fol. 102.

56. CLRO, Rep. 12 (1), fol. 104v.

57. CLRO, Letter Book R, fol. 12.

58. CLRO, Letter Book R, fol. 11v.

59. CLRO, Rep. 12 (1) fol. 105v.

60. CLRO, Rep. 12 (1), fol. 107v., Journal 16, fol. 20v. Companies that sent men for the "winning of Boulogne" were to arm the same number for the defense of the City; see Rep. 12 (1), fol. 108 and Journal 16, fol. 24v.

61. CLRO, Rep. 12 (1), fol. 106v.

62. CLRO, Rep. 12 (1), fol. 108.

63. CLRO, Letter Book R, fol. 13.

64. CLRO, Rep. 12 (1), fol. 106v.

65. *TRP*, pp. 475-76.

66. Wriothesley, 2: 15-16,

67. W. S. Holdsworth, *A History of English Law*, 7th ed. (London, 1956), 1: 575-76.

68. Holdsworth, *A History of English Law*, 2nd ed. (London, 1938), 10: 709-10. See also Roger B. Manning, "The Origins of the Doctrine of Sedition," *Albion*, 12 (1980), 107-10.

69. *TRP*, pp. 475-76.

70. Wriothesley, 2: 18-20; *Chronicle of the Grey Friars of London*, p. 59.

71. *Stow's Survey*, p. 131. Cf. F. Rose-Troup, *The Western Rebellion of 1549* (London, 1913), p. 322.

72. CLRO, Journal 16, fol. 23; Rep. 12 (1), fol. 112.

73. Wriothesley, 2: 16.

74. CLRO, Journal 16, fol. 24v.

75. CLRO, Rep. 12 (1) fol. 117v.; Letter Book R, fol. 24.

76. Wriothesley, 2: 20; Fletcher, *Tudor Rebellions*, p. 55.

77. *Stow's Survey*, p. 20.

78. CLRO, Journal 16, fol. 25v.

79. Wriothesley, 2: 20; *Chronicle of the Grey Friars of London*, p. 61.

80. CLRO, Journal 16, fol. 32; Letter Book R, fol. 31v.

81. *TRP*, pp. 464-69.

82. There were complaints about excessive charges to military forces; see CLRO, Letter Book R, fol. 28 and Journal 16, fol. 28v.

83. CLRO, Letter Book R, fol. 14v.

84. CLRO, Letter Book R, fol. 32.

85. CLRO, Journal 16, fol. 26.

86. CLRO, Rep. 12 (1), fol. 126v.

87. *Stow's Survey*, pp. 95-96; R. J. Mitchell and M. D. R. Leys, *A History of London Life* (Harmondsworth, Middlesex, 1964), pp. 135-38.

88. CLRO, Rep. 12 (1), fol. 130v.

89. *Grey Friars*, p. 62; cf. Wriothesley, 2: 21.

90. CLRO, Rep. 12 (1), fol. 138v.; Wriothesley, 2: 23.

91. Executions during July and August, 1549:

NOTES, CHAPTER 7

July 22

Bailiff of Romford, Essex, executed at Aldgate.

A man from Boulogne executed at Southwark.

A man "that came out of Kent at the brygge fotte into Southwark on another gibbet."

August 16

A man named Church executed at Bishopsgate.

A man named Payne executed at Waltham.

A man executed without Aldgate.

A man executed at Tottenham Hill.

August 22

John Allen, peddler of Southwark, executed at Tyburn.

Roger Baker, falconer of Southfield, Suffolk, executed at Tower Hill.

William Gates of Hampton, Wiltshire, executed at Tottenham.

James Webbe, vicar of Barford, Oxfordshire, executed at Aylesbury.

August 27

Three persons executed at Tyburn that came out of the West Country.

Sources: Wriothesley, *Chronicle of England; Grey Friars;* John Stow, *Summary of the Chronicles* (London, 1570), and *The Annales of England* (London, 1592).

92. Sharpe, *London and the Kingdom,* 1: 433.

93. Jordan, *Edward VI,* pp. 511-12. Jordan refers to the "considerable and devoted sentiment in the City favouring Somerset in this struggle for power . . . ." John Foxe, who was quite partial to Somerset, wrote that after the Aldermen received letters from both Somerset and the leaders of the Privy Council asking for support, "the case seemed hard to them, and very doubtful (as it was indeed) what way to take, and what were best for the citizens of London to do. On the one side, the power and garrisons of the lords, lying then in London, was not little, which seemed then to be such as would have no repulse." John Foxe, *Actes and Monuments* (London, 1844), 2: 912-13.

94. CLRO, Rep. 12 (1), fols. 99-99v.

95. CLRO, Rep. 12 (1), fols. 135-135v.

96. CLRO, Rep. 12 (1), fol. 139v.

97. Although sheriffs were traditionally elected on June 24 and sworn in on September 28 (Pearl, *London and the Outbreak of the Puritan Revolution,* p. 52), it is possible that York was not chosen until August 1. The year before, the sheriffs had been elected on that date, according to Wriothesley, 2: 5; moreover, the dating of Somerset's letter would also suggest that York had only recently been elected.

98. CLRO, Rep. 12 (1), fol. 120v.

99. Wriothesley, 2: 24-25; Stow, *Annales,* pp. 1007-8; Foxe, *Actes and Monuments,* 2: 910-11; Richard Grafton, *This Chronicle of Briteyn* (London, 1568), p. 1311; Hollinshed, p. 1017. Cf. Sharpe, *London and the Kingdom,* 1: 433-35, and Jordan, *Edward VI,* pp. 508-11. Jordan incorrectly states that October 6 was Saturday. According to Grafton, the Aldermen informed the Privy Councillors that London could provide armed men to be used against Somerset only after obtaining consent of Common Council. See also *APC,* 2: 330-32.

100. Grafton, *This Chronicle of Briteyn,* p. 1311; Foxe, *Actes and Monuments,* 2: 909; Wriothesley, 2: 25.

101. CLRO, Journal 16, fols. 36-37. Italics are mine. Cf. Sharpe, *London and the Kingdom,* 1: 435-36.

102. Wriothesley 2: 25-26; Stow, *Summary,* fols. 353v-354; *APC,* 2: 336-37.

103. Among the various versions of George Stadlow's speech are the following: BL, Hargrave MS, 134; Harl. MS, 1749, fols. 174v. and 253; Foxe, *Actes and Monuments,* 2: 913;

John Hayward, *The Life and Raigne of King Edward the Sixth* (London, 1636), pp. 220-23; and William Maitland, *History of London* (London, 1772), 1: 240. See also George Norton, *Commentaries on the History, Constitution . . . of London*, 3rd ed. (London, 1869), p. 198.

104. CLRO, Rep. 12 (1), fol. 151v.

105. CLRO, Journal 16, fol. 37.

106. CLRO, Journal 16, fol. 37v. See also Stow, *Summary*, fol. 354. Wriothesley, 2: 26, states that on October 10 there was also "an assembly of all the commons of the city having liveries. . . ."

107. Wriothesley, 2: 26-27.

108. Wriothesley, 2: 26; *APC*, 2: 337. The other sheriff, Richard Turke, also participated. It was Turke who read the proclamation against Somerset on October 8, and his house was the scene of a meeting of the privy councillors on October 10.

109. Stow, *Summary*, fol. 355; Wriothesley, 2: 28.

Chapter 8

1. Holinshed, p. 960. John Foxe, *Acts and Monuments* (London, 1684), 2: ix, 13, lists eight Cornish clergy who were executed. An inventory of the goods and chattels of two priests who were executed, PRO, E 199/6/52, includes John Wolcock, one of the eight listed by Foxe, and another man, Robert Raffe, vicar of St. Kirians. David H. Pill, *The English Reformation, 1529-58* (Totowa, N.J., 1973), p. 140, notes that most of the incumbents of the 520 parishes in the diocese of Exeter did not take an active part in the rebellion.

2. A. L. Rowse, *Tudor Cornwall* (London, 1969), p. 283. Richard Grafton, *A Chronicle at Large* (London, 1569), p. 519. Holinshed, pp. 925-26.

3. Pocock, pp. 53-55, 73. M. M. Rowe, ed., *Tudor Exeter, Tax Assessments 1489-1595* (Torquay, Devon, 1977), p. 49. Robert Tothill obtained a pardon for John Stowell, clerk, from Lord Russell. Stowell and William Salter promised to pay Tothill 26s. 8d. for his efforts but later refused. PRO, C 1/1272/49.

4. PRO, E 368/327. In August Cecil wrote to Sir John Thynne that there would be no assizes for the remainder of the year. Longleat, Thynne MS 2, fol. 116.

5. Neville, K3v. Holinshed, pp. 926-61. John Bellamy, *The Tudor Law of Treason* (London, 1979), p. 50, n. 4.

6. *CPR*, 2: 248; 3: 31. Neville, K4r.

7. C. H. Cooper, *Annals of Cambridge* (Cambridge, 1843), 2: 43-44.

8. PRO, SP 10/8/61; SP 10/8/32.

9. Edmund Lodge, *Illustrations of British History* (London, 1838), 1: 163. A. G. Dickens, "Some Popular Reactions to the Edwardian Reformation in Yorkshire," *Yorkshire Archaeological Journal*, 34 (1939), 151-69.

10. Pocock, p. 63. PRO, SP 10/8/47. Extant records are silent as to the fate of Maunder, who was captured at Sampford Courtenay. Nicholas Boyer of Bodmin was executed by Sir Anthony Kingston.

11. PRO, SP 10/8/54. *APC*, 2: 354.

12. Longleat, Thynne MS 2, fol. 140. *Fourth Report of the Deputy Keeper of the Public Records* (London, 1843), App. 2, 222.

13. Wriothesley, 2: 30. Russell, p. 161, says that the Ketts reached Norwich on December 1; but the *Inquisition Post Mortem*, printed by Russell, p. 230, states that they left London on December 1.

14. Rose-Troup, p. 349. Wriothesley, 2: 32.

15. John Stow, *The Annales of England* (London, 1605), pp. 1005-6. *APC*, 2: 311. Wriothesley, 2: 21. J. G. Nichols, ed., *Chronicle of the Grey Friars of London* (London, 1852), p. 62.

16. PRO, SP 10/9/48.

17. *Fourth Report of the Deputy Keeper*, App. 2, 223-24. *APC*, 2, 381; 3, 21. *CPR*, 4, 13.

18. For an introduction to the debate over the peasantry and the early modern social structure see R. H. Hilton, *The English Peasantry in the Later Middle Ages* (Oxford, 1975), pp. 3-19; Alan Macfarlane, *The Origins of English Individualism* (New York, 1979), pp. 7-61; and Margaret Spufford, *Contrasting Communities* (London, 1974). Buchanan Sharp, *In Contempt of All Authority: Rural Artisans and Riot in the West of England, 1586-1660* (Berkeley, 1980), places great emphasis on the role of artisans. He writes, p. 257, "The people who engaged most intensely in the popular disorders characteristic of Elizabethan and early Stuart times — the forest riots, food riots and related insurrections — were artisans, skilled men in rural areas of small towns working in non-agricultural employments."

19. *Chronicle of the Grey Friars of London*, p. 62.

20. *The Works of Thomas Cranmer*, ed. J. E. Cox (Cambridge, 1846), 2: 194-95.

21. Udall's "Answer" was not printed until 1884 when it was included in Pocock's collection of materials relating to the Western Rebellion.

22. *The Hurt of Sedition* printed in Holinshed, pp. 988, 1003.

23. PRO, SP 10/15/11. BL, Microfilm of Hatfield Manuscripts M485/59, vol. 230 and Harl. MS 353, fols. 90r-102v. An interesting example of local expenditures may be found at the Devon Record Office, Exeter Receiver's Vouchers, Box 1.

24. Jeremy Goring, "Social Change and Military Decline in Mid-Tudor England," *History*, 60 (1975), 185-97. D. M. Loades, ed., *The Papers of George Wyatt* (London, 1968). Diane Willen, "Lord Russell and the Western Counties, 1539-1555," *Journal of British Studies*, 15 (1975), 26-45.

25. PRO, SP 10/9/46. Lawrence Stone, *The Crisis of the Aristocracy, 1558-1641* (Oxford, 1965), p. 207, stresses the revival of aristocratic military power. His view is not easily reconciled with Goring, "Social Change and Military Decline," *History*, 60 (1975).

26. *The Works of Hugh Latimer*, ed. G. E. Corrie (Cambridge, 1844), 1: 247. Thomas Becon, *Jewel of Joy* (London, 1550), p. 432. *The Fortress of the Faithful* (London, 1550), pp. 596, 598.

27. *Thomas Lever, Sermons 1550*, ed. E. Arber (Westminster, 1895), pp. 40, 57, 69, 88-89, 95.

28. *The Select Works of Robert Crowley*, ed. J. W. Cowper (London, 1892), pp. 21-22, 43, 92, 95, 99, 146.

29. Ibid., p. 108.

30. *Tudor Economic Documents*, ed. R. H. Tawney and E. Power (London, 1924), 3: 62-63.

31. *A Discourse of the Commonweal of This Realm of England, Attributed to Sir Thomas Smith*, ed. Mary Dewar (Charlottesville, Va., 1969), pp. ix, 95-96, 101, 118.

32. B. L. Beer, *Northumberland* (Kent, Ohio, 1973), pp. 140-42; "Northumberland: The Myth of the Wicked Duke and the Historical John Dudley," *Albion*, 11 (1979), 1-14. G. R. Elton, *Reform and Reformation* (London, 1977), p. 358. For a critical analysis of the Royal Commission see James Alsop, "The Revenue Commission of 1552," *Historical Journal*, 22 (1979), 511-33.

33. R. W. Heinze, *The Proclamations of the Tudor Kings* (Cambridge, 1976), pp. 225-49.

34. *The Works of Hugh Latimer*, 1: 248.

35. *TRP*, pp. 520-22; cf. Heinze, p. 236. C. S. L. Davies, *Peace, Print, and Protestantism, 1450-1558* (Frogmore, St. Albans, Hertfordshire, 1977), p. 287. Joan Thirsk, ed., *The Agrarian History of England* (Cambridge, 1967), 4: 224.

36. See John Pound, *Poverty and Vagrancy in Tudor England* (London, 1971), p. 43.

37. R. R. Sharpe, *London and the Kingdom* (London, 1894), 1: 449-52. E. M. Leonard, *The Early History of English Poor Relief* (Cambridge, 1900), pp. 31-35.

38. J. W. F. Hill, *Tudor and Stuart Lincoln* (Cambridge, 1956), p. 67. Pound, p. 61.

39. *APC*, 2: 407; 3: 198-99, 206. *Journal of Edward VI*. James E. Oxley, *The Reformation in Essex* (Manchester, 1965), pp. 164-66.

40. *A Breuiat Chroncile Contaynynge All the Kinges from Brute to This Day* (Canterbury, 1551), n.p. (*STC* 9968). John Stow, *The Annales of England* (London, 1605), p. 1019. *Calendar of State Papers, Spanish*, 10: 109, 116.

41. *APC*, 3: 181; 4: 115-16. William Potts, *History of Banbury* (Banbury, 1958), pp. 99-100.

42. *APC*, 3: 31, 34.

43. PRO, DL 5/8, fol. 292. Cf. BL, Royal MS 18C 24, fols. 252-53.

44. R. C. Anderson, ed., *Letters of the Fifteenth and Sixteenth Centuries from the Archives of Southampton* (Southampton, 1921), pp. 78-79. *APC*, 3: 35. *Journal of Edward VI*.

45. CLRO, Repertory 12 (1), fols. 228f.

46. *APC*, 3: 6. See also J. C. Jeaffreson, *Middlesex County Records* (London, 1887), 1: 3.

47. *APC*, 2: 421; 3: 6-7.

48. Norfolk and Norwich Record Office, Book 12 a (1), fols. 1-11.

49. *APC*, 2: 385; 3: 18, 31, 131, 198.

50. PRO, REQ 2/18/106.

51. *Chronicle of the Grey Friars of London*, p. 4. *APC*, 2: 400; 3: 324-25. Wythe was excluded from the parliamentary pardon, 3 and 4 Edward VI, c. 24. *Calendar of Patent Rolls, Elizabeth*, 2: 567. PRO, DL 1/89, p. 43; DL 3/46, p. 7.

52. *APC*, 3: 247, 252, 410. D. Wilkins, *Concilia Magnae Britanniae* (London, 1737), 4: 68.

53. CLRO, Repertory 12 (2), fols. 298, 321, 323v., 324, 333, 355. *Calendar of State Papers, Spanish*, 10: 279, 290. *APC*, 3: 256.

54. BL, Royal MS 18C 24, fol. 88v. *CPR*, 4: 343.

55. HMC, Salisbury 1, 92 [Samuel Haynes, *A Collection of State Papers . . . Left by William Cecil, Lord Burghley . . .* (London, 1740), pp. 114-15.] PRO, SP 10/13/37.

56. BL, Royal MS 18C 24, fol. 34v. PRO, DL 42/96, fol. 49v.

57. PRO, DL 42/96, fol. 66f; DL 5/9, fols. 103r-104.

58. PRO, DL 42/96, fol. 62r.

59. PRO, DL 42/96, fols. 70v-71r.

60. PRO, E 315/479, fols. 29r-30v. Instructions from the king to the Earl of Oxford, Lord Darcy, and the commission for the survey of church goods in Essex, June 10, 1552.

61. W. Gurney Benham, *The Red Paper Book of Colchester* (Colchester, 1902), p. 23.

62. Miles Coverdale became Bishop of Exeter and Thomas Thirlby Bishop of Norwich. Lists of clerical appointments and preaching licenses may be found in BL, Royal MS 18C 24, fol. 137f.

63. E. H. Phelps Brown and Sheila V. Hopkins, "Seven Centuries of the Prices of Consumables, Compared with Builders' Wages," in *The Price Revolution in Sixteenth-Century England*, ed. Peter H. Ramsey (London, 1971). Peter Bowden, "Statistical

Appendix," in *The Agrarian History of England and Wales*, 4, ed. Joan Thirsk (Cambridge, 1967).

64. *APC*, 4: 38, 40. *Stow's Survey of London* (London, 1965), p. 330.
65. CLRO, Repertory 12 (2), fol. 521v.
66. *APC*, 4: 109, 225.
67. PRO, REQ 1/9, fols. 137r-139r. *CPR*, 3: 319. *APC*, 4: 45.
68. PRO, DL 42/96, fol. 54r.
69. PRO, REQ 1/9, fols. 152v-153r.
70. *APC*, 3: 462. Colthurst was a former auditor of the Court of Augmentations, who was not reappointed when the Court was reorganized in 1547; W. C. Richardson, *History of the Court of Augmentations 1536-1554* (Baton Rouge, 1961), p. 154 n. 118.
71. Beer, *Northumberland*, pp. 135-38.
72. A. G. Dickens, *The English Reformation* (London, 1964), pp. 236-40. Irvin B. Horst, *The Radical Brethern, Anabaptism and the English Reformation to 1558* (Nieuwkoop, 1972), pp. 108-40.
73. BL, Cotton MS Titus Fiv, fol. 323r.

Conclusion

1. Fernand Braudel, *The Mediterranean and the Mediterranean World in the Age of Philip II*, (New York, 1973), 2: 704.
2. *The New Cambridge Modern History*, ed. R. B. Wernham (Cambridge, 1968), 3:3. See also J. Hurstfield, "Social Structure, Office-Holding and Politics, Chiefly in Western Europe," ibid., 126-28.
3. Guy Fourquin, *The Anatomy of Popular Rebellion in the Middle Ages* (Amsterdam, 1978), p. 129.
4. Two excellent examples of this type of research are David G. Hey, *An English Rural Community: Myddle under the Tudors and Stuarts* (Leicester, 1974) and Keith Wrightson and David Levine, *Poverty and Piety in an English Village, Terling, 1525-1700* (New York, 1979).
5. A recent study that places great emphasis on artisans is Buchanan Sharp, *In Contempt of All Authority, Rural Artisans and Riot in the West of England, 1586-1660* (Berkeley, 1980).
6. Lawrence Stone, "Patriarchy and Paternalism in Tudor England: The Earl of Arundel and the Peasants' Revolt of 1549," *Journal of British Studies*, 13, no. 2 (1974), 19-23.
7. See Fourquin, pp. 63-79.
8. John Stow, *The Annales of England* (London, 1605), pp. 1013-14.

BIBLIOGRAPHY

I. Manuscript Sources

The following manuscript collections have been examined:

British Library
    Additional MSS
    Cotton MSS
    Hargrave MSS
    Harleian MSS
    Hatfield MSS (microfilm)
    Lansdowne MSS
    Royal MSS

Corporation of London Records Office
    Journals
    Letter Books
    Repertories

Devon Record Office, Exeter

Essex Record Office, Chelmsford

Guildford Museum and Muniment Room

Inner Temple Library
    Petyt MSS

Kent Archives Office, Maidstone

Longleat, Manuscripts of the Marquis of Bath
    Thynne Papers

Norfolk and Norwich Record Office, Norwich

Northamptonshire Record Office, Northampton
    Fitzwilliam of Milton MSS, Paget Letter Book

Public Record Office
    Chancery (C)
    Duchy of Lancaster (DL)
    Exchequer (E)
    Requests (REQ)
    Star Chamber (STAC)
    State Papers (SP)

Surrey Record Office, Kingston upon Thames

Wallington Public Library
    Carew MSS

BIBLIOGRAPHY

II. Printed Sources

Anderson, R. C. ed. *Letters of the Fifteenth and Sixteenth Centuries from the Archives of Southampton.* Southampton, 1921.

Arber, Edward, ed. *Thomas Lever, Sermons 1550.* Westminster, 1895.

Becon, Thomas. *Jewel of Joy.* London, 1550.

Beer, Barrett L., ed. " 'The Commoyson in Norfolk 1549': A Narrative of Popular Rebellion in Sixteenth-Century England," *Journal of Medieval and Renaissance Studies,* 6 (1976), 73-99.

————, ed. "A Critique of the Protectorate: An Unpublished Letter of Sir William Paget to the Duke of Somerset," *Huntington Library Quarterly,* 34 (1971), 277-83.

Beer, Barrett L. and Jack, Sybil M. (eds.). *The Letters of William, Lord Paget of Beaudesert, 1547-1563. Camden Miscellany XXV.* London, 1974.

Benham, W. Gurney, ed. *The Oath Book or Red Parchment Book of Colchester.* Colchester, 1907.

————, ed. *The Red Paper Book of Colchester.* Colchester, 1902.

A Breuiat Cronicle Contaynynge All the Kings from Brute to This Day. Canterbury, 1551. [*STC* 9968].

Burnet, Gilbert. *The History of the Reformation.* 2 vols. London, 1841. Includes journal of Edward VI.

Calendar of the Patent Rolls Preserved in the Public Record Office, Edward VI, 1547-53. 5 vols. and index. Ed. R. H. Brodie. London, 1924-29.

Calendar of the Patent Rolls Preserved in the Public Record Office, Philip and Mary, 1553-58. 4 vols. Ed. M. S. Giuseppi. London, 1936-39.

Calendar of State Papers, Domestic. Vol. 1. Ed. Robert Lemon. London, 1856.

Calendar of State Papers, Foreign, Edward VI and Mary. 2 vols. Ed. W. B. Turnbull. London, 1861.

Calendar of State Papers, Spanish. 13 vols. and 2 supplements. Eds. M. A. S. Hume, Royall Tyler et al. London, 1862-1954.

Carew, Richard. *The Survey of Cornwall.* London, 1602.

Carion, John. *The Thre Bokes of Cronicles.* Ed. Gwalter Lynne. London, 1550. [*STC* 4626].

Certain Causes Gathered Together Wherein is Showed the Decaye of England. London, c. 1548. [*STC* 9980].

Christmas, H., ed. *Select Works of John Bale.* Cambridge, 1849.

Clifford, Henry. *The Life of Jane Dormer, Duchess of Feria.* London, 1887.

Cooper, Charles H., ed. *Annals of Cambridge.* 5 vols. Cambridge, 1842-1908.

Corrie, G. E., ed. *The Works of Hugh Latimer.* 2 vols. Cambridge, 1844-45.

Cowper, J. W., ed. *The Select Works of Robert Crowley.* London, 1872.

Cox, J. E., ed. *The Works of Thomas Cranmer.* 2 vols. Cambridge, 1844-46.

Cresswell, Beatrix, ed. *The Edwardian Inventories for the City and County of Exeter.* London, 1916.

Dasent, J. R., ed. *Acts of the Privy Council of England.* 32 vols. London, 1890-1907.

Deputy Keeper of the Public Records, *Fourth Report.* London, 1843.

Dickens, A. G., ed. "Robert Parkyn's Narrative of the Reformation," *English Historical Review,* 62 (1947), 58-83.

Elton, G. R. *The Tudor Constitution, Documents and Commentary.* Cambridge, 1960.

Foxe, John. *Acts and Monuments.* 3 vols. London, 1684.

Grafton, Richard. *A Chronicle at Large.* London, 1569.

Hall's Chronicle. London, 1809.

Harrison, William. *The Description of England.* Ed. G. Edelen. Ithaca, 1968.

Havinden, M. A., ed. *Household and Farm Inventories in Oxfordshire, 1550-1590.* London, 1965.

Haynes, Samuel. *A Collection of State Papers . . . Left by William Cecil, Lord Burghley.* London, 1740.

Hayward, John. *The Life and Raigne of King Edward the Sixth.* London, 1630.

Historical Manuscripts Commission. *Reports.* London, 1870-.

Holinshed's Chronicles of England, Scotland, and Ireland. 6 vols. London, 1808.

The Holy Bible containing the Old and New Testaments with the Apocryphal Books in the Earliest English Versions made from the Latin Vulgate by John Wycliffe and his Followers. 4 vols. Ed. J. Forshall. Oxford, 1850.

[Hooker] Vowell alias Hoker, John. *The Description of the Citie of Excester.* 3 parts. Ed. H. Tapley-Soper et al. Exeter, 1919-47.

Hooker, John. *The Discourse and Discovery of the Life of Sir Peter Carew,* in *Calendar of the Carew Manuscripts at Lambeth.* Vol. 1. Ed. J. S. Brewer and William Bullen. London, 1867.

Hughes, P. L. and Larkin, J. F., eds. *Tudor Royal Proclamations.* Vol. 1. New Haven, 1964.

Jeaffreson, John Cordy. *Middlesex County Records.* 2 vols. London, 1887.

Kingsford, C. L., ed. *Two London Chronicles. Camden Miscellany XII.* London, 1910.

Lamb, John. *A Collection of Letters, Statutes and Other Documents from the Manuscript Library of Corpus Christi College.* London, 1838.

Lambard, William. *The Duties of Constables, Borsholders, Tythingmen, and Such Other Lowe Ministers of the Peace.* London, 1587.

Lamond, Elizabeth, ed. *A Discourse on the Commonweal of This Realm of England.* Cambridge, 1929.

Letters and Papers, Foreign and Domestic of the Reign of Henry VIII, 1509-47. 21 vols. Ed. J. S. Brewer et al. London, 1862-1910.

Loades, D. M., ed. *The Papers of George Wyatt.* London, 1968.

Lodge, Edmund, ed. *Illustrations of British History.* 3 vols. London, 1838.

Merson, A. L., ed. *The 3rd Book of Remembrance of Southampton, 1514-1602.* Vol. 2. Southampton, 1955.

Neville, Alexander. *Norfolkes Furies or a View of Ketts Campe.* Trans. Richard Woods. London, 1615.

Nichols, John Gough, ed. *Chronicle of the Grey Friars of London.* London, 1852.

————, ed. *The Literary Remains of Edward VI.* 2 vols. London, 1857.

Pocock, Nicholas, ed. *Troubles Connected with the Prayer Book of 1549.* London, 1884.

The Prayse and Commendacion of Such as Sought Comonwelthes. London, c. 1548. [*STC* 20182].

Robinson, H., ed. *Original Letters Relative to the English Reformation.* Cambridge, 1846.

Rowe, M. M., ed. *Tudor Exeter, Tax Assessments 1489-1595 including the Military Survey of 1522*. Torquay, Devon, 1977.

Smith, Thomas. *De Republica Anglorum*. London, 1583.

Stow, John. *The Annales of England*. London, 1592, 1605, 1615.

————.*A Summary of English Chronicles*. London, 1565.

Stow's Survey of London. London, 1965.

Strype, John. *Ecclesiastical Memorials*. 3 vols. Oxford, 1822.

Tawney, R. H. and Power, E. *Tudor Economic Documents*. 3 vols. London, 1924.

Tytler, P. F. *England under the Reigns of Edward VI and Mary*. 2 vols. London, 1839.

Worth, R. N., ed. *Calendar of the Plymouth Municipal Records*. Plymouth, 1893.

Wriothesley, Charles. *A Chronicle of England*. 2 vols. Ed. W. D. Hamilton. London, 1875-77.

III. Selected Secondary Sources

Alsop, James. "The Revenue Commission of 1552." *Historical Journal*, 22 (1979), 511-33.

Bak, Janos, ed. *The German Peasant War of 1525*. London, 1976.

Beer, Barrett L. "London and the Rebellions of 1548-1549." *Journal of British Studies*, 12 (1972), 15-38.

————. *Northumberland*. Kent, Ohio, 1973.

————. "Northumberland: The Myth of the Wicked Duke and the Historical John Dudley." *Albion*, 11 (1979), 1-14.

Beer, Barrett L. and Nash, R. J. "Hugh Latimer and Lusty Knave of Kent: The Commonwealth Movement of 1549." *Bulletin of the Institute of Historical Research*, 52 (1979), 175-78.

Bell, H. E. *An Introduction to the History of the Court of Wards and Liveries*. Cambridge, 1953.

Bellamy, John. *The Tudor Law of Treason*. London, 1979.

Beresford, M. W. "The Poll Tax and Census of Sheep, 1549." *Agricultural History Review*, 1 (1953), 9-15 and 2 (1954), 15-29.

Bindoff, S. T. *Ket's Rebellion, 1549*. London, 1949.

————. *Tudor England*. Harmondsworth, Middlesex, 1950.

Blake, William J. "The Rebellion of Cornwall and Devon in 1549." *Journal of the Royal Institution of Cornwall*, 18 (1910), 147-96 and 300-338.

Blanchard, Ian. "Population Change, Enclosure, and the Early Tudor Economy." *Economic History Review*, 2nd ser. 23 (1970), 427-45.

Blench, J. W. *Preaching in England in the Late Fifteenth and Sixteenth Centuries*. New York, 1964.

Blomefield, Francis. *An Essay Towards a Topograpical History of the County of Norfolk*. 11 vols. London, 1805-10.

Braudel, Fernand. *The Mediterranean and the Mediterranean World in the Age of Philip II*. Vol. 2. New York, 1973.

Bridbury, A. R. "Sixteenth-Century Farming." *Economic History Review*, 2nd ser. 27 (1974), 538-56.

Bush, M. L. *The Government Policy of Protector Somerset*. Montreal, 1975.

_____. "Protector Somerset and Requests." *Historical Journal,* 17 (1974), 451-64.

Carthew, G. A. *The Hundred of Launditch and Deanery of Brisley.* 3 parts. Norwich, 1877.

Challis, C. E. *The Tudor Coinage.* Manchester, 1978.

Chauncy, Henry. *Historical Antiquities of Hertfordshire.* 2 vols. Bishop's Stortford, 1826.

Clark, Peter. *English Provincial Society from the Reformation to the Revolution: Religion, Politics, and Society in Kent, 1500-1640.* Hassocks, Sussex, 1977.

_____. "The Ownership of Books in England, 1560-1640: The Example of Some Kentish Townsfolk." In *Schooling and Society,* ed. L. Stone. Baltimore, 1976.

_____. "Popular Protest and Disturbance in Kent, 1558-1640." *Economic History Review,* 2nd ser. 29 (1976), 365-82.

Clark, Peter and Slack, Paul. *English Towns in Transition, 1500-1700.* London, 1976.

Clark, Peter; Smith, A. G. R.; and Tyacke, N., eds. *The English Commonwealth, 1547-1640.* New York, 1979.

Clarkson, L. A. "English Economic Policy in the Sixteenth and Seventeenth Centuries: The Case of the Leather Industry." *Bulletin of the Institute of Historical Research,* 38 (1965), 149-162.

_____. "The Organization of the English Leather Industry in the Late Sixteenth and Seventeenth Centuries." *Economic History Review,* 2nd ser. 13 (1960-61), 245-56.

Collinson, John. *History and Antiquities of the County of Somerset.* Bath, 1791.

Cornwall, Julian. "English Population in the Early Sixteenth Century." *Economic History Review,* 2nd ser. 23 (1970), 32-44.

_____. *Revolt of the Peasantry 1549.* London, 1977.

Coyle, Mary. "Sir Richard Rich, First Baron Rich (1496?-1567), A Political Biography." Ph.D. diss., Harvard, 1967.

Craik, T. W. *The Tudor Interlude.* Leicester, 1958.

Cressy, David. *Literacy and the Social Order.* Cambridge, 1980.

Cross, Claire. *Church and People, 1450-1660.* Atlantic Highlands, N.J., 1976.

Davies, C. S. L. *Peace, Print, and Protestantism.* St. Albans, Hertfordshire, 1977.

_____. "Peasant Revolt in France and England: A Comparison," *Agricultural History Review,* 21 (1973), 122-34.

_____. "Slavery and Protector Somerset: The Vagrancy Act of 1547," *Economic History Review,* 2nd ser. 19 (1966), 533-49.

Davis, Natalie Z. *Society and Culture in Early Modern France.* Stanford, 1975.

Dewar, Mary. *Sir Thomas Smith: A Tudor Intellectual in Office.* London, 1964.

Dickens, A. G. *The English Reformation.* London, 1964.

_____. *Robert Holgate.* London, 1955.

_____. "Some Popular Reactions to the Edwardian Reformation in Yorkshire." *Yorkshire Archaeological Journal,* 34 (1939), 151-69.

Dodds, M. H. and Ruth. *The Pilgrimage of Grace 1536-1537 and The Exeter Conspiracy 1538.* 2 vols. Cambridge, 1915.

Elton, G. R. *Policy and Police.* Cambridge, 1972.

_____. *Reform and Renewal.* Cambridge, 1973.

_____. *Reformation and Reform.* London, 1977.

Ericson, C. G. "Parliament as a Legislative Institution in the Reigns of Edward VI and Mary." Ph.D. thesis, London, 1973.

Fletcher, Anthony. *Tudor Rebellions*. 2nd ed. London, 1973.

Foster, Frank F. *The Politics of Stability: A Portrait of the Rulers in Elizabethan London*. London, 1977.

Fourquin, Guy. *The Anatomy of Popular Rebellion in the Middle Ages*. New York, 1978.

Gilbert [Giddy], Davies. *The Parochial History of Cornwall*. 4 vols. London, 1838.

Goring, Jeremy. "Social Change and Military Decline in Mid-Tudor England." *History*, 60 (1975), 185-97.

Guy, J. A. *The Cardinal's Court: The Impact of Thomas Wolsey in Star Chamber*. Totowa, N.J., 1977.

Hatcher, John. *English Tin Production and Trade before 1550*. Oxford, 1973.

————. *Plague, Population, and the English Economy 1348-1530*. London, 1977.

Heinze, R. W. *The Proclamations of the Tudor Kings*. Cambridge, 1976.

Henderson, Charles. *A History of the Parish of Constantine in Cornwall*. Truro, 1937.

Hill, Christopher. "The Many-Headed Monster in Late Tudor and Early Stuart Political Thinking." In *From the Renaissance to the Counter-Reformation*, ed. C. H. Carter. New York, 1965.

Hill, J. W. F. *Tudor and Stuart Lincoln*. Cambridge, 1956.

Hilton, R. H. *The English Peasantry in the Late Middle Ages*. Oxford, 1975.

Hoak, D. E. *The King's Council in the Reign of Edward VI*. Cambridge, 1976.

Hoare, R. C. *The History of Modern Wiltshire*. 14 parts. London, 1822-44.

Holdsworth, William. *A History of English Law*. 16 vols. London, 1936-66.

Horst, Irvin B. *The Radical Brethren: Anabaptism and the English Reformation to 1558*. Nieuwkoop, 1972.

Hull, Felix. "Agriculture and Rural Society in Essex, 1560-1640." Ph.D. thesis, London, 1950.

Hurstfield, Joel. *The Queen's Wards*. Cambridge, Mass., 1958.

James, Mervyn. *Family, Lineage, and Civil Society*. Oxford, 1974.

Jones, Whitney R. D. *The Mid-Tudor Crisis, 1539-1563*. London, 1973.

————. *The Tudor Commonwealth, 1529-1559*. London, 1970.

Jordan, W. K. *Edward VI: The Young King*. London, 1968.

————. *Edward VI: The Threshold of Power*. London, 1970.

Kerridge, Eric. *Agrarian Problems in the Sixteenth Century and After*. London, 1969.

————. *The Agricultural Revolution*. New York, 1967.

Kett, L. M. *The Ketts of Norfolk: A Yeoman Family*. London, 1921.

Lake's Parochial History of Cornwall. 2 vols. Truro, 1867.

Land, Stephen K. *Kett's Rebellion*. Ipswich, 1977.

Leonard, E. M. *The Early History of English Poor Relief*. Cambridge, 1900.

Le Roy Ladurie, Emmanuel. *The Peasants of Languedoc*. Urbana, 1974.

Levine, Mortimer. *Tudor Dynastic Problems, 1460-1571*. London, 1973.

Lewis, George R. *The Stannaries*. Boston, 1908.

Loades, D. M. *Politics and the Nation, 1450-1660*. London, 1974.

MacCaffrey, W. T. *Exeter, 1540-1640*. 2nd ed. Cambridge, Mass., 1975.

MacCulloch, D. "Kett's Rebellion in Context." *Past and Present,* 84 (1979), 36-59.

Macfarlane, Alan. *The Origins of English Individualism.* New York, 1979.

Manning, Roger B. "The Origins of the Doctrine of Sedition." *Albion,* 12 (1980), 99-121.

———. "Patterns of Violence in Early Tudor Enclosure Riots." *Albion,* 6 (1974), 120-33.

———. "The Rebellions of 1549 in England." *Sixteenth Century Journal,* 10 (1979), 92-99.

———. "Violence and Social Conflict in Mid-Tudor Rebellions." *Journal of British Studies,* 16 (1977), 18-40.

Manship, Henry. *A Book of the Foundations and Antiquity of the Town of Great Yarmouth.* Ed. C. J. Palmer. Great Yarmouth, 1854.

Mollat, Michel and Wolff, Philippe. *The Popular Revolutions of the Late Middle Ages.* London, 1973.

Murphy, Terence R. "The Maintenance of Order in Early Tudor Kent, 1509-1558." Ph.D. diss., Northwestern, 1975.

Norden, J. *Speculi Britanniae Pars, A Topographical and Historical Description of Cornwall.* London, 1728.

Oman, C. W. C. *The Great Revolt of 1381.* Oxford, 1906.

Oxley, James E. *The Reformation in Essex.* Manchester, 1965.

Patten, J. H. C. *English Towns, 1500-1700.* Folkestone, Kent, 1978.

Pearl, Valerie. *London and the Outbreak of the Puritan Revolution.* Oxford, 1961.

Pill, David H. *The English Reformation, 1529-58.* Totowa, N.J., 1973.

Pollard, A. F. *England under Protector Somerset.* London, 1900.

Pound, John. *Poverty and Vagrancy in Tudor England.* London, 1971.

———. "The Social and Trade Structure of Norwich, 1525-1575." *Past and Present,* 34 (1966), 49-64.

Ramsay, G. D. *The City of London in International Politics at the Accession of Elizabeth Tudor.* Manchester, 1975.

Ramsey, Peter H., ed. *The Price Revolution in Sixteenth-Century England.* London, 1971.

Ravensdale, J. R. "Landbeach in 1549: Kett's Rebellion in Miniature." In *East Anglian Studies,* ed. L. M. Munby. Cambridge, 1968.

———. *Liable to Floods: Village Landscape on the Edge of the Fens AD 450-1850.* New York, 1974.

Rose-Troup, Frances. *The Western Rebellion of 1549.* London, 1913.

Rowse, A. L. *Tudor Cornwall.* 2nd ed. London, 1969.

Russell, F. W. *Kett's Rebellion in Norfolk.* London, 1859.

Schofield, R. S. "The Geographical Distribution of Wealth in England, 1334-1649." *Economic History Review,* 2nd ser. 18 (1965), 483-510.

———. "The Measurement of Literacy in Pre-Industrial England." In *Literacy in Traditional Societies,* ed. J. Goody. Cambridge, 1968.

Scribner, Bob and Benecke, Gerhard, eds. *The German Peasant War 1525 — New Viewpoints.* London, 1979.

Sharp, Buchanan. *In Contempt of All Authority: Rural Artisans and Riot in the West of England, 1586-1660.* Berkeley, 1980.

Sharpe, R. R. *London and the Kingdom.* 3 vols. London, 1894-99.

BIBLIOGRAPHY

Shrewsbury, J. F. D. *A History of Bubonic Plague in the British Isles.* London, 1970.

Slavin, A. J. *Politics and Profit: A Study of Sir Ralph Sadler, 1507-1547.* Cambridge, 1966.

Smith, A. Hassell. *County and Court: Government and Politics in Norfolk, 1558-1603.* Oxford, 1974.

Smith, Lacey Baldwin. "Henry VIII and the Protestant Triumph."*American Historical Review,* 71 (1966), 1237-1264.

Stone, Lawrence. *The Crisis of the Aristocracy, 1558-1641.* Oxford, 1965.

————. "Patriarchy and Paternalism in Tudor England: The Earl of Arundel and the Peasants' Revolt of 1549." *Journal of British Studies,* 13 (1974), 19-23.

Swinden, Henry. *The History and Antiquities of the Ancient Burgh of Great Yarmouth.* Norwich, 1772.

Tawney, R. H. *The Agrarian Problem in the Sixteenth Century.* London, 1912.

Thirsk, Joan, ed. *The Agrarian History of England and Wales.* Vol. 4. Cambridge, 1967.

Thomas, Keith. *Religion and the Decline of Magic.* Harmondsworth, Middlesex, 1973.

Tittler, Robert and Loach, Jennifer, eds. *The Mid-Tudor Polity, c. 1540-1560.* Totowa, N.J., 1980.

Victoria History of the Counties of England. Westminster, 1900—.

Willen, Diane. "The Career of John, Lord Russell, First Earl of Bedford: A Study in Tudor Politics." Ph.D. diss., Tufts, 1972.

————. "Lord Russell and the Western Counties, 1539-1555." *Journal of British Studies,* 15 (1975), 26-45.

Williams, Penry. *The Tudor Regime.* Oxford, 1979.

Woodman, A. Vere. "The Buckinghamshire and Oxfordshire Rising." *Oxoniensia,* 22 (1957), 78-84.

Worth, R. N. *History of Plymouth.* Plymouth, 1890.

Youings, Joyce. "The Economic History of Devon, 1300-1700." In *Exeter and Its Region,* ed. Frank Barlow. Exeter, 1969.

Zeeveld, W. Gordon. "Social Equalitarianism in a Tudor Crisis." *Journal of the History of Ideas,* 7 (1946), 35-55.

INDEX

Agricultural laborers, 7
Aldrich, Thomas: collaborates with Kett, 93, 102; at Tree of Reformation, 95; returns to Norwich, 99; imprisoned, 101; signs Kett's demands, 104
Allen, John, 187
Amcottes, Sir Henry, 172
Amicable Grant of 1525, 165
Anabaptists, 167, 209
Anticlericalism, 165
Antwerp, 20
Appleyard, Alice, 85
Appleyard, Roger, 85
Armstrong, John, 167
Artisans: role in Edwardian rebellions, 189-90
Arundel, Earl of. See Fitzalan, Henry
Arundell, Humphrey, 50, 188, 215; Cornish rebel, 7; leads Cornish rebels, 49; opposition to court party, 69; captured, 81; trial and execution, 185-86
Ashbourne, Derbyshire, 151
Ashford, Kent, 202
Aske, Robert, 7
Askew, Anne, 15
Atkinson, John, 101
Attleborough, Norfolk, 82-83
Aucher, Sir Anthony, 152
Audley, James, Lord Audley, 6, 43
Audley, Thomas, 86

Bacon, Henry, 101
Baker, Roger, 187
Banbury, Oxfordshire: enclosure riot (1550), 202
Barker, John, 104
Barlow, William, 25
Barnstaple, Devon, 45
Barret, Dr. John, 125
Bartholomew Fair, 177
Becon, Thomas, 195-96
Bedford, Earl of. See Russell, John
Bedingfield, Sir Henry, 121
Bell, Robert, 142, 188

Beresford, M.W., 36
Berkshire: disturbances (1549), 158; order for repressing disorder, 162
Bible, 8
Bideford, Devon, 45
Bilney, Thomas, 15, 90
Bindoff, S.T., 108, 109
Bishopsgate, London, 166
Blackaller, John, 57, 59
Black Death, 19
Blakman, Andrew, 155
Bloch, Marc, 10
Bocher, Joan, 209
Bocking, Essex, 201-2
Boconnoc, Cornwall, 47
Bodley, John, 78
Bodmin, Cornwall, 7, 40, 43, 48, 50, 69; rising of 1549, 48-49
Body, William, 46-48
Bonner, Edmund, Bishop of London, 66; illegal celebration of mass, 115; does not join rebels, 214
Book of Common Prayer, 31, 50, 52; repudiated by Western rebels, 66-67; effect on popular unrest, 212
Bordeaux, France, 11
Bothom, John, 184
Boulogne, 22
Bowlar, William, 150
Bowldrey, Thomas, 150
Bowthorpe, Norfolk, 92
Boyer, Nicholas, 183
Brampton, Anthony, 91
Brampton, William, 101
Brandon, Charles, Duke of Suffolk, 166
Brandon Ferry, Norfolk, 142
Brandon, Katherine, Duchess of Suffolk, 94
Bray, John, Baron Bray, 128, 129
Bray, Sir Reginald, 43
Bristol: disorder at, 158-59
Brook, Robert, recorder of London, 180
Bucer, Martin, 115
Buckingham, Duke of. See Stafford, Edmund

INDEX

Buckinghamshire: protests against enclosure (1548), 150-51; order for repressing disorder, 162; enclosure dispute (1551), 205

Bunting, Robert, 141

Burnam, Robert, 203

Bury, John, 159; trial and execution, 186-87

Bury St. Edmunds, Suffolk; center of discontent (1549), 142

Calais, 22

Cambridge: rendezvous of Warwick, Grey of Powis, and Bray, 129; complaints of townspeople, 143-44; gallows at, 185

Cambridgeshire: saffron growing area, 110; disorder (1549), 143-46

Cambridge University, 143

Canterbury, 153; disorder (1550), 202

Cardmaker, John, 25

Carew, Sir Gawen, 54, 74

Carew, Sir Peter, 74, 75; dispatched to Exeter, 54; blamed for burning of Crediton, 55; advances to Clyst St. Mary, 56

Carew Manuscripts, 233-34

Carew, Richard, 41, 42, 49

Carye, Gregory, 78; location of windmill, 225

Castle Kynock, Cornwall, 49, 50

Castle Rising, Norfolk: rebel camp, 141

Catherine of Aragon, Queen of England, 68

Cecil, Sir William, 5, 32; protects Thomas Hancock, 27; obtains pardon for rebels at Cambridge, 144

Chagford, Devon, 61

Chantries: dissolution of, 31

Charles V, Emperor, 22, 126

Charles I, King of England, 8

Chaundeler, Sir John, rebel priest, 141, 142, 147

Cheauers, Italian mercenary, 122

Cheke, Sir John: tutor to Edward VI, 18; compares citizens of Norwich and Exeter, 96-97; *The Hurt of Sedition*, 190-91

Cheshunt, Hertfordshire, 148

Chipping Norton, Oxfordshire, 149, 150; tanner in, 86

Clark, Peter, 153

Clere, Sir John, 121; dispute with Sir William Paston, 91

Clerkenwell, Middlesex, 177

Clyst Heath, Devon, 79-80, 210

Clyst St. Mary, Devon: fortifies itself against gentry, 55-57; battle of, 78-79

Codd, Thomas: mayor of Norwich, 92; collaborates with Kett, 93, 102; at Tree of Reformation, 95; refuses Kett's demand to pass through Norwich, 98; returns to Norwich, 99; imprisoned, 100; signs Kett's Demands, 104; at Mousehold Heath, 121

Colchester, Essex, 147, 207

Colthurst, Matthew, 208-9

Commonwealth reformers: writings from 1547 to 1549, 23-31; writings after 1549, 196-97

Coniers, Thomas, 95

Constable, Sir Marmaduke, 129

Constantine, Cornwall, 48

Cook, Robert, 201

Corbett, John, 93

Cornwall: social and economic conditions, 40-42; rebels against Henry VII, 2, 4, 6, 42-44; Western Rebellion in, 38-81; pacification, 183; lack of support for government, 212

Cornwall, Duchy of, 42, 48

Cornwall, Julian, 108

Cornwallis, Sir Thomas, 121, 124

Courtenay family, 5, 213

Courtenay, Henry, Marquis of Exeter, 6, 42, 45, 51, 68

Courtenay, Sir Piers, 56

Coverdale, Miles, 25, 32, 48, 57, 78

Cowdrey, Avys, 208

Cox, Richard, 18, 25

Cranmer, Thomas, Archbishop of Canterbury: member of Council, 14; attack on, 16; commitment to Protestantism, 23; author of prayer book, 31; marriage of, 32; preaches against rebellion, 71, 114-15, 190

Crediton, Devon, 53-55, 70

Cringleford, Norfolk, 92, 96

Crispin, Richard, 67-68

Cromwell, Thomas, 5, 44, 46; architect of Henrician Reformation, 15; reform program, 23; house in London, 165

Crowley, Robert, 29-30; Commonwealth writer, 23, 27; views social unrest as a disease, 196

Crugge, William, 87

Cutts, Sir John, 121

252

INDEX

INDEX

More, Sir Christopher, 155
More, Nicholas, 147, 185
More, Sir Thomas: *Utopia*, 1, 21, 23;
  humanism of, 16; opinion on literacy,
  28
Moreman, John, 67-68
Morley, Norfolk, 83
Morton, John, Archbishop of Canterbury,
  43
Morton, Simon, 183
Morval, Cornwall, 47
Mousehold Heath, Norfolk, site of Kett's
  camp, 93, 94-95
Myddle, Shropshire, 87
Mytton, Thomas, 145

Neall, John, 86, 87
Neville, Alexander, 82, 94; refers to rebel
  sympathizers at Norwich, 97; description
  of hangings, 184; narrative published
  (1575), 209
Neville, Charles, Earl of Westmorland, 5, 6
Newcombe, John, 58
Newmarket, Suffolk, 129
Norden, John, 40
Norfolk: rebellion of 1549, 82-112; gentry
  accompany Northampton to Norwich,
  121; pacification of, 113-39, 184-85;
  failure of gentry to maintain order, 212;
  bondmen in, 206
Norfolk, Duke of. *See* Howard, Thomas
Northampton, Marquis of. *See* Parr,
  William
Northamptonshire: disorder of 1548-49, 151
Northaw, Hertfordshire, 148
North Elmham, Norfolk, 94
Northumberland, Duke of. *See* Dudley,
  John
Northumberland, Earl of. *See* Percy,
  Thomas
Norton, John, 157-58
Norwich: social and economic conditions,
  97-98; tensions in, 91-92; failure of city
  leaders, 212, 213-14; program of poor
  relief, 201; officials appeal for assistance,
  116; defended against Kett, 99-100;
  bombardment of, 122; burned, 124-25,
  133-34; effect of fall on London, 176;
  fighting in, 131-34; arrival of Swiss
  troops, 135; civilian casualties, 231;
  thanksgiving service, 137-38; rebuilding,
  138; artisans remember Kett, 203
Norwich Cathedral, 91

Odiham, Hampshire, 157
Ombler, William, 160-61
Order of Communion, 31
Ottery St. Mary, Devon: burned (1549), 78
Overton, Hampshire, 157
Oxfordshire: disturbances of 1549, 149-51;
  order for repressing disorder, 162-63;
  executions, 185

Paget, Robert, 80, 184
Paget, Sir William, Baron Paget of
  Beaudesert, 32, 73, 76, 117, 148, 178;
  member of Council, 14; recalls German
  Peasant War, 12; letter to Somerset
  (Christmas, 1548), 13; depressed with
  affairs of state, 22-23; opinion of poor,
  30; critic of Somerset's enclosure policy,
  35; advises against sheep tax, 36
Palmer, Sir Thomas, 129, 136
Paris, 11
Paris, George van, 209
Parker, Sir Henry, 121
Parker, Matthew: preaches to Norfolk
  rebels, 95-96; meets with Warwick at
  Cambridge, 129; prevents violence at
  Landbeach, 146
Parkyn, Robert, 161
Parr, Catherine, Queen of England, 51
Parr, William, Marquis of Northampton,
  14; commands army sent to Norwich,
  119-21; casualties suffered by army, 123;
  retreats from Norwich, 124; Warwick
  offers to serve under, 127
Paston, Anne, 204
Paston, Sir Thomas, 121, 122
Paston, Sir William, 91
Patchyn, John, 154, 188
Paulet, Sir Hugh, 159; report of rebel
  deaths, 80
Paulet, William, Baron St. John, 32, 178
Paul's Cross, London, 25
Peasantry: debate over, 240
Peasants' Revolt of 1381, 89
Penwith, Cornwall, 46
Penyngton, Gilbert, 169
Percy, Thomas, Earl of Northumberland,
  5, 6
Periam, John, 78
Peter, John, 59
Petibone, John, 99
Petre, Sir William, 32
Philip II, King of Spain, 5, 9
Pickering, Sir William, 168-69

INDEX

53, 76; and Norfolk Rebellion, 117, 118-19, 120, 125-27, 128; relations with London, 167, 173, 177-81; domestic policy, 20, 23, 30, 32, 34, 35, 36, 73, 141, 162-63; religious policy, 24, 45; foreign policy, 22; fall of, 4, 5, 191; imprisoned at Tower of London, 181; takes armed force to Wokingham (1551), 205; trial and execution, 208-9
Seymour, Thomas, Baron Seymour of Sudeley, 33, 74
Sharke, John, 59
Sheffield, Edmund, Baron Sheffield: accompanies Northampton to Norwich, 120; killed, 123-24, 214
Sherborne, Dorset, 75
Sherfield-upon-Loden, Hampshire, 208
Shoreditch, Middlesex, 166
Shrewsbury, Earl of. See Talbot, Francis
Slader, Mark, 52
Smith, Lacey Baldwin, 17
Smith, Richard, 25
Smith, Robert, 78
Smith, Sir Thomas, 32, 146, 197-98; opposes use of royal proclamations, 76; sends advice to Somerset, 117; servants involved in London disturbances, 169
Sneyde, Sir William, 152
Somerset, 45; rising in, 159; execution of rebels, 184
Somerset, Duke of. See Seymour, Edward
Somerset House, London, 166
Sotherton, Leonard, 101, 118, 229
Sotherton, Nicholas, 82, 94; speaks of falsehood of Norwich citizens, 96
Southampton, 157
Southampton, Earl of. See Wriothesley, Thomas
Southwark, 166
Southwell, Sir Richard, 120-21
Spencer, John, 204
Stadlow, George, 180
Stafford, Edmund, Duke of Buckingham, 6
Staffordshire, 151-52
Star Chamber, Court of, 9, 10
Statutes: abolishing and putting away divers books and images (1550), 194; fond and fantastical prophecies (1550), 194; improvement of commons and waste grounds (1550), 199; leather (1549), 87; poor (1552), 200; relief (sheep tax, 1549), 36, 72, 199; repeal (1547), 33; retaining of journeymen (1550), 194; six

articles (1539), 15, 17, 23, 25, 31, 66; uniformity (1549), 31; unlawful assemblies (1550), 194; vagrancy (1547), 33, 200
Stephenson, John, 142
Steward, Augustine, 101, 121, 124, 130
Stone, Lawrence, 7, 153, 54
Stow, John, 71
Stratton, Cornwall, 47
Suffolk: disturbances of 1549, 142-43
Suffolk, Duchess of. See Brandon, Katherine
Suffolk, Duke of. See Brandon, Henry; Grey, Henry
Sulyard, Sir John, 121
Surrey, Earl of. See Howard, Henry; Howard, Thomas, third Duke of Norfolk
Surrey: unrest in (1549), 154-55
Surrey Place, Norfolk, 101
Sussex: population growth, 19; disorder of 1549, 153-54
Sutton, Ralph, 100, 104
Swannington, Norfolk, 137
Swinden, Henry, 103
Sylver, Richard, 155

Tailler, Thomas, 169
Talbot, Francis, Earl of Shrewbury, 126, 129, 178
Taylor, Richard, 59
Thame Park, Oxfordshire, 149
Thetford, Norfolk, 142
Thirsk, Joan, 41; evaluation of agrarian legislation, 200
Thomas, Keith, 6
Thorpe Wood, Norfolk, 139, 204
Thynne, Sir John, 157-58, 184; criticized by Paget, 32
Tomson, Richard, tilemaker, 154
Tomson, Richard, vicar, 150
Tonge, Joseph, 48, 57
Tonge, Roger, 25
Totnes, Devon, 45
Townshend, Sir Roger, 90
Trematon Castle, Cornwall, 50
Trevian, Pascoe, 47
Truro, Cornwall, 42
Tylby, Charles, 167

Udall, Nicholas, 71, 190
Underhill, Thomas, 52, 70, 81
Upcharde, Thomas, 201-2
Uppingham, Rutland, 206
Urban discontent, 213-14

258

Barrett L. Beer, Professor of History at Kent State University, is the author of *Northumberland: The Political Career of John Dudley, Earl of Warwick and Duke of Northumberland* (KSU Press, 1971), and *The Letters of William, Lord Paget of Beaudesert, 1547-1563, Camden Miscellany, Volume XXV,* with Sybil M. Jack, as well as numerous articles on the Tudor era. He will be a Fulbright Professor in British Studies at the University of Tromso in Norway during the 1983 academic year.